MVFOL

AA

DISCOVER AMERICA

DISCOVER
AMERICA

AA

Produced by the Publications
Division of the Automobile Association
Fanum House, Basingstoke, Hampshire RG21 2EA

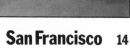

*The Statue of Liberty Enlightening the
World, designed by the French sculptor
Frédéric Auguste Bartholdi, was erected on
Liberty Island in New York Harbour and
unveiled on 20th October 1886. It symbolizes
the link forged between France and America
during the American Revolutionary War*

Contents

Produced by the Publications Division of the
Automobile Association

Researched and written by Roland Weisz

Editors Barbara Littlewood,
Donna Wood, Julia Brittain,
Pat Rowlinson and Gail Harada

Art Editors Keith Russell,
M A Preedy MSIAD
Dave Austin

**Editorial
Adviser** Professor Esmond Wright,
Director of the
Institute of
United States Studies

Maps produced by the Cartographic
Department of the Automobile Association.
Based on cartography supplied by the
American Automobile Association.
All maps © 1981 The American Automobile
Association

*Carved from the solid rock of
the mountainside, gigantic
portraits of George
Washington, Thomas Jefferson,
Theodore Roosevelt and
Abraham Lincoln decorate
Mount Rushmore in the Black
Hills of South Dakota.*

Acknowledgements
The publishers would like to acknowledge the
extremely valuable help given to them in the
preparation of this book by the American Automobile
Association (AAA), National Headquarters, 8111
Gatehouse Road, Falls Church, Virginia, 22047.
  The AAA has prepared all the town plans, route
maps, and the distance and location maps on pp. 10 to
13. They have also devised the routes followed by the
motor tours and the route information has been
checked by AAA road reporters, who make an annual
survey of all US roads. The names, addresses and
telephone numbers of museums, places of interest and
public buildings are based on the information
available to the AAA at the time of going to press
(Spring 1981), and are therefore as up-to-date as it is
possible to make them.
  The individual Automobile Clubs listed in the
directory of each city are affiliated to the AAA and will
provide maps and touring information to members of
the British Automobile Association under a reciprocal
agreement between the associations. You will need to
have with you your British AA membership card.
  The publishers are also grateful to the following for
providing facilities and help during the preparation of
material for this book: Pan American World Airways,
Inc., the Hertz Corporation, Hyatt Regency Hotels,
Exchange Travel, the United States Travel Service.
  Professor Esmond Wright, Director of the Institute of
United States Studies, the University of London, has
provided valuable help in reading the manuscript.

Filmset by Bi-print Studio Ltd
Printed and bound by New Interlitho SPA, Milan
Published by the Automobile Association,
Fanum House, Basingstoke,
Hampshire RG21 2EA

Introduction

Discover America is not only an indispensable guide for the tourist paying his first visit to the United States, it will also be invaluable to those who already know a small part of the North American continent and now want to discover more about it.

The book concentrates on eight major cities — San Francisco, Los Angeles, Las Vegas, New Orleans, Miami, Washington, New York and Boston — which have been selected because of their distinctive and contrasting character, and for their popularity with visitors. All make excellent centres from which to explore some of America's most magnificent

scenery: the giant redwood forests of California; the surfing beaches of the west coast; the Grand Canyon; Death Valley; the plantation homes of the Old South; the Everglades and the Florida Keys; the eastern seaboard and the quiet charm of the New England countryside.

Each city has been divided into three sections. The first describes its unique character, highlights the major attractions, and includes a detailed street plan of the centre. The second consists of a directory of places of interest, selected hotels and restaurants, and useful addresses and telephone numbers. The third section consists of carefully planned motor tours of one to three days' duration. The route and the main places of interest are clearly marked on the road map accompanying each tour, and route directions are given in the text.

Information for Tourists

There is much to enjoy, much to appreciate, and much to admire on a visit to the United States. Despite the fact that both British and Americans speak the same language, America is a foreign country, and attitudes and customs differ radically from those common in Europe. The mixture of peoples is far greater than anywhere in Europe: San Francisco, for example, is famous for its Chinatown, but in Los Angeles, Japanese influence is strongly felt; Blacks predominate in New Orleans; in Miami, Spanish is the second language and New York has taken something from everywhere.

In most of the big cities, street violence is more prevalent than in Europe, but provided that tourists are sensible, and stay away from the trouble spots (local tourist offices will advise you), they should not experience any unpleasantness. The four cardinal rules are: Do not act oddly, or draw undue attention to yourself; do not stare pointedly at strangers, or pass remarks about them; do not get into arguments; do not walk in deserted streets.

ENTRY REGULATIONS

Essential documents permitting entry to the United States are a visa, and a full British passport, which must be valid for at least six months after your intended return from the USA. The one-year British Visitor's Passport is not valid for the USA. Visa application forms are held by most travel agents and they may undertake to obtain a visa for you. You can apply yourself by post to the: American Embassy, Visa Branch, 5 Upper Grosvenor St, London W1A 2JB, tel. 01 499 3443 (recorded information), enclosing a stamped addressed envelope, your passport and evidence of your intent to leave the United States after your holiday (your return ticket, or a letter from your employer confirming that you are returning to work, will be sufficient). Allow at least four weeks to complete the application. In an emergency, personal application may be made at the Visa Branch (open 8am to 3pm, Monday to Friday, except for public holidays, 25th May and 3rd July) but you may have to wait a long time — anything up to three hours. Visas may also be obtained from the American Consulates in Edinburgh and Belfast. The addresses are: American Consulate General, 3 Regent Terrace, Edinburgh EH7 5BW; American Consulate General, Queen House, 14 Queen St, Belfast BT1 6EQ.

If you intend to drive a car you will need your British Driving Licence and an International Driving Permit, obtainable from any AA Service Centre or Travel Agency. To obtain your IDP you will need to produce your Driving Licence and a passport-size photograph.

Customs regulations allow non-residents to bring the following items into the USA duty-free: a litre of spirits or wine (persons aged 21 and over), local state laws permitting; 200 cigarettes or 50 cigars or 3lbs of tobacco, or proportionate amounts of each; gifts to the value of $100, providing that you intend to stay more than 72 hours in the States and that you have made no previous claim during the past six months. You may bring up to $5000 in personal funds into the USA.

All visitors to the USA have to pass through immigration on arrival. This is usually just a formality, but long queues do build up, and there is nothing to do but wait your turn. Immigration officials will want to know where you intend to stay — the address of your hotel will usually be sufficient.

CURRENCY

The dollar bill (buck) is the basic unit of currency ($1.00 = 100 cents). Paper notes are available in denominations of $1, $2, $5, $10, $20, $50, $100, $500 and $1000. All notes are the same colour. You may have difficulty in changing anything greater than $20. Coins are minted in 1¢ (penny), 5¢ (nickel), 10¢ (dime), 25¢ (quarter) and 50¢ denominations.

Your currency may be exchanged into US dollars at your port of entry. Most major banks exchange currency, hotels generally do not. It is advisable to change your currency where possible at airports or in larger cities, where you will receive a better rate of exchange. Normal banking hours are 9am to 3pm, Monday to Friday. Travellers' cheques in sterling or dollars are usually accepted by banks, hotels, restaurants or shops. Credit cards such as American Express, Access (American Master Card), Barclaycard/VISA and Diners Club are almost universally acceptable.

TRAVEL

Air: All major airlines have frequent services into most of the cities directly from London. British Airways call at all except Las Vegas; Pan Am at all except Boston; Laker Airways Skytrains fly to New York, Miami and Los Angeles, and operate a weekly charter flight to San Francisco. Air travel is the best way to cover very large distances within the USA. The internal flight network is very good and covers more than 600 cities. Special discount fares for foreign travellers can be obtained from many airlines. A Visit USA Fare (VUSA) giving 40% discount is operated by many domestic airlines, and there are also several go-as-you-please packages. Ask your travel agent for details. Special shuttle flights operate between some cities — San Francisco-Los Angeles, New York-Washington for example — and are so frequent that you need not book and should not have to wait long for a flight. You obtain a boarding pass when you arrive at the airport, take a seat on a waiting plane, and pay your fare.

Rail: AMTRAK is the major American rail network for passengers. Inter-city trains are generally cheaper than planes over shorter distances. Long-distance trains often follow scenic routes — an example is the spectacular 'San Francisco Zephyr' which runs from Denver through the Rockies and Sierra Nevada to the coast.

USA Rail Passes and Family USA Rail Passes, offering unlimited travel for a specified length of time, may only be bought outside the USA. Thomas Cook (England and Wales) and Thistle Air (Scotland) are AMTRAK agents in the UK. Your travel agent will also be able to make the arrangements for you.

Road: The most economical long-distance travel is by luxurious, efficient buses. Greyhound and Trailways are the largest bus companies, and together with more than a hundred smaller companies they cover over 120,000 miles (193,000 kilometres) of excellent highways. Reclining seats enable you to sleep during the journey.

Passes entitling you to unlimited, nationwide travel are available and should be bought in advance in the UK. Your travel agent can obtain them for you.

Motoring: Major roads in America are well-surfaced, wide, and well signposted, although it is helpful sometimes to know north from south and east from west. Distances are calculated in miles, but Americans usually think in terms of how long it takes not how far away it is. Local roads are often narrow and not so well surfaced.

CAR HIRE

Many air package tours include car-hire costs, on a fly-drive basis. This may be a convenient arrangement, but hire cars are available in most cities at airports and in rental offices in hotels or from car hire agencies. Local AAA clubs will recommend reputable agencies. There is usually a wide choice of vehicles, and you have the added advantage of being able to inspect the vehicle first. If you plan to go camping, campers — touring vehicles equipped with all mod cons — are readily available, but it is sensible to reserve these in advance to avoid disappointment. A list of approved camping sites, all well equipped, is available to members of the British AA from the American Automobile Association (address on p. 6). Some major companies will rent to tourists at 18 years of age, others require the driver to be over 21 and in some places drivers must be over 25. Major credit cards are universally acceptable and travellers' cheques are taken. Your passport and driving licence (see Entry Regulations) must be produced. Prices vary from one region to another and include oil, maintenance and liability insurances. State and local taxes are additional and petrol is usually extra. Most American cars have automatic transmission, and are sometimes air-conditioned. As summers in some regions are very much hotter than in Britain, this can be more of a necessity than you might think.

When buying petrol (gas), remember that American pints, quarts and gallons are smaller than their Imperial equivalents by one-fifth — i.e. there are 16 fluid ounces in US pint, and a US gallon is about four-fifths of a British one.

It is quite common at gas (petrol) stations to find the cashier sitting behind a bullet-proof kiosk. He may insist on being paid before he allows you to fill up. Most hire-cars use only lead-free petrol. This is a more expensive grade, and there is usually a notice about it in the car.

HIGHWAYS

Controlled-access highways are variously known as interstates, turnpikes, expressways or toll roads. Interstate roads are, roughly speaking, equivalent to motorways. Roads designated US, followed by a number — e.g. US 90 — are the old Federal Highways, similar to the British main trunk roads. State Routes are main roads within each state, and Local Routes are minor roads. Tolls of 2-3 cents per mile are charged on toll roads and turnpikes. Access is limited on these super-highways, as on our motorways, so exit points and rest stops should be planned well in advance.

DRIVING REGULATIONS

Driving in America is not difficult, but it would be wrong to expect Americans to make allowances for foreign motorists, so it is wise to know a few of the rules they take for granted. Each state has its own traffic regulations, and only general rules and hints are listed here. Local AAA offices will give advice about local regulations.
1 Drive on the right of the road.
2 Keep to the speed limits; 20-25 miles per hour in cities and congested areas, 55 miles per hour on open roads.
3 Report any accident to the nearest police department immediately.
4 Strictly observe all traffic lights and stop, slow and caution signs. Normally, however, cars can filter right on red, providing they have first halted and checked that the road is clear. This does not apply in New York.
5 Do not pass on bends, at junctions or near the top of hills.
6 Do not pass school buses which have stopped

to allow children to get on or off. This applies both when you are following the bus and when you are approaching it.
7 Observe reduced speed limits in all school zones.
8 Do not park on the highway in rural areas. If you must stop, pull right off the road.
9 Observe parking zone laws in cities, or your car may be towed away. Always park facing the flow of traffic and never double-park. Kerbside colour codes are: red for no parking; yellow for unloading commercial vehicles; white for unloading passengers; blue for parking for handicapped people; green for short-term (this often means literally 12 minutes).
10 Always signal when you turn, stop or change lanes. Remember, however, that on many multi-lane highways Americans may overtake you on both sides, and may themselves change lane without signalling.
Watch your positioning on near-side lanes of highways. These sometimes become exit lanes only, and you may not see the sign saying 'Right Lane Must Exit' until too late. Many stretches of roadway on fast highways are heavily studded. This is an effective deterrent to speeding, as the noise of the drumming of the tyres is most alarming. On urban highways, keep an eye on the speed limits.
11 Cars carrying fewer than four people may be barred from certain privileged lanes of highways, especially at rush hours. These express lanes by-pass hold-ups at junctions, and are designed to encourage car-sharing.
12 Keep a lookout for cyclists — they are allowed to ride towards oncoming traffic.
13 Always lock your car when it is unattended.
14 Never pick up hitch-hikers.
15 Never call a sidewalk a pavement. To an American, the pavement is the roadway, and using

the English term could lead to confusion if you have to have dealings with the police.

MEDICAL TREATMENT

If a doctor or a dentist is required, your hotel will call one for you. Alternatively your embassy or consulate can supply a list of approved doctors. Medical charges in the States are high. Get yourselves insured before you leave.

HOTELS & RESTAURANTS

American food at its best is excellent. By British standards, restaurants are not over-expensive, but remember that portions may be larger than you are used to, and salad is often served without question as a first course. Except for self service restaurants, it is common to wait for a 'hostess' to usher you to a table, and send someone to take your order. Tipping in restaurants is expected — 12½ or 15% is normal. Sometimes restaurants have a 'happy hour' usually between 4 and 7 pm when meals cost less.
Hotels seldom include the cost of breakfast in the price of a room, but in cities hotels often offer

cheap weekend rates to keep the rooms filled.

PUBLIC HOLIDAYS

Americans celebrate a number of public holidays which will not be familiar to tourists. The principal holidays are as follows:

New Year's Day	1 January
Washington's Birthday	Third Monday in February
Memorial Day	Last Monday in May
Independence Day	4 July
Labor Day	First Monday in September
Columbus Day	Second Monday in October
Armistice Day	11 November
Thanksgiving Day	Fourth Thursday in November
Christmas Day	25 December

Other commemorative days such as Lincoln's Birthday, Veterans' Day and Yom Kippur, are celebrated as holidays in certain states or areas.

TOURIST INFORMATION

Every state has a State Tourist Department from which tourist literature and maps are available. Addresses of these departments may be

obtained from the United States Travel Services, US Department of Commerce, 22 Sackville Street, London W1.

TELEPHONES

Public telephones are found everywhere in the USA: in most restaurants, garages, tobaconnists and drugstores, as well as in pavement telephone boxes, hotel foyers, bus and railway stations and airports. Instructions for use are clearly printed beside the telephone. Local calls cost from 10 to 20 cents, and when making long-distance calls, a plentiful supply of quarters (25¢ pieces) will be useful. Many large hotels and other organizations have freephone numbers, for which the code is 800, and these you may phone without charge. Some hotels also have 'courtesy phones' at airports, and these are also free.
The STD system is universal, but if you need the operator, dial 0. Telephone codes for the cities described in this book are:

San Francisco:	415
Los Angeles:	213
Las Vegas:	702
New Orleans:	504
Miami:	305
Washington:	202
New York:	212
Boston:	617

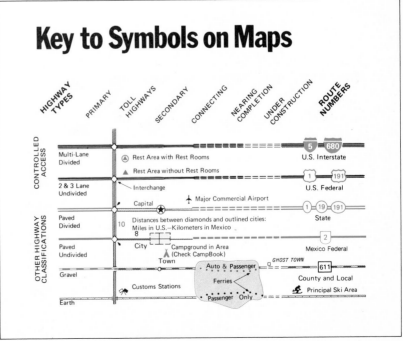

Key to Symbols on Maps

TIME ZONES:
Continental USA has four major time zones. Eastern Standard Time is three hours ahead of Pacific Time, two hours ahead of Mountain Time and one hour ahead of Central Time. The map shows the extent of the different time zones and tells you what time it is in each when it is noon by Eastern Standard Time. In April, clocks are put forward one hour to take advantage of extra daylight, and they are put back again in late October. British time is five hours ahead of Eastern Standard Time.

DRIVING DISTANCES:
Distances and driving times are compiled by AAA road reporters driving the most often-used routes under normal conditions. The driving times take account of speed limits but not of any stops en route. Distances and driving times are estimated from city centre to city centre.

Time Zones and Driving Distances

Distances are shown in red
Driving times are shown in blue

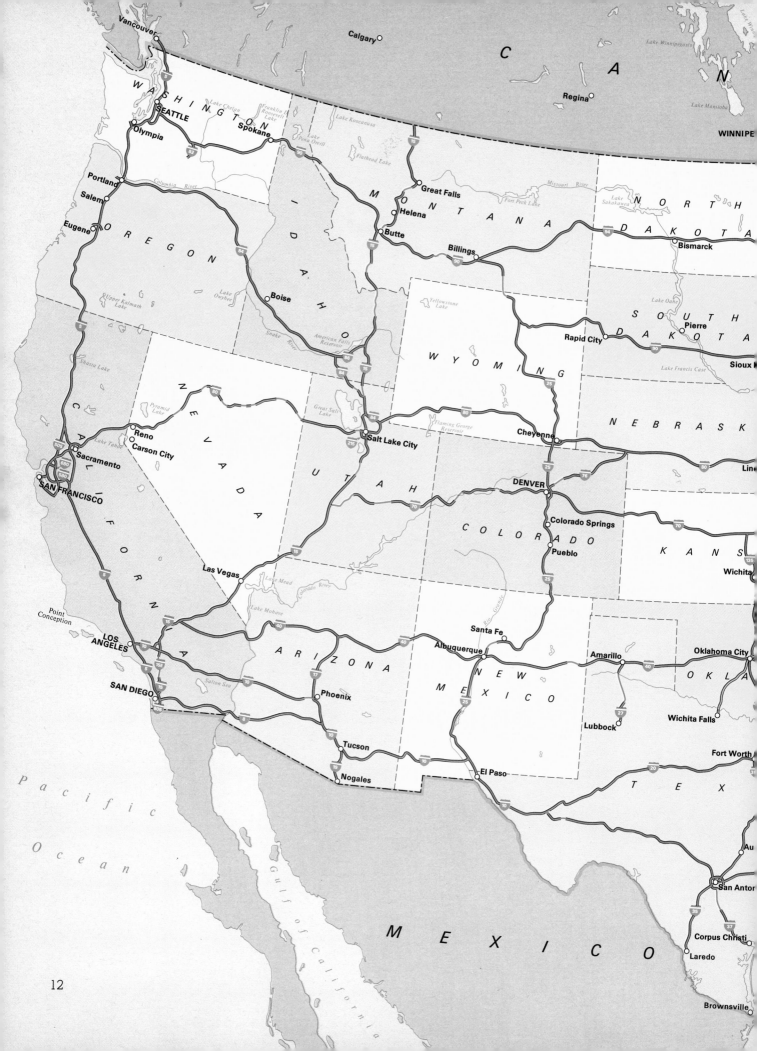

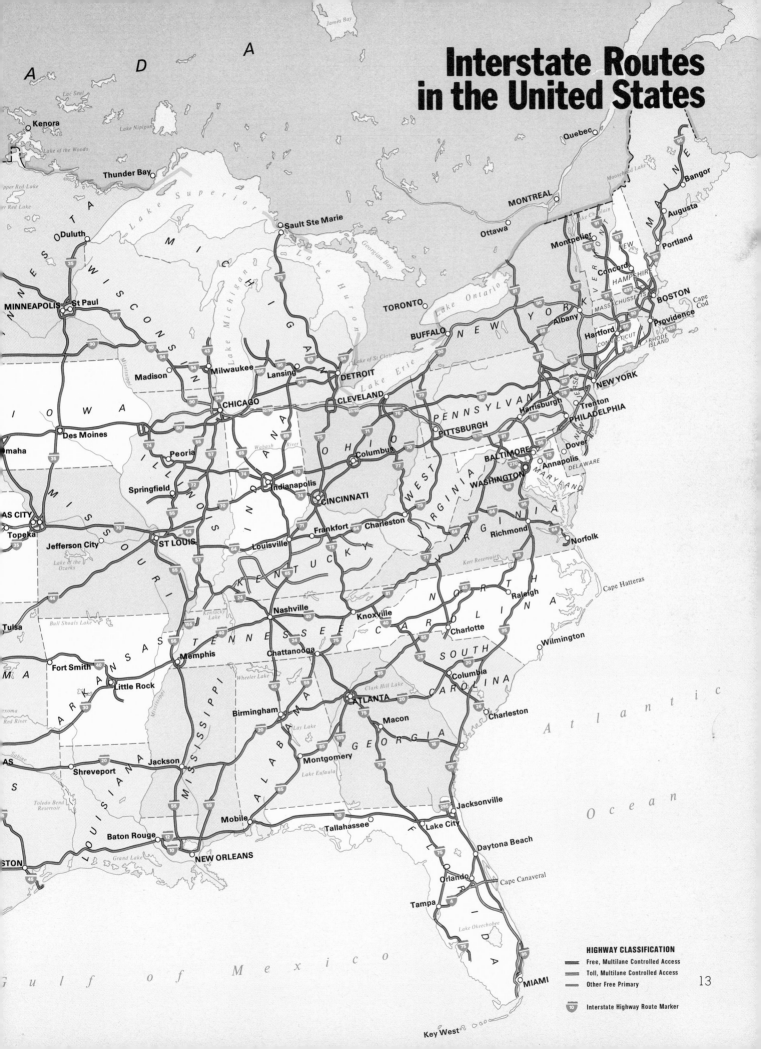

Interstate Routes in the United States

HIGHWAY CLASSIFICATION

— Free, Multilane Controlled Access
— Toll, Multilane Controlled Access
— Other Free Primary

🛡 10 Interstate Highway Route Marker

13

Completed in 1937, Golden Gate Bridge, which spans the entrance to San Francisco's harbour, has become one of the world's most famous landmarks. In the background, the misty outline of the Oakland Bay Bridge, and Alcatraz island

San Francisco

San Francisco is a city most Western nations might have been glad to call their own. It is truly an international city, not because it attracts more foreign tourists or diplomats or jet-setters than any other comparable metropolis, but because it is so easy to feel at home here. People come from all over the world to live in San Francisco.

The city has dignity, emanating from its many old-style buildings, its elegant Golden Gate Bridge, its undulating streets, its anachronistic cable-car system. Rebuilt seven times after devastating fires — the last one caused by a cataclysmic earthquake in 1906 — San Francisco truly enjoys the task of preserving what is left of the past. It is a good place for the European tourist to make his first acquaintance with America, but it is also hard to leave. As an anonymous wag once said: 'I'd rather be a broken lamp-post on San Francisco's Battery Street than the Waldorf-Astoria in New York.'

The automatic motor car might have been developed specially for San Francisco. Like the cable car, it suits the roller-coaster contours of the streets. The city's garages would do a roaring trade in burnt-out clutches if motorists had to do a hill start in bottom gear at the lights.

In San Francisco (never, never call it Frisco, particularly in earshot of an inhabitant), the hills are alive with the sound of screeching brakes, tooting horns and clanging cable cars which hurtle through busy junctions miraculously cleared of traffic in the nick of time. To the visitor it must at first seem a highly perilous place to motor in. But it is not, provided you remember two important traffic regulations in the city: first, that cable cars always have the right of way, and secondly, that if you park on a hill you must turn your wheels into the kerb to prevent rolling. If you remember these two cardinal rules, you will find that driving in the city is just different — and very rewarding.

The hills on which San Francisco stands offer an endlessly captivating variety of viewpoints. There are few places in the world where one can watch a sunset more spectacular than that seen from Sutro Heights Park. Smog permitting — although to British visitors, accustomed to a semi-permanent blanket of overcast skies, California's notorious smog is little more than a damp mist — a car park conveniently gives a grandstand view as the ball of fire sinks out of sight behind the ocean. Nobody can say for certain how many hills there are. Forty is the number most people agree on, but some say more. The problem is that one man's mountain is another man's molehill. And the argument is simply about what part of the city should be considered up and what down.

The cable cars take all the hills in their stride. Outdated and uncomfortable though they are, they are still the most practical mode of transport for San Francisco. Recognition of their value to the community was made in 1964 when the US Government designated the cable-car system a historic landmark, preserving the rolling stock for posterity and the tourists.

Indeed, the tourist derives more than a nostalgic thrill from these antiquities. The control centre of the cable-car system is open to visitors, who can watch the 10½ miles of wrapped steel cable moving over the giant winches at a steady 9½ miles an hour. Fed under the street surface, the cable is grabbed by each car and the cars are literally pulled along.

It was all the brainchild of a London-born engineer and wire-rope manufacturer. In 1869 Andrew Hallidie watched in outrage as a team of four horses struggled up a steep San Francisco slope hauling a heavily laden cart. One horse slipped on the cobbles, the other horses couldn't hold the cart, and the whole combination slipped back, tumbling the horses and cart down the hill. Vowing to find a way to prevent the cruel exploitation of these animals Hallidie took four years to perfect his idea. On 2 August 1873 the first cable car made its maiden run down Nob Hill's perilous east side. Now there are three routes, some with gradients as steep as one in five. But cable cars have a good safety record. Among four separate braking devices is an emergency brake

California Street and Lombard Street — they call Lombard Street 'the crookedest street in the world' because it takes in ten tight 'S' bends as it descends a precipitous hill — have probably been photographed more often than any other streets in the world. No wonder so many film makers, tempted by the lure of San Francisco's innumerable photographic surprises, have built the city into the framework of their motion pictures.

Captivated by its life-style, many artists and writers have been enslaved by it, too. Somerset Maugham called it 'the most civilized city in America.' Rudyard Kipling complained it had only one drawback: 'tis hard to leave.' John Steinbeck, though not a native of San Francisco, regarded himself as part of its fabric and likened it to 'a golden handcuff with the keys thrown away.' His words perhaps best express the problems of a tourist

choosing San Francisco as the first American city to visit. He may just never want to go anywhere else.

To the European and in particular to the British, some of the attraction of San Francisco is its European texture — its Victorian houses, the narrow nooks and crannies hiding behind its streets, a sanguine appreciation by many of its residents that it is a city for living in. Above all the tourist is captivated by San Francisco's magnificent location. Caught between a bay and an ocean, with a coastline of unparalleled beauty, it is just a few hours' drive from some of the world's most awesome forests and the muted grandeur of the deserts.

(Above) Outsoaring even the skyscrapers, the 853ft-tall Transamerica pyramid towers over Jackson Square

which, once applied, can be dislodged only by a welding crew.

Passengers also usually manage to escape injury, despite their apparent total disregard for safety. Travelling at nine and a half miles an hour is not very fast, but every cable car, at most times of the day, is festooned with people hanging on wherever they can find a foothold. Sometimes as many as ninety have found room on a car with only twenty-nine seats.

There is no better way to cut yourself an unforgettable slice of San Francisco's panorama than to climb aboard the No. 60 cable car at the corner of Powell and Market streets and let it transport you on the most thrilling switchback ride you will ever have outside a fairground, over Nob Hill and Russian Hill north towards the bay. Or stand at the bottom of California Street and look up as it stretches like a colossal escalator towards the horizon before dipping out of sight.

The California Street cablecar, seen from Nob Hill. Beyond, the 8½-mile-span of the Oakland Bay Bridge

San Francisco

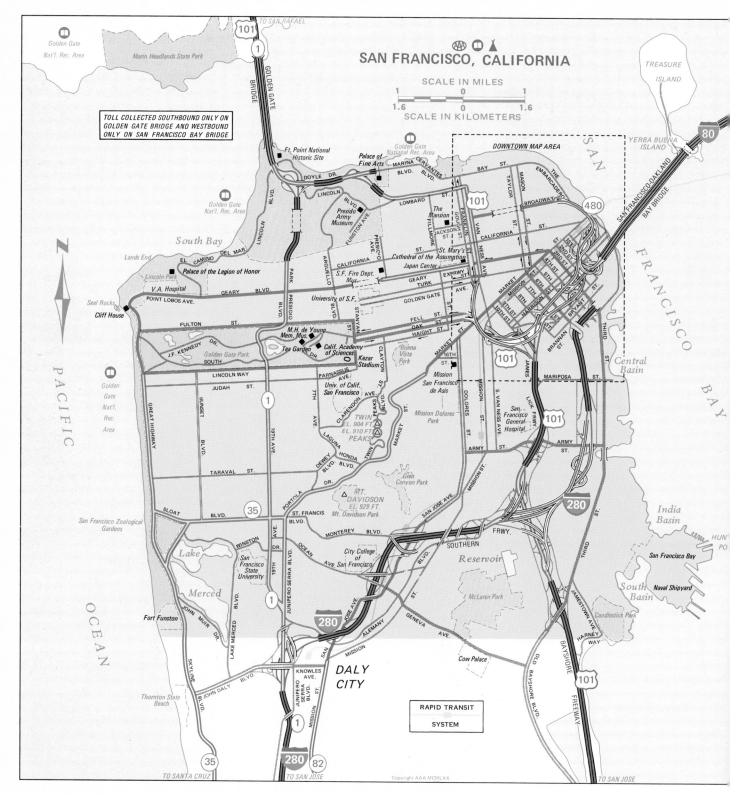

Because there are no great industries in and around the city, tourism is San Francisco's principal business. In the late 1970s, it accommodated more visitors per year than there were people living in the whole metropolitan area. Its appeal lies not only in its beautiful setting and European flavour, but also in its equable climate. Temperatures rarely rise far into

the seventies. The highest rainfall, and that is not very much, is in December, January and February, and it rains hardly at all from May to September. Indeed, the best time to see San Francisco is in October and November, when on many days the view of the bay stands out crystal clear, the sun is warm and the wind cool. If the city's radio commentators are any-

thing to go by, San Franciscans have a fixation about rain. Expectations of a shower are measured in percentages — a forty per cent chance of rain is given apocalyptic treatment. In San Francisco, rain is an intrusion; 'Haven't we got enough to worry about with the smog?' they seem to ask.

In 1980, San Francisco completed its

tively modernistic Hyatt Regency in the Embarcadero Center at the foot of California Street. Its enormous atrium lobby is an entertainment complex in itself, drawing hundreds of passers-by through its doors every day. But even in the Nob Hill neighbourhood you can find a room for a modest price — sometimes including free breakfast, a luxury that most large American hotels still deny their guests. 'B and B', however, is catching on with the smaller hotels which aim at more modest European standards, but are able to provide these services in attractive settings, often retaining the Victorian or Edwardian character of the building.

The Victorian architectural influence is overwhelming in San Francisco. If you decide to hire a car, you can get the measure of this influence on a forty-nine-mile scenic drive that the San Francisco Visitors' Bureau has mapped out with signposts marked by a blue, white and orange seagull motif along the route. The drive takes in all the major landmarks, such as the Golden Gate Bridge, Nob Hill, Chinatown, Golden Gate Park, Japan Town (Nihonmachi to the initiated), which has its own shops, restaurants, theatres and hotels; Fisherman's Wharf, (that famous — or, some people might say, infamous — tourist haunt where the quality of the food is sometimes matched by the banality of the souvenirs), a handful of museums ranging from San Francisco's military showplace, the Presidio, to the quaint cable-car museum next to the engine room.

Alternatively, you can park the car in

twentieth new hotel for the tourist in ten years. Still more are planned to add to the 50,000 rooms that are available in the city. Prices are, of course, highest in the city's dozen luxury hotels. Four of them (the Fairmont, Huntington, Mark Hopkins and Stanford) sit astride Nob Hill, 400ft up. Nob Hill — its name derived from 'nabob' — was once the quarter of the super-rich, many of whom now prefer to live outside the city away from the hubbub. But the hotels on Nob Hill retain their air of aloof and discreet exclusivity, despite growing

Large American cars find difficulty in negotiating Lombard Street, 'the crookedest street in the world'

competition from the big, brash 'townships' of hotels created by the large chains like Hyatt and Hilton.

The Hilton in the city (there is another at the airport) claims to be the largest hotel on the West Coast, with 1800 rooms. Hyatt has two in the city centre — a traditional hotel in Union Square and the imagina-

---

There are three price categories of hotels and restaurants listed: expensive, moderate and reasonable. Prices cannot be specified as they are subject to change and to fluctuations in the exchange rate. Hence the categories are intended only as a rough guide.

Hotels

HOLIDAY INN: Fisherman's Wharf, 1300 Columbus Ave, tel. 771 9000, 339 rooms, price range: moderate
Impressive glass-walled suites, public rooms looking out on Telegraph Hill and the Bay. Small swimming pool and restaurant in greenhouse setting; seafood bar.

THE MANSION HOTEL: 2220 Sacramento St. Pacific Heights, tel. 929 9444, 18 rooms, price range: reasonable
One of a dozen or more new 'neighbourhood inns' opened in refurbished property, this

was once a hostel for hippies. In its new role, it capitalizes on its home-from-home atmosphere. Stylish Victorian decor with brass beds and handmade quilts compensate for shared bathrooms. Free sauna and room service breakfast.

MIYAKO HOTEL: Japan Center, Post St, tel. 922 3200, 208 rooms, price range: moderate
Japanese-style accommodation makes this a delightfully different experience. There are miniature indoor gardens, and an attractive Japanese garden layout is overlooked from the Garden Bar. The restaurant provides Japanese cuisine, but Western dishes and conventional rooms are also available.

THE RAPHAEL: 386 Geary St, tel. 986 2000, 150 rooms, price range: moderate
Although not large, the Raphael has a well-bred elegance. Situated in the heart of theatreland, it

displays modern art posters, including works by Matisse, Chagall, Picasso and Henry Moore. The Pam Pam East restaurant has booths for secluded dining. The walls of the cocktail bar are hung with theatrical souvenirs.

Restaurants

PAPRIKAS FONO HUNGARIAN RESTAURANT: 900 North Point, Ghirardelli Sq, tel. 441 1223, price range: moderate
Really authentic Hungarian food, distinctively different from other European cuisine. Soup is cooked in traditional peasant fashion on an open fire in a special kettle.

Pastries are prepared in the adjoining pastry shop. Popular choices are chicken paprikas, veal and lamb tokany and, of course, goulash. Open daily.

SAM'S GRILL AND SEAFOOD RESTAURANT: 374 Bush St, tel. 421 0594, price range: moderate
Good seafood in a traditional American atmosphere with 13 curtained booths giving it that 'speakeasy' look. Mainly a lunchtime draw for business people close to the city's financial district, it is also suitable for early dinner, served until 8.30pm. Closed weekends.

LE TRIANON RENÉ VERDON: 242 O'Farrell St, tel. 982 9353, price range: expensive
René Verdon has impeccable credentials. A master chef of France, he was picked as the official White House chef during President Kennedy's era. Since they opened their own restaurant Verdon and his wife, Yvette, have

established an irreproachable reputation for high cuisine in an informal 18th-century setting. Specialities include Salade Yvette, mousse au chocolate René, his own dessert, filet d'agneau en croute Trianon and globi de volaille au poivre vert. Evenings only. Closed Sundays.

THE WATERFRONT: Pier 7, Embarcadero, tel. 391 2696, price range: expensive
Seafood at its best combined with a magnificent view of San Francisco bay makes a meal here something rather special. Oak panelling and stained-glass windows give the place a period atmosphere. Try Pacific salmon, Gulf prawns, and Waterfront scampi (they are baby lobster tails sautéed in a blend of garlic lemon butter, shallots and white wine). Drink the local Californian wines with your meal. Brunch served Saturday and Sunday. Eggs Benedict and a fresh seafood omelette are popular choices. Open daily.

San Francisco

the city centre for a small fee (taking care to observe the parking signs and avoid 'tow-away zones'), and explore parts of the route at more leisure on foot. The two major squares, Union and Jackson, are good starting points.

From Union Square, the heart of the shopping and hotel district, some of the finest shops in the world are only a few steps away. Bounded by the fashionable streets of Powell, Post, Geary and Stockton, Union Square is the hub of the city, and the shops are immaculate. I. Magnin occupies eight floors, offering Californian and European designs in furs, sportswear, shoes — luxury items that only a major store with an international clientele can hope to sell at top prices.

In Post you will find Gumps, another famous department store where rare antiques, Chinese and Japanese porcelains, jade and stone carvings vie for attention with rare furniture, lamps, crystals, and almost priceless jewellery by leading American, European and Asian designers. Wander along Post to the junction of Grant Avenue and you come across a touch of Scotland at the Scotch House, which sells cashmere, lambswool and Shetland sweaters — even Irish handknits.

Jackson Square will probably appeal more to the antique and art buff, as becomes its handsome nineteenth-century façade. A seedy souvenir of the city's early beginnings, the square was nurtured into new life in the 1950s. Restoration of the 400 blocks that make up this narrow, oblong area of Jackson Street has now made it a fashionable centre, but nevertheless the innate charm of San Francisco is deeply rooted here.

In contrast, the Embarcadero Center, near the waterfront, affects the style of so many undercover shopping 'malls' which have been such a success all over the States. This one is tucked away behind tall office buildings, so its shops have to offer glossy brochures at street corners to attract customers.

Make sure you see the new St Mary's Catholic Cathedral — a strident piece of architecture in Italian marble which, according to its critics, looks like a washing-machine agitator. More than ten years after the foundations were laid, the city is still arguing whether such a controversial design should have had a place on the San Francisco skyline. It rose, like a phoenix out of the ashes, after fire had destroyed the seventy-two-year-old mother church in 1962. When the new cathedral was finished, the then archbishop of San Francisco, who had helped to steady the architects' nerves, was presented with what must be regarded as San Francisco's supreme accolade: a tiny, silver cable car.

In concept, the design is a long way from what remains of Mission Dolores at 16th and Dolores Streets. One of the first six of the twenty-one Spanish missions established on the Californian coast between

Erected in 1776, Mission Dolores, influenced by Moorish architecture, was founded by Father Junipero Serra

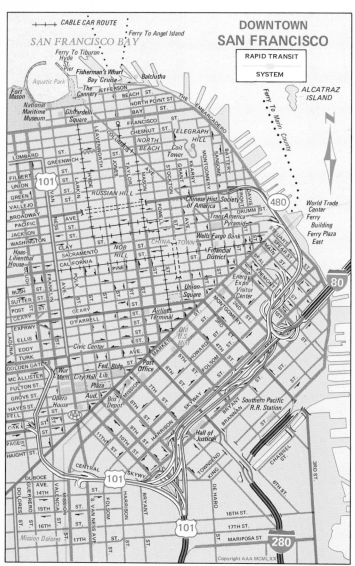

Shops

America's most famous names in shops are nearly all represented in San Francisco, and the majority can be found in the central area in and around Union Square and a network of fashionable streets leading off into leafy alleyways and discreet cul-de-sacs where some of the smartest shops are to be found. But the city has several other important and highly distinctive shopping areas to visit.

SUTTER STREET: one street north of Union Square, has vogue boutiques, and stylish furnishing, haute couture and rare accessories shops.

EMBARCADERO CENTER: foot of Market Street, is an impressive office block in which shops and restaurants on three levels have been incorporated with landscaped plazas and promenades. High fashion, exciting gifts, exotic foods.

CHINATOWN: bounded by Broadway, Bush, Kearny and Stockton Streets, specializes in porcelains, rattan and bamboo ware, teak furniture, carved ivory and, of course Chinese food. Start your exploration at Chinatown Gate, at the junction of Bush and Grant Streets.

KINTETSU SHOPPING CENTER: in the Japan Center bordered by Post, Geary, Languna and Fillmore Streets, has oriental specialities on a two-level shopping 'mall', and an arcade where the arts of Japanese flower arranging, ceramics and pearl culture are demonstrated.

1769 and 1823, it once included shops, stables and a barracks for the mission soldiers. Now only the church — its redwood timbers still lashed together with rawhide as they were a century ago — and the cemetery garden are left.

Some of the most rewarding places to make for (and, of course, the ubiquitous cable cars or buses will save your legs) are the hills. There are stunning views of the city from 300ft-high Russian Hill. On Telegraph Hill, also 300ft high, the 210ft Coit Memorial Tower, built in memory of the city's volunteer firefighters, offers an even better view. Alternatively, there is a choice of hotels where you can take a leisurely drink with a view: the Top of the Mark in the Mark Hopkins Hotel; forty floors up at the Hyatt on Union Square; the Hyatt Regency, which has the city's only revolving restaurant, or the top of the Hilton tower, forty-six storeys high. Above the rooftops, the vista, with its predominance of nineteenth-century architecture, is overwhelming. Of the 14,000 houses that survived the 1906 earthquake (and subsequently the activities of the developers), about half have been restored to something of their former splendour.

In the quake and the three days of fires that followed, 600 people died and 28,000 buildings were destroyed. The entire north-east side of the city was wiped out, and a rich vein of Victoriana reduced to rubble. Much of what had been left was neglected or pulled down in the next half-century, but then wisdom prevailed. Thanks to a foundation formed to redevelop the run-down areas of the city, paint and design businesses are flourishing, and an entire industry has sprung up to supply replicas of the nineteenth-century stone and wood.

On the waterfront, where most of the piers are thoughtfully numbered (Fisherman's Wharf, squeezed between two piers, is 45), a disused chocolate factory has become a thriving 'community' centre housing in four buildings quaint specialist shops, art galleries, restaurants and even a theatre. Called Ghirardelli Square, after the man who built up the

chocolate empire, the seventy-year-old factory has been sensitively restored and is now a multi-level complex, each building retaining its turn-of-the-century character. In one building, dominated by a clock tower (a replica from a French chateau), the famous chocolate can still be seen being made. Different in character, but similar in aim, is the reincarnation of the Del Monte fruit cannery building. Called the Cannery, it opened in the late 1960s as a smaller and more arty version of Ghirardelli Square.

These centres have been so successful in drawing shoppers, gourmets and crowds of young people looking for somewhere to

On the San Francisco waterfront: (right) Ghirardelli Square, (left) the Cannery, two old factories now converted to shops, cafés and theatres

'do their own thing' that the idea has spread to another pier. Unlike the others, Pier 39 has been tailor-made to attract tourists and provide a platform for young musicians, jugglers and mimers who give impromptu performances to indulgent family audiences. It opened in 1978 to a fanfare of civic pride. At the bottom of Columbus Avenue, Cost-Plus is an immensely practical, though less imaginatively built emporium of Indian brass, china, glass and gourmet specialities within reach of the street-market shopper.

One of the pleasures of shopping in any American city is that so many shops stay open late — useful if you are on the way to sample the restaurants and the nightlife.

San Francisco has a staggering variety of good restaurants and a total of 2600 to choose from. If you order a French wine in some of the more prestigious

places, then expect the waiter to disapprove of your choice automatically. California's grape harvest makes for excellent table wines and any wine waiter worth his diamond-studded corkscrew would be proud to recommend a wine bottled just up the road in the Napa and Sonoma valleys. The names on the labels will be more familiar if you have already spent a day up in the wine country. Nearly all the vineyards welcome visitors, and there is no problem about sampling the wines. Many vineyards offer tables and chairs for visitors' picnics. At the Wine Country Restaurant in Healdsburg you can eat at a table in a wine barrel!

For more conventional surroundings American, French, Italian and English cuisine is available in almost every neighbourhood of the city, or within easy driving distance. In Chinatown — the largest Chinese community outside Asia is concentrated here — you can find some of the finest oriental food in the world. In downtown, the fashionable shopping and business area, you can also eat well in German, Moroccan, Armenian/Russian or Polynesian restaurants.

For the British who miss the taste of English beer, Rosebud's English pub offers a moderately priced English-style dinner in a reasonably authentic English atmosphere. For the really genuine article (well, as genuine as landlord Charles Felix, an expatriate Englishman, and his wife can make from what they still regard as a hobby), the Pelican Inn on Highway 1 (a mere twenty minutes from the Golden Gate Bridge) keeps a good cellar of Bass, Watneys, John Courage and Guinness. The sixteenth-century panelled bar, with its brasses, low beams, dart boards, and bar snacks, appeals enough to passing American motorists for them to stop in increasing numbers at the beamed, white-painted cottage and stand shoulder to

shoulder in the bar with the stalwart English regulars.

Why Pelican? It was the original name of the *Golden Hind,* in which Sir Francis Drake beached at the Marin coast just a few miles away. The fact that he didn't actually find the bay is partly due to his unconcealed relief at making landfall, and partly to California's persistent fog, which hid the bay from the view of passing mariners for another 200 years. What really matters about the city's past is that, just like its millions of modern disciples, the earliest colonizers fell for the charms of its bayside location.

The first white settlement on the site where San Francisco now stands was established in 1776 by a Spanish officer, Colonel Juan Batista de Anza. Soon after he had put up a Spanish military post on the southern shore of the Golden Gate, a group of Franciscan Fathers founded the first Mission several miles up the coast. Having hacked out a trail linking the two stations it was only a matter of time before a halting place sprang up half way. It took another sixty years for it to develop into the town of Yerba Buena, later to be called San Francisco. At first there were only 100 inhabitants, but the discovery of gold in

Museums

CALIFORNIA ACADEMY OF SCIENCES: Music Concourse, nr 8th Ave, Golden Gate Park, tel. 752 8268. Open daily.
An enormous complex, with several halls, each with its own line in wonder. You can see dinosaurs in Cowell Hall; Man, under exciting anthropological examination in the Wattis Hall; fossils, flora, birds and mammals in their myriad guises on display in the Halls of Science, the North American Hall and the African Hall; and 197 tanks filled with 10,000 specimens of sealife at the Steinhart Aquarium.

EXPLORATORIUM: Palace of Fine Arts, 3601 Lyon St, tel. 563 7337. Open Wed-Fri

1-5pm; weekends 12-5pm; Wed. eve only 7-9.30pm. Free except for Tactile Gallery.
Here you may 'Look, touch, feel, smell and hear'. Marvellous for young people. Some 400 scientific, technological and artistic exhibits can be activated at the push of a button. The museum is housed in the only building still remaining from those put up for the San Francisco World Fair of 1915.

NATIONAL MARITIME MUSEUM: Aquatic Park, Polk St, tel. 556 8177; The *Balclutha,* Pier 43; Hyde St Pier, 2905 Hyde St, tel. 556 6435. Open daily.
Figureheads, ship models and photographs illustrate West Coast maritime history and the city waterfront. See a lot

more about it on board the *Balclutha,* a three-masted square-rigged sailing vessel of the Cape Horn fleet built in Scotland almost 100 years ago. At Hyde Street Pier is a floating museum of fine historic ships.

OLD MINT: 5th & Mission Sts, tel. 556 6270. Closed Sunday and Monday. Free.
A million dollars stacked in a pyramid of 71 bars of pure gold and 1000 ounces of gold nuggets worth over £5 million on the open market are the highlight of a tour through this late 19th-century building. A collection of privately minted gold coins includes some from gold dug by the pioneers of the Old West. You can strike your own souvenir medal during your visit, on an 1869 press.

RIPLEY'S BELIEVE-IT-OR-NOT MUSEUM: 175 Jefferson St, tel. 771 6188. Open daily.
If you want to see the world's smallest violin, the largest shoe, or a two-headed goat you will find them among cartoonist Robert L. Ripley's 2000 oddities. His private hoard reflects his life-long fascination with the unbelievable and unimaginable.

WAX MUSEUM AT FISHERMAN'S WHARF: 145 Jefferson St, tel. 885 4975. Open daily.
Madame Tussaud had more than a finger in this pie, and the idea will be familiar to British visitors who have been to the London waxworks. Like Madame Tussauds, the museum has a Chamber of Horrors, and also a Hall of Fame. It also has a full-size

replica of the Tutankhamen treasures. Seventy-four tableaux feature 275 authentically costumed wax figures.

Guided City Walks

GUIDED CITY WALKS: For information and, where necessary, reservations, for: Chinese Heritage Walks, Culinary Walk with lunch (fee) tel. 986 1822; City Guide Walks (including City Hall, Civic Centre, Fire Dept. Museum, etc), tel. 558 3949; Golden Gate Park Walks (weekends only, May-October), tel. 543 4664; Heritage Walks (fee) Sundays only, tel. 441 3046.

A gateway crowned by 2 dragons (left) marks the entrance to Chinatown, whose colourful streets are often strung with paper lanterns (above)

the American River in 1848 was the magnet for thousands of gold-rush prospectors. Thirteen years later San Francisco had a population of 10,000. By the time the city was reached by the first transcontinental railroad in 1869, the world wanted to beat a path to its door. Even though the gold rush was over, there was still a lot of silver in 'them thar hills' just a few days' ride away. Over 100 years later more than three million people live in the metropolitan area, but only about

twenty per cent of them in the city itself.

San Francisco supports a noble musical tradition and a theatrical culture only marginally less impressive. The demand for seats at the War Memorial Opera House and the new 3000-seater Louise M. Davies Symphony Hall usually far outstrips what is available on any one night. Even a new extension to the Opera House (home of the San Francisco Opera and ballet companies), and a new rehearsal hall for the San Francisco Symphony Orchestra are expected to be inadequate provision for the city's growing audiences. For film enthusiasts, the Palace of Fine Arts houses a 1000-seater theatre where the prestigious San Francisco Film Festival is held every year. The major significant stage output is concentrated at the American Conservatory Theater in Geary Street. The resident repertory company offers a wide range of plays and shows to a consistently high standard.

If your taste in nightlife is for what the Americans call burlesque — a term for

San Francisco Bay in 1868. Before the railway was built, the city was most easily reached by sea

anything between a sleazy strip show and a spectacular revue — San Francisco offers a rich choice to its devotees.

With so much going on, it is hard to recognize the fact that San Francisco has only over recent years developed its cultural life, and to remember that its origin was as a rumbustious watering hole. An area of Union Street, where 100 years ago the first dairy herd grazed in a dip between two hills, still clings to its name of Cow Hollow. Today shoppers have replaced the dairy maids, and the cash registers in the specialist shops that have sprung up in the meantime ring more briskly than the cow bells ever did. Situated between Russian Hill and the Presidio, Cow Hollow hides behind flower-filled courtyards, passages bordered by boutiques, and backyard barns stocked with antiques. Some of the cluster of old Victorian houses, artfully refurbished for the smart shops, are reminiscent of London mews. Cows were banished from Union Street early this century, but they still appear from time to time at livestock shows in the Cow Palace — a derisory name bestowed on one of the largest indoor sports stadiums in the West. It was built as a farmers' showplace and these days it is used more

San Francisco

for rodeos and livestock exhibitions than as the venue for the main spectator sports.

Most baseball and football home fixtures are held in Candlestick Park, a stadium rather than a park. But San Francisco has an abundance of parkland, thanks to an Act of Congress in 1972 which set aside 35,000 acres in San Francisco and Marin County as parkland. Now increased to 39,000 acres, its boundaries encompass vast areas that fringe the ocean and cut deep swathes into the square pattern of roads. Parks with evocative names — Pine Lake, Glen Canyon, Lincoln, Buena Vista. Perhaps the best loved is Golden Gate Park, 1000 acres of drives, walks, lawns and gardens. There is enough to see there to justify several visits, such as the Japanese tea garden, a conservatory modelled after London's Kew Gardens, the music concourse with a band concert every Sunday, and museums.

Echoing John Steinbeck, the real problem about visiting San Francisco is to summon up the determination to saw through the handcuffs and get out of the city for long enough to explore the countryside.

Though the great Californian redwood forests are too far away to explore in a day's drive out of the city, a small, lovingly preserved cluster of giant *sequoia sempervirens* — the world's tallest tree — is on San Francisco's doorstep. To drive the seventeen miles to Muir Woods *(see p.39)* takes you over the Golden Gate Bridge to Marin County,

home of San Francisco's commuters. In the 1970s the bridge was the number one tourist attraction in America, and owes its appeal as much to its opulent name as to its elegance of design and its beautiful location. When it opened in 1937, it was the longest single-span suspension bridge in the world, spanning more than one and a half miles across the entrance to one of the world's largest land-locked harbours. This great engineering feat was accomplished with a main span of 4200ft and two massive towers which, rising 746ft above the water, are still the highest bridge towers ever built.

Disappointingly the bridge is not painted gold — more a rust red. You can sweep across the bridge out of the city free of charge, though to come back into the city you must pay. First right after the bridge takes you to Vista Point, where the panoramic view of the city is superb. Once through the charming rainbow-striped tunnel entrance beyond, you can drive a short circular route which takes in the other two main bridges across the bay. Travelling clockwise, you can also avoid tolls on the Richmond-St Rafael bridge and only pay for the drive across Oakland Bay Bridge back into the city. The cost saving is minimal, and is typical of the indulgent attitude of San Francisco to its countless attractions.

Another example of San Francisco's tolerance, the cable car is only the flamboyant part of an extensive municipal transport system in the city. MUNI, as it

likes to be called, still clings to its few trams, and the city area is well served by buses; maps of bus routes will be found at the front of the Yellow Pages in the telephone book.

The pride and joy of the MUNI system are the three new subway lines linking nine San Francisco subway stations with twenty-five across the bay. Among them is Berkeley, where the University of California occupies a beautiful 720-acre campus. Impeccably clean, airy and speedy, the seventy-one-mile Bay Area Rapid Transport railway (better known, in the fashion of modern acronyms, as BART) is neglected and unloved by the community. Commuters complain that it should never have been built where it was; that it would have been better to spend the millions of dollars it cost to relieve pressure on the commuters who have to use ferries across the Golden Gate Strait when they can no longer bear the rush-hour queues on the bridge. Others, remembering a disastrous fire on one of the trains, still condemn it for being a fire hazard even though the authorities have since replaced the inflammable upholstery of the seats which was blamed for the blaze.

The cynics, on the other hand, say that it is just another sign of San Francisco's

Victorian timbered houses, as characteristic of old San Francisco as the Hyde Street cable car

'Occupation: gangster' defiantly wrote Al Capone, most notorious of Alcatraz prisoners. The island is now a popular San Francisco resort

reluctance to embrace the twentieth century. (Many San Franciscans still visibly shudder at the sight of the Transamerica Corporation's 34-million-dollar pyramid-shaped folly rising 853ft above all else in the heart of the city. It does look out of place — rather more so than the half-acre of Redwood trees planted along the east side of the Pyramid base.) BART's main drawback for the tourist is discovering how to operate its automatic ticket machines. There is a list of instructions, and it pays to study them carefully. Fortunately trains run every twelve minutes for most of the day.

The ferry companies that ply the bay have none of these new-fangled contraptions. You pay a man in a kiosk, and as long as you have got on the right boat, they will take you on a bracing and beautiful trip north to Sausalito, Larkspur or Angel Island, or, most popular of all, to the fortress of Alcatraz, just a stone's throw out in the bay. Sullen and brooding, Alcatraz was for nearly 100 years a grim penal settlement, almost as notorious a legend as Devil's Island, to which French prisoners were shipped. It housed such Very Important Prisoners as Al Capone, Machine Gun Kelly and the Birdman, all immortalized by Hollywood.

Ironically, since Alcatraz (the innocuous translation of the Spanish is 'island of the pelicans') opened to the public in 1973, it has been almost as difficult for tourists to get on to it as it was for the convicts to get off. Only three inmates ever managed to escape, but as nothing has been heard of them since, no one can be certain that they didn't end up somewhere at the bottom of the bay.

As an entertainment Alcatraz has very little to commend it. In the claustrophobic confines of the carefully preserved cells, it is easy enough for the mind to tune in to the echoes of the despairing voices of men long gone, and to feel the violence, frustrations and miseries of human beings tantalizingly close to a civilized city only just over a mile away and yet irrevocably denied a part of it.

Alcatraz still makes demands on those who set foot on it. The tour takes in steep climbs and stone steps, and at least a mile of walking around the perimeter road. 'Please consider your physical condition before visiting the island,' warns the leaflet they hand out to you. Such a show of solicitude was not extended to the twenty-seven pale men who were led in handcuffs, leg irons and waist chains down to the wharf for the last time on 21 March 1963 when the Alcatraz cell doors finally closed for business. But it was not the last time the place was occupied. A group of disgruntled Indians took it over in 1969 and squatted there for two years.

Sail on for a few minutes more, and you land at the pretty wooden jetty on Angel Island. As a former army stronghold for many years it has had a less gruesome though no less stern past. In the last war it was an enlistment and later a discharge centre. Today army huts, their windows shuttered, still huddle together as if in a ghost town, their white clapboard walls shimmering in the heat. San Francisco has long cast covetous eyes on the islands.

The elegant conservatory in Golden Gate Park, a three-mile-long oasis of flowers and shrubs, created on a sandy waste in 1868

Since the army left in 1962, this 740-acre wildlife preserve full of trails, coves and bike paths (no cars allowed) has become a popular weekend haunt for San Franciscan families. During the three top summer months the Red and White fleet provide a daily ferry service to Angel Island, but for most of the year it is accessible only at weekends.

The ferries also call at Tiburon, which, like Sausalito at the southern tip of Marin County, has a timeless charm compounded of winding wooden streets, a one-block main drag, and a village-like character such as one might expect to find in the villages of France or Cornwall. Both communities attract the visitor who wants to shop and eat in style and at modest cost.

You can rent a car in San Francisco from dozens of firms, with very few formalities. The larger companies like Hertz and Avis can even arrange your booking as soon as you step into the airport arrival lounge. You can pick the car up there or in the city and return it at any prearranged location.

It is no use expecting to find the efficient Californian multi-lane highways surviving inside the metropolitan area, in the way so many freeways spectacularly speed up traffic in Los Angeles and other large American cities. San Francisco once tried to build its statutory network of elevated motorways — roads intended to sweep majestically over the bumpy, twisting alleys which were never built for the motor car. But they gave up in the end, and now the pathetic short stretches of new road either end abruptly above the rooftops, leading nowhere, or take the traffic half-heartedly for a few miles before dropping it back to earth and to the familiar problem of crossings and lights.

Within a day's drive of San Francisco,

San Francisco

you can find an unparalleled variety of scenery. Highway 1, which runs down the coast to the Monterey Peninsula, gives a breathtaking view of the Pacific coastline. Once there, you can have more of the same or a seventeen-mile signposted scenic drive which starts at Pacific Grove and winds along the rugged coastline. Further south are the bold cliffs of Big Sur. Further south still, at San Simeon, is Hearst Castle. This rococo mansion, former seat of the newspaper tycoon Randolph Hearst, complete with its art collection, is preserved as a colossal monument to the colossus who dominated Californian life for so many years. It is open to the public (see the Los Angeles motor tours, p.61).

If you don't want to venture that far, less than forty miles from the city along the Pescadaro Road are three parks, each of which is worth exploring for its majestic trees. The main Californian redwood forests lie much further north on Highway 101, but the Redwood Coast and the Avenue of the Giants are on the way.

Alternatively, you can go east across the Nevada border to Lake Tahoe, and on to the larger-than-life marriage and gambling mecca of Reno — notorious as the divorce capital of the States — where you can win and lose your money as easily

Byzantine splendour — gilded mosaics, rich tiles and marble statues — surround the pool at Hearst Castle

as you can dissolve your marriage.

South of Lake Tahoe is the Yosemite (pronounce it Yo-se-me-ty) National Park, with its valleys hemmed in by 4000ft ravines, and waterfalls that sparkle as they cascade down the sides *(see pp.32-4)*.

California is a land where the soil is still untamed, and where sometimes the earth erupts. Small tremors occur somewhere in the state at least once a month, but in San Francisco nobody takes much notice. Defiantly, San Franciscans seem to enjoy living on this turbulent patch of earth which might one day give way and collapse beneath their feet.

San Francisco Directory

Hotels

The hotels and restaurants listed here are either recommended by the American Automobile Association (AAA) or have been selected because they are of interest to tourists. As a rough guide to cost, they have been classified as either expensive, moderate or reasonable. Hotels, unless otherwise stated, all have private bathrooms and colour television.

BEST WESTERN AMERICANIA: 121 7th St, tel. 626 0200. 145 rooms. Parking: garage and open. Dining room and coffeeshop. Swimming pool. Motor inn, central, moderate.

BEST WESTERN EL RANCHO: 1100 El Camino Real, tel. 588 2912. 250 rooms including 14 kitchen apartments. Restaurants. Swimming pool. Motor inn, near San Francisco International Airport, reasonable.

FAIRMONT HOTEL & TOWER: 950 Mason St, tel.

772 5000. 595 rooms. Pay garage. Restaurants and coffee shop. Luxury hotel on Nob Hill. Only AAA 5-star hotel in San Francisco. Expensive.

HOLIDAY INN: Airport, 245 South Airport Blvd, tel. 589 7200. 332 rooms. Restaurant and coffee shop. Swimming pool. Standard hotel, near San Francisco International Airport, moderate.

HOLIDAY INN: Golden Gateway, 1500 Van Ness Ave, tel. 441 4000. 500 rooms. Garage parking. Restaurant and coffee shop. Swimming pool. Standard hotel, central, moderate.

HYATT ON UNION SQUARE: 345 Stockton St, tel. 398 1234. 710 rooms. Pay valet garage. Restaurants. Luxury hotel, central, expensive.

HYATT REGENCY: 5 Embarcadero Center, tel. 788 1234. 806 rooms. Pay valet parking. Restaurants. Luxury hotel, central, expensive.

MARK HOPKINS HOTEL: 1 Nob Hill Circle, tel. 392 3434. 366 rooms. Pay garage. Restaurant and coffee shop. Luxury hotel, central, expensive.

PACIFIC PLAZA: 501 Post St, tel. 441 7100. 140 rooms.

Pay valet garage. Restaurant. Motor inn, central, moderately expensive.

QUALITY INN: 2775 Van Ness Ave, tel. 928 9500. 140 rooms. Limited garage. Restaurant. Motor inn, near Bay shore, moderate.

SAN FRANCISCO HILTON: 330 O'Farrell St, tel. 771 1400. 1800 rooms. Swimming pool. Pay garage. Restaurants. Luxury hotel, central, expensive.

SHERATON PALACE HOTEL: 639 Market Street, tel. 392 8600. 600 rooms. Pay garage. Spectacular, domed, glass-roofed restaurant where Sunday brunch buffet at fixed price is a bargain. Standard hotel, 19th-century decor, central, moderate.

Restaurants

ALEXIS RESTAURANT: Mason & California Streets, tel. 885 6400. Russian and French cuisine. Closed Sundays. Central, expensive.

ALLATO'S: 8 Fisherman's Wharf. Seafood. Valet parking. Moderate.

CHARLEY BROWN'S: 1550 Bayshore Highway, Burlingame, tel. 697 6907. Steak and lobster specialities. Limited menu. Sunday brunch. Reasonable.

CHIC'S PLACE: 202A Pier 39, tel. 421 2442. American cuisine. Boat berthing for customers. Reasonable.

EMPRESS OF CHINA: 838 Grant Avenue, China Trade Center Building, Chinatown, tel. 434 1345. Excellent Chinese cuisine. Central, moderate.

GRISON'S STEAK HOUSE: 2100 Van Ness Avenue, tel. 673 1888. Roast beef served from trolley. Maine lobsters a speciality. Closed Tuesdays. Moderate.

LEHR'S GREENHOUSE: Canterbury Hotel, 740 Sutter St, tel. 474 6478. Garden setting, salad buffet speciality. Sunday brunch. Reasonable.

ONDINE RESTAURANT: 558 Bridgeway, Sausalito, tel. 332 0792. French specialities. Panoramic views. Valet parking. Expensive.

SCHROEDER'S CAFE: 240 Front St, tel. 421 4778. Highly esteemed, old established German restaurant. Closed weekends. Valet parking. Central, reasonable.

TRADER VIC'S: 20 Cosmos Place, tel. 776 2232. Exotic Polynesian cuisine. Valet parking. Moderate.

VENETO RESTAURANT: 389 Bay St, tel. 986 4553. Italian cuisine. Four dining rooms with rare doll collection. Closed Mondays. Valet parking. Moderate.

YAMATO RESTAURANT: 717 California St, tel. 397 3456. Superb Japanese food and decor. Central, moderate.

Transport

SAN FRANCISCO INTERNATIONAL AIRPORT:

About 30 international and domestic airlines use San Francisco International Airport, about 16 miles south of the city near San Mateo, on US Federal highway 101. You can have direct flight connections to most major cities in the United States, including the 7 other cities featured in this book. Frequent buses and coaches ply between city centre and airport and the journey takes about 45 minutes, but traffic congestion can sometimes make the trip much longer. The three public service carriers, Airporter, Sam Trans and Greyhound, charge each passenger less than one-tenth of many taxi or private limousine services.

AIRPORTER services information, tel. 673 2432. Buses depart from the terminal at the corner of Taylor and Ellis Streets in San Francisco.

LIMOUSINES: tel. Associated Limousines, 824 2660; Airport Limousines, tel. 595 3636; Holiday Limousines, tel. 447 3129

TAXIS: DeSoto Cab, tel. 673 1414; Luxor Cab, tel. 552 4040; Veteran's Cab, tel. 552 1300; Yellow Cab, tel.626 2345.

CAR HIRE: Five major car-hire firms have facilities for renting and returning cars at San Francisco International Airport: Hertz, Avis, Dollar National and Budget. But you do not need to rent the car at the airport in order to return it there. Generally every effort is made to give you the best deal. Yellow pages list other car-hire firms in and around the city. Many are cheaper than the leading firms, but may not provide such comprehensive service or do not inspire the same degree of confidence.

Avis Rent-A-Car, tel. 885 5011; Budget Rent-A-Car, tel. 928 7863; Dollar Rent-A-Car Systems, tel. 673 2137, Hertz Rent-A-Car; tel. 771 2200; National Car Rental System, tel. 474 5300.

CITY TRANSPORT SERVICES: The San Francisco Municipal Railway System (MUNI) operates the cable cars, buses and trams (streetcars). The exact fare is required on all public transport, as no change is given. A bus transfer ticket (from the driver) saves paying twice if you wish to break your journey or change lines. Information, tel. 673-MUNI.

THE BAY AREA RAPID TRANSIT SYSTEM: (BART) operates between the East Bay and San Francisco via a tunnel under the bay. Information, tel. 788 BART.

GOLDEN GATE FERRIES: run frequent ferry services to Marin County. Routes link Sausalito and Larkspur from the terminal at the foot of Market Street. Information, tel. 332 6600. Tiburon ferry leaves from Pier 43½. Information, tel. 546 2815. Ferry cruises of San Francisco bay: Blue & Gold Fleet, tel. 781 7877; Gold Coast Fleet, tel. 775 9108; Red & White Fleet, tel. 546 2815.

RAIL SERVICES: are provided by America's interstate rail system, AMTRAK. Shuttle buses take passengers from city centre ticket office (at 1st and Mission Streets) to terminal. AMTRAK also offers all-inclusive tours to many destinations in the United States. Tel. 800 648 3850 (no charge).

Touring Information

CALIFORNIA STATE AUTOMOBILE ASSOCIATION: Main office, 150 Van Ness Ave. Open in office hours, tel. 565 2012. District offices: Berkeley Dale City, Fremont, Greenbrae, Hayward, Oakland, Palo Alto, Redwood City, San Leandro, San Mateo, San Pablo, Santa Clara, Sunnyvale and Vallejo. Open in office hours.

SAN FRANSCISO CONVENTION & VISITORS' BUREAU: 1390, Market St, tel. 626 5500.

Places to See

BOWLES/HOPKINS GALLERY: 47 Beach St, tel. 885 4550. Graphics and special exhibitions. Open daily 10am-11pm.

CHINESE CULTURE CENTER: 750 Kearny St (3rd floor of the Holiday Inn), tel. 886 1822. Opened in 1974, it has become a popular centre for Chinese arts and culture, reflecting the customs and traditions of the city's Chinatown community. Arts performances are held in a 650-seater theatre. Open Tuesday-Saturday 10am-5pm. Free.

CORY GALLERIES: 377 Geary St, tel. 397 0966. 360 Jefferson St, tel. 771 3664. Traditional and contemporary paintings, graphics and sculpture. 19th-century English landscapes. Open daily 9am-10pm.

M.H. DE YOUNG MEMORIAL MUSEUM: Golden Gate Park, tel. 558 2887. San Francisco's most extensive collection of fine and applied arts. Priceless display of paintings. Closed Monday and Tuesday. Admission free on first Wednesday of month.

GUINNESS MUSEUM OF WORLD RECORDS: 235 Jefferson St, tel. 771 9890. Evidence of the existence of the biggest, widest, finest, etc., and a chance for visitors to beat a record or two themselves. Open daily. Check times.

WINE MUSEUM: 633 Beach St, tel. 673 6990. Exquisite glass and rare artefacts in praise of wine and its history.

Open 11am-5pm, Sunday 12-5pm, closed Monday. Free.

SAN FRANCISCO ZOOLOGICAL GARDENS: Zoo Ave, off Sloat Blvd, tel. 661 4844. In 70 acres, Fleishacker Zoo is populated by more than 1000 creatures. Among them are snow leopards, pigmy hippopotamus, white rhinoceros, monkeys, birds and reptiles. In the Children's Zoo, popular attractions are a carousel, a zebra train, and tame animals. Also on site — a deer park and a nature trail. Open daily. Children under 15 accompanied by an adult admitted free.

Sport

CANDLESTICK PARK: is the venue for most major spectator sports. Situated 8 miles south of the city on Route 101, the stadium draws thousands to see the San Francisco Giants at baseball, and the San Francisco 49ers at Football. Information and tickets, tel.467 8000 (baseball); 468 2249 (football).

COW PALACE: hosts San Francisco's newest spectator sport, indoor soccer. Some 40 games are played at home during the winter season. For information tel. 928 5FOG. Big tennis tournaments and wrestling bouts are also held there from time to time.

OAKLAND-ALAMEDA COUNTY COLISEUM COMPLEX: which includes an indoor arena, exhibit hall and a stadium seating up to 52,000 people, is where San Francisco's professional basketball team, the Golden State Warriors, play. The complex is reached via the Nimitz Freeway across the Bay. Information, tel. 776 9404.

The city has two 18-hole and two 9-hole municipal golf courses. There is also an abundance of fishing. Boats leave from Fisherman's Wharf. Equipment can be hired.

Music

MIDSUMMER MUSIC FESTIVAL: Sigmund Stern Memorial Grove, Sloat Blvd & 19th Ave. Free Sunday afternoon programmes, ballet, symphony, opera, jazz, ethnic dance groups and musicals. Season: June to August.

SAN FRANCISCO BALLET: War Memorial Opera House, Van Ness Ave, Civic Center, tel. 431 1210. Main season: spring. Summer season: Geary Theater, 415 Geary St, tel. 673 6440.

SAN FRANCISCO OPERA: War Memorial Opera House, Van Ness Ave, Civic Center, tel. 432 1210. Season: mid September to November. Light opera repertoire in March at Curran Theater, 445 Geary St, tel. 673 4400.

SPRING OPERA THEATER: Palace of Fine Arts Theater, 3601 Lyon St, tel. 431 1210. Three-week season: March to April by San Francisco Opera.

SAN FRANCISCO SYMPHONY ORCHESTRA: Louise M. Davies Symphony Hall, Van Ness Ave, tel. 431 5400. Season: mid September to May. Pop concerts in summer.

Theatres

AMERICAN CONSERVATORY THEATER, 415 Geary St, tel. 673 6440. Prestigious repertory company with guest artists and varied programme. Main season: late October to May. Summer season nightly except Sunday. Special productions, Marines Memorial Theater, 609 Sutter Street.

CANNERY THEATER, The Cannery at 2801 Leavenworth St, tel. 441 6800. All kinds of theatrical presentations.

GOLDEN GATE THEATER: Golden Gate & Taylor Streets, tel. 673 4400. Pre- or post-Broadway productions.

THE ORPHEUM: 1192 Market St, tel. 552 4002. Pre- and post-Broadway spectaculars.

Migrant Monarch butterflies winter on the California coast

dipper and a cave train among its attractions.

Facing the plaza is Mission Santa Cruz, a reproduction of the original, which was founded by Father Serra in 1791. Old mission books and vestments are on display, and the chapel is open to visitors.

On Broadway, in the Santa Cruz Art League Galleries, is a three-dimensional replica, with life-size wax figures, of Leonardo da Vinci's painting of the Last Supper.

About two miles north of the town, on Branciforte Drive, is a section of redwood forest called Mystery Spot, where the laws of gravity seem to be defied. It has been suggested that this is due to a meteor or minerals with magnetic properties buried deep underground. Whatever the cause, the effects are astonishing. Animals avoid the area and no bird will choose a nest site in the vicinity. Visitors can experience them for themselves — for example, there is a sloping plank along which a ball will roll uphill, and climbing the hillside feels exactly like walking on level ground.

Drive north on State Route 9, through redwood country for 29 miles, turning left onto State Route 236 which leads to Big Basin Redwoods State Park.

Big Basin Redwoods State Park, California
The first of the redwood groves to be declared a state park, Big Basin was established in 1902. Some trees are as high as 330ft, with a diameter of 18ft — particularly magnificent specimens. You may hike, picnic or camp here. Swimming is a summer activity, and winter pursuits in the area include ice skating, skiing, sledging and tobogganing. There is hunting and fishing in season, and several winter sports centres are close by.

Drive south on State Route 236 for 9 miles to rejoin State Route 9. Continue southwards, back to Santa Cruz. Leave the town, heading south on State Route 17, passing spectacular begonia gardens 3 miles south in Capitola. Continue for another 39 miles on State Route 1 to Monterey.

Magnificent beaches, spectacular coastal scenery, towering redwoods and lush vineyards are irresistible ingredients of this tour south of the city. Beloved of artists, the Monterey Peninsula, as well as haunting cypresses silhouetted against the sky and sea, has delightful, timeless communities such as Monterey and Carmel. Reminders of a religious past abound in the beautiful missions founded in the 18th century by the pioneering Franciscan friar, Father Serra. Children are catered for in various amusement parks en route.

Head southwards from San Francisco on the scenic coastal State Route 1 and drive for 30 miles beside the dazzling San Mateo Coast State Beaches, past Montara, a picturesque artists' colony. The road hugs the coastline for another 39 miles to the bustling resort of Santa Cruz.

The Monterey Peninsula and San Jose

3 days — 325 miles

San Francisco — Santa Cruz — Big Basin Redwoods State Park — Monterey — Pacific Grove — Seventeen Mile Drive — Carmel — Salinas — San Juan Bautista — San Jose — Los Gatos — Saratoga — Santa Clara — Palo Alto — Redwood City — San Francisco.

Santa Cruz, California
Surrounded by redwoods, Santa Cruz is approached from the north by Natural Bridges State Beach, with its fascinating surf-carved sandstone arches and rock pools. From mid October to the end of February, Monarch butterflies may be observed here. These unusual migrant butterflies cover enormous distances, spending the winter in parts of California and Mexico and flying north — sometimes as far as Canada — in the spring.

By contrast, Santa Cruz Beach Boardwalk is an extensive family playground, and includes a giant

Monterey, California

This charming old city, once capital of Alta California under the Spanish, Mexican and American flags, is largely preserved as a State Historic Park. A 'Path of History' is marked out by a line of orange dots on the pavements. It links more than 40 buildings built before 1850 which have been reconstructed in their original styles. The Old Custom House on Fisherman's Wharf dates back to Spanish Colonial times. The Larkin House, on Calle Principal, was the home of the first American Consul here. The house was the first of many similar buildings in Monterey — an architectural mix of Spanish Colonial and New England. Stevenson House, on Houston Street, is the old French Hotel where Robert Louis Stevenson wrote *Vendetta of the West* during the autumn of 1879. The house is furnished in period style. Pacific House, on Calle Principal, is a museum of Californian history and Indian relics. The attractive garden is also open to visitors. First Theater on Pacific Street was once a lodging house for sailors, and in 1847 became the first building in California to charge admission for a theatrical performance. These buildings and a number of others may be visited by purchasing a single ticket.

Other places of interest include Colton Hall, on Pacific Street, where the first Constitution of California was written in 1849.

Spanish paintings and sculptures may be seen on guided tours of the San Carlos Cathedral in Church Street. The cathedral has been in continuous use since 1795.

Down in the bay is Cannery Row, renamed in honour of John Steinbeck, who used the colourful locale in his novel of that name. Now galleries and restaurants have replaced all but one of the fish canneries, but you may still watch fishermen unloading their silvery catch of herring, cod, tuna, anchovy and salmon on City Wharf. Along Fisherman's Wharf, a theatre, a handicraft shop and an art gallery have largely replaced the commercial fishing of half a century ago.

Another concession to the present is the Dennis the Menace Playground in the park on El Estero. Hank Ketcham, creator of awful Dennis — anti-hero of the *Beano* — helped to devise the play equipment.

Carmel Valley. The rolling landscape of gentle fields gives way to a distant prospect of high mountains

Drive further into the Monterey Peninsula along Lighthouse Avenue and Central Avenue to Pacific Grove.

Pacific Grove, California

As well as being the starting point for the famous scenic Seventeen-Mile Drive, this town is of interest to naturalists. The 'butterfly trees' on Lighthouse Avenue are pine trees, which from October to March are covered with masses of orange and black Monarch butterflies. The Museum of Natural History, on Forest Avenue, portrays the wildlife of the Monterey Peninsula.

Seventeen-Mile Drive, California

Twisted, strange-shaped Monterey pines are strewn along this spectacular drive past the homes of many film stars and celebrities. Highlights along the way include Seal Rock and Cypress Point. The route is flanked by top-class golf courses — Monterey Peninsula, Spy Glass Hill, Cypress Point and Pebble Beach — scene of the Crosby Pro-Am Tournament each spring. The resort of Pebble Beach is the enclave of the very rich. There is a toll at both ends of the drive, which ends at Carmel.

Carmel, California

This forest village and artists' paradise is encircled by

Lone Pine Rock is one of the highlights of Seventeen-Mile-Drive, which is famous for its magnificent seascapes

mountains, rolling hills and sparkling white beaches bordered by the beautiful Monterey cypresses. The unspoilt quality of the village is not accidental — in 1929 rigid zoning laws prohibited neon signs, traffic signals and other 20th-century intrusions on the quaint village scene. Narrow streets are lined with tasteful little boutiques, souvenir shops and no fewer than 65 art galleries. Some of California's finest restaurants are here. The most perfectly preserved of Father Junipero Serra's missions is also here, alongside State 1 just south of the town: the Mission San Carlos Borromeo de Carmelo. Serra, who pioneered the Mission Trail with 21 mission hostels from Baja California to Sonoma, is buried beneath the chancel floor of the church.

Four miles south of Carmel is Point Lobos Reserve — well worth a visit if you have time for the detour. This rugged sea-coast area of 1276 acres has some of the most beautiful scenery along the Californian coast, with marvellous stands of gaunt cypress. Chinaman's Beach and Bird Island

should not be missed. Colonies of seals and sea lions live on the rocks. The barking of the seals gave the place its name 'Lobos', which is Spanish for 'wolf'.

Drive north from Carmel on State Route 1 for about 3 miles and join State Route 68, following it for about 15 miles east to Salinas.

Salinas, California
California's biggest rodeo is held here every July. The gigantic celebration, packed into four days, is known locally as Salinas Big Week. A night parade with bands, drill teams and clowns is the highlight, and other events include a street dance and a public breakfast. More than 1000 horses and riders parade down Main Street prior to each day's rodeo.

Also of interest is the Steinbeck House on Central Avenue, which was the birthplace and boyhood home of novelist John Steinbeck (1902-68).

Head north on US 101 for 17 miles and turn on to State Route 156 at the second interchange. Drive for about 4 miles south to San Juan Bautista.

San Juan Bautista, California
The largest of Serra's mission churches, Mission San Juan Bautista, was founded here in 1797. Three of the original five bells in the chapel area remain and decorations by Indian converts are still visible on the interior walls.

A State Historic Park centred around the Plaza includes the old Plaza Hotel, built in 1813 for Spanish soldiers, and Castro House, where officials of the Mexican government stayed. A stable and carriage house and horse-drawn vehicles are other attractions. A Spanish orchard and garden complete the park.

Return to US 101 and continue north for 31 miles, then take State Route 82 into San José.

San José, California
The oldest incorporated city in California, this community was founded in 1777 and named Pueblo de San José de Guadalupe. It is internationally famed for its table wines, and is surrounded by interesting countryside.

Six miles east, on State Route 130, is Alum Rock Park, lying in the foothills of Black Mountain. Marked trails, picnicking spots and mineral springs punctuate the 776 acres. Frontier Village, on Monterey Road, is an Old West amusement park with staged

This elaborate house in Central Avenue, Salinas was the birthplace of John Steinbeck. He spent much of his childhood here

San Juan Bautista grew up around the mission church founded here in 1797. The area is now a State Historic Park

gunfights and bank robberies.

In the city, Kelley Park offers some of the most popular attractions. Happy Hollow is a childrens' playground with a steamboat model, a treehouse and a baby zoo. Japanese culture is represented in the landscaping and lanterns of the Japanese Friendship Tea Garden. On Phelan Avenue, and part of the park, is the San José Historical Museum, which exhibits the effects of Indian, Spanish, Mexican and American influences on the development of Santa Clara Valley. A print shop, bank, hotel, doctor's office, blacksmith's forge, reconstructed stables and restored homes may be seen in the grounds. Indian baskets, mining tools and wagons are also on display.

Other notable museums include the Egyptian Museum in Rosicrucian Park. A collection of antiques and rare modern pieces includes a full-size replica of an Egyptian rock tomb, scarabs, jewels, mummies and paintings.

San José Museum of Art, on Market Street, offers changing exhibitions of modern and traditional art. On Almaden Road is the unusual New Almaden Mercury Mining Museum, which portrays the history of mercury mining, with pictures, machinery and equipment. Some Indian relics found during mining

operations are also exhibited.

On the way out of San José, near the junction of Interstate 280 and State Route 17, a bewildering experience awaits you. Winchester Mystery House, open to visitors, is among the most bizarre buildings in the world. Beautifully and expensively appointed, the house is the unfinished design of Sarah Winchester, widow of the famous rifle magnate's son. She was convinced by a medium that she would be haunted by the spirits of all those killed by Winchester rifles, and that she could keep evil and death away only by continual building. Sarah became obsessed with the house. The rambling, 160-roomed Victorian mansion covers six acres and took 24 carpenters over 38 years to build. Thirteen is a key number in its construction — there are 13 bathrooms, ceilings with 13 panels; rooms with 13 windows — and 40 stairways, every one with 13 steps and all the turned posts installed upside down! Some stairs lead nowhere, doors open onto blank walls or into space — was Sarah trying to trick the evil spirits? Even the servants had to use a map to get around the house.

Drive south-west on State Route 17 for 7 miles to Los Gatos.

Los Gatos, California
The restored array of Spanish and Victorian architecture which dominates Old Town on University Avenue is the principal attraction in this pleasant community. Shops, restaurants, the California Actors' Theater and studios where craftsmen demonstrate their skills may all be seen.

The Los Gatos Museum on Main and Tait Streets has exhibits ranging from art to local and natural history.

Children will be amused by the Billy Jones Wildcat Railroad in the park.

As befits a town in this area, Los Gatos also offers tours of winemakers' premises ('wineries', as the Americans call them). One mile south, on State Route 17, is Novitiate Wines, where the tasting room can be visited.

Head north-east out of Los Gatos on State Route 9 and drive 4 miles to Saratoga.

Saratoga, California
While you've got a taste for wine you would do well to head for Saratoga Avenue and visit the Paul Masson Champagne and Wine Cellars.

A good way to sober up is to stroll in Hakkone Gardens on Big Basin Way. This 15-acre park has formal Japanese gardens and a tea room.

Drive east along Saratoga Avenue for 5 miles to Santa Clara.

Santa Clara, California
At the heart of this old Spanish town is the campus of the University of Santa Clara. One of the major attractions on the campus is the Mission Santa Clara de Asis, founded in 1777. The present building is a replica of the third mission, built in 1825. Three bells donated by the King of Spain are still to be seen, as is the original garden.

Also on the campus is the De Saisset Gallery and Museum, which displays paintings, sculptures and an Early California collection.

Another museum, on Warburton Avenue, is the Triton Museum of Art. Its four buildings — a blend of Oriental and Spanish architecture — house permanent and temporary exhibits including American paintings, ceramics and glass.

As you leave Santa Clara, you will come upon Marriott's Great America at the junction of Great America Parkway and US 101. If spills and thrills are not to your taste, drive on, but the children will never forgive you. This 200-acre family entertainment park seeks to evoke the diverse spirits of America through its landscaping, boutiques, restaurants, craft shops and amusements. Several areas have been built to a specific 'theme'; for instance, there is a replica of New Orleans' famous French

Stanford Memorial Church, on the campus at Palo Alto, was built as a memorial (1893) to Leland Stanford Jr, founder of the university

Quarter and one of an 1890s Gold Rush town in the Klondike. Among 28 thriller rides, the Tidal Wave is a looping roller coaster which catapults riders forwards and backwards through a 75ft-high vertical loop at 50 miles per hour. Williard's Whizzer, another roller coaster, spins riders into 70-degree banked turns. The Logger Run and Yankee Clipper flume rides propel masochists on a sinuous nautical journey that includes a 60ft plunge into a lagoon. The ultimate experience is The Demon Awaits . . . For children there is Fort Fun — a play area with pools, tunnels, slides and nets, dodgems, a narrow gauge railway and a zoo. Bugs Bunny and other cartoon characters appearing in the park's theatre stroll around all day. Visitors are spoilt for choice in ethnic eating and you can round off the day at Lockheed's Pictorium — a cinema with the largest motion picture screen in the world, nearly 100 feet wide.

Continue north on US 101 for 10 miles to Palo Alto.

Palo Alto, California
Palo Alto is dominated by Stanford University, standing in an estate of 8200 acres known as 'Stanford Farm'. The university was founded in 1891 by Leland Stanford, the 19th-century railway magnate and senator.

The main university buildings are about a mile from the city. A bird's eye view of the campus may be had from the observation platform of Hoover Tower. The building houses the Hoover Institution of War, Revolution and Peace, which is devoted to the study of world conflict. It is named after President Herbert Hoover, himself a graduate of Stanford, who was elected to the White House in 1928.

The university boasts a particularly fine art gallery, and the Leland Stanford Jnr Museum displays mementoes of the Stanford family, a collection of Egyptian antiquities and oriental art, Rodin bronzes and the original 'golden spike', ceremoniously hammered by Leland Stanford into the last sleeper to complete America's first transcontinental railway in 1869.

A unique exhibit on the campus is the two-mile long linear electron accelerator, which explores the particles of an atom. It took four years and cost $114 million to build and is the largest scientific instrument in the world.

Continue north on US 101 for 6 miles to Redwood City.

Redwood City, California
This city is best known for an animal extravaganza about four miles to the north, east of US 101. Marine World/Africa USA is a 65-acre complex combining zoo and oceanarium. Many of the animals roam freely behind natural barriers formed by waterways. Seals, lions, elephants, chimps and dolphins perform in live shows, and other popular attractions include killer whales and a 'jungle raft safari'. Refreshments, a free supervised playground and camel and elephant rides are also available.

Return to San Francisco on US 101 for 20 miles to the centre.

Yosemite Valley

3 days — 475 miles

San Francisco — Livermore — Columbia — Big Oak Flat —
Yosemite Valley — Yosemite Village — Mariposa — Merced — San
Francisco

Yosemite Valley is a small part of the astonishing 1200-square-mile Yosemite National Park. Snow-covered mountains, spectacular, plunging waterfalls, lofty granite domes, glaciated canyons, alpine meadows and endless stretches of forest are features of this wilderness of the Sierra Nevada mountains. Beautiful redwood groves at Tuolumne and Mariposa are extra wonders of nature to complete this most scenic of tours.

Cross the San Francisco Bay-Oakland Bridge and drive through Oakland on Interstate 580 for 49 miles east to Livermore.

Livermore, California

The principal community in Livermore Valley, this town is surrounded by cattle lands and vineyards and is well known for its dry white wines. The famous Del Valle Dam is visible about five miles to the south on Arroyo Road.

Three miles to the south, off Vasco Road, are two wineries where you can sample the local vintage: Concannon Vineyards and Wente Brothers, both in Tesla Road.

The Lawrence Livermore Laboratory Visitors' Center, off Greenville Road, is about two-and-a-half miles south of Interstate 580. New energy sources are the subject of research here, and imaginative exhibitions and audio-visual presentations enable visitors to learn about the laboratory's work.

Drive east on Interstate 205 for 22 miles to Manteca, then on State Route 120 for 57 miles, turning off onto State Route 49 to Sonora. Head north on State Route 49 for about 3 miles, then take an unclassified road for 1 mile to Columbia.

Columbia, California

Picturesquely situated in the foothills of the Sierra Nevada, this community was one of the largest and most important mining towns in California. Here gold was extracted from the sand and gravel in stream-beds, a process known as placer-mining. Around $87 million in gold was extracted here between 1850 and 1880.

Part of the old business area has been restored to look much as it did in the days of the gold rush. The area is known as Columbia State Historic Park, and the buildings include saloons, a newspaper office, a barber's shop, two old hotels, a bank, a school, the famous Wells Fargo Express company and the City Hotel, which offers tours and accommodation. The Masonic

Temple has been reconstructed on its original site, and an old theatre presents stage shows. Stage-coach rides are available daily in summer and on fine weekends in winter.

Return to Sonora and Jamestown. About 3 miles south of Jamestown, turn left, following State Route 49 for 13 miles and branching off onto State Route 120 to Big Oak Flat.

Big Oak Flat, California

This town was originally called Savage Diggings, after James Savage, who founded it in 1850 and later discovered the Yosemite Valley. A large valley oak, 11ft in diameter, which grew in the centre of the town, inspired the present name. A monument now stands in its place, with two pieces

Distant views of the snow-capped Sierra Nevada beckon the traveller on the road from San Francisco to Yosemite National Park

of the original tree preserved for all to see. Apart from this, a few old stone and brick buildings are all that remain of the old gold-mining centre. South of the town, on Big Oak Flat Road, is Tuolumne Grove, which contains 25 giant sequoias, including one known as the 'Dead Giant'. Access is by a one-way road beginning at Crane Flat.

Strike east for the Yosemite Valley along the beautiful Big Oak Flat Highway — State Route 120 — and follow this road through wild and mountainous country for 41 miles to Crane Flat. Continue south on New Big Oak Flat Road for about 8 miles to the entrance of the Yosemite Valley.

Yosemite Valley, California

This mile-wide valley was carved by glaciers and is flanked by sheer granite cliffs and lofty mountain peaks. Carpeted with

SCALE

20.5 MILES TO 1 INCH

10 0 10

10 0 10 20 KILOMETRES

meadows and forests through which the silver Merced River threads, the valley is seven miles long. The most striking outcrop at the western end is El Capitan, which towers to over 7500ft above sea level and comprises a 3500ft single block of shining granite with a completely unbroken perpendicular wall. The eastern end of the valley is dominated by massive Half Dome which reaches nearly 9000ft. Sentinel Basket and North Dome complete the semi-circle of vast granite domes at the upper end of the valley. Unbelievable waterfalls spill from the rim of the valley, the most spectacular of them being Yosemite Falls. Split into two cascades, Upper Yosemite Fall plunges 1430ft over the north wall — a height equal to nine Niagaras. Lower Yosemite, immediately below, is a drop of over 320ft. Other beautiful falls include Ribbon, misty Bridalveil, Illilouette, Vernal and Nevada. Ribbon, at 1612ft, is the highest single fall. The falls are at their fullest in May and June, and fairly abundant up to mid-July, but are practically non-existent during high summer.

Driving along North Valley Road, the striking pinnacles seen south of the Merced River are Cathedral Spires, which top 6000ft. The road leads to the head of the valley and Yosemite Village.

Yosemite Village, California
Surrounded by giant forests clothing the mountain flanks, the road reaches this tourist centre. It is packed with attractions of its own, but the dramatic topography is still the overwhelming feature.

The most remarkable viewpoint is Glacier Point, a lofty peak over 7000ft, reached by a road which

winds through red fir and pine forest and meadows. Unfortunately, this road is closed in winter. The panoramic view of the High Sierras includes El Capitan, Half Dome, Upper Yosemite, Nevada and Vernal Falls, with a backdrop of snowy peaks beyond.

The visitors' centre in the village is open all year. Audio-visual programmes explain how the unique Yosemite scenery was formed, and nearby is an Indian Cultural Museum. Maps and information are available here. Trips to Glacier Point operate from Yosemite Village daily during summer, and a free shuttle bus service operates in the valley. Camp sites abound, and hotels and restaurants are plentiful. Children may be left in a supervised play area — Curry

Village in summer, and Ski Tots Club, further away at Badger's Pass, in winter.

Mountaineering is encouraged with guided climbs, and hiking trails are numerous. Guided tours on horseback are also available. At Happy Isles Nature Center, south of the village, a naturalist will conduct you on a nature walk lasting from half an hour up to a whole day (summer only). Bicycles may be rented from Curry Village or Yosemite Lodge, and an open tram tours the valley during summer. In winter, skiing and skating are popular activities and there is an outdoor skating rink near Curry Village. Skiing is best at Badger's Pass Ski Center, where instruction is available.

The valley and the village get overcrowded in the high season

Meltwater from the high Sierra Nevada — which means 'snowy mountains' — feeds spectacular torrents such as Yosemite Falls

and you would be well advised to make a detour to Tuolumne Meadows if you intend to stay overnight. Overlooking the valley from the north, these high alpine meadows are accessible by car during the summer along the Tioga Pass — a spectacular, if sometimes hair-raising mountain road. A camp-site is open in summer, and meals are served under canvas, family-style. Vast stands of pine and lakes, partly hidden by mountains, add interest to this largest meadow of the High Sierras.

The drive out of the valley, along South Valley Road, gives

Yosemite Valley

splendid views of the Three Brothers — imposing peaks over 6000ft high and of El Capitan, north of the river.

Cross the valley over the road bridge and head west on State Route 140 for 40 miles to Mariposa.

Mariposa, California

This historic town boasts the oldest courthouse in California, built in 1854 and still in use. Wooden pegs were used in the building of this two-storey, white pine building, with its charming square clock tower. The old clock was brought to California via Cape Horn. Visitors may view original furnishings on the second floor.

On State Route 140 is the Mariposa County History Center, which contains relics of gold rush days, including a five-stamp mill, horse-drawn vehicles and mining and printing equipment. Also on view are replicas of a school room, a print shop, an apothecary's shop, a miner's cabin and an Indian village.

Mariposa Grove lies some distance to the east of the town. This spectacular sequoia grove is accessible through Wawona by taking the Wawona Tunnel out of Yosemite Valley. Grizzly Giant, the oldest tree in the grove, has a base diameter of 34·7ft, a girth of 96·5ft and is over 200ft high. The famous Wawona Tunnel Tree fell during the 1968-9 winter storms, but the tunnel in the 'California Tree' may still be driven through, though not in a private car. Trips from Yosemite Village are scheduled every day in summer. Exhibits of giant redwoods are displayed in the Mariposa Grove Museum, which is open to coincide with the tram tours that operate within the grove in summer.

Continue on State Route 140 for 36 miles west to Merced.

Merced, California

This large town is principally known as the western gateway to Yosemite National Park for travellers from the south. It is set in the fertile San Joaquin Valley. Sixteen miles south-west is the Merced National Wildlife Refuge, and water sports are available at Yosemite Lake, seven miles to the north-east.

Leave Merced on State Route 99, turning left at the next interchange on State Route 140. In about 35 miles turn right on Interstate 5. About 30 miles further on, join Interstate 580 at the interchange. This road takes you through Livermore again and back into San Francisco.

Glacier-carved canyons hemmed in by awesome granite summits like Half Dome are characteristic of Yosemite rock formations

The glinting waters of San Francisco and San Pablo Bays and the Pacific Ocean highlight this tour of the north of California. Great cities such as Oakland and Berkeley give way to the peaceful vineyards of the Napa Valley and in Marin County are the picturesque artists' havens of Tiburon and Sausalito. Dramatic scenery may be enjoyed in Muir Woods, where Mount Tamalpais is rivalled by the mighty redwoods.

Leave San Francisco by driving east along Interstate 80 over the San Francisco-Oakland Bay Bridge. Continue on Interstate 580 for 1 mile into Oakland, turn right on to Interstate 980 and drive down to Broadway.

Oakland, California

The East Bay area has been transformed during the last few years. Once the poor relation of San Francisco, Oakland is now a

California's Vineyards and Marin County

2 days — 146 miles

San Francisco — Oakland — Berkeley — Martinez — Benicia —
Vallejo — Napa — Sonoma — San Rafael — Tiburon — Mill Valley —
Muir Woods National Monument — Stinson Beach — Sausalito —
San Francisco.

star in its own right. This large city varies in altitude from sea level to over 1500ft, and a skyline boulevard follows its perimeter, passing through magnificent parks and private estates. On a clear day, the view of the bay is

spectacular. The port of Oakland has splendid dock facilities, and shipbuilding is only one of the city's thriving industries.

At the centre of the city is Broadway, which leads down to the Inner Harbour. Jack London

Square is the colourful waterfront area, named after the author of countless adventure stories such as *White Fang* and *The Call of the Wild*. He grew up in the neighbourhood and spent many hours in the First and Last Chance Saloon, which is built from the remains of an old whaling ship. You can also see the log cabin — originally from the Yukon — where the author spent the harsh winter of 1897-8. Just south of London's favourite saloon is Jack London Village, a shopping complex designed in turn-of-the-century style.

On Broadway itself is the Paramount Theatre of the Arts. Built in 1931, it is an extraordinary example of Art Deco architecture and decor. The restored picture palace is now a centre for the performing arts.

Close to the city centre is attractive Lake Merritt. Lakeside Park envelopes the north shores of the 155-acre salt-water lake. Among the attractions here are free Sunday concerts, a children's Fairyland, a miniature stern-wheeler riverboat which cruises on the lake, boats for hire, and bowling and putting greens. Lakeside Park Garden Center is surrounded by a variety of specialist gardens. They include a Japanese garden, a Polynesian garden and cactus, chrysanthemum and dahlia gardens. There are flower shows in season. Visitors to the Rotary Natural Science Center may attend free lectures and see exhibits of insects, birds and mammals as well as displays of flowers. Thousands of wild ducks and other waterfowl seek sanctuary outside the museum in winter, and are fed every afternoon.

South-west of the lake, on Tenth and Oak Streets, is the Oakland

Born in San Francisco in 1876, novelist Jack London spent much of his childhood in Oakland

Views from the University of California's Campanile extend to Berkeley town and San Francisco Bay

Museum, which contains a complex of gardens and galleries, including the new Breuner Gallery. The ecology, history and art of California are reflected in the museum's exhibits.

North-east of the lake, west of Grand Avenue, is the stunning Morcom Amphitheater of Roses. Here colourful blooms may be seen throughout the year, though April to December is the peak season.

Dominating Lincoln Avenue, and visible even from the San Francisco Bay Bridge, is the Mormon Temple. Only the gardens are open to visitors.

A mile above the Mormon Temple, on Joaquin Miller Road, is the Woodminster Amphitheater, situated in the centre of Joaquin Miller Park. Concerts by the Oakland Symphony and other orchestras and light operas are presented here during the summer.

Return on Interstate 980 and rejoin Interstate 580. After 1 mile, turn right on to Interstate 80 and drive for about 5 miles to Berkeley.

Berkeley, California
Best known for its magnificent university, Oakland's neighbour is lively, inquiring and experimental, reflecting the radical activities of the campus. The university is particularly famous for politics and philosophy, and fishing is also an important activity in Berkeley. At the foot of University Avenue is the Berkeley Marina, home of a large charter boat fleet. There is also a free fishing pier. Water sports and model yacht racing are popular on the mile-long salt-water lake in Aquatic Park.

East of Oxford Street, between Hearst Street and Bancroft Way, is the 720-acre campus of the University of California. A landmark is the graceful 307ft-high Campanile, also called the Sather Tower. There is a lift to the observation platform, from which you can enjoy a marvellous view of the campus. The 12-bell carillon is played three times daily, and each hour is chimed.

The University Art Museum on Bancroft Way is very impressive architecturally, and the Lowie Museum of Anthropology in Kroeber Hall features fascinating exhibits on ethnology, archaeology and biology. On the east side of the campus is the Lawrence Hall of Science, a research centre where various exhibits are on view to visitors at certain times. The Hearst Creek Theater is also worth a visit. In Strawberry Canyon is a Botanical Garden which covers nearly 30 acres. Plants are labelled, and some of the flowers are in bloom most of the year.

Guided walking tours of the campus leave the visitors' centre in the lobby of the Students' Union from Monday to Friday at 1pm.

Continue north on Interstate 80 for 15 miles past Albany and San Pablo, then turn right on to State Route 4 and drive 9 miles to Martinez.

Martinez, California
The most interesting feature of this small town is the John Muir National Historic Site on Alhambra Avenue. This monument to the great Scottish-American conservationist, naturalist, scientist and author consists of his house — built in 1882 and furnished in turn-of-the-century style — and the surrounding orchards and vineyards, which are also open to visitors. Muir crusaded for the preservation of the nation's wilderness, and his ideas resulted in the establishment of the national parks and forests system.

Drive north to join Interstate 680 and cross Suisun Bay. Join Interstate 780 and drive north to the first interchange, turning off here to Benicia.

Benicia, California
Founded in 1847, this small city was the site of California's first capitol. In the city are many well-preserved old houses, some built over a century ago. Early events in Californian history are commemorated by historical markers in the city. You may visit Benicia Capitol State Park, where the capitol building has been restored and furnished in period style. It served as state capitol from 4 February 1853 to 25 February 1854.

Return to Interstate 780, drive north through Benicia State Reservation Area, continuing for about 6 miles to Vallejo.

Vallejo, California
Founded by General Mariano Guadalupe Vallejo in 1851, this city served as state capitol twice between 1851 and 1853. Because of its position on San Pablo Bay and at the mouth of the Napa River, the city is famous for ship building. The first US warship on the Pacific was built in 1859 at the Mare Island Naval Shipyard, on a point between the bay and the river. The California Maritime Academy is housed in the city.

Drive north from Vallejo on State Route 29 for 12 miles to Napa.

Napa, California
A fertile valley and fields of the wine country surround this town. Napa County cultivates over 100 varieties of grapes and is renowned for its table wines. North of the town, the Napa Valley is California's most famous vine-growing region. Sunny days, tempered by cooling ocean breezes and fog, give optimum conditions for many varieties of grape. Literally dozens of vineyards are open daily for tours, but those nearest the town are open by appointment only. If you want a bird's-eye view of the vineyards, drive north to Yountville early in the morning and take a hot air balloon ride along the beautiful Napa Valley.

Drive west on State Route 121 and across into Sonoma County. Continue north on State Route 12, through Vineburg, reaching Sonoma after about 12 miles.

Sonoma, California
A walk around the historic plaza is a glimpse into California's chequered past. A flagpole and a bronze figure stand where the Bear Flag, proclaiming the state an independent republic, was raised in 1846, and the little shops have the look of a bygone era. You may wander into the old Toscano Hotel on the north side of the plaza — a part of the Sonoma State Historic Park — and view

The fertile slopes of the beautiful Napa Valley are ideally suited to vineyards, and produce some of California's finest wines

California's Vineyards

some upper rooms furnished in the style of the mid 19th century.

Other buildings in the Historic Park that are open to visitors include the Vallejo Home, half a mile west of Sonoma Plaza. This charming Gothic-style home of General Mariano Guadalupe Vallejo, the Mexican founder of Sonoma and half of California, is set in a garden which also contains a Swiss chalet displaying mementoes of the great man. The Barracks, to the north of the plaza on Spain Street, were erected by Vallejo in 1836. Built of redwood timbers and adobe brick, in 1846 they became the headquarters of the Bear Flag Party, who wanted an independent California. Blue Wing Inn is an ancient building constructed by the General in 1840 as a hotel for emigrants and travellers.

The Mission San Francisco Solano, on East Spain Street, was the last of California's 21 missions to be built — by Father Junipero Serra in 1823. A religious and cultural centre during General Vallejo's time, today it is well restored and houses an outstanding collection of Californian historical relics. A colourful pageant is held here each autumn during Sonoma's Vintage Festival.

Today Sonoma is best known as a centre of the wine country, and wine-tasting tours, combined with

meals in restaurants of every conceivable character, are perhaps the star tourist attraction. Two miles east, on Old Winery Road, is the Buena Vista Winery, a State Historical Landmark. Count Agoston Haraszthy, a Hungarian vintner expelled from his country following a rebellion in 1840, scoured America for a suitable valley in which to grow vines. His search ended when he glimpsed the Sonoma Valley, and by 1860 his Buena Vista Winery was one of the largest in the world. The Father of the Californian grape industry did not live to see the collapse of the winery after the 1906 earthquake. The old stone wine cellars, the oldest in the state, have now been restored and can be toured. Visitors are also welcome in the tasting room.

One of the oldest family wineries, to the east of the Plaza, is Sebastiani Vineyards at 4th Street East. On guided tours of this sprawling winery, visitors will see a tasting room in the corner of the original stone cellar. A special feature is a huge collection of ornate, hand-carved oak casks. A new attraction is the Sebastiani Indian Museum, which contains unusual arrowheads, pipes, tools, pestles and mortars discovered by various Sebastianis as they worked in the vineyards.

The attractive main street at Tiburon, a popular resort

A mile south of the Plaza, at Broadway, is Train Town, a 10-acre railway park and home of the Sonoma Gaslight and Western Railroad — a superb scale reproduction of a complete railroad 'mountain division' of the 1890-1930 period.

North of Sonoma, near Glen Ellen, is the 800-acre Jack London State Historic Park. Here are the author's 26-room dream castle, Wolf House (gutted by fire before he could occupy it), his widow's cobblestone mansion complete with secret passages and a collection of his manuscripts, rejection slips and South Sea trophies. His grave is under a giant red rock. Also on the ranch is the modest cottage where he actually lived, his 'scientific' barns and his concrete 'pig palace', with a suite for each family of porkers. Visitors may recall this larger-than-life author by hiking the trails where he galloped, seeing the mountain lake where he rowed and the bath-house he built.

Drive south for about 5 miles on State Route 12, then turn right on to State Route 121 and continue south for 12 miles to Sears Point. Join State Route 37 and drive west for 8 miles to join US 101. Drive south for about another 8 miles to San Rafael.

San Rafael, California
The administrative, commercial and transport hub of Marin County, San Rafael hugs the western shores of San Pablo Bay and is known for its attractive waterfront homes. The Marin County Civic Center, just north off US 101, was the last major project of the famous architect Frank Lloyd Wright, who died in 1959.

A replica of the Mission San Rafael Arcangel stands on the site

of the original complex, built in 1817. The mission proper consisted of a hospital, a chapel and a monastery. There is also a museum.

On Albert Park Lane, the Marin Wildlife Center houses ill or injured animals native to Marin County.

Continue south on US 101 for about 7 miles. Take State Route 131 — Paradise Drive — at the second interchange, and drive for about 4 miles to Tiburon.

Tiburon, California
Known also as the Shark, Tiburon lies on Raccoon Strait. It has a picturesque village-like Main Street which is a blend of Cape Cod and early Californian in its architectural simplicity. Its colourful harbour shelters the exalted Corinthian Yacht Club as well as a cluster of open-deck restaurants.

Less than a mile from Tiburon is wooded and hilly Angel Island, the largest in the bay. It can be reached by an 800-passenger sightseeing boat, the *Countess*. The boat lands at Ayala Cove, where there are facilities for picnics and barbecues, and the island offers 12 miles of scenic roads and fascinating trails.

Ferries run all week in the summer, but only at weekends for much of the year.

Drive north on State Route 131 for 6 miles along the west side of the peninsula and continue north-west to Mill Valley.

Mill Valley, California
This small community, west of the Redwood Highway, nestles in wooded canyons which lead up to Mount Tamalpais. Quaint houses, shops and architectural landmarks complete the scene. Mount Tamalpais State Park, 6 miles west

The present chapel of the Mission San Francisco Solano at Sonoma was built in 1840. It has been a State Historic Monument since 1903

Muir Woods National Monument: the tallest trees on earth — California redwoods

California's Vineyards

Stinson Beach, California

This long, sandy beach lies within the Golden Gate National Recreation Area. Only the more hardy will enjoy swimming here, as the water is rather cold. Surfing is popular and fishing, picnicking and other beach activities are encouraged.

Continue south on State Route 1 for about 12 miles past beautiful beaches and wooded country to US 101. Turn right on to this road and at the next interchange follow signs to Sausalito.

Sausalito, California

Rustic houses spill down the steep hillsides overlooking San Francisco Bay in this artists' haven and major tourist magnet. Some of the narrow streets of 'Little Willow', as the town is known, become broad steps winding down between the houses. Some houses are precariously supported over space. Shops and restaurants hug the waterfront, and the wooded streets overlook a thicket of boat masts in the harbour. San Francisco and the entire bay area are visible from Sausalito and from Vista Point, at the northern end of the Golden Gate Bridge. Silversmiths, potters and other craftsmen may be seen at work at the complex of shops, restaurants and gardens known as the Village Fair.

At the foot of Spring Street, in the Old Marinship area, is a hydraulic model of San Francisco Bay and Delta. Tidal action, flow and currents of water and mixing of salt and freshwater are cleverly simulated.

At weekends, Little Willow is more crowded than Piccadilly Circus, so it is best visited during the week.

Rejoin US 101 to cross over the spectacular Golden Gate Bridge for the last 2 miles to San Francisco.

of the town, offers 6233 acres of rugged mountain scenery. A historic old mill and a mountain theatre are among the park's attractions. Plays are produced in spring and summer and there is an art festival in autumn.

Continue north-west for 3½ miles into Muir Woods National Monument.

Muir Woods National Monument, California

On the south-west slopes of Mount Tamalpais is this 550-acre redwood grove. The awesome giants which tower up to 240ft are coastal redwoods — *sequoia sempervirens.* The redwoods were threatened with destruction at the turn of the century, when a water company tried to dam life-giving Redwood Creek, but in 1908 William Kent, local landowner and friend of President Theodore Roosevelt, persuaded the President to declare Muir Woods a National Monument. Cars are allowed into the woods only for the drive to the summit of the 2600ft east peak of Mount Tamalpais, from which there is a panoramic view of the north bay country. Visitors to the woods can see a cross-section of a fallen tree whose growth rings testify that it was standing even before William the Conqueror invaded England in 1066. Nature trails carpeted with needles from the great conifers lead alongside sparkling brooks, and deer, chipmunks, raccoons and sometimes skunks are seen. Under the massive redwoods grow delicate azaleas, oxalis and swordferns. There are many miles of nature trails in the forest, including two that lead to the top of Mount Tamalpais. There is a 'Braille Trail' for blind visitors, and wheelchairs are catered for. Another trail leads to 'family circle', where you can see the propagation of young trees, growing in a circle round the parent redwood. Other facilities include a restaurant.

Drive north-west of Muir Woods and join State Route 1, following it southwards for 4 miles along the coast to Stinson Beach.

Exclusive hillside villas overlook a thicket of boat masts in the attractive harbour at Sausalito

The new downtown skyline, with its gleaming towerblocks, rises dramatically out of the desert sands and marks out Los Angeles as a true city of the future

Los Angeles

'LA's the Place' was the slogan that introduced the city's recent bicentennial celebrations. In those 200 years Los Angeles has grown from a Spanish settlement founded in 1781 by eleven Mexican families into the third most populous city in the United States. The city itself covers more than 400 square miles, and Greater Los Angeles about 4000 square miles. For most of this century it — or rather its offshoot, Hollywood — has been the centre of the film industry, the home of a host of glamorous stars, the core of a tough commercial world, the playground of millionaires and the holiday destination for millions of tourists every year.

So what kind of a place is LA? There are probably as many answers as there are people who have visited the place, for Los Angeles has the stuff that dreams are made of, and everyone's dream is different.

Los Angeles

Whatever else it might mean to the sophisticated jet-setter, Los Angeles is still the place where the fantasies of millions of people throughout the world are seen to come true. It would be impossible to assess how much Hollywood's influence has changed the attitudes of society this century, or to what extent this sprawling suburb of Los Angeles is the real reason so many tourists come to the city. Despite this, there seems to be no apparent enthusiasm for Hollywood among Angelenos; indeed, a visitor might be forgiven for thinking that the entertainment industry a few miles up the road is the last topic of conversation he should raise. A tourist could look in vain for signs of the city's appreciation, or even recognition, of the role Hollywood has played in the prosperity of the west coast. There are no theatres or public buildings named after the giants of the silver screen. For a community accustomed to dispensing sentimentality, it is surprising that there are no shrines built out of the homes where these tinselled gods and goddesses lived, and where for years coachloads of star-struck tourists have been stopping, staring, envying, admiring, and praying for a glimpse of their idols. The coachloads still come today, but somehow there is less enthusiasm for worshipping the present owners of these magnificent mansions. There is, after all, much else —

and much more permanent — to see in Los Angeles, though the city with its eighty-eight communities (some say more) is too big, too fragmented, too unwieldy to have a clearly defined identity. Stretching across 464 square miles it is California's largest city and has the third biggest population — 7,000,000 people live in the metropolitan area — in the States. The distinguished journalist Jack Smith, its affectionate and compassionate critic, once wrote in his *Los Angeles Times* column that he needed to remind himself that the city 'had a pastoral beginning and was not created overnight by some dreadful Southern Pacific train wreck!'

The city's reputation for being shrouded in smog has not helped, but in fact its climate is mild and it has its fair share of sunshine. Summer temperatures average 83°F, winter, 67.5°F. Rainfall is moderate, and the worst months are between November and March.

LA's central area, called downtown, after years of neglect, has recently begun to smarten itself up, and in the now fashionable part contained by Pico Boulevard, Figueroa Street, Sunset Boulevard and Broadway, several luxury hotels, shops, office blocks, apartment houses and parks have helped to bring a new vitality to this neglected section of the city. As one observer put it: 'Things are sure improving down here. The pretty

girls are back in town'. Geographically, downtown hardly rates in the overall sprawl of Los Angeles. Its boundaries give the city an odd shape. Viewed in outline it resembles a handgun, with the grip somewhere in the San Fernando Valley, the trigger around Beverly Hills, the breech in the central area and the barrel, with its sights over the restless Black community of Watts, reaching south to San Pedro on the coast.

The city is often denigrated for the very reason that it has been so successful — for its entertainment industry. Yet Los Angeles is not, as its critics would say, 'a cultural wasteland.'

There are plenty of museums and theatres, a stunning new Music Center, and wide squares overlooked by polished buildings like the World Trade Center with its shops selling goods from nearly 100 nations.

In the central area, Olvera Street and Broadway both in their different ways express Los Angeles' past. Both have a rich Spanish and Mexican atmosphere — in Olvera Street, it is the historic houses dating from the founding of Los Angeles, and the Mexican shops selling the

The bright lights of Hollywood's Sunset Strip entice many would-be stars with hopes of fame and fortune

traditional costumes and foods that appeal; and in Broadway, the coarse gutsy brashness of the crowds imparts an invigorating Latin flavour to the streets and shops. Broadway is also the place where the local film industry likes to show off its wares from time to time; many of the cinemas here are landmarks in the history of films (see the Directory).

Various stretches of Wilshire Boulevard, among several major arteries linking the coast with the city centre, have become fashionable shopping districts, too. On the Miracle Mile — that's on Wilshire Boulevard between La Brea Avenue and San Vicente Boulevard — the exclusive clothing boutiques and children's wear shops rub shoulders with tall luxurious hotels. There are also fine shops and restaurants on La Cienega Boulevard, with its rows of art galleries and antique shops. For a different mood and price bracket, try Farmers' Market, a conglomerate of nearly 200 outdoor and indoor shops and stalls. Situated east of Beverly Hills, just one main junction north from Wilshire Boulevard, it has a genuine street-market charisma.

The choice of nightlife in a cosmopolitan city such as Los Angeles is inexhaustible. Most nightspots are in the Wilshire Boulevard area between Rampart Avenue and Western Avenue, and on Sunset Strip. Most of the big hotels cater for dinner and dancing.

Though hotels can always supply current information on theatres, cinemas and concerts in Los Angeles, a useful telephone inquiry service called Experience, tel. 660 5700, will help with advice and bookings in restaurants and for other nightlife activities.

But without generally needing to book you can confidently try many of the wide range of ethnic restaurants in the city. The largest Japanese colony outside the Orient offers plenty of chances to sample genuine sushi — raw fish on a bed of vinaigrette rice — an acquired taste for the Western palate.

The city also has a large Chinatown, but so numerous are the Japanese — they have been coming in increasing numbers since the war — that many guides and leaflets for tourists are printed in Japanese when one might expect the foreign version to be in Spanish, because the predominant influence on the city came originally from Mexico.

Though a Spanish expedition in search of Monterey had landed on the coast of what was to become Los Angeles in 1769 it was twelve years later that forty-four Mexicans under Governor Felipe de Neve founded El Pueblo de Nuestra Senora la Reina de Los Angeles de Porciuncula, which translates as 'the village of our lady the Queen of the Angels of Porciuncula.' California remained a Mexican province until, after a brief campaign, the USA annexed it in 1846.

Early settlers on the west coast, the Chinese preserve their traditional way of life and style of building

Although the actual anniversary fell in September 1981, Los Angeles launched its Bi-Centennial Year in September 1980. The peremptory slogan 'LA's the Place', heralded celebrations including festivals, exhibitions, concerts and parades, but the cost was relatively modest compared with the bill expected for the 1984 Olympic Games.

Fortunately, the real souvenirs of its 200-year-old past are already well established. El Pueblo de Los Angeles State Historic Park, its forty-four acres bounded by Main, Arcadia, Los Angeles and Macy Streets, is full of historical landmarks. Olvera Street, part of the park, is believed to be the oldest street in the city. On it stands Avila Adobe, the oldest house in the city. Built around 1818 it has been restored to its 1840 condition because at that time, the years of the famous '49 Gold Rush, it was used as a private house. The Pico House, named after the last Mexican governor of California who built it in 1869, was once a hotel, but it has now been partially restored and can be toured.

The old Plaza Church on North Main Street is the oldest religious building in the city. Among nearly 2000 churches are an A-Di-Da Buddhist temple, the First Temple of Astrology, the serene lakeside shrine of the Self-Realization Fellowship and the Garden Grove Community Church, nicknamed the 'Crystal Cathedral' because it seats 4000 people in an all-glass, star-shaped design, 124ft tall.

These small and exotic-sounding sects reflect Los Angeles' tolerance for anything unusual. Whether flower children or weirdies, they belong firmly to a community that allows reality and fantasy to exist side by side, and where the difference is not always noticeable.

To assess Hollywood's influence over Los Angeles, one must first visit the places with romantic-sounding names made familiar by films and television: Malibu, Bel Air, Long Beach, Marina del Rey, San Fernando Valley.

Where better to make the acquaintance of Hollywood than at Mann's

Places of Interest

RANCHO LA BREA TAR PITS & GEORGE C. PAGE LA BREA DISCOVERIES MUSEUM: 5801 Wilshire Blvd, tel. 936 2230, closed Mondays.

Ever since the Ice Age these tar pits, a murky swamp of molten asphalt, disguised with a thin covering of water, have been a death trap for thousands of animals, birds and insects which came to the pits to drink or bathe. Once trapped in the sticky substance they drowned and have been preserved as fossils in the tar. Although the existence of the tar pits was known for centuries and the asphalt removed for commercial purposes, it was not until the early years of this century that scientists realized what treasures lay in the depths. G. Allan Hancock, the owner of the La Brea ranch, gave permission for excavation and in 1915 presented the site to the County of Los Angeles. More than half a million specimens have been recovered, including the perfectly preserved skeleton of the Imperial Mammoth, the largest land mammal ever to have existed. Mastodons, sabre-tooth tigers, ground sloths, huge vultures and innumerable types of insects have also been found. The most interesting exhibits are now housed in the George C. Page La Brea Discoveries Museum at 5801 Wilshire Boulevard. At the tar pits themselves there is an Observation Pit where visitors can see work in progress.

AAA: 2601 South Figueroa St at Adams Blvd, tel. 741 3111. A historic house, in Californian terms, is the impressive Spanish-colonial-style headquarters of the Automobile Club of Southern California (part of the American Automobile Association). Built in 1923, it is worth a visit, not only for the range of services the club provides for AAA members and automatically affiliated tourists with AA or other foreign motoring club membership, but also for its beautiful gold ceiling under the regal, domed rotunda. A plaque outside proclaims that the building was declared a Historic Cultural Monument by the Cultural Heritage Board of the Municipal Arts Department.

WATTS TOWERS: 1765 E. 107 St, Watts, Los Angeles. This extraordinary and flamboyant example of folk art is the creation of one individual, a poor Italian immigrant from Rome named Simon Rodia who settled in the Watts area of Los Angeles and worked as a tile setter. When he was about 40 he became obsessed with the desire to build for himself a lasting memorial, and this weird group of three towers, one over 40ft high, and two topping 100ft, constructed of every kind of scrap material he could scavenge around the city, is the result of 30 years of single-minded

Simon Rodia's fantastic towers in the Watts district

devotion. Scrap metal, old bottles, fragments of china, and sea shells make up the towers, which were finished in 1954. Rodia then left Los Angeles, taking no further interest in his creation. In the 1960s the Municipal Building Department decided to demolish them, but in the aftermath of a public outcry in 1963 they were designated a cultural monument by the City Cultural Heritage Board. Simon Rodia died in 1965.

Imperial Mammoth skeleton at the George C. Page La Brea museum

Chinese Theater where the hand and foot prints of more than 150 stars are set in the pavement cement? Countless glittering premieres and sneak previews over many years have drawn the stars to this famous theatre which is still better known as Grauman's, after the name of its former owner (see also p.61). A solemn ceremony is also held at the Walk of Fame every month to embed the name of a celebrity (suitably encased in a five-pointed bronze star) in the pink terazza squares of Hollywood Boulevard. Look for them between Sycamore Avenue and Gower Street, and both sides of Vine Street, from Yucca Street to Sunset Boulevard. Already more than 1700 stars have been given this accolade and as long as the list of stars holds out, there is no reason why the monthly ritual shouldn't go on for another fifty years until the five-acre site is a fair approximation of the Milky Way.

To explore the roots of the film industry, and to see how it matches up today to the enduring image, you need not linger in Hollywood itself. Within a short drive of the city centre, you can wander round Beverly Hills where the pavements are wide and uncrowded, or stroll along Rodeo Drive, which since Gucci opened his shop there in 1969 has become the ultimate in fashionable shopping streets. Success in these parts is measured by the number of Rolls Royces in driveways — there are rumoured to be more Rolls in Beverly Hills than in the whole of London.

Alternatively you may prefer the twenty-five mile-long drive along Sunset Boulevard which, rising like a river in the upper reaches of the city, offers a marvellously varied panorama around every turn. It passes through a garish neighbourhood of nightclubs where briefly it becomes Sunset Strip, slowly emerges from these restless waters at the foot of Beverly Hills before reaching the heights of Bel Air, skirts the fine UCLA (University of California at Los Angeles) campus with its sculptured gardens and fine art gallery, and where 40,000 students add colour to the elegant neighbourhood of Westwood, cuts through the smart area of Brentwood and ends at the coast. On the way it passes the wealthy estates owned for generations by families whose bronzed offspring frolicked in the blue waters of the Pacific on their doorsteps and sunbathed on the white sandy beaches.

For a change of mood you can drive to Burbank where a community of 85,000 people supports a large aviation and film industry side by side. This is the home of the mighty Lockheed Aircraft Corporation and the headquarters of the no less important Walt Disney Productions. Here, too, is where two major film studios, Warner Brothers and Columbia Pictures, have combined to form Burbank Studios, and where the television output of a major network, the National Broadcasting Company (NBC) keeps up with an insatiable demand. Both studios can be visited. They make a fascinating study in contrasts, the former offering a glimpse of the more traditional film-making techniques (although they also make television series at Burbank Studios), and the latter geared to producing instant programmes for television.

A rather different way of looking at the movie world is on offer at Universal Studios. Here you can see the exploitation of the glamour and glory of the picture business. A day at Universal is like a day at the fair, and the 3,500,000 people who spend the equivalent of a three-course meal on the visit are, it is rumoured, bringing in more money than many of the films and television shows for which the studio is renowned. The guided tour takes four-and-a-half hours and while the attractions may vary in detail from time to time, the effect is the same. From the moment you step aboard the Glamortram, accosted by an absurdly oversized figure who might be the Incredible Hulk of comic and television series fame, but looks more like a mutated Frankenstein's Monster, you can leave reason behind and let your mind freewheel into fantasy. In the first two-and-a-half hours, while the Glamortram winds through the 420-acre studio lot, nothing much that they show you is real. If you can survive Battlestar Galactica, based on a spectacular science-fiction film, your nerves will be tested by the proximity of the giant shark reincarnated from the film *Jaws*, which leaps out of the water a few feet from you,

Special effects at Universal: the weir that parted the Red Sea in De Mille's epic, **The Ten Commandments**

children are catered for.

Stars, human or animal, have always been Hollywood's most lucrative commodity, and it was their foresight in inventing the star system that allowed the Hollywood pioneers to flourish. In the early part of the twentieth century, Chicago was the centre of the new film industry, but with the Mid-West weather so unpredictable for location shooting, Colonel William Selig became the first film-maker to move his operations to the West Coast. In 1907 he started shooting *The Count of Monte Cristo* in the photogenic hills around Los Angeles and on the beaches of the West Coast. The first fully operational film studio in the city opened in Blondeau's Tavern in 1911. It eventually became Paramount Pictures and, like Universal, has survived the film-industry slump of the 1960s under its own identity. Others, like Twentieth Century Fox, although still making films, have sold off several studio lots in Los Angeles. On those acres now stands Century City, a hotel, shopping and commercial complex of steel and glass that leaves nothing to the imagination.

If you are looking for the imperishable glamour of yesteryear's stars, the place to go is Disneyland. Not the film studio, the playground. Here Disney's magic cast of stars show that they are as young and as real as on the day each first appeared on the screen. Disneyland is not strictly in Los Angeles although it is in the metropolitan area of the city, at Anaheim, twenty-seven miles away in Orange County. There Disney's Vacationland has drawn nearly 200,000,000 admirers since it opened in 1955 at a cost then of around £10,000,000. On the first day alone, more

than 30,000 people converged on the seventy-six acre site to pay homage to Disney's own superstars. In the first year there were 3,800,000 visitors. In 1980, 11,500,000 people came to see Disney's seven 'theme' lands, with fairy-tale names such as Bear Country, Frontierland, Adventureland, and Tomorrowland. A visionary to the last, Walt Disney indulged his passion for the future in a projection of the shape of things to come. The monorail system, its sleek and elegant trains gliding at rooftop height on a two-and-a-half mile track, was the first real passenger-carrying monorail system of its kind in the world. It is still used to capacity, not as a novelty, but as a working transport network linking various attractions in the park.

One of Disney's unfulfilled ambitions was to create EPCOT, the Experimental Prototype Community of Tomorrow, and at Disneyworld in Orlando, Florida, this concept is being developed (see Miami section). In Disneyland, a part of Disney's 'living blueprint of the future' is a rather solemn demonstration of a new animation technique. An entire theatre is given over to a ten-minute speech, delivered, rather pompously, by a life-sized Abraham Lincoln. Moving his limbs and lips as if he had just been dragged out of a deep sleep, the three-dimensional Lincoln acquits himself less well than many of the cartoon characters who have also been given Disney's elixir of life. The technique, known as 'audio animatronics'

A cruise with Donald Duck, Mickey Mouse and other cartoon favourites is a popular Disneyland amusement

its plastic teeth whiter than white, or you will gasp with shock as a bridge appears to collapse under the weight of the tram. It is a stunt, of course, and even more exciting seen from afar. One of the highlights of the tour is a twenty-minute film show which uses volunteers from the audience to act out new scenes for an early 1970s disaster movie, *Airport*. These scenes are then videotaped, cleverly inserted into the relevant parts of the film and played back. There are many side shows too, all well thought out and aimed at family audiences and even small

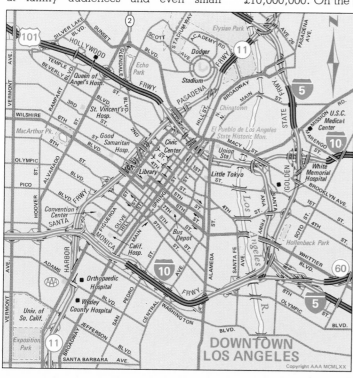

The death-defying rollercoaster ride tests the nerves at Knotts Berry Farm

is best demonstrated by an endearing all-singing all-dancing display of animal show-offs. Pigs, frogs, foxes, porcupines are all in three-dimensional substance in 'America Sings'. The show is programmed by computer.

Every so often, the main street with its quaint early-American-style shops, is lined with hundreds of people watching the fancy-dress parade of floats, musicians and dancers. The Disney characters, this time under human propulsion, weave in and out to the overwhelming delight of the wide-eyed children. It is this cartoon world of unforgettable characters that sets Disneyland apart from other big family entertainment parks. But it also is not without its heart-stopping thrills and spills. What must be the world's most scaring rollercoaster, Space Mountain, takes you on a gravity-defying ride through the cosmos in almost total darkness through tight figurations — curling, twirling, twisting, through what the senses are supposed to identify as space. Judging from the screams of fright and cries of delight emanating from the darkness, it is a great success (see also p.56).

Another colossal playground nearby is Knott's Berry Farm which, contrary to its rustic name, is a commercial amusement park with a higher than usual proportion of thrilling novelties. It began modestly in the 1920s when Walter and Cordelia Knott leased twenty acres of land to grow boysen berries and also opened a roadside diner and an Old West Ghost Town, still part of the amusements. A particularly sensational contraption is the rollercoaster called Montezuma's Revenge. It turns the carriage in a 360-degree vertical loop and is awful to watch, though marginally less terrifying to experience. The same applies to the jump from a parachute tower. To those whose head for heights is good, the skyjump from a cabin suspended on top of a mast is a spectacular thrill. Knott's Berry Farm celebrated its half-century in 1980, and is no less impressive in its size and the numbers it attracts than its more illustrious neighbour. The Movieland Wax Museum, Movieworld, the Californian Alligator Farm and the Anaheim Vacation Park are other distractions, all within easy reach of each other in that area.

If you crave for a cultural morsel of movie nostalgia, drive to the San Fernando Valley and stop off at the Hollywood Bowl. It is an undeniably genuine reminder of the 1940s and 1950s when it was first featured in films that dared to weave classical music into the plots (with Jose Iturbi conducting well and acting rather less well). More recently it has been the much publicized arena for pop and rock concerts — the Beatles did a memorable concert there. As a concert platform, the Hollywood Bowl is unique. One of the largest amphitheatres in the world, it seats more than 17,000 people outdoors in a wide arc facing a stage covered by what looks like half a coconut shell and was designed by the celebrated architect, Frank Lloyd Wright. Floodlit at night, much of the illumination coming from lights hidden on creeper-covered pillars, it is a spectacular sight, and a dramatic auditorium for music such as that played by the Los Angeles Symphony

Parks and Gardens

FOREST LAWN: 1712 S. Glendale Ave, Glendale, tel. 254 3131.

Cemeteries don't spring to mind as obvious tourist attractions, but the famous four Forest Lawn Memorial Parks in the Los Angeles area are required touring for their uniquely American blend of commercial and cultural reverence. The original Forest Lawn is the place Evelyn Waugh cruelly satirized in his novel *The Loved One*. A treasure trove of rare paintings, sculptures and historical relics, each Forest Lawn also offers to make the delicate arrangements on the spot for funerals and interments to come. To quote the rather less delicately worded brochure which urges visitors not to miss the opportunity while they are there: 'Because everything is under one management costs are lower.' The grounds of the original Forest Lawn at Glendale, north of the city centre, are lovingly landscaped. On 300 acres

stand three churches and a museum for displays of stained-glass, marble statues, jewels and an original collection of every coin mentioned in the Bible. Dramatic presentations of a stained-glass recreation of Leonardo de Vinci's *The Last Supper* are made in the Memorial Court of Honour, and in a hall named after its exhibits, one of the world's largest religious oil paintings, Jan Styka's *Crucifixion* (195ft by 45ft), is permanently mounted with *The Resurrection* (51ft by 70ft) by the American artist, Robert Clark.

HOLLYWOOD HILLS FOREST LAWN: 6300 Forest Lawn Drive, Los Angeles, tel. 984 1711. Here is displayed America's largest historical mosaic, *The Birth of Liberty* which portrays 25 scenes in America's colonial history. It is made up of 10,000,000 pieces of Venetian glass. The independence theme features in most exhibits here.

COVINA HILL FOREST LAWN: 21300 Via Verde Drive, Covina, tel. 966 3671. Thirty miles east of LA city centre, Covina Hill has the largest religious mosaic in America, depicting 26 scenes of the life of Christ. It is mounted on a hilltop, and can be seen for miles.

CYPRESS FOREST LAWN: 4471 Lincoln Avenue, Cypress, tel. 828 3131. The highlights of this Forest Lawn, west of Anaheim, are the marble statues towering over sweeping lawns, and the magnificent *Ascension* mosaic, from a painting by John La Farge.

GRIFFITH PARK: Los Feliz Blvd and Riverside Dr., tel. 665 5188. Observatory open 7pm-10pm on clear nights only. Planetarium open daily. Laserium closed Sunday and Monday. Science Hall closed Monday, except in summer.

Here, from the top of Mount Hollywood, you can see the stars come out in a way that no Hollywood premiere could match. At the Observatory you can use a twin-refracting

Life-size marble monuments are a feature of Forest Lawn

telescope and projectors that reproduce the stars visible in the sky, show eclipses, and the moon and the planets. There is also a fully-equipped 500-seat planetarium, a laserium (for laser beam shows), and a Hall of Science where the weather satellite tracking station may be seen free of charge.

Covering 4063 acres on the green south and east slopes of Mount Hollywood, Griffith Park is the largest municipal park in America. Befitting its giant proportions, it has a dazzling range of attractions, including a bird sanctuary, golf courses, tennis courts, athletic fields and lots of walking trails and picnic sites. The park is also home to Los Angeles Zoo — 113 acres accommodating more than 2000 mammals, birds and reptiles, with a children's zoo featuring an animal nursery and petting yard. The Greek Theatre located in the natural plateau below the pine-covered slopes of the mountains, is the venue for popular shows and attracts leading showbiz personalities. The park also has room for Travel Town, a transport museum which shows old aircraft and veteran railway rolling stock. To ride on an old locomotive costs a few cents, but admission to the exhibition is free.

Orchestra in the summer season. The auditorium, carved out of the Hollywood hills, stands in a park of 116 acres with 2000 trees, fountains and a splendid statue to the muse of music at the entrance.

Almost as old as the film business, the Bowl has miraculously survived for sixty years to become part of the Hollywood legend. At the time when W. D. Griffith's *Birth of a Nation* turned motion pictures almost overnight from being a sideshow into the Goliath of mass entertainment, a small group of actors, producers and musicians wanted to develop an artistic outlet for the unused talent that had converged on Hollywood. They needed a hall where they could put on classical plays and music. Hoping to rival the festival standards of Oberammergau, the German village where the passion play is held every ten years, they decided to build their own hall. The site they found not only had natural charm, but had its inbuilt acoustic properties — a benefit that derived from the ring of mountains in which the Bowl was to be set. The first performance, on a crude, makeshift stage, was Wagner's *Parsifal*. It began at dawn on a Sunday morning in March 1921, the Wagnerian chords augmented by the dawn chorus of the birds. An impressive occasion that must be hard to equal these days. It has also made its share of stars. At the age of ten, internationally renowned

maestro Lorin Maazel conducted the Los Angeles Philharmonic Orchestra on the Hollywood Bowl stage.

By keeping alive a tangible interest in music, the Hollywood Bowl has, in a sense, spawned the Los Angeles Music Center. A complex of three theatres in Los Angeles' Civic Center Mall, it is the winter home of the Philharmonic. Since the 1960s, the 3000-seater Dorothy Chandler Pavilion has drawn packed houses to symphony concerts, opera, recitals and dance programmes. Like the 2000-seat Ahmanson Theatre, and the more intimate Mark Taper Forum, the Pavilion has a pleasing modern architectural style, with sculptured fluted columns faced in white quartz, and Bavarian crystal chandeliers in the Grand Hall. The Pavilion auditorium has been designed so that every seat on the four tiers is within 105 feet of the stage.

The Music Center is the jewel of the downtown revival which over recent years has changed the face of the city's central area. Until the early 1960s, the building of skyscrapers — at least those with more than thirteen floors — was banned, since Los Angeles sits virtually on the notorious San Andreas fault. The only exception was City Hall, which grew and grew until when it was finished in 1928 it had a twenty-eight-storey tower described as 'Italian Classic'. The rule was relaxed as

Aptly named, the Hollywood Bowl, a vast amphitheatre built in the 1920s, occupies a magnificent site at the foot of the Hollywood Hills

building techniques and materials improved, allowing for more flexibility in the design and construction of ever more elaborate high-rise buildings.

Although San Francisco is more closely associated in the public mind with earthquakes, the Los Angeles area is just as vulnerable to them, and hotels reflect this passive concern by stressing on notices that lifts should not be used in case of fires or earthquakes. Now that monster buildings are clawing the sky wherever you look, Los Angeles is able to offer excellent rooftop views of the city from towering pillars like the World Trade Center, the Stock Exchange Building, or the Atlantic Richfield Plaza (a twin-towered fifty-two-storey edifice in the heart of downtown, with the world's largest subterranean shopping centre, where there are also restaurants and offices on several levels, and streets depicting scenes from famous European thoroughfares, Piccadilly and the Champs Elysées, among others). Criss-crossing the customary American pattern of numbered roads are streets with charming names like Flower, Hope, Grand, Spring

Civic Centre Walk

Distance can be very misleading in a city where 'blocks' — buildings between two parallel roads — are so long that they can stretch a pleasurable walk into a marathon. The following tour is about four miles and may be best covered in stages, but it is compact enough to allow for a stroll between some of the highlighted attractions. You will find details about most of them in the directory on pages 49-51, or in the main text.

Start at Hope Street where the magnificent Music Center dominates the Civic Center area. Across the street, fountains surround the Department of Water and Power Building which at night is usually floodlit.

After crossing Grand Avenue through the underpass, walk the length of the Music Center Mall, turn right into Hill Street and first left into First Street. Pass the Law Library, and the State Office building, then turn left into

Spring Street.

At City Hall, take the lift to the 27th floor where there is an observation platform, giving a grandstand view of the city. Leave the building at the Main Street exit and turn left. You will soon pass the US Courthouse, and the Los Angeles Mall, a subterranean shopping arcade. It has a museum for children. At El Pueblo de Los Angeles State Historic Park, you may be able to look over Pico House, once an elegant hotel, and the Old Plaza Fire House. You will find them in Olvera Street, believed to be the oldest street in LA.

Return to Main Street, turn right to the junction of Macy Street, turn left to Spring Street. This is where Sunset Boulevard begins. Return via Spring Street, turn right at Aliso Street, left at Broadway, right at Temple Street and left at Grand Avenue, then right at First Street back to the corner of Hope Street.

Stalls selling Mexican produce line Olvera Street, LA's oldest district

EL PUEBLO DE LOS ANGELES STATE HISTORIC PARK: bordered by Arcadia, Los Angeles, Macy and Main Streets.
The heart of this fascinating old area of town is Olvera

Street, thought to be the oldest street in Los Angeles. It was restored in the 1930s as a Mexican market place. Shops, stalls, cafes, etc. all specialize in Mexican produce.

AVILA ADOBE: 10E, Olvera St. An early 19th-century adobe mansion and the oldest house in LA, built in 1818 by Don Francisco Avila, a ranch owner, can be visited. Closed Mondays.

and Geranium. But the roads dominating and overshadowing so much of Los Angeles are the sweeping curves of elevated multi-lane freeways.

The most extensive of all America's network of urban highways, the Los Angeles freeway system has shaped the life of the city. Dubbed the 'commuter capital of the world' LA is really the consumer end of the Detroit motor vehicle production line. Angelenos use the 620 miles of city freeways boldly, confidently, and certainly make no apology for their reliance on the motor car. Public transport is available, but it doesn't fit too happily into the highly developed personal transport philosophy of the city. Apart from the distinctive striped-roof minibuses operating a shuttle service at ten-minute intervals through the business centre and shopping areas, the main bus line, the Southern Californian Rapid Transport District, is not greatly in evidence, except in the rush hour. The taxis are not economical for day to day use. (The twenty-five-mile trip to a downtown hotel from LAX, the Los Angeles international airport, can be as much as the price of a medium-sized hotel room for a night). Hiring a car is usually worthwhile. Some hotels, like the Hyatt Regency which shares its guest garage with a Hertz rental pool, are particularly adept at arranging car-hire facilities.

Happily for the stranger, Los Angeles provides generously large and legible street signs, particularly at major junctions. The local motorist is unlikely to bully the stranger on the road, and as long as he hasn't stilled the roar of LA traffic by

parking in the middle of the road to study the map, he will find that courtesy on the streets prevails. On the freeways, the rules of the road are strictly observed. If you fail to fall in with the traffic flow properly when you enter the freeway, or keep changing lanes, the sheer weight of traffic behind you will eventually seem to overwhelm you. It will snap at your heels, lunge at your sides, snarl and bark all around you. Of course if you speed, the law may get you first. It is a sobering fact that police enforce the speed regulations from the air, and there are warning signs that the road is patrolled by aircraft on many stretches. All the road furniture is worth studying — signs range from the terse 'OK to drive on shoulder 3.30-7pm', to overhead computerized lighted signs that, when they are not warning of hold-ups, flash cajoling messages such as 'Take a bus holiday for fun', or 'Try motorcycling. It's quicker and saves $$$'. Other signs invite you to check your speedometer and conveniently mark the start and finish of a measured mile. The national fifty-five mph speed limit which has been in force since the oil crisis began in 1973 is generally accepted and is only rarely flouted. Now and again, a high-speed merchant will take on the rest of the pack in a spectacular outside-lane pass.

The best way to negotiate the freeways is to study the special freeway maps available from the AAA, to work out first where to get on the freeway and when to come off. It also helps to know the points of the compass and left from right. Best not to ask, 'How far?' Much more relevant is the question, 'How long does it take?' If the

trip is supposed to take two hours it is folly to try and cut twenty minutes off the journey time.

Parking presents no problems — but you must be prepared to pay for it almost everywhere in the central areas. There are adequate parking lots and garages, but be warned: to use a parking meter on a busy thoroughfare is asking for trouble. It exposes the car needlessly to damage from passing traffic, and to the far greater danger of being towed away or fined on the spot if the car, irrespective of whether it has outstayed its time or not, is still at the meter during the rush-hour when most meters are automatically suspended.

It takes fifty minutes, give or take a few minutes each way, to pick up your car from the Downtown parking lot, join the freeway to Long Beach, make for the docks and arrive at the shipside of the former Cunard liner, *Queen Mary*.

Among California's six largest cities, Long Beach is not only an important business and industrial centre, but is the home of the US Navy's major fleets. It is also where Howard Hughes's giant flying boat, nicknamed 'The Spruce Goose' is on show. Only flown once, this eight-engined monster had not been seen in public for nearly thirty years until in 1980 it was wheeled out of its hangar to take its place beside the *Queen Mary* — now the biggest show afloat.

A relic of Britain's maritime glory the *Queen Mary* has been permanently anchored in these southern Californian waters since 1967 — lured across the Atlantic for the last time for the princely sum of £1,500,000 to give Long Beach,

Los Angeles' lifeline is its extensive, high-level freeway system

prefer the pervasive charm of the West Coast beaches, of course.

From Malibu to Redondo Beach, California's shoreline is alive with the vibrant voices of young people (and some not so young), all with that deep golden tan reflecting a sense of well-being and prosperity. Fishing, surfing, swimming, cycling and jogging are the main activities on beaches everywhere. The Venice beach, just a few miles south of Santa Monica, is the place to see impromptu juggling, magic acts, and acrobatics performed on the sand by impoverished students with an articulate line in drawing a crowd. The cafes are packed, moderately priced, and full of students with rude tee-shirts and tight jeans. Venice was once a very fashionable watering hole. It went into decline between the wars, and is now attracting professional people, who are slowly reviving the neighbourhood causing great anger among the Black community.

Close by, at Marina del Rey, is the world's largest man-made yachting harbour which can accommodate more than 10,000 yachts, dinghies and sloops at one time. This is the rich man's paradise — the playground for one of the wealthiest communities in the States. Some have come from LA's Bunker Hill, once the city's affluent area, but which is now downtown's newest development of offices, apartments, parks and shops.

One day, if LA's core continues to grow as it has done in the downtown area over the past few years, the city will shake itself free of its alter ego, Hollywood, and acquire an identity of its own, a personality that everyone who comes to the city can recognize.

one suspects, an edge over LA's own tourist attractions. Despite early misgivings and a recent change of ownership, the *Queen Mary*'s new role is drawing the crowds. Her new boss, head of an industrial corporation, had a sentimental reason for taking her over. With his wife, he had crossed the Atlantic on the *Queen Mary* a dozen times. Holder of the Blue Riband Atlantic speed record at thirty-three mph (thirty knots) for sixteen years — between 1936 and 1952 — in her thirty-year old career at sea, she

carried 2,100,000 fare-paying passengers across 3,800,000 miles of ocean; since she has had nowhere to go she has been boarded by five times as many people. A passable attempt is also made to re-create the Changing of the Guard ceremony at the shipside. Another of the more successful features is typically American, however, a wedding chapel and since 1972 about 500 couples a year have waited until they were on board the *Queen Mary* to tie the nuptial knot. The 'Brits', a pejorative that even the 50,000 permanent residents in the British 'colony' in Los Angeles don't seem to mind, need not go far to find a touch of home. Many of them, having settled in the Santa Monica area,

Los Angeles Directory

Hotels

The hotels and restaurants listed here are either recommended by the American Automobile Association (AAA) or have been selected because they are of interest to tourists. As a rough guide to cost, they have been classified as either expensive, moderate or reasonable. Hotels all have private bathrooms and colour television.

BEVERLY HILLS HOTEL: 9641 Sunset Blvd, Beverly Hills, tel. 276 2251. 325 rooms, swimming pool, parking lot and pay valet garage, 2 restaurants and coffee shop, expensive. The Polo Lounge Bar is LA's most glamorous drinking spot, and the Coterie Restaurant is celebrated.

BEVERLY HILLCREST: Pico Blvd, Beverly Hills, tel. 277 2800. 150 rooms, swimming pool, valet garage, 2 dining rooms, moderate. A well-appointed hotel, with fine views from the restaurant over the city to the ocean.

BILTMORE HOTEL: 515 S. Olive St at 5th St, tel. 624 1911. 1000 rooms, pay valet garage, central, expensive. Convenient for downtown LA, the Biltmore is a byword for elegance and personal service. Bernard's restaurant

is rated one of the best in Los Angeles.

BONAVENTURE: 350 S. Figueroa St. tel. 624 1000, freephone 800/228 3000. 1500 rooms, swimming pool, rooftop bars, central, expensive. Among Los Angeles' most distinctive landmarks are the five gleaming golden towers of this futuristic extravaganza. Inside are a lake, gardens, shopping arcades, bars and restaurants.

FIGUEROA HOTEL: 939, S. Figueroa St, tel. 627 8971, central, good quality and comfort, reasonable.

GALA INN TOWNE MOTOR HOTEL: 925 S. Figueroa St, tel. 628 2222. 170 rooms, swimming pool, central, reasonable.

HACIENDA HOTEL: 525 Sepulveda Blvd, tel. 322 1212. 660 rooms, swimming pool, parking, moderate. Near airport.

HOLIDAY INN — International Airport: 9901 S. La Cienega Blvd, tel. 649 5151. 403 rooms, swimming pool, motor hotel, moderate. Near airport.

HOLIDAY INN: N. Highland Ave, Hollywood Blvd, Hollywood, tel. 462 7181. 462 rooms, carparking, swimming pool, revolving rooftop restaurant. Motor Hotel, moderate.

HYATT REGENCY: Los Angeles, 711 S. Hope St, tel. 683 1234. 487 rooms, valet pay garage, central, expensive. Three restaurants, and revolving rooftop bar.

LOS ANGELES HILTON: 930 Wilshire Blvd, tel. 629 4321. 1200 rooms, swimming pool, pay valet garage, central, expensive.

MAYFLOWER: 535 S. Grand Ave, tel. 624 1331. 350 rooms, pay garage, moderate. An old-fashioned and solidly comfortable hotel.

NEW OTANI HOTEL: 120 S. Los Angeles St, tel. 629 1200. 448 rooms, pay valet garage, central, expensive. The most charming feature of the elegant Japanese hotel is its gardens, modelled on those of the famous Otani in Tokyo.

OASIS MOTEL: 2200 W. Olympic Blvd, tel. 385 4191. 70 rooms, swimming pool, reasonable. Attractive rooms in a quiet area of town.

RAINBOW HOTEL: 536 S. Hope St, tel. 627 9941. Reasonable. Comfortable and quiet, situated in the business area.

UNIVERSITY HILTON: 3540 S. Figueroa St, tel. 746 1531. 241 rooms, swimming pool, pay parking, motor hotel, expensive.

Restaurants

ANGELS' FLIGHT: Hyatt Regency Hotel, 711 S. Hope St, tel. 683 1234. A revolving restaurant with particularly interesting lunchtime menu. Central, moderate.

BROWN DERBY RESTAURANTS: 1628 Vine St, Hollywood, tel. 469 5151; 9537 Wilshire Blvd, Beverly Hills, tel. 276 2311. The one on Wilshire is the original Brown Derby, and part of the exterior is shaped like a Derby hat. Sunday brunches, American cuisine. Cobb salad, a famous American speciality, originated here. Moderate.

EL CHOLO MEXICAN RESTAURANT: 112 S. Western Ave, tel. 734 2773. Established since the 1920s, specialities include crabmeat

enchilada and other Mexican dishes. Central, reasonable.

EMILIO'S: 6602 Melrose Ave, tel. 935 4922. One of Los Angeles' most elegant restaurants, offering European dishes, with an emphasis on Italian. Excellent pasta and seafood. Central, expensive.

FAMOUS ENTERPRISE FISH CO: 174 Kinney St, Santa Monica, tel. 392 8366. Mexican-style fresh seafood, especially shellfish, charcoal grilled. Moderate.

HARRY'S RESTAURANT & DELI: 416 W. 7th St, tel. 622 3311. Excellent choice of delicatessen food. Central, reasonable.

HUNGRY TIGER, 7080 Hollywood Blvd, Hollywood, tel. 462 1323: One of a chain of restaurants serving seafood. Whole Maine lobster is a speciality. Moderate.

LEON'S KITCHEN & YOGURT & ICE-CREAM PARLOUR: 201, N. Los Angeles St, tel. 613 0747. Closed Sundays and 7pm evenings. Specializes in health foods. Central, reasonable.

McHENRY'S TAIL O THE COCK: 477 S. La Cienega Blvd, tel. 273 1200, and 12950 Ventura Blvd, North Hollywood, tel. 877 0889. Two restaurants specializing in American food. La Cienega has old-world atmosphere and flower gardens. Moderate.

MADAME WU's GARDEN: 2201 Wilshire Blvd, Santa Monica, tel. 828 5656. Authentic Cantonese cuisine.

MUNICH HOFBRAU TURNER INN: 645 W. 15 St, tel. 747 8191. Old-established Bavarian tavern with American and European cuisine. Moderate.

NEW OTANI HOTEL: 120 S. Los Angeles St, tel. 629 1200. Two restaurants, 1. A THOUSAND CRANES RESTAURANT; 2. GRILL KURO FUNE: The former is a charming restaurant specializing in Japanese food. Japanese-style gardens provide a delightful setting, the latter specializing in grills, is decorated to create the atmosphere of an 18th-century trading ship. Central, moderate.

PACIFIC DINING CAR: 1310 W. 6th St, tel. 483 8000. Decorated to look like an old

railway dining car, American food. Central, moderate.

PERINO'S RESTAURANT: 4101 Wilshire Blvd, tel. 383 1221. Founded in 1932, this is one of the best known restaurants in the US. International cuisine and meticulous service. Valet parking. Closed Sundays, central, expensive.

PUB INN THE ALLEY: 607 S. Hill St, tel. 622 5794. 'Authentic' English pub with beer and English dishes such as Welsh Rarebit. Dartsboard, too. Closed weekends and 8pm evenings. Reasonable.

SERGE'S STOP INN: 201 N. Los Angeles St, tel. 629 3543. Inexpensive hot meals; wide variety of sandwiches. Closed weekends and 6pm evenings. Reasonable.

SMITH BROS FISH SHANTY: 8500 Burton Way, La Cienega, tel. 272 4241. An old established seafood restaurant. Moderate.

TOWER RESTAURANT: 1150 S. Olive St, tel. 746 1554. On the 32nd storey, with panoramic views of Los Angeles. Central, moderate.

Shopping

LA's Little Tokyo (bordered by 1st, Los Angeles, 3rd and Alameda Sts) and Chinatown (entrance on N. Broadway, near College St) districts, La Cienega Boulevard, Melrose Avenue and the ultra-fashionable Rodeo Drive out in Beverly Hills, are all exciting and interesting shopping streets. Olvera Street in El Pueblo de Los Angeles is described in the City Walk box, p.48, and a few of the other most notable shopping centres in and around LA are listed below.

ARCO PLAZA: 5th and Flower Sts. Beneath the Atlantic Richfield building, the Arco Plaza is the largest subterranean shopping centre in the USA.

BONAVENTURE SHOPPING GALLERY: 404 S. Figueroa St. Inside the Bonaventure Hotel, the Shopping Gallery is an Aladdin's Cave of expensive specialist boutiques.

FARMER'S MARKET: 6333 W. 3rd St, has all manner of colourful, exotic food stalls and craft shops where you can buy the best of the world's produce.

FLOWER MARKET: 775 S. Wall St, is an old-fashioned flower market, established

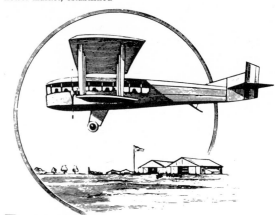

nearly 60 years ago, which sells 95 per cent of local flower growers' crop.

JAPANESE VILLAGE PLAZA: 350 E. 1st St, specializes in Japanese ware.

PORTS O CALL VILLAGE (off Harbor Freeway): Port of Los Angeles, Berth 77, San Pedro, tel. 831 0287 for information. A reconstructed old-world village with a wealth of craft shops and tempting boutiques.

Transport

LAX INTERNATIONAL AIRPORT: In anticipation of traffic for the 1984 Olympic Games, a new four-storey international terminal at LAX, Los Angeles's main airport, some 20 miles out on Century and Sepulveda Blvds, has been designed to relieve the pressure on the existing two buildings through which 24,000,000 passengers pass every year.
Frequent airport bus and coach services link all the major communities in and around central LA. Taxis are numerous and expensive. Check that the cab carries the LA franchise seal to validate his right to ply for hire at the airport. If you are staying at one of the six AAA-listed hotels in the airport area, use the hotel's free coach transportation. Taxi drivers do not like short trips, but if one refuses to make the journey, you can complain to the authorized taxicab supervisor, tel. 646 9177.
A useful service, between 7am and 11pm, if you are driving to the airport is to listen to the car radio on frequency 530 (far left on the dial) for traffic and parking bulletins.

CAR HIRE: Hertz and Avis have depots throughout

southern California, and at LAX, Los Angeles airport. Tel. (Hertz) 385 7151, freephone 800/654 3131; (Avis) 481 2000 or freephone 800/331 1212. Econo-car, tel. 776 6184, freephone 800/228 1000; Budget Rent a Car, tel. 645 4500, freephone 800/228 9650; American International Rent a Car, tel. 674 4780, freephone 800/527 6346, are all well known car-hire firms.

BUSES: Southern California Rapid Transit District (RTD) operates local and express buses. The information office at 425 S. Main St has maps and timetables. Tel. 626 4455. You can also phone them from anywhere in the city and ask them how to get from where you are to where you want to be. Tourist passes can be bought from kiosks at the International Airport terminal on production of evidence (passport, for example) that you are not a resident. Travelling by bus takes a long time, and will probably involve several interminable waits to change buses, but there is a frequent minibus service (about 10-minute intervals) around the downtown area of Los Angeles. Exact fare is required on buses.

TAXIS: Because Los Angeles is so spread out, taxis can prove expensive. Best known in the downtown area are the Los Angeles Red Top, tel. 870 5311, 822 4100; A & W, tel. 466 0328; United Independent, tel. 653 5050; Independent, tel. 380 7236, 955 5959; Checker, tel. 258 3231; Red and White, tel. 654 8400; Yellow, tel. 670 1234, 652 5111.

ORGANIZED BUS TOURS: Several bus companies run sightseeing tours in and around LA. Gray Line Tours 1207 W. 3rd St, tel. 481 2121, picks up from major hotels. Starline Sightseeing Tours, 6845 Hollywood Blvd, tel. 463 3131, is another well known company, and others are listed in the Yellow Pages of the telephone directory.

AMTRAK: the American passenger train service offers trips along the coast to San Francisco by a train romantically named the Coast Starlight; to Las Vegas on the Desert Wind, or to Flagstaff, Arizona, where there is a bus connection to the Grand Canyon. If you intend to travel far by train, a USA Rail Pass for unlimited travel is a good investment.

Touring Information

AAA, 2601 S. Figueroa St (at Adams Blvd), tel. 741 3111. The Automobile Club of Southern California. The Main office is open during office hours. District offices within the metropolitan area are to be found in: Burbank, Century City, Compton, Culver City, Downey, El Monte, Fullerton, Gardena, Garden Grove, Glendale, Hacienda Heights, Highland Park, Hollywood, Huntington Beach, Huntington Park, Inglewood, La Habra, Long Beach, Los Angeles, Manhattan Beach, Monrovia, Montebello, Montrose, North Hollywood, North Long Beach, Northridge, Norwalk, Pasadena, San Fernando, San Gabriel, San Pedro, Santa Monica, South Los Angeles, Temple City, Torrance, Van Nuys, Whittier, Woodland Hills.

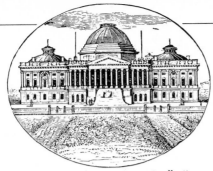

Museums

CASA DE ADOBE: 4605 N. Figueroa St. Close to the South-west Museum, the Casa de Adobe is a faithful replica of an early 19th-century Spanish colonial ranch, furnished throughout in period. Open Wednesdays, and weekends.

HUNTINGTON LIBRARY, ART GALLERY AND BOTANICAL GARDENS: 1151 Oxford Rd, San Marino. Henry Huntington, a former railway magnate, gave his magnificent collection of rare books, manuscripts and paintings to the county. Paintings include works by John Constable and Thomas Gainsborough. The library's outstanding treasures are the Ellesmere manuscript copy of *The Canterbury Tales* and a Gutenberg Bible (1450-55). The buildings are surrounded by extensive and beautiful gardens, divided into types — Desert, Palm, Japanese, Australian, Sub-tropical, Jungle, Shakespearean, etc.

J. PAUL GETTY MUSEUM: 17985 Pacific Coast Highway, Malibu, tel. 454 6541. The fabulous collection of the former oil magnate, who never actually visited his museum, features art treasures from ancient Greece and Rome and all periods of Western civilization, housed in a reconstructed Roman villa. Closed weekends in summer, Sundays and Mondays the rest of the year. Parking by reservation only (see also p.60).

LOS ANGELES CHILDREN'S MUSEUM: 310 N. Main St (Los Angeles Mall), tel. 687 8800. Specially for children, who are encouraged to explore and touch displays, this informal museum includes a replica city street and a 'grandma's attic' to rummage in.

LOS ANGELES COUNTY MUSEUM OF ART: 5905 Wilshire Blvd, tel. 937 2590 for recorded information. The permanent collection ranges from prehistoric times to the 20th century and covers Asian, African and European art. Closed Mondays.

NATURAL HISTORY MUSEUM: 900 Exposition Blvd. Superb exhibitions of fossils, minerals, birds, mammals, insects and the history of mankind are on show at this museum, the largest of its kind in the West. Closed Mondays; free films, Saturday afternoons; chamber music concerts, Sunday afternoons in summer.

NORTON SIMON MUSEUM OF ART: 411 W. Colorado Blvd, Pasadena, tel. 449 6840. The museum is a 1930s-style building, housing a superb collection of Renaissance art, works by the German Expressionists and South-east Asian sculpture.

SOUTH-WEST MUSEUM: 234 Museum Drive, tel. 221 2163. The museum is devoted to American-Indian arts and crafts. There are outstanding displays of the cultures of the Nomadic Plains Indians, the basket-making tribes of the south-west, and the Eskimos and tribes of the north-west.

Places of Interest

HOLLYWOOD WAX MUSEUM: 6767 Hollywood Blvd, Hollywood, tel. 462 8860. Also called Spoony Singh's after its Indian proprietor, the Hollywood Wax Museum displays lifelike wax figures of 170 of the most famous Hollywood film stars.

HUNTINGDON-SHERATON HOTEL: 1401 S. Oak Knoll Ave, Pasadena. Built in 1907, the hotel is an early example of reinforced-concrete construction, now romantically covered in creepers, and is set in magnificent gardens covering 23 acres. One of the most delightful features of the grounds is the Japanese garden.

Parks & Gardens

DESCANSO GARDENS: 1418 Descanso Dr., La Canada Flintridge, tel. 790 5571. Roses and more than 100,000 camellia bushes blooming in shady oakwoods are the major attraction of these lovely gardens. Roses and fuchsias are at their best between May and December; camellias, azaleas and rhododendrons from November to May.

ELYSIAN PARK: bordered by N. Broadway, Stadium Way, Academy Rd. The Chavez Ravine Arboretum, South California's first botanic garden, takes up a large part of this park. Trees from all over the world can be seen here.

LOS ANGELES STATE AND COUNTY ARBORETUM: 301 N. Baldwin Ave, Arcadia, tel. 446 8251. The Arboretum is also a horticultural research centre, with 127 acres of trees and shrubs, and greenhouses full of orchids and begonias. There is a bird sanctuary in the grounds, and several reconstructed historical buildings, the most interesting of which are the ornate 'Queen Anne' Cottage, the Santa Fe Railroad Depot and the Hugo Reid Adobe.

Sport

BASEBALL: the Los Angeles Dodgers can be seen at Dodger Stadium, 1000 Elysian Park Ave, tel. 224 1400; AMERICAN FOOTBALL: the Los Angeles Rams play at Anaheim Stadium, 2000 State College Blvd, Anaheim, tel. 999 8990; BASKETBALL: the Los Angeles Lakers play at the Forum, 3900 W. Manchester Blvd, Inglewood, tel. 674 6000; ICE HOCKEY: the Los Angeles Kings also play at the Forum. There are two horse-racing tracks, Hollywood Park, 1050 S. Prairie Ave, Inglewood, tel. 419 1500, and Santa Anita, Arcadia, 285 W. Huntington Drive, Arcadia, tel. 574 7223.

Theatres & Cinemas

Many historic cinemas are located on Broadway. The Cameo Theater, 588 S. Broadway, is a good example of one of the early nickelodeons, dating from 1910. The Los Angeles Theater, 615 S. Broadway, and the Million Dollar Theater, 307 S. Broadway, are both true cinema palaces erected in the heyday of the motion picture industry and opulently decorated. Mann's Chinese Theater (formerly Grauman's) 6925 Hollywood Blvd, tel. 464 8111, is the most famous of them all and is where many of the major film premieres are held. Its oriental-style architecture and forecourt decorated with the hand and footprints of the stars have made it a must on any sightseeing tour (see p.60).

EBONY SHOWCASE THEATER: 4720 Washington Blvd, tel. 936 1107. This is the oldest, Black-owned independent theatre in Los Angeles.

HOLLYWOOD BOWL: 2301 N. Highland Ave, Hollywood. Home of the Los Angeles Philharmonic Orchestra (see also p.61).

JOHN ANSON FORD THEATER: 2850 Cahuenga Blvd, tel. 469 3974. Run by Los Angeles County, the theatre offers musical programmes as well as plays and has an annual Shakespeare festival.

THE MUSIC CENTER: 135 N. Grand Ave, tel. 972 7485. Pride and joy of Los Angeles' downtown revival, the Music Center contains three separate theatres: the Dorothy Chandler Pavilion, the Ahmanson Theatre and the Mark Taper Forum.

PANTAGES THEATER: 6233 Hollywood Blvd, tel. 469 7161. The interior of this former cinema, now a 'straight' theatre has been meticulously restored in the original Art Deco style of the 1930s.

church built in 1797-1806 and shattered in the 1812 earthquake. It was one of the most ambitious and elaborately decorated of all the mission churches. The lovely gardens, often filled with flocks of white pigeons, and the pure simplicity of the place, bring many photographers and tourists, but perhaps its greatest attraction is its 'Legend of the Swallows' Every year on 19 March, St Joseph's Day, hundreds of swallows arrive at the mission and leave again for their winter home punctually on 23 October.
6 miles further south on Interstate 5 lies San Clemente.

Contrast is the essence of this far-reaching tour through south-east California to the Mexican border. It takes you through the arid white sands of the Colorado Desert, stopping on the way to view luscious palms, olives and citrus oases, rare and beautiful shrubs and plants. Sleepy old Spanish mission towns, steeped in legend, contrast sharply with the atomic research centres and moon and Mars scanners of a space-age America.

Rich in natural beauty and phenomena, the south-eastern part of California has rugged mountains, life-giving spa waters, wonderful beaches and mysterious caves.

Interstate 5 takes you through the Laguna Hills to San Juan Capistrano, 30 miles away.

The Southern Coast and the Mexican Border

5 days — 630 miles

Los Angeles — San Juan Capistrano — San Clemente — Oceanside — Carlsbad — Encinitas — Del Mar — La Jolla — Point Loma — Coronado — Tijuana — San Diego — San Pasqual — Joshua Tree National Monument — Palm Springs — Big Bear Lake — San Bernardino — Claremont — Arcadia — Pasadena — Glendale.

San Juan Capistrano, California
The classic beauty of Mission San Juan Capistrano, the seventh of

Father Junipero Serra's missions, founded in 1776, has earned it the name the 'Jewel of the Missions'. It is unusual in having two churches; one restored adobe building in use daily, and the ruins of a stone

San Clemente, California
This town was 'put on the map' when Richard Nixon retired here after resigning his presidency in 1974. There is a fine state beach, and the town is dotted with the original Spanish style buildings, white walled and red-roofed

SCALE 20.5 MILES TO 1 INCH

structures. At the Basilone Road exit of Interstate 5 is the San Onofre Nuclear Generating Station, where displays and self-operating exhibits explain the conversion of atomic power for peaceful uses.

Interstate 5 becomes a gently rolling coastal road from San Clemente. This road was first established by the Spanish and named El Camino Real, or the King's Highway. Follow it for 22 miles to Oceanside.

Oceanside, California
Oceanside has a wide, four-mile stretch of beach, and deep-sea fishing boats operate from its harbour. The 125,000 acres of Camp Pendleton, the largest Marine naval base in the country, are nearby and tours of the camp and also of the many beautiful orchid gardens in the area, are available through the Chamber of Commerce.

Mission San Luis Rey de Francia at 4050 Mission Avenue was eighteenth in the chain of twenty-one missions, and is named after Louis IX of France, the only French King to be canonized. Its spacious interior has lofty beamed ceilings and original decoration done by the Indians. An annual fiesta is held in July.

3 miles further along Interstate 5 is Carlsbad.

Carlsbad, California
Named after the famous Czechoslovakian spa because of the similarity of its mineral waters to those of the Czech resort, Carlsbad USA is a popular seaside holiday place and an important flower-growing centre. The best time to visit is in the spring when the flowers are in bloom.

9 miles further down Interstate 5 is Encinitas.

Encinitas, California
The Quail Botanic Gardens at 230 Quail Gardens Drive hold an amazing variety of rare plants, and a thicket of dwarf evergreen oak provides a natural and popular bird refuge. The dawn chorus is an extraordinary symphony of birdsong.

6 miles out of Encinitas is Del Mar.

Del Mar, California
Stunted, deformed and twisted into sinister shapes by the force of the Pacific winds, Torrey pines are the descendants of primeval trees that existed before the Ice Age. The Torrey Pines State Reserve, a 1000-acre park at Del Mar, and Santa Rosa Island near Santa Barbara, California, are their only surviving natural habitats.

Leave Der Mar and travel for 8 miles on Interstate 5 to La Jolla.

San Juan Capistrano: 4 bells remain from the old mission church which was destroyed in the 1812 earthquake

La Jolla, California
Over the years, Pacific waves have carved seven caves out of the soft cliffs of La Jolla. One of these may be explored via an inland underground stairway, the other six are reached only from the ocean. This accounts for the name of this popular resort and artist's colony — it is a confusion of two Spanish words, *la joya,* meaning jewel, and *la hoya,* meaning hollow. A three-and-a-half mile bicycle tour along the sea front, takes you to explore the caves, passing the pretty seaside homes and Bird Rock, a nesting place for pelicans and cormorants.

An important tennis centre, the La Jolla Beach and Tennis Club has ten championship courts and is host to the venerable La Jolla Tennis Tournament, held annually since 1916.

The aquarium museum at the Scripps Institution of Oceanography is one of only two of its kind in the world and forms a research base for the famous undersea explorer Jacques Cousteau.

Leave La Jolla on Interstate 5 but turn off at Ocean Beach to pick up the unclassified coast road to Point Loma, jutting from the mainland between the Pacific Ocean and San Diego Bay.

Point Loma, California
A lighthouse built in 1891 crowns the tip of finger-shaped Point Loma. At certain places along the front the ocean's powerful waves have carved the precipitous cliffs into fantastic shapes, earning them the romantic name of Sunset Cliffs.

Overlooking the city and harbour of San Diego is the Cabrillo National Monument, commemorating the voyage of the Portuguese sailor employed by Spain, Juan Rodriguez Cabrillo, who landed here in 1542. There is

The elegant resort of Coronado lies across the bay from San Diego. This graceful, swooping bridge links it to the mainland

Joshua trees, a rare species of lily, growing in the Colorado Desert

a vantage point here from which, at the right time of year, you can see grey whales migrating.

Drive away from Point Loma on State Route 209, and turn right along Harbour Drive until you reach the San Diego-Coronado Bay Bridge. This will take you to the attractive town of Coronado

Coronado, California
On a peninsula between San Diego Bay and the Pacific Ocean is this small resort noted for its recreational facilities. Boats may be hired for fishing and sightseeing; on land the favourite form of transport is the two-wheeled kind, and bicycles and mopeds are also available for hire. The Coronado Municipal Golf Course, bordering the San Diego and Glorietta Bays, and the public tennis centre cater for sports enthusiasts. Silver Strand State Beach, seven miles south of the town is an ideal picnic area and safe for swimming.

Take State Route 75 out of Coronado to pass by Imperial Beach and join Interstate 5 once more before reaching Tijuana.

Mexican hats piled up for sale in the market at Tijuana

Tijuana, Mexico
You are now in Mexico, though Tijuana, a growing industrial complex and the main port of entry to the Baja Peninsula, is, however, by no means typical of the rest of the country.

Bullfights are held every Sunday during the mid-May to mid-September season, and spectator sports such as horse and dog racing or *jai alai* (a fast and dangerous variant of the ancient Basque game of pelota) inspire intense betting at ever-changing odds.

Mexican handicrafts make good souvenirs and the Avenida Revolucion is the main shopping street; the US dollar is accepted in Tijuana.

Leave on Interstate 5, and once over the border again take Interstate 805, drive for 15 miles to reach a major intersection. Here take State Route 15, which later broadens out to become Interstate 15, and head for San Diego.

San Diego, California
The second largest city in the State, San Diego is often referred to as 'the place where California began.' The Portuguese captain Juan Cabrillo, first sailed into the bay in 1542, but it was not until 1769 that Father Junipero Serra established the first of his 21 missions here and planted the State's first palm and olive trees. From that moment on San Diego has never looked back, and today it is counted as a popular holiday resort as well as a thriving manufacturing and shipping centre.

The city's many places of interest include Balboa Park, a vast recreation and cultural centre at the edge of the business district. Among the Park's exhibition halls are some fine examples of Spanish architecture. The Botanical Building, in which sub-tropical plants are housed, is a reconstructed Santa Fe railway station, and many ornate buildings from the Panama-California

International Exposition, held in 1915, remain. Subjects covered in other parts of the complex include natural history, art, space, sport, science and mankind.

San Diego Zoo, also in Balboa Park, is one of the largest in the world with over 5000 animals on display, all living in simulated natural habitats. Escalators take visitors from the deep, landscaped canyons to the upper levels and an 'aerial tramway' operates from the main entrance.

The old town of San Diego is remembered by the restored adobe building at 2656 San Diego Avenue, the old town plaza, and a six-block historic park containing many original structures and early American relics has been preserved as a traffic-free area.

Leave San Diego on Interstate 15 and branch off on State Route 78, which leads east to San Pasqual, about 15 miles from the centre of San Diego.

San Pasqual, California
The San Diego Wild Animal Park, 1800 acres of desert land that looks as if it has been imported from Africa or Asia, lies in San Pasqual. Here, an electric monorail transports visitors from one delight to the next. Elephants, lions, rhinos, zebras, giraffes and many other colourful creatures roam freely.

Animal and bird shows and other entertainment take place in 'Nairobi Village'.

From San Pasqual take State Route 78 for 60 miles through the desert to Salton Sea, a vast lake more than 200ft below sea level, nestling beneath the steep slopes of the Chocolate Mountains. Turn left on State Route 86 to drive along the lake shore, then take State Route 195 to Joshua Tree National Monument.

Joshua Tree National Monument, California
This is a living, growing monument in the form of the rare and beautiful Joshua Tree, a species of the lily family which grows 20-40ft high and lives for

up to 300 years. The Joshua Tree was given its name by early pioneers who felt that the strange plant, with its very greenish-white flowers, resembled the prophet Joshua raising his arms in supplication to God. Surprisingly, the monument, an arid desert park, is the home of many forms of wildlife, lizards, wood-rats, birds and the largest animal in the area, the desert bighorn, live among the Joshuas. Nine campsites exist in the 870 square miles of the park.

State Route 195 crosses the park, and at the junction with State Route 62, turn left for Twentynine Palms, a small town whose name was chosen in 1870 when it was bordered by exactly that number of palms. Take State Route 62 through Yucca Valley. In 14 miles, turn left on to Interstate 10 to Palm Springs intersection.

Palm Springs, California
You are now in the heart of Colorado, California's southernmost desert land. Palm Springs, known as the 'playground of the wealthy' was developed from a single natural oasis with hot water springs into a spa, and later, an internationally famous holiday resort.

An 80-passenger aerial tramway runs to the top of the precipitous Mount San Jacinto, or, as it is affectionately known, Old San Jack, where there are gift shops, a games room, a restaurant and picnic area. Views are spectacular. More down-to-earth enjoyment might be star spotting in the local boutiques and exclusive restaurants, many of which are owned and run by television and film personalities.

A seven mile drive over the desert will bring you to Palm Canyon, a grove of 3000 palms along a trickling stream on the Aqua Caliente Indian Reservation. Some of the native Washington palms are estimated at 2000 years old. Also here is the Andreas Canyon with its many spectacular rock formations.

Leave Palm Springs on State Route 111, turning left on Interstate 10, a semi-arid desert road. Once through Beaumont, about 20 miles, turn right on an unclassified road through Cherry Valley and Yucaipa. At the junction with State Route 38, turn right and travel through the rugged San Bernardino Mountain range to Big Bear Lake, 44 miles away.

Big Bear Lake, California
Those who love 'the great outdoors' flock to Big Bear Lake and Valley, one of California's largest all-year-round recreation areas. Its craggy location in the eastern mountain range makes it

an ideal place for riding and swimming in summer and skiing, ice skating, tobogganing and sledge riding in winter. Camping and picnic sites abound, and nearby are several winter sports centres.

At the end of the lake, turn right on to State Route 18 and drive for 14½ miles to Lake Arrowhead where State Route 18 takes you into San Bernardino and you join US 15E.

San Bernardino, California
In San Bernardino National Forest are the highest mountains in southern California, including the 11,502 ft San Gorgonio. Wide variations in scenery, climate and vegetation are found within the massive area covered by the forest, and the walking and driving tours attract many visitors. Campsites, picnic places and six winter sports areas exist here.

Take Interstate 10 out of San Bernardino and drive for 16½ miles, turning off at junction 47 to Claremont.

Claremont, California
Claremont is largely a college community with the Scripps College for Women, Pomona College, Claremont Men's College, Harvey Mudd College, The Pitzer College for Women and the Southern California School of Theology within its confines. It lies at the base of the graphically named Mount Baldy in the Angeles National Forest.

An excellent collection of native Californian plants and flowers are on show at the Rancho Santa Ana Botanic Garden at 1500 North College Avenue.

From Claremont, take State Route 66 to reach Interstate 210 which takes you into Arcadia.

Arcadia, California
At 301 Baldwin Avenue is the Los Angeles State and County Arboretum, a horticultural research centre. 127 acres are devoted to orchid and begonia greenhouses, all kinds of rare and interesting trees and shrubs, a bird sanctuary and a library.

Arcadia is also the home of Santa Anita Park, a famous horse-racing track, which, since it first opened for business in 1934, has introduced and developed the starting gate, photo finish, electrical timing and the totalizer. Morning workouts may be viewed during the racing season.

From Arcadia drive 7 miles along Interstate 210 to Pasadena.

Pasadena, California
This elegant city has a fine residential district with rows of stately old houses.

Every New Year's Day the 'Tournament of the Roses' football match, is played in Pasadena's Rose Bowl stadium in Brookside Park. The Tournament of the Roses is also the name of a colourful annual carnival, when flower-covered floats process through the city streets. The site of the Rose Bowl, and that of the California Institute of Technology on East California Boulevard, have lately become the home of NASA's Jet Propulsion Laboratory where Moon and Mars-scanning satellites are designed.

The Norton Simon Museum of Art has exhibits of tapestries, sculpture and painting from early Renaissance to the 20th century. Don't miss the Monet, Renoir and Van Gogh works.

6 miles away, still on Interstate 210, is Glendale.

Glendale, California
Glendale lies at the entrance of the San Fernando Valley and was the first piece of land to be granted to settlers in California by King Charles IV of Spain in 1784. The state remained a Mexican province, and thus a Spanish possession, until America annexed it in 1846.

The Forest Lawn Memorial Park at 1712 South Glendale Avenue (see also p.46) comprises over 300 beautifully landscaped acres. Among the attractions of the cemetery is a collection of large white marble statuary and stained glass windows, including a re-creation of Leonardo de Vinci's 'The Last Supper'. The Hall of the Crucifixion-Resurrection contains religious oil paintings, while rare gems and coins are on show in the museum.

Take State Route 2 and Interstate 5 back to Los Angeles, 8 miles away.

Palm Springs, playground of the wealthy, lies in the Colorado Desert

Disneyland and LA's Coastal Resorts

2 days — 90 miles (plus ferry).

Los Angeles — Anaheim — Costa Mesa — Newport Beach — Santa Catalina Island — Long Beach — San Pedro — Palos Verdes — Redondo Beach — Marina del Rey — Santa Monica — Los Angeles.

Driving south from the city of Los Angeles, this 90-mile tour makes its first stop at fabulous Disneyland. From that point onwards the tour is a series of high spots. Inland, it moves through the hilly country of San Joaquin to reach the Pacific Coast, where the flower-decked hills of beautiful Santa Catalina Island are just a ferry ride away. Back on the mainland, the route follows the coastal road through the idyllic resorts of Southern California. Long Beach, Marina del Rey, Santa Monica — the palm-fringed beaches unfold, one after the other, on the return journey to LA.

Take Interstate 5 (Santa Ana Freeway) out of Los Angeles city and drive for 22 miles through the spectacular scenery of south-western California to Anaheim.

Anaheim, California
Not many people will have heard of Anaheim in its own right, for it is completely overshadowed by the fame of the fantasy kingdom it plays host to — Disneyland. At 1313 Harbor Boulevard, visitors find themselves walking through the entrance and on to 'Main Street' — a reconstruction of a typical American street in the 1890s. From here it is wise to select the area you are most interested in — 'Tomorrowland', 'Frontierland', 'Fantasyland', 'Adventureland', 'Bear Country' or 'New Orleans Square' and head straight for it, as the areas are so vast, it would take several days to see them all.

Tomorrowland is a space-age extravaganza, featuring electronic and aeronautical exhibits. Space Mountain, which takes you on a breathtaking voyage through space, is the most spectacular attraction. Frontierland goes back in time to the early 19th century and the explorations of the pioneers. Big Thunder Mountain Railroad will take you back to the days of the Gold Rush, through a spectacular mine with rainbow-coloured waterfalls. Tom Sawyer Island, named after the hero of Mark Twain's novels, can be explored by boat, with rides on rafts or canoes for the adventurous. In Fantasyland is the best known of all Disneyland's attractions — Sleeping Beauty's Castle — the pastel colours and glittering spires of which make it the park's most photographed site. Alice in Wonderland, Peter Pan and Dumbo are just a few of the much-loved characters who live here. Adventureland offers a tour of the Indian Jungle through Rudyard Kipling's 'Mowgli' stories, while in Bear Country Davy Crockett Explorer canoes will take you to watch the bears caper at their country jamboree (see also p.45-6).

Rejoin the Santa Ana Freeway and drive for 7 miles to the Tustin exit, where the Costa Mesa Freeway will take you the remaining 8 miles to Costa Mesa itself.

Costa Mesa, California
Costa Mesa boasts an excellent municipal golf course and ex-racing driver and car constructor Briggs Cunningham runs an Automotive Museum at 250 East Baker Street. Around 100 sports, classic and racing cars, some dating back to 1898 are housed here, including a 1927 Bugatti 'Royale' one of the largest and most expensive cars ever made.

About 2 miles away on the Pacific Coast is Newport Beach.

Newport Beach, California
With a population of 64,200, the city of Newport Beach embraces Balboa, Balboa Island, Lido Isle, Corona del Mar, Newport Heights, Harbor Island, Bay Shores and Linda Isle.

Newport Harbor is a leading rendezvous for yacht enthusiasts, and regattas are held almost every weekend of the year. The six-mile stretch of sand that leads into the warm, blue Pacific makes Newport

Sleeping Beauty's Castle appears like a story-book illustration above the trees in Fantasyland (left)

(Right) 20 miles from the California coast, the island of Santa Catalina was for centuries a smugglers' hideout

SCALE 7.75 MILES TO 1 INCH

Beach a popular holiday resort.
Newport Dunes Aquatic Park on Upper Newport Bay includes a 20-acre lagoon, sports courts, amusements and picnicking facilities.

A 2-hour ferry crossing will take you across the 22-mile channel to Catalina Island. For details of crossing times and fares phone the Avalon Chamber of Commerce (213) 510 1520.

Santa Catalina Island, California

Once a base for smugglers and pirates, Santa Catalina Island, with its sandy bays and crystal-clear water, was transformed into a fashionable holiday resort at the end of the last century. In 1915 it was sold to the chewing gum king William Wrigley Jr, and it became the playground of the wealthy and famous. Facilities for sailing, fishing, swimming and scuba-

Luxury hotels surround the Queen Mary, which lies in stately retirement at Long Beach

diving abound, and inland, among the flower-covered hills, there are miles of trails through lush countryside for horse-riding and bicycling.

The main town, Avalon, takes its name from the mystical Isle of Avalon in Celtic mythology, an enchanted realm to which King Arthur is said to have been carried after his death.

An evening boat trip to watch the antics of the flying fish — the world's largest specimens inhabit these waters — is a memorable experience.

By day, glass-bottomed boats tour the Californian State Marine Preserve, an underwater garden of exotic marine plants, fishes and other forms of sea-life.

From Santa Catalina, catch the ferry back to Newport Beach and continue north on State Route 1 to Long Beach.

Long Beach, California

This is California's sixth largest city, bustling with life and counting as one of its main attractions a five-and-a-half mile beach. The Market Place on East Pacific Coast Highway, and

Seaport Village at the end of Marina Drive, are the best places to eat or shop. The Long Beach Convention and Entertainment Center houses two theatres and an arena for sporting events and trade shows. Anyone spending an evening in Long Beach should consult the Center's varied programme of events.

The *Queen Mary*, once one of Britain's most famous luxury liners for the rich and famous, launched in 1934, is docked at Pier J, specially built to accommodate her. The 81,000 ton ship, one of the largest ever built, is now a floating museum, and the interior has been restored to its original 1930s splendour. In the furnishing of the cabins and gangways, for example, 57 different woods were used. You can even stay overnight in one of the 400 elegant state rooms, which are now run as a luxury hotel. Several excellent boutiques and restaurants are open on board, as well as underwater explorer Jacques Cousteau's Living Sea Museum.

Other 'British' attractions on the dockside are two red double-decker London buses and a

traditional black London taxi. Soon to be built, apparently, is a replica English village (see also pp.48-9).

An unclassified coastal road leads straight to San Pedro, 4 miles away.

San Pedro, California

Together with Wilmington and Terminal Island, San Pedro constitutes the Port of Los Angeles. The man-made harbour is one of the largest deep-water ports in America, and it is guarded by formidable Fort MacArthur, one of the country's foremost coastal defences. Don't miss Ports O'Call Village, on the main channel of Los Angeles harbour at the south end of the Harbour Freeway. It is a total re-creation of life in a 19th-century port community, with gaslit streets and 'olde worlde' shops and restaurants. You may even encounter a pirate or two! Narrated-tour cruises operate daily.

Excursions to watch the grey whales migrating are available when the time is right; usually in December or January.

Take the coastal road for 7 miles to Palos Verdes Peninsula.

Palos Verdes Peninsula, California

20th Century Fox own Palos Verdes' world famous Marineland, so as expected, the antics of the performing killer whales, dolphins and acrobatic sea lions are stage-managed with more than a touch of show-biz razamataz. Those who know how to snorkel can dive into a 540,000 gallon tank where a trained diver will point out rare undersea sights. The less adventurous can watch the diver's progress on television.

Marine Animal Care Center houses and cares for wounded sea creatures on the premises. Children are well catered for with stage shows and a playground and there are picnic facilities.

Continue northwards along the coast to Redondo Beach.

Redondo Beach, California

At the southern end of Santa Monica Bay, Redondo Beach is a popular resort where an international surf festival is held each August. At Fisherman's Wharf on Monstad Pier are fresh fish stalls, seafood restaurants, souvenir shops, penny arcades, and other seaside attractions.

9 miles further north along the coast is Marina del Rey.

Marina del Rey, California

This is the largest marina in the Los Angeles area, with sailing craft of all sizes berthed in its harbour. A coastguard air-rescue base operates from the shore. Sailing and fishing boats can be hired from 13723 Fiji Way. Fishermen have caught excellent halibut, bonito and bass off this part of the LA shoreline.

On the seafront, at 13755 Fiji Way, is Fisherman's Village, where speciality shops, nightclubs and restaurants can be found.

Still moving northwards, drive 5 miles to Santa Monica.

Santa Monica, California

Santa Monica is a residential city stretching along the coastline to include the beaches of Ocean Park, Will Rogers State Beach and the exclusive sands of Malibu. For magnificent vistas of the Pacific, make for one of the many viewpoints and well-placed picnic sites scattered over the promenade or venture along the sea-front cliffs to Palisades Park.

The Donald Douglas Museum and library at 2800 Airport Avenue is dedicated to the history of aviation. Features include scale models of aircraft and mementoes of famous fliers.

From Santa Monica join Interstate 10 and drive 11 miles to return to Los Angeles city.

The Spanish Mission Trail

3 days — 440 miles

Los Angeles — Beverly Hills — Pacific Palisades — Malibu — Port Hueneme — Ventura — Santa Barbara — Solvang — Lompoc — San Luis Obispo — San Simeon — San Miguel — Lebec — Valencia — Newhall — San Fernando — Hollywood — Los Angeles.

The tour takes you north from Los Angeles through spectacular coastal and mountain scenery, following part of the Spanish mission trail, which dates from the early history of California when Father Junipero Serra began in 1768 a chain of 21 missions for the conversion of the Indians. The old towns contrast vividly with the opulent mansions of the stars which draw tourists in their thousands to Beverly Hills, and with the brash, showbiz personality of Hollywood.

From the centre of Los Angeles, drive 7 miles down Hollywood Freeway before joining State Route 2, which connects with Sunset Boulevard. Ten miles down Sunset Boulevard, towards the coast, is Beverly Hills.

SCALE 20.5 MILES TO 1 INCH

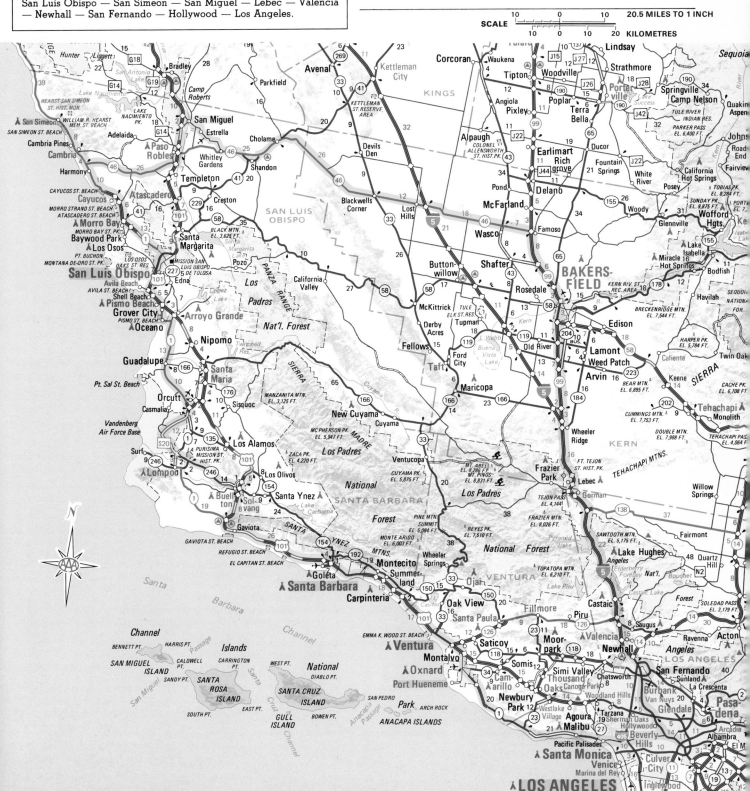

Spanish Mission Trail

The J. Paul Getty Museum was built on the plan of a Roman villa which was discovered at Herculaneum in Italy

Beverly Hills, California
The most affluent and elegant residential suburb in Southern California, Beverly Hills is famous as the home of many film and television stars. Southern California Visitors Council at 705 West 7th Street issue a free tour pamphlet for those who wish to identify the stars' homes on foot, though many bus and limousine tours operate.

Travel on Sunset Boulevard for 12 miles, then take the local road to Pacific Palisades.

Pacific Palisades, California
Here is the 186-acre home of late humorist and film star Will Rogers. Now a State Historic Park at 14253 Sunset Boulevard, the house and grounds are open daily.

Coastal State Route 1 takes you 18 miles to Malibu.

Malibu, California
The splendid sands of Malibu stretch several miles alongside the coastal road, wedged between the Santa Monica Mountains and the sea. Many artists, writers and members of the 'jet-set' have homes here, and sun-bronzed beach boys ride the surf all day. Visit the J. Paul Getty Museum at 17985 Pacific Coast Highway (see also p.51). The museum exhibits the collection amassed by the late oil magnate over a long lifetime. Art treasures start with Greek and Roman antiquities and range over the whole of Western civilization.

Follow coastal State Route 1 for 64 miles before reaching an interchange where you take the Hueneme Road to Port Hueneme.

Port Hueneme, California
The CEC/Seabee Museum is part of the US Naval Construction Battalion, and battle scenes, weapons, models of equipment and uniforms pertaining to the Civil Engineer Corps and the Seabees are on show. Call at the Ventura Gate for a free visitor's pass.

From Port Hueneme climb northwards away from the coast to join US 101 and drive 20 miles to Ventura.

Ventura, California
One of the oldest towns in the state, Ventura was once the site of a Chumash Indian settlement. Today it is a typical holiday town, with beautiful beaches, a public pier and a marina.

Mission San Buenaventura was the last mission to be dedicated by the pioneering Franciscan Padre, Father Junipero Serra, before his death in 1784. Father Serra walked nearly 5000 miles and founded a chain of 21 missions along the Californian coast. The present church has been restored.

Father Serra also erected the Padre Serra Cross on Mission Hill. The views from this point are impressive, and at Easter services take place at sunrise.

Ventura County Historical Museum (closed Mondays) at 100 East Main Street reflects the influence of Indian, Spanish and Pioneer settlers, and in the grounds there is an agricultural display.

Take coastal US 101 for a straight ride of 60 miles of beautifully landscaped freeway to the palm-fringed beaches of Santa Barbara.

Santa Barbara, California
A major holiday resort, Santa Barbara is perched on a narrow shelf between the picturesque Santa Ynez Mountains and the Pacific Coast. Spanish influence came to the town as early as 1782 and, after an earthquake in 1925 had destroyed virtually the whole town, it was rebuilt in the classic adobe style, with warmly coloured stucco and terra-cotta tiles. Made from unburnt, sun-dried materials, the adobe dwellings are crowned with rounded red clay roof tiles which were moulded on the thighs of the Indian women. Many of these white-washed, tile-roofed buildings still stand, and are in active community use today. The vine-hung streets with Spanish names such as Camino Cielo (Street of the Sky) or Los Olivos (The Olives) do much to remind the visitor of Santa Barbara's past.

A magnificent example of Spanish-Moorish decoration can be seen at the County Courthouse at 1120 Anacapa Street, where the murals, exotic decorations and sunken gardens seem an incongruous setting for a place where justice is meted out. Tours take place Friday at 10.30am, the rest of the week you may visit by appointment only. Phone (805) 966 1611 ext 7600.

Also worth a visit is the Mission Santa Barbara, occupying a queenly position high above the sea and city. Excellent exhibits of Greek, Roman and Egyptian sculptures are housed here, and a 'Little Fiesta' is held in August. In the wooded canyon behind the Mission is the Museum of Natural History at 2559 Puesta de Sol Road, where mounted specimens of the largest flying bird in North America, the California Condor, can be found.

Continue along the coast on US 101, past Goleta, a coastal town surrounded by lemon groves, to Solvang, which means 'Sunny Valley', 20 miles away.

Solvang, California
Known as Little Denmark, Solvang was established in 1911 as a settlement for Danish immigrants. Much of the town's architecture is in the Scandinavian style, and Danish festivals are held each September. The beautifully restored mission of Santa Ines was founded here in 1804 and housed California's first seminary. A few miles south-west, picnic facilities are available, near the rushing waters of dramatic Nojoqui Falls.

From Solvang take State Route 246 for 15 miles to Lompoc.

Lompoc, California
Flower-seed fields are big business in Lompoc, and through the summer the fields are ablaze with colour. La Purisima Mission was rebuilt here by Franciscan priests in 1813 after it had been demolished by an earthquake. Demonstrations of traditional crafts take place regularly in the summer season.

From Lompoc take County Route 20 to Orcutt where the road becomes State Route 1. Follow this road to Grover City, where US 101 will take you into San Luis Obispo.

San Luis Obispo, California
A delightful old town tucked away in the Los Padres mountains, about half-way between Los Angeles and San Francisco, San Luis grew up around an 18th-century mission. Charactistically, the Sinsheimer Brothers Drygoods Store, founded in 1876, is doing good business by selling the same kind of stock as it sold to the pioneers over 100 years ago. Its original cast-iron colonnaded front was made in San Francisco. Also of interest is the Ah Louis Store, opened in 1874 by a Cantonese family who had come to California in search of gold. It still specializes in Oriental goods.

The white-walled adobe Mission San Luis Obispo de Tolosa, built in 1772, is often called the 'Prince of Missions' and was the first to resort to tiled roofing to thwart the Indians who used to set fire to the original rush roofs. It is now used as the parish church and there is a museum attached, displaying relics of the early mission days and many items relating to Cherokee and Chumash Indian culture. The mission gardens stretch down to a secluded creek.

In the County Historical Museum is a wonderful collection of folklore and interesting objects, not least of which is a book from 1853 called *The Matchmaker*, which gives valuable advice on how to 'woo, win and wed', how to have pleasant dreams and other such essential information.

Take State Route 1 out of San Luis. After Morro Bay, the road runs along the coast to San Simeon, about 20 miles away.

San Simeon, California
San Simeon sits on top of La Cuesta Encantada (the enchanted hill) in the lush countryside of the Santa Lucia Mountains. The Hearst-San Simeon State Historical Monument is a sight not to be missed, for it incorporates Hearst Castle, the fabulous estate of the late newspaper tycoon William Randolph Hearst, memorably portrayed by Orson Welles in his most famous early film, *Citizen Kane*. La Casa Grande, a twin-towered Hispano-Moorish castle, was Hearst's home, and his $50,000,000 collection of art treasures is housed here in 100 lavishly decorated rooms, packed with paintings, books and precious

One of the most distinctive and famous buildings in Hollywood, Mann's Chinese Theatre

Spanish Mission Trail

and monastery. An Indian craft room forms part of the attached museum and the old gardens, known as Brand Park, are filled with flowers and shrubs which have come from the other 20 missions. Open daily.

State Route 118 takes you 8 miles west to join Interstate 5 (the Golden State Freeway) and then the Hollywood Freeway, 25 miles from Hollywood.

Hollywood, Los Angeles
Hollywood is the undisputed glamour capital of the world. It's a place that has entertained millions since the beginning of the century and it still pulsates with the excitement and creative energy that make it a 'must' on every tourist's itinerary. Fascinating tours through the 'back lots' and sound stages of the motion picture studios take place regularly at Universal City and Burbank. Highlights include stunt shows, special-effects demonstrations and set construction.

The most visited site in Hollywood is certainly Mann's Chinese Theatre at 6925 Hollywood Boulevard, where the handprints and footprints of world-famous celebrities have been preserved in concrete since 1927, when a star called Norma Talmadge started the fashion (see also p.44).

In a natural amphitheatre in the foothills is the Hollywood Bowl, a gigantic stadium designed by America's most famous architect, Frank Lloyd Wright (see also pp.46-7).

From Hollywood take US 101 back to Los Angeles.

objects from all over the world. The landscaped Italian gardens are studded with pools, statues, fountains and magnificent guesthouses, also sumptuously furnished.

Retrace your path down State Route 1 for approximately 12 miles. Here take State Route 46 for 10 miles to Paso Robles, then join US 101 for 5 miles to San Miguel.

San Miguel, California
The Mission San Miguel Arcangel is still used as a parish church and boasts beautiful frescoes dating from 1821. An annual fiesta is held on the third Sunday in September.

From San Miguel an unclassified road takes you south to join State Route 46. Approximately 60 miles away, at the Famoso interchange, join State Route 99 and drive 10 miles south to Bakersfield. From Bakersfield take State Route 99 and journey 40 miles to Lebec.

Lebec, California
In Lebec is a restored US Army Dragoon post, in use from 1854-64 from which the US Camel Corps hauled supplies all the way from San Antonio, Texas, between 1857 and 1861. It has now been preserved and fitted out as a museum.

From Lebec drive south to join Interstate 5 and travel to Valencia.

Valencia, California
Something for the children here at Six Flags Magic Mountain — a 200-acre playground and entertainment extravaganza on magic Mountain Parkway. Attractions include the

'Revolution' and 'Colossus' roller coasters, craft demonstrations, a theatre and live music shows. Refreshments are available.

5 miles south of Valencia along an unclassified road off Interstate 5, is Newhall.

Newhall, California
Hero of the early Westerns, the late William S. Hart had his home and a 253-acre ranch here, now open to the public as a county park. Hart's original furnishings can be seen in the house, plus displays of Indian and western artefacts and objects of historical

interest. Bring a picnic and watch the bison graze nearby. The park is open daily and the house on certain weekdays and at weekends.

Leave Newhall on the unclassified road which joins State Route 14. From there drive 20 miles alongside Placerita Canyon State and County Park on Interstate 210 to San Fernando.

San Fernando, California
The handsome Mission of San Fernando Rey de Espana, founded in 1797, boasts a restored church

Hearst Castle, on 'the enchanted hill' stands as a magnificent monument to William Randolph Hearst

Las Vegas by night is a dazzling spectacle of multi-coloured neon lights. Casinos never close, and the nights are for gambling, high-style cabaret shows, eating and drinking, in a non-stop merry-go-round of entertainment

DEWAR'S
White Label

MOTEL
WELCOMES

T
E
X
A
C
O

SHELL

Gulf

Smith's
FOOD
KING

Las Vegas

It is tempting to dismiss Las Vegas with an indulgent smile or a faint sneer. The popular notion that it is a sin city and a playboy's paradise is not so much inaccurate as unfair. It can appear to be all of these things, but it is also much more.

Nowhere else in the world is there such a concentration of top-line entertainment or such a cluster of pleasure palaces with so many opportunities for making and losing money at the toss of a dice or a turn of a card. And nowhere are these activities so well controlled and so smoothly operated.

This is a city for fun and games, and tourists who do not want to enter into the laisser-faire spirit had better not go to it. At once frenetic and casual, Las Vegas never sleeps. A truly twenty-four hour city, it has no clocks to watch. Timeless, too, is the awesome terrain of mountains and desert beyond its boundaries. They not only add an entirely different dimension, but also impose a unique and fitting isolation for this twentieth-century phenomenon.

Las Vegas

Whether you approach it by road or from McCarran International Airport, barely ten minutes away from the Strip, Las Vegas hits you right between the eyes. The intensity of the flashing lights, the cacophony of noise, the bustle of the crowds and the clamour of the traffic add up to an incongruous carnival atmosphere in striking contrast to the thousands of square miles of silent desert which start just beyond the last winking neon sign. If you arrive by air and come upon Las Vegas suddenly, the impact is a crude assault on the senses, but you can alleviate the shock if you come across the state line into Nevada by car. Just a few yards away from the border, the hoardings begin to beckon with promises of untold delights. As the tufts of desert scrub give way to the first signs of urban sprawl, the enticements become progressively more hysterical.

FREE is the most familiar four-letter word in the Las Vegas vocabulary. Casinos, hotels, bars, cafés, all exploit it to tempt, taunt and tout for your business.

Faced on all sides by such apparent generosity, it is not surprising if the tourist feels his pulses quicken. '99c Breakfast, 24 Hours Daily!'; 'FREE room, FREE 1000-dollar Money Machine Play!'; 'FREE $1 LUCKY BUCK!'.

This, for instance, is what Vegas World Hotel offers the stunned visitor:

FREE $277 GAMBLING CERTIFICATE. $9 in nickels (5-cent pieces) $18 in dollars . . . play as you wish! $39 in lucky bucks for table play! $180 in $1000 money machine play! Three free breakfasts including champagne! Three free dinners. Three free old-fashioned foot-long hot dogs. Free cocktails and 24-hour lounge shows. Free guaranteed slot wins . . . win up to $75 cash; six $25,000 King Ransom match plays; three $1000 Shower of Money match plays.

Despite the unfamiliarity of the terms, the tourist gets the message loud and clear — the giveaways are all designed to encourage visitors to gamble. Surprisingly,

the only really useful free facility the hotels forget to include in their spiel is free parking. There are few parking meters in Las Vegas. Most place have large enough parking lots (unsupervised), and some hotels even offer guests free garage parking. Certainly, this is one of several ways a tourist can benefit in Las Vegas.

Reputedly too, with clever planning and single-minded determination, it is possible for a visitor to leave Las Vegas with more spending money than he had when he arrived, without once pulling a fruit machine handle, turning a card or cashing a chip. Admittedly there is not much to be made out of it, other than the satisfaction of winning in Las Vegas without gambling. The system largely depends on how many 'fun packs' you can acquire on your way into the city. A 'fun pack' is a bundle of free tokens, usually given away at commercial reservation bureaux or in cafés. The 'fun packs' contain all kinds of inducements; a meal at a particular restaurant, a seat at a show — some free, some at substantial discounts.

How to Play the Games

There are nine main ways to win — and lose — money in Las Vegas, but the most popular betting games in the casinos are baccarat, blackjack, craps, roulette and keno. You can also play bingo, poker and the slot machines, and place virtually any kinds of bets with a bookmaker. Three golden rules to remember before you try your luck.

1. If you don't know the rules of any game, don't join in until you have seen what goes on. You may learn something.
2. There are certain skills you can acquire which will shorten the odds in your favour on almost any game. Try to learn them before taking the plunge.
3. Never be tempted to recoup your losses by putting more on than you are prepared to lose.

The top people's game is **baccarat** (also known as chemin de fer). It is usually played for high stakes. Six packs of cards are dealt from a box called a 'shoe'. Players pair up — one acting as bank. Each player is dealt two cards from the shoe. All tens and picture cards count zero, and the object is for either player to get a hand totalling nine. Other players at the table bet on either the banker or the player.

Blackjack is better known as 'twenty-one' or 'pontoon'. Up to six players sit at a horseshoe-shaped table, pitting their luck (and memory) against the house. The dealer hands out two cards to each player, and deals two to himself. Each player decides from counting the face value of the cards if he should call for further cards. The object of the game is to get closer than the dealer to a total hand of 21. A hand over 21 loses.

The most complicated game is **craps.** Ideal for an extrovert to play, it is often noisy. It is fun to watch and listen to, but difficult to follow. The object is to throw dice on a segmented board which offers different odds. You can bet on your own or other people's throws. Altogether there are more than ten different ways to bet, and you have to be quick to join the right action at the right time.

Roulette is the most universally played casino game. It is easy to learn and provides the beginner with many interesting betting opportunities. Small stakes are popular. Playing with chips you can bet on any of the 38 black or red numbers of the roulette wheel, the house zeros, a group of numbers or a colour. A ball thrown on to the revolving wheel determines the winning number once the ball and the wheel come to rest.

Like a combination of the pools and bingo, **keno** allows players to win up to £20,000 for a stake of less than £1. You may mark a coupon of numbers with eight selections and put your stake with it. Soon a selection of 20 winning numbers is announced and if you have five or more right you win a progressively larger dividend. The numbers are drawn almost continuously, so you need not wait long to know the fate of your stake.

Apart from saving money in this way, certain tokens can actually be exchanged for money at the casino. The test of willpower then is not to drop the coins into the machines. In truth, to resist these enticements is rather pointless if you want to enjoy Las Vegas. The city's attitude of 'anything goes' certainly has paid off. Since 1979, the State of Nevada has earned more than two billion dollars at the gaming tables every year, two-thirds of which has come from Las Vegas. That is over three times what it was ten years ago. Las Vegas is not a collection of strip joints, and the streets are not littered with the debris of desperate gamblers. Nor are they paved with gold. Like any city it has its sleazy area, its unsavoury hotels and bars, its pornographic bookshops. But that part of the tourist trade is irrelevant. What matters is that every night of the year 30,000 tourists are entertained at more than forty major hotels in and around Las Vegas Boulevard — the throbbing five-mile-long artery which in part is the famous Strip. Where the boulevard enters downtown, the glamour barely fades, but hotel and food prices are even more modest than on the fashionable part of the Strip. At Casino Center, where gambling first got its foothold, the corner of Fremont Street and Casino Center Drive is brighter at night than in daylight. Las Vegas is a city without public clocks. Time represents reality, and reality is not a commodity the city has time for. And because the gambling never stops, the casinos at, say, four o'clock in the morning look the same as they did at six o'clock the previous evening. Even the

Win or lose, the wheels of fortune spin ceaselessly in most of Las Vegas's brightly-lit casinos, where roulette is one of the most popular games

people at the tables, and the robot-like figures endlessly pulling the slot-machine handles, look indistinguishable from each other — a steely pallor of face and a glazed gleam of eye is common to them all.

The casinos attached to most hotels have no windows, and offer free and expensive-looking drinks to gamblers at the tables (sometimes also to the regulars of the one-armed bandit parlours). Cocooned in a cosy, anonymous shell, people are soon lost in the gloom of the place, isolated by the seclusion of their private thoughts and ambitions. The outside world and its problems are rigorously kept out.

At your first visit to a casino, you may sensibly decide just to watch for a while, but sooner or later, the fruit machines with their insistent machine-gun rattle as they spew out somebody's winnings, are likely to claim your attention and your loose change. Almost everywhere the public goes, the fruit machines stand in wait. They will take nickels (five cents), dimes (ten cents), quarters (twenty-five cents) and dollars in large, round, silver-dollar pieces dispensed at the change kiosks in the casinos. For a glimpse of the inner workings of these contraptions, you can visit the Mint Hotel at Fremont Street and First Street where there is an interesting display (see p. 73).

With competition fierce, hotels (many big ones are called 'resorts' because of the complexity of their entertainment facilities) go to sensational lengths to lure the visitor. Most, of course, pander to adult tastes, but one has recently tried to cater for the family, too. Children are allowed to watch the show at the Circus Circus Hotel, which lives up to its name by having a Big Top virtually above the casino, where frequent performances are

Las Vegas

given by high-wire acrobats, jugglers, clowns and animals. Taking the Big Top theme very literally, Circus Circus has been decorated like a circus tent, but is something of a fairground as well. Shooting galleries and other sideshows are part of the hotel services. The shops include a novelty photographer's where you can be made to look like Wyatt Earp one day and Mae West the next. The hotel also offers instant weddings at the 'Chapel of the Fountain'. The half-hour ceremony can cost twenty dollars for the marriage licence, forty dollars for the use of the chapel, twenty-five dollars for the organ music, five dollars for a cassette recording of the ceremony, and another five dollars for a choice of ribbons. A recording of the wedding march comes free! At the last count there were thirty wedding chapels in Las Vegas, with names like Cupid's Wedding Chapel, Silver Bells, Wee Kirk o' the Heather and Hitching Post. More than 50,000 couples a year surrender to the blandishments of these places over which ministers nicknamed 'Marrying Sams' officiate.

At most 'resorts' the attractions are more conventional. Nearly every great entertainer has played Las Vegas, and on any week, some half-dozen stars are performing at different hotels, usually in lavish shows. At Caesars Palace there are two theatres. The 1300-seat Circus Maximus has a glamorous spectacular twice

nightly, the second show starting as late as 12.30am. The other theatre holds 380 people. Its seats are carefully angled to facilitate the view of a giant screen. A six-track stereophonic sound system has sixteen speaker banks and fifty-six individual speakers hidden under the seats. They hold seventeen film shows there every day.

One of the more memorable features of any of the late cocktail shows (where they only serve drinks) is the way you can be made to sit still for close on three hours at a time on each side of long tables placed at right angles to the stage. Although the arrangement is better suited to a school canteen, it has the advantage of giving a close-up view of the performance in your immediate field of vision. If you happen to sit on a middle table, you virtually need the co-operation of the neighbours on each side before you can turn around to follow the action behind you. This feeling of oneness is even more apparent when you watch the valiant efforts of the serving staff before the performance starts, to cut their way between the tables, precariously balancing overladen trays of drinks above their heads, and under the anxious gaze of the thirsty crowds. Each drink order is a double — that is, each person gets two glasses, as if two orders had been placed, and is charged accordingly.

There are, of course, other categories of seats available at the box office. You can also book by telephone, but neither of these methods ensures you a reserved seat. To secure the seat you want, you need to arrive early enough (an hour before the show starts is cutting it fine), and accurately assess the amount of

'folding favour' needed to win the maître d'hotel's support. 'Folding favour', the euphemistic term for tipping, is the passport to all kinds of ancillary services. The system is very practical, very efficient and ideally suited to the circumstances. The shows are always so superbly staged and so lavishly presented that despite a few inconveniences, such as this well-tried custom, the audience keeps coming back for more.

The restaurants in these palatial hotels match the luxurious appointments. At Caesars Palace, the Bacchanal, appropriately named after the God of Wine, looks like the gardens of a private Roman villa. At the Hilton, Benihana Village, a Japanese fantasyland, comes to life in five restaurants set in lush gardens (see p. 72).

Food in Las Vegas can be very good, but is often not appreciated enough by guests impatient to make the next show, or find the nearest gaming table. The city has an extensive choice of cosmopolitan restaurants, although the variety of cuisine is not as wide as in some cities where a truly ethnic or continental culture exists. Most cafés are either part of the hotel scene or branches of the many fast-food chains so beloved by tourists and city folk alike.

Las Vegas has earned a reputation for giving visitors a good time, but it doesn't do badly by its own people. Thanks to the gambling bonanza, the thriving community pays lower taxes and has a wider choice of schools for its children than cities in many other American states. The population of nearly half a million also supports about 200 churches.

An 'instant' wedding chapel, one of many such establishments in Las Vegas. Ceremonies take place to the romantic accompaniment of soft lights and music

Las Vegas

Las Vegas has rather more conventional cultural attractions, too. Helped by the range of talent the city employs, classical ballet and dance theatre get some of their support, and recruit many of their performers, from the showgirls who nightly kick their legs in unison. With their encouragement, the off-Strip theatres like the Nevada Dance Theater enjoy a high standard and attract enthusiastic audiences from the community and the tourists. The dancers perform throughout most of the year at the 600-seat Judy Bayley Theater on the campus of the University of Nevada, Las Vegas. Also on the campus, and just a few minutes' drive from the Strip, is a concentration of cultural facilities, among them the Artemus Ham Concert Hall, where 2000 music lovers can go every concert night and where prominent musicians such as Aaron Copland, Isaac Stern, Andrés Segovia and Eugene Ormandy have performed in front of distinguished visiting orchestras. Opera companies, jazz ensembles, ballet troupes, folk and pop stars also appear there from time to time.

The university is the pride and joy of a city that betrays an understandable concern about broadening the intellectual horizons of its young generation. Founded in 1957, it stands on 300 acres and accommodates up to 9000 students at a time. It also plays host to Nevada's Museum of Natural History, which houses collections of prehistoric Indian artefacts from Southern Nevada, a mineral collection containing more than 1000 items from all over the world and, at the nearby Juanita Greer White Hall, tropical plants, mammals, reptiles and exotic birds.

Art exhibits, plays and concerts are staged periodically at the Reed Whipple Cultural Center on Las Vegas Boulevard, and the Charleston Heights Arts Center, east of Decatur Boulevard between Charleston Boulevard and the Las Vegas expressway. The Las Vegas Art Museum in Lorenzi Park on West Washington Avenue holds exhibitions by local artists and encourages children's competitions, paintings, sculptures and ceramics under the umbrella of the Allied Arts Council of Southern Nevada. The Council's Cultural Focus Division, which raised funds to promote culture 'as another interesting dimension of the Las Vegas area', arranges tours of the city's historical areas, even briefly including a skirmish through the Casino Center.

That Las Vegas has a compulsion to show off its historic monuments is not really surprising, but unfortunately there is not a lot left to see of the city's past. If it had not been for America's bicentennial celebrations in 1976, the main historic site — the Las Vegas Mormon Fort, at the corner of Las Vegas Boulevard North and Washington Avenue — might not even be standing today. Fortunately it was taken over and refurbished by the city's newly-formed Preservation Association.

Circus Circus (above) offers 'big top' amusement for children while parents gamble. Wax figures of Liberace (right), seated at pianos in the Liberace Museum

Las Vegas can claim numerous distinguished citizens, among them the late Howard Hughes, the airline and film-industry tycoon who in a blaze of non-publicity devoted three years of his reclusive life to living in one of Las Vegas's hotels. For a time he also lived on a ranch which had once been owned by Vera Krupp, widow of the famous munitions manufacturer. Spring Mountain Ranch is about twenty miles out of the city, and is open to the public in the summer. The eccentric Vera Krupp is said to have had a secret passage built from a wardrobe in her bedroom to another bedroom. The motive was not explained, but she was once tied up by robbers who stole her fabulous jewellery, including the million-dollar Krupp diamond, later recovered and bought by Richard Burton for Elizabeth Taylor.

Another long-standing Las Vegas personality is the piano-playing Liberace. The self-styled Mr Showmanship, he is the embodiment of Las Vegas's flamboyance. Much of the success and the bizarre spoils of his career are due to his innate gift for self-exploitation — a talent that thrives better in Las Vegas than anywhere else. The city certainly helped to make him something of a legend. In 1979 he established the Liberace Foundation for the Performing and Creative Arts, a non-profit-making organization with the aim of giving financial support to promising young musicians. Much of the money comes from the proceeds of admission charges at the Liberace Museum, a treasure-trove of exotic clothes, cars,

pianos and extravagant bric-à-brac. Like the man himself, the museum flourishes because it is part of the life-style of Las Vegas.

In the first two years, nearly 200,000 visitors have approached its piano-shaped reception desk, paid their entrance fee and entered this Ali Baba's den. Among several classic cars on display is a red, white and blue Rolls Royce, used for a time by Liberace for his regular Hilton Hotel shows. There is also a London taxi, together with a licence, which a visiting London taxi-driver donated to the museum as a token of appreciation for the star. Liberace's own collection of costumes includes the most outrageous exhibits — a stunning wardrobe revealing his taste in clothes. There can be seen the full array of those twinkling, sequinned extravagances created for his TV shows or for his Royal Variety Performance appearances in London. There is a Czar Nicholas uniform with 22-carat-gold braiding, and a regal cape modelled on the coronation robe of King George V and covered in $60,000-worth of rare chinchilla. Among his collection of pianos is one that Chopin played, a concert grand owned by George Gershwin, and a truly remarkable range of miniature pianos.

Mining Tours

Las Vegas's heritage is bound up with the tough mining communities which, more than 100 years ago, opened up parts of the uncompromising desert and mountains in Nevada. Many mining sites are still preserved, several within 60 miles of the city. Most of them can be reached by paved roads, but some, which have become ghost towns, might need four-wheel drive vehicles to cover the rough terrain. Potosi, 25 miles south and west of Las Vegas on the old Spanish Trail, is the state's oldest lode mine. Its tramway ruins are particularly worth exploring. Goodsprings, 35 miles south-west of Las Vegas, was a booming camp, mining lead and zinc at the start of the century. A railway line and some of the mine workings are preserved and can be toured. Sandy, 13 miles west of Goodsprings in the Sandy Valley, is a ghost town where once a gold mill flourished. Apart from old mine ruins, the area is full of interesting desert plant life within walking distance of the road, and is noted for its sand-dunes.

Eldorado Canyon lived up to its name until as recently as 1942. By then the Techatticup mine, one of several in the narrow, rugged canyon, had alone produced more than $2,500,000 in gold. It is 40 miles south-west of Las Vegas, near the hamlet of Nelson. Searchlight might have become the original Las Vegas, for soon after the turn of the century this now sleepy town in the heart of the gem fields 55 miles from Las Vegas, was a tough, bustling mining centre. Tourists now stop there on the way to view Lake Mohave and to cross Spirit Mountain via the picturesque, winding Christmas Tree pass.

In 1850 a small group of Mormons constructed a 150ft-long adobe-walled settlement to give refuge to travellers, many of whom had already used the site as a stopping place on the way to and from the Californian goldfields. But the gold rush was over, and few stayed at the settlement for long. After eleven years, the entire population of the Las Vegas valley was still less than fifty. Most were Indians, so the Mormons left the settlement to the elements and the Indians and moved on to Utah.

By that time, however, the area was becoming a favourite hunting ground for miners, and when an enterprising miner from the gold camps along the Colorado River stumbled on it, he and his partners decided to develop the fort and the meadows around it (Las Vegas in Spanish means 'the meadows' and Spanish influence was strong all over the south-west) into a ranch with blacksmith and supply services for the increasing number of people passing on the road between California and Utah. At last it began to attract the nucleus of a new community. By the early twentieth century, the fort was thriving enough to be acquired by the forerunner of the Union Pacific Railroad, which wanted it as a junction post linking Los Angeles and Salt Lake City. With the railroad came not only more land prospectors, but also speculators, who soon built up a tent town beside the track to exploit the passing passenger traffic trade. It was a tough town. Saloons and gambling parlours sprang up overnight. Miners, their pockets bulging, poured money into the city. At the turn of the century, Las Vegas boasted five lawyers, three doctors, two dentists, one plumber and eleven saloon keepers.

When, in 1928, the decision was taken to build the Hoover Dam, twenty-nine miles east of Las Vegas, the city's future was assured. This 726ft-high concrete marvel, which has tamed the worst excesses of the Colorado River, took five years to build, and gave jobs to 5000 men. More then 4,000,000 cubic yards of concrete were poured into the dam, creating a base 220 yards thick. The dam, like a giant hoarding waiting for someone to paste up slogans for Las Vegas, has several observation platforms which give striking views of the majestic sweep of concrete that fills a deep canyon of the fast-flowing Colorado. Now nearly fifty years old, the dam has virtually repaid the $175,000,000 development costs from the growing income it earns by creating enough electrical energy from its seventeen water-driven turbines to provide power for Arizona, Southern California and the southern half of Nevada. The water released in the process helps to irrigate more than 1,000,000 acres of land in the states and in Mexico. It has also spawned the 255-square-mile Lake Mead — one of the largest artificial lakes in the world (see pp. 78-9).

Hoover Dam had an important effect on Las Vegas's fortunes, for it persuaded Nevada, which saw the potential of the growing community drawn to Las Vegas, to make gambling legal in 1931. At this time America was still emerging from the prohibition era and there was a strong puritanical resistance to liberalizing changes. Certainly no other state dared to make such a momentous decision at the time — or indeed for forty-five years afterwards, since it was only in 1976 that

Kyle Ranch

Carey Avenue at Crown Drive, tel. 649 5811.

Kyle Ranch played a significant role in Nevada's quickie divorce market in the forties and fifties when it quickly became a popular 'heartbreak house' for couples needing the essential legal residential qualifications in Las Vegas. Because only wealthy couples (they included several film stars) could afford this convenient shelter, Kyle Ranch became a fashionable kind of guest house, and a small pool was even constructed for their use, so they wouldn't miss too many home comforts. Named after Conrad Kiel, who courageously established the place as a cattle ranch in the 1880s at a time of turbulence and lawlessness, it was one of only two major cattle complexes in the Las Vegas Valley in the 19th century. It was eventually sold to a banker who built a plantation-style white house near the original 19th-century, one-room, adobe building which the Kiels put up and probably used as a general store. This and a shed is all that remains of that period. The house is of unusual design with a deep porch, a split roof and a semi-open cellar. Other more recent buildings added include a play house, intended for the banker's children, but later popular with the divorce-era guests, and the willow house, a large wooden-framed house with a

gabled roof. Several other features on the site worth exploring include the reservoir, once used to irrigate the land, and a modern concrete fountain, built in 1939 to help amuse and distract the guests. Eventually, the ranch was sold off to developers, but in 1976, as part of the bi-centennial programme, Las Vegas acquired 27 acres of the ranch. It is now listed as a historic site.

Atlantic City started to operate three casinos. To a frontier town like Las Vegas, where illegal saloon gambling had been a way of life, its new-found legal respectability took years to exploit fully. Nor did anyone at first really anticipate the bonanza it would create.

In 1940, a group of Los Angeles investors opened the first hotel casino at the junction of Sahara Avenue and the Strip, opposite where the Sahara Hotel now stands. Soon others followed, and with them came the competition which

Scarcely less brilliant than the cactus flowers, the red rocks of Red Rock Canyon seem to belong to another world

was to lure a plethora of international showbiz stars to the city at enormous fees. Shops began to proliferate, and the growing numbers of tourists from all over the world soon attracted several large department stores to the city. Many shops are to be found in hotels, and nobody is likely to miss the giant shopping complex on the Strip at Spring Mountain Road, which opened in 1981. Two large shopping malls worth visiting are the Boulevard and the Meadows (see p. 73).

Though geared for glamour and the concept of plenty, Las Vegas, surprisingly, is also the centre of a vast military presence. Just beyond the outskirts of the city, and only eight miles from the Strip, the famous American Air Force

training base, Nellis, occupies a truly vast acreage. Named after a 28-year-old Las Vegas fighter pilot killed in action over Luxembourg in December 1944, Nellis is said to be the largest airbase in the free world, with more than 8000 airmen and other personnel, and 11,000 dependants making a substantial contribution to Las Vegas's prosperity. But the military presence is barely noticeable in the streets, and there are few airmen in uniform mingling with the crowds.

Much further away, beyond the other end of town, is the Nevada Nuclear Test Site, a vast tract of land deep in the desert. Roads go by it, cutting through a desolate world where places like Devil's Hole, Funeral Mountain and Death Valley

Las Vegas

express the awful loneliness and the unforgiving nature of the terrain. Gauntly beautiful, particularly around autumn and winter, Death Valley is one of the hottest and driest places in the world (see pp. 75-8). Much of the vast desert area is now a national park, with a visitor's centre, a golf course and museums.

Some fifty miles north-east of Las Vegas — an hour's drive away on Interstate 15 — is the Valley of Fire, a favourite location for Hollywood westerns. Burt Lancaster, Lee Marvin, Gregory Peck and George Peppard are among the stars who have been filmed there. Strange, colourful rock formations are responsible for the valley's name, and the area is also well-known for its petroglyphs — pictures etched into the fiery-coloured sandstone by Paiute Indian tribes more than 2000 years ago. Good examples of these early rock carvings can be found at Mouse's Tank, while Elephant Rock, near the eastern entrance to the Valley of Fire State Park, resembles in shape a prehistoric animal. The Lost City Museum in Overton, a few miles further north, exhibits a range of archaeological relics found in the area.

Another worthwhile trip from Las Vegas is to the Grand Canyon. It is too far by car if you do not want to be away from the city for most of the week, but Scenic Airlines offer an afternoon's outing to this 'eighth wonder of the world'. Seen from the air, it makes a panorama of such awesome splendour that no worm's eye view can match it. The flight from McCarran, in a small Cessna plane, passes over the Hoover Dam and Lake Mead, and joins the course of the Colorado River, which has helped to create this miracle of nature over millions of years. The images change endlessly as the aeroplane dips dramatically below the rim of the gorge, hemmed in by nature's largest amphitheatre. From

above, the jagged gashes in the earth's crust create a fantastic landscape of weird shapes. Some are like crinoline skirts others like pagodas. At one side, a rock stands proudly like a cathedral, balanced on a precipice; on another side majestic sweeping walls curve away, and on a plateau below the rim, 100ft-high trees look no bigger than blades of grass on a rough lawn.

Landing at Grand Canyon airport, you can take a coach trip to the South Rim. Looking across, the North Rim seems no taller, yet it is 900ft higher than the South Rim, and in winter has about 200 inches of snow compared with South Rim's average of 10 inches. At one point the canyon bottom is 2400ft above sea level yet it is still about a mile below the North Rim. The scale of nature's handiwork at the Grand Canyon is measured by statistics which are almost beyond comprehension. Scientists estimate that the Colorado had gouged out about 500,000 tons of sand and lime from the earth every day for the last 6,000,000 years. Since 1963, when the Glen Canyon Dam, 100 miles upstream, was completed, the Colorado's voracious appetite has been diminished to a meagre 80,000 tons a day. Flowing at an average speed of 12 miles an hour, the river has cut a chasm 277 miles long through the rocks. At one point the canyon is 18 miles wide; at another, near the spot where a suspension bridge has been thrown across the canyon, it is only about 300ft wide.

Animal and plant life flourish in the canyon. There are some 70 species of mammal, 250 species of bird, 25 different reptiles and 5 kinds of amphibian creatures inhabiting the region.

Tourists with stamina, strong legs and iron resolve can pick their way down on inner canyon trails which have been carved out of the sides of the cliffs. For

Camping

There is room for more than 80,000 tourists in the hotels and guest houses of Las Vegas, but even so, there is a continually increasing demand for camping and caravanning sites for the families who may prefer watching the stars in the sky to those on the stage. Several hotels in the city provide space for campers and caravanners in parks adjacent, or close, to their premises. The Hacienda Hotel, at the south end of Las Vegas Boulevard, has an AAA-approved site of 27 acres with 451 places adjoining the hotel, and a laundry, a store, a pool, playgrounds and tennis courts. Circusland RV Park a few minutes' walk west of the Strip and just north of Sahara Avenue, has 421 places on six acres near the Circus Hotel. Laundry, heated swimming pool, wading pool, sauna, whirlpool and recreation room are also on the site, which has been inspected by the AAA. Another AAA-approved site within a few minutes' drive is the Holiday Travel Trailer Park, provided by Holiday Inn hotels, on Nellis Boulevard. It has 265 places, and is spacious and level. The 22-acre site has a laundry, a pool and a recreation room. Other AAA-approved sites with names derived from Las Vegas's better-known hotels include the Riviera Travel Trailer park, with 134 places on six acres at 2200 Palm Street, and the Silver Sands Travel Trailer Park with 210 places on 11 acres at 4295 Boulder Highway. Known throughout the United States as R/Vees (Recreational Vehicles), all kinds of campers, motorized caravans and mobile homes can be rented for short or long periods. Sometimes, operators will arrange bookings as part of a package before you leave home, but it is easy to arrange on-the-spot rentals of an R/Vee at many outlets. Further information for affiliated members from the AAA, 3312 W. Charleston Blvd, tel. 870 9171.

Sport

In keeping with its showmanship traditions, Las Vegas stages several spectacular sporting events, and prides itself also on its own sports facilities. Principal among them are ten municipal golf courses, hundreds of tennis courts (eight municipally owned) and several swimming pools in public parks as well as scores more in the major hotels.

Among many top sporting events is the £40,000 desert car race held around the city in May, a £100,000 tennis tournament which draws the top tennis stars to Caesars Palace every April, and a professional bowls tournament with a £50,000 purse staged at the Showboat Hotel's 106-lane bowling alley. Several international boxing encounters take place in the city every year, mainly at Caesars Palace, and in late May there is a particularly colourful four-day rodeo which recreates the early pioneering days of the American West.

The Grand Canyon of the Colorado River is one of the world's most majestic natural phenomena, a gigantic rift 277 miles long in the earth's crust

those with a good seat, conducted trips on muleback are also available.

The Havasupais, one of the five Indian tribes whose ancestors built cliff-dwellings on the canyon slopes, are today much in evidence whenever a tourist coach arrives at a viewpoint on the Rim. They sell necklaces and jewellery, some made from the fruits of the Utah juniper tree, from pinion pines or wild date trees. These trinkets cost very little.

Scenic Airlines is among several operators who fly the Grand Canyon route. One of the largest, it offers three tours — one for the flight only, another with lunch included, and the third involving an overnight stay. The rates are expensive — equivalent to a week's stay at some hotels — but in a city accustomed to large sums

of money changing hands very quickly, there are always plenty of customers and few empty seats. Since its operations began in 1962, Scenic Airlines has flown more than 1,000,000 passengers on the Grand Canyon route, and now has a large terminal at McCarran, with twenty flights a day during the height of the season.

Another trip from Las Vegas — and of particular interest to British visitors — is to Lake Havasu City, 150 miles away, just over the Arizona state line on the banks of the Colorado. It can be reached by air, but it is preferable to hire a car so as to enjoy the desert and mountain routes leading to the site of the miraculous reincarnation of London Bridge. (see p. 79).

A shorter trip than the 150-mile drive to Lake Havasu is to drive 20 miles west to find breathtaking high-desert scenery at Red Rock Canyon. The scenic road built there offers a 60-mile round trip and gives a tantalizing glimpse of the mysteries of Nevada's prehistoric times. The Red Rock

escarpment, 3000ft high, is a sculpture of rainbow-coloured pinnacles and boulders — far removed in mood from the brash vigour of Las Vegas, yet near enough in distance to make it a simple trip away from it all. But before returning to the city, turn off to Bonnie Springs, Old Nevada, a commercial 'ranch' where you can watch make-believe lynchings and shoot-outs. If you patronize the restaurant there, remember that the menfolk are not allowed to wear ties, which have to be left at the reception desk.

Gimmicks like this are part of the fun-and-games philosophy of Las Vegas. It is all reminiscent of the old-fashioned holiday camp approach, and one's critical faculties are never seriously tested. Puns are always popular. 'Slots of Fun' is the name of a small fruit-machine casino. 'Watch your step a Litter bit' say notices on street waste baskets. The streets are tidy, so the appeal must work. The corny choice of words simply matches the mood of Las Vegas.

Las Vegas Directory

Climate

As one might expect in a desert resort, the summers in Las Vegas are hot and dry, with very high midday temperatures in July and August, but the low humidity and good air-conditioning do much to dispel discomfort. Winters are usually mild and ideal for outdoor activities. It can, however, be cold at night and it is often windy.

Hotels & Restaurants

The hotels and restaurants listed here are either recommended by the American Automobile Association (AAA) or have been selected because they are of interest to tourists. As a rough guide to cost, they have been classified as either expensive, moderate or reasonable. Hotels all have private bathrooms and colour television (and, in Las Vegas, casinos).

Hotels

ALADDIN HOTEL: 3667 Las Vegas Blvd South, tel. 736 0111. 1000 rooms. Parking lot. Two swimming pools, shopping arcade. Luxury hotel, central, expensive.

CIRCUS CIRCUS HOTEL: 2880 Las Vegas Blvd South, tel. 734 0410. 800 rooms. Parking lot. Restaurants, health club and sauna, live circus acts. Motor hotel, central, moderate.

DEL WEBB'S SAHARA HOTEL: 2534 Las Vegas Blvd, tel. 737 2111. 1000 rooms. Valet parking. Five restaurants, coffee shop, golf. Motor hotel, central, moderate.

DESERT INN HOTEL: 3145 Las Vegas Blvd South, tel. 733 4444. 839 rooms. Valet parking. Luxury hotel. Golf, floodlit tennis courts, jacuzzi baths, shops. Motor hotel, expensive.

DUNES HOTEL: 3650 Las Vegas Blvd South, tel. 737 4110. 1000 rooms. Valet parking. Sauna, golf course, shops, restaurants. Motor hotel, moderate.

FLAMINGO HILTON AND TOWER: 3555 Las Vegas Blvd South, tel. 733 3111. 1250 rooms. Parking lot. Putting green, restaurants, coffee shop. Motor hotel, moderate.

FRONTIER HOTEL: 3120 Las Vegas Blvd South, tel. 734 0110. 589 rooms. Valet parking. Once owned by millionaire-recluse Howard Hughes. Tennis courts, restaurants. Motor hotel, moderate.

GOLDEN NUGGET HOTEL: 129 East Fremont St, tel. 385 7111. 579 rooms, Victorian decor, wild-west theme. Parking, three bars, two restaurants. Downtown area, moderate.

HACIENDA HOTEL: 3950 Las Vegas Blvd South, tel. 739 8911. 522 rooms. Tennis courts. Near airport, motor inn, reasonable.

HOLIDAY INN — CENTER STRIP: 3475 Las Vegas Blvd South, tel. 732 2333. 511 rooms, riverboat-theme decor. Parking lot. Coin-operated laundry service. Motor hotel, moderate.

LAS VEGAS HILTON: 3000 Paradise Rd, tel. 732 5111. 2783 rooms. Parking lot. Putting green, tennis courts, health club with sauna, supervised 'children's hotel', Japanese and Italian restaurants, coffee shop. Expensive.

MINT HOTEL: 100 East Fremont St, tel. 385 7440. 300 rooms. Pay valet garage. Twenty-six-storey-building with panoramic views of the city. Three restaurants. Motor hotel, reasonable.

RIVIERA HOTEL: 2901 Las Vegas Blvd South, tel. 734 5110. 1209 rooms. Sauna and health club, floodlit tennis courts, restaurants, coffee shop. Motor hotel, expensive.

SAM'S TOWN HOTEL: 5111 Boulder Highway, tel. 456 7777. 200 rooms. Has an 'old west' theme. Restaurant and coffee shop. Motor hotel, reasonable.

TROPICANA HOTEL: 3810 Las Vegas Blvd South, tel. 739 2222. 1107 rooms. Outdoor and indoor tennis courts, handball and racquetball courts, golf, health club, restaurant and coffee shop. Moderate.

Restaurants

In Las Vegas you can indulge your every eccentricity — if you yearn for lunch at three o'clock in the morning or breakfast at five in the afternoon go ahead — no one will bat an eyelid. Many restaurants are located within the major hotels and stay open 24 hours a day.

THE BACCHANAL: Caesars Palace, 3570 Las Vegas Blvd South, tel. 731 7110. Named after Bacchus, the Roman god of wine, this sumptuous restaurant is a re-creation of an opulent garden in Rome's heyday. Good flambé desserts. Expensive.

BENIHANA VILLAGE: Las Vegas Hilton, 3000 Paradise Rd, tel. 732 5111. No need to go all the way to Japan when you can visit Benihana Village. Five restaurants allow you to dine amidst running streams and Japanese gardens. Try the sukiyaki steak. Moderate.

CARSON CITY RESTAURANT: Circus Circus Hotel, 2880 Las Vegas Blvd South, tel. 734 0410. Diners are allotted ringside seats at this circus-restaurant. Popular with family parties, Carson City restaurant serves Western food and is probably the only establishment to offer a Las Vegas dinner show for children. Reasonable.

DA VINCI'S: Maxim Hotel, 160 East Flamingo Rd, tel. 731 4300. Situated on the Strip's 'Golden Corner' this restaurant offers excellent food and service. A speciality of the house is Chicken da Vinci. Reasonable.

DELMONICO ROOM: Riviera Hotel, The Strip, tel. 734 5110. Decor is elegant, cuisine is French-based. Reasonable.

DOME OF THE SEA: Dunes Hotel, 3650 Las Vegas Blvd South, tel. 737 4254. Dinner at the court of King Neptune is quite an experience as portrayed by this restaurant. A mermaid in a gondola will serenade you while you sample the speciality sea food. Expensive.

LILLIE LANGTRY'S: Golden Nugget, 129 East Fremont St, tel. 385 7111. Named after the English actress whose beauty captivated the crowned heads of Europe in the Edwardian era, this restaurant is decorated in period style. The food, however, is incongruously Cantonese. Open evenings only. Moderate.

QUARTERDECK RESTAURANT: Mint Hotel, 100 East Fremont St, tel. 385 7440. Everything is ship-shape in this handsome restaurant with a nautical theme. The Sunday champagne buffet is particularly recommended. Open evenings only. Moderate.

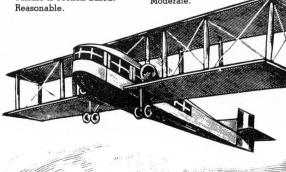

Transport

AIRPORT: All flights to Las Vegas land at McCarran International Airport, 5 miles south of the business district of the city via Paradise Road and the Strip. There are 15 major airlines all over the United States that operate regularly into McCarran International, and offer more than 230 flights daily. Eleven million people pass through the airport every year, and its modernization programme (to be completed over the next 20 years at a cost in excess of $800,000,000) should give it the capacity to handle 30,000,000 passengers, and make it equivalent to New York's Kennedy and LA's LAX airports in importance and size.

CAR HIRE: Many car-hire firms have offices at McCarran International Airport and along the Strip, but the yellow pages of the Las Vegas telephone directory or local 'throwaway' newspapers such as *Vegas Visitor* give a complete list. Hertz and Avis offer AAA discounts to members at participating locations. The major agencies are: Avis-Aiport, tel. 739 5595, Strip, tel. 736 1935; Budget, tel. 735 9311; Hertz-Airport, tel. 736 4900; Strip, tel. 735 4597; National-Airport, tel. 739 5391, Strip, tel. 734 2222.

TAXIS: Taxis are plentiful, particularly at the entrances of the major hotels, so little or no waiting need occur. Fares are determined by both mileage and number of passengers. The major companies are: ABC Union and Ace Cab Companies, tel. 736 8383; Checker and Vegas Western Cab Companies, tel. 736 6121; Desert and Western Cab Companies, tel. 384 1672; Whittlesea Blue Cab, tel. 384 6111; Yellow Cab Company, tel. 382 4444.

BUSES: The Las Vegas Transit System covers the downtown area to the Hacienda Hotel at the southernmost point of the Strip. Buses run 24 hours a day, usually every 15 minutes. If you plan to use the buses frequently, a commuter ticket can represent a large saving. For individual journeys exact fare is required.

Touring Information

AAA Clubs: Nevada is served by the California State Automobile Association. Las Vegas office, 3312 West Charleston Blvd, tel. 826 8800, open in office hours.

LAS VEGAS CHAMBER OF COMMERCE: 2301 E. Sahara Ave, tel. 457 4664, and **LAS VEGAS CONVENTION AND VISITORS BUREAU:** 3150 S. Paradise Rd, tel. 733 2323. Both provide information for visitors. Offices open daily in office hours.

Museums & Galleries

ADOBE GALLERIES: 3110 Las Vegas Blvd, tel. 733 2941. The complex includes 6 different galleries exhibiting a wide range of art from Indian crafts to abstract paintings. Open daily.

LIBERACE MUSEUM: 2½ miles east of the Strip at 1775 East Tropicana Ave, tel. 731 1775. Closed Sunday morning. (see p.67).

Shopping

LAS VEGAS PLAZA: 3025 Las Vegas Blvd South. Most shops in this area, right in

THE BOULEVARD MALL AND SHOPPING CENTER: 3528 Maryland Parkway, tel. 735 8268. This is an entire, air-conditioned shopping complex open 7 days a week and just 3 minutes away from the Strip. With over 72 speciality shops, including a pet centre, health food shops, boutiques and 4 full-scale department stores, it is unlikely that you will need to look any further afield for special purchases. A bonus is the huge car park with space for more than 5800 cars.

Places of Interest

BINION'S HORSESHOE: 128 Fremont St. This casino features 100 rare US bank notes, bound between sheets of bullet-proof glass, and suspended from a giant golden horseshoe. Each note displays the head of Salmon Portland Chase, secretary of the treasury from 1861-4, during the American Civil War. A respected statesman, he began his career as counsel for the defence of fugitive slaves from the deep south of America in the mid 19th century. In 1864, he was appointed Chief Justice of the US, and as such presided at the trial of Andrew Johnson, the only president to be impeached. Each separate note is valued at $10,000.

CIRCUS CIRCUS: The Strip, tel. 734 0410. A pink-and-white striped, tent-shaped casino with a circus gimmick. The circus can be viewed in comfort, from an observation gallery lined with carnival stalls and food tables (see pp.55-6).

MINT HOTEL AND CASINO: First and Fremont Sts, tel.

the heart of the Strip, close on Sunday mornings only. Not to be missed at the Plaza is **Suzy Creamcheese**, tel. 732 3533. A go-go dancer turned dress designer, owner Suzy's sequinned creations have been worn by Shirley Maclaine and Sammy Davis Jr amongst other famous names. Clothes are displayed in surroundings of almost decadent Victorian opulence.

THE MEADOWS: 4300 Meadows Lane. Newest and largest of the Vegas shopping complexes is the Meadows. This multi-million-dollar investment boasts restaurants, coffee bars and hundreds of interesting shops in an ultra-modern building.

385 7440. An 'inside look' at the workings of a casino is offered at this downtown hotel. One-way mirrors enable spectators to view the gaming tables and the mechanical workings of old-fashioned slot machines are on display.

OLD VEGAS: 2440 Boulder Highway, Henderson, tel. 564 1311. A theme park built around an original Mormon adobe fort, Old Vegas offers a fascinating glimpse into the early history of a Nevada settlement. Among the many attractions is a railway museum, a narrow-gauge steam train, an old fairground roundabout, a Wild West shooting gallery and a selection of reconstructed frontier stores selling souvenirs. The town of Henderson (see p.78) is about 15 miles away from Las Vegas on US 93 and 95.

RED ROCK RECREATION AREA: On West Charleston Blvd, 15 miles west of Las Vegas. The dramatic desert scenery at Red Rock (see p.69) is composed of beautiful red and white sandstone formations and spectacular views of steep, stark canyons.

Sport

In order to give visitors a change from the atmosphere of the dark, smoky, gaming tables, the space devoted to outdoor activity in and around Las Vegas is as large as in any city in America. The most popular sports are golf and tennis, and many of the major hotels have their own facilities. Away from the hotels, on the outskirts of the city you will find any number of golf courses and country clubs. More specialized facilities can be found at the places listed below.

LAS VEGAS SPORTING HOUSE: 3025 Industrial Rd, tel. 733 8999. This luxurious health farm offers a comprehensive range of facilities, including a full gymnasium, a 60ft-long swimming pool, saunas, steam rooms, massage parlours, sports courts, jacuzzi baths and skin care and hairdressing salons. Though many of the Strip hotels have some of these facilities, none offers such complete service. Spotting the stars who 'work out' here adds to the fun.

THE ROLLER PALACE: 800 East Karen Ave, tel. 732 1046. Open evenings only. Proof that the nationwide craze of roller skating has reached Las Vegas, this stadium vibrates to the sound of small wheels hitting the floor, occasionally to the accompaniment of a live orchestra.

SHOWBOAT HOTEL: 2800 East Fremont St, tel. 385 9123. If bowling is your game, the Showboat is one of the world's most modern, best-equipped bowling alleys, with an amazing total of 106 lanes. There is a snack bar and a free, attended playroom for the children.

Theatres & Cinemas

MEADOWS PLAYHOUSE: 4775 S. Maryland Parkway, tel. 739 3131. Contemporary plays and the classics are staged by a resident professional theatre company.

UNIVERSITY OF NEVADA: Plays and ballet are staged at the Judy Bayley Theater on the university campus. Also on campus is the Artemus Ham Concert Hall (see p.67).

About a dozen 'drive in' cinemas exist in and around Las Vegas, the best of which are the **Sunset**, 3800 Cheyenne Ave, tel. 648 7550 and the **Nevada**, 3873 Las Vegas Blvd North, tel. 643 3333.

RED ROCK THEATERS: 5201 West Charleston Blvd, tel. 870 1423. This is a complex of 11 cinemas each offering a different film.

Night Clubs

Aside from gambling, the one other area in which Vegas excels is 'big name' entertainment. The three-and-a-half miles of the Strip play host to million-dollar extravaganzas and polished productions straight from Broadway. International stars such as Frank Sinatra, Dean Martin, Ann-Margret and Diana Ross entertain from time to time at the major hotels. Dinner shows usually start at 8pm and late shows at midnight. Reservations must be made.

More energetic visitors may prefer to visit Las Vegas's plush disco called **Jubilation** at 75 East Harmon Avenue, tel. 733 8822. Entertainer Paul Anka owns this masterpiece of design in a modernistic structure, with its elegant decor and views over desert rock gardens. There is a good chance of rubbing shoulders with well known celebrities on the dance floor.

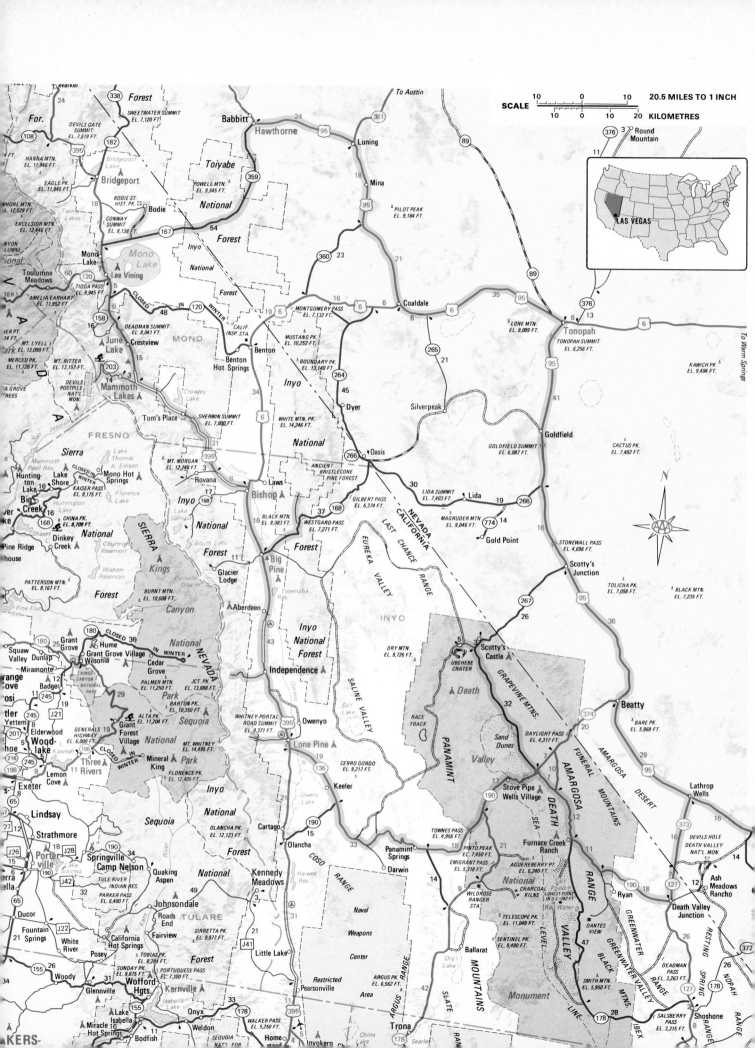

Death Valley and the 'Ghost Town Trail'

847 miles — 4 days

The awesome scenery of Death Valley. Creosote bushes are among a surprising variety of plants that flourish in desert conditions

This is a tour of extremes and superlatives. Although rather long, it passes within a few miles of both the highest mountain and the lowest spot in the USA, and runs right through the middle of notorious Death Valley, one of the hottest places in the world. You can see trees that are among Earth's oldest — the gnarled Bristlecone Pines — and giant sequoias, which are among the most massive.

The tour is lent added colour by visits to old towns that were built by the gold-seeking 'forty-niners'. One of them, Bodie, has been preserved as a historic park where visitors can experience the atmosphere of a typical ghost town.

Geological wonders abound, and much of the drive is characterized by unforgettable views, providing a fine introduction to the vast expanses of unspoilt and beautiful country that await the visitor to the American West.

From downtown Las Vegas take the Las Vegas Expressway and travel north-west for 84 miles on US 95 to Lathrop Wells. The road runs through bare, mountainous desert country. To the left are the Spring Mountains, their lower flanks scattered with yucca and cactus while, higher up, evergreens clothe the slopes. At Lathrop Wells turn left on to State Route 373. After 16 miles the road crosses the border into California and becomes State Route 127, continuing for 7 miles to Death Valley Junction.

Death Valley Junction, California

This town is one of the principal eastern gateways to the area that has been known as Death Valley since 1849, when a group of prospectors and their families set off to cross it on their way to the goldfields. At that time no roads crossed the valley, and the party spent almost three months lost in the desert. Several of them died — victims of hunger, thirst and the punishing heat.

Now, Death Valley Junction is only one of several towns from which the valley can be reached by road. A notable attraction in the town is Marta Becket's Amargosa Opera House, where dance-mime performances are staged.

Leave Death Valley Junction on State route 190, entering the Death Valley National Monument after 16 miles. Continue for 13 miles, crossing the Amargosa Range and passing on the left Zabriskie Point — famous for the splendid views it offers across the desert and, in recent years, for the feature film that was named after it.

Soon the road reaches the oasis of Furnace Creek Ranch and, just to the north, the park headquarters of the Death Valley National Monument.

Death Valley National Monument, California

This is the third largest national monument in the USA, covering more than 3000 square miles. It is a land of extremes; almost one-fifth of the ground is well below sea level — as much as 282ft below at Badwater, the lowest place in the States — whilst elsewhere the land rises above 10,000ft. The valley is also one of the hottest and driest places in the world. Rainfall averages only 2″ per annum, and ground temperatures as high as 200°F have been recorded — though it can become very cold at night. To the Panamint Indians the valley was known as Tomesha, which means 'ground afire'.

Although the valley is perhaps best known for its fierce heat and dryness, it is well worth a visit to experience the spectacular natural phenomena that it has to offer. The dry atmosphere and clear air help to preserve the natural colours of the rocks, so the landscapes are often a blaze of brilliant reds, oranges and purples — unforgettable in the early morning or late afternoon when the sun is low. There are geological wonders galore, ranging from breathtaking canyons to towering rock pinnacles, vast sand dunes and glittering crystal formations. Death Valley also boasts a surprisingly wide range of wildlife. Over 600 species of plant are found here, 21 of which are not found anywhere else in the world. These include the Death Valley sandpaper plant and the Panamint daisy. Animal life is also abundant, and even includes fish that have adapted themselves to the heat — one species is known as the 'desert sardine'. As one would expect, most creatures are nocturnal, emerging after the punishing sun has set to drink from the springs which rise in the valley.

The area is rich in minerals. Silver and gold were mined here in small quantities by determined pioneers, but it was the discovery of extensive deposits of borax — used in the chemicals, paint and drugs industries — which drew larger numbers of prospectors in the late 19th century. This early industry was responsible for the opening up of this inhospitable area. Roads were built and wells dug, and today Death Valley is well served by highways and offers a wide range of accommodation from luxury hotels to camp sites. But do not under-estimate the climate: Death Valley in summer is no place for the faint-hearted, and travellers should always carry plenty of water. From November to April, however, the area is a popular tourist attraction, drawing large numbers of visitors.

The visitor centre at Furnace Creek will tell you all you need to know about the Death Valley area with a range of leaflets and suggestions for walks, and occasional slide shows. There are also guided walks and evening natural history lectures in winter, and the centre houses an interesting museum.

Continue northwards from Furnace Creek along State Route 190, driving through the heart of Death Valley. When you reach the junction with State Route 374 after 19 miles, you can make a detour northwards for 35 miles along a local route to Scotty's Castle.

Death Valley

Scotty's Castle, California

Death Valley's most famous man-made landmark, this extraordinary Moorish-Spanish palace was the desert showplace of an eccentric millionaire from Chicago. He built it in the 1920s for Walter Scotty, a performer in Buffalo Bill's Wild West Show, who always liked to tell people that the castle had been built with the proceeds from his secret gold mine. The elaborately furnished castle and its grounds are open to visitors, and guided tours are sometimes available.

Some 5 miles to the west is the Ubehebe Crater, an 800ft-deep pit formed during a volcanic eruption more than 3000 years ago.

Return to State Route 190 and turn right on to it. Continue for 68 miles, passing through Stove Pipe Wells, whose name is derived from the old prospectors' habit of marking springs with pieces of stove pipe stuck into the sands. Leave Death Valley and pass through Panamint Springs, then join State Route 136. After 4 miles the road runs through Keeler, now a ghost town but once a thriving mining community and railway terminus. Some of the original buildings and railway carriages can still be seen. Turn right after 15 miles on to US 395. At the junction is the Interagency Visitor Center, where information is available on the Owens Valley, Inyo National Forest and surrounding area. Two miles from this junction the route reaches Lone Pine.

Lone Pine, California

This town is known as the starting point of a trek up Mount Whitney, whose summit, some 15 miles to the west, is the highest point in the USA (excluding Alaska) at 14,495ft. Whitney Portal Road

A fantasy palace in the Moorish style, Scotty's Castle was built for an eccentric showman

(closed in winter) leads westwards from Lone Pine, enabling would-be climbers to drive to a height of 8371ft. From the end of the road a 10½-mile trail leads to the summit. Those intending to climb Mount Whitney must have a permit, obtainable from the Forest Ranger Station in Lone Pine.
To the west and north-west of Lone Pine are the Alabama Hills, a barren, rocky area which devotees of Western films may recognize, for parts of the hills are often used as film sets.

Continue northwards for 16 miles along US 395 to Independence.

Independence, California

This town is set in the Owens Valley, with the Inyo National Forest to the east and the dramatic slopes of the Sierra Nevada to the west. A road (closed in winter) leads westwards from the town towards King's Canyon National Park, a natural wonderland of canyons, waterfalls and rushing rivers. (The park is accessible from this side by trail only.) The

famous sequoias of King's Canyon include the General Grant Tree, which is 267ft high with a girth of 107ft. These trees belong to the species *sequoia gigantea,* not to be confused with the coastal redwood, or *sequoia sempervirens,* which are taller but not as massive.

Independence is the home of the Eastern California Museum, on Grant Street, where the history, anthropology, botany and geology of the area are illustrated by a varied collection of exhibits. Nearby, to the north-west, is the Mount Whitney State Fish Hatchery, which is open to visitors daily, free of charge.

From Independence continue northwards up the Owens Valley along US 395 for 27 miles, passing through Aberdeen, to reach Big Pine.

Big Pine, California

From here a detour may be made eastwards along State Route 168 — known as the Westgard Pass — into the heart of the Inyo National Forest. A paved road leads northwards off State Route 168 to

the Ancient Bristlecone Pine Forest, an area of about 28,000 acres where you can see ancient, gnarled conifers that are even older than the redwoods — an astonishing 4500 years, in some cases. The trees are quite different from redwoods, seldom reaching heights of more than 25ft, with stubby branches and short needles. There is a picnic site and an information centre where visitors may obtain details of planned nature trails in the area.

Continue northwards along US 395 for 16 miles to Bishop.

Bishop, California

Set in the upper Owens Valley, between the Sierra Nevada and the White Mountains, Bishop is a popular base for exploring the magnificent countryside that surrounds it. To the west of the town is Bishop Creek Canyon, hemmed in by spectacular 1000ft cliffs. Bishop Creek has been dammed several times to generate power which is transmitted across the Mojave Desert to the towns of southern California.

Not counting Alaska, Mt Whitney, seen here from Lone Pine, is the highest peak in America. From the summit can be seen the wild hills of the Sierra Nevada

Five miles north-east of Bishop, off US 6, is the Laws Railroad Museum. The old railway settlement of Laws has been restored and the 11-acre area is now preserved as a historic site.

Drive on from Bishop along US 395 for 39 miles, then turn left on to State Route 203 for a detour to Mammoth Lakes.

Mammoth Lakes, California
This popular resort is part of a specially designated 200,000-acre recreation area in Inyo National Forest. Several long-distance mountain trails pass through the area, including the Pacific Crest Trail System and the 220-mile-long John Muir Trail, named after the 19th-century naturalist and conservationist who campaigned for the preservation of America's wilderness. Mammoth Lakes is well known for winter sports, and

11,000ft Mammoth Mountain offers ski-slopes for both beginners and experts. There are facilities for fishing and boating, and guided walks are available, as well as suggestions for planning your own. From nearby Minaret Summit, 9000ft up, there are excellent views of the Forest, taking in peaks such as 13,000ft Mount Ritter, and an earthquake fissure.

From Mammoth Lakes the detour can be extended by driving on along State Route 203 for 14 miles to the Devil's Postpile National Monument. (The road is narrow and winding, and the last stretch is unmetalled.)

Devil's Postpile National Monument, California
Another of California's stunning geological wonders, Devil's Postpile is a series of sheer, symmetrical columns of blue-grey basalt. Some of them, resembling huge organ pipes, reach a height of 60ft. The columns are remnants of a lava flow, and their tops — which can be reached by a fairly

easy path — have been worn smooth by glaciers so that the surface gives an unusual tiled effect.

A 2-mile walk from the Postpile leads to Rainbow Falls, where one channel of the San Joaquin River plunges more than 100ft. Devil's Postpile National Monument is usually open only from about mid June to October.

The main tour continues northwards on US 395 for 33 miles, reaching a height of 8041ft at Deadman Summit. At the junction with State Route 167 shortly past Mono Lake, turn right. After 7 miles a detour can be made by turning left on to a gravel road which leads to Bodie.

Bodie, California
Once reputed to be one of the most lawless gold-mining settlements in the West, Bodie produced almost $100 million worth of gold from its 30 mines after the metal was discovered here in 1859. What is left of the original town has been preserved as a state historic park, but the buildings have not been restored, and the eerie atmosphere is distinctly that of a ghost town. Visitors can follow a specially mapped-out walking tour of the old buildings, many of which remain as they were when Bodie was abandoned. Bodie is usually accessible only in summer, because winter conditions make the road dangerous.

Rejoin State Route 167 and continue eastwards to the California-Nevada state boundary, where the road

becomes State Route 359. Continue for 33 miles to Hawthorne, then join US 95 and follow it for 133 miles to Goldfield. The road runs through mountainous country, passing the occasional old mining settlement — hence the nickname given to US 95, the 'Ghost Town Trail'. The road reaches 6256ft at Tonopah Summit, shortly past the town of Tonopah where a rodeo is held every July.

Goldfield, Nevada
Often referred to as the 'Silver State', Nevada also has its fair share of gold deposits. This early 20th-century mining settlement, dramatically set among bare, rugged peaks, stands amid some of the richest gold deposits in the American West. The workings and the town were abandoned many years ago, but are now gradually being opened up again. Many of the original buildings are still intact.

Continue southwards from Goldfield along US 95, reaching 6087ft at Goldfield Summit, just south of the town. Pass through Scotty's Junction after 28 miles and continue for another 36 miles to Beatty.

Beatty, Nevada
This attractive old mining town is set in the valley of the Amargosa River. Two miles to the north-west is the ghost town of Rhyolite, and also nearby is Chloride Cliff, an excellent viewpoint.

From Beatty continue along US 95 for 113 miles to return to Las Vegas.

Bodie's streets once echoed to the sound of gunfire and saloon brawls in the heyday of the gold-prospecting era. Now deserted and silent, this 'ghost town' has been preserved as a historic monument

Hoover Dam
and Lake Havasu

2-3 days — 372 miles

Las Vegas — Henderson — Hoover Dam and Lake Mead — Kingman — Lake Havasu City — Lake Mohave — Las Vegas

Three great lakes feature on this tour through southern Nevada and Arizona. Lake Mead, more than 115 miles long, was created by one of the great engineering feats of the 20th century — the building of the Hoover Dam. Around Lake Mead and Lake Havasu, wild countryside offers superb leisure facilities and is a paradise for nature lovers, since a vast nature reserve has been created where many rare birds and wild animals such as the puma are to be found.

Sixteen miles out of Las Vegas on US 93 and US 95 (the two roads run together) is the town of Henderson.

Henderson, Nevada

On Boulder Highway is Old Vegas, an entertainment centre featuring an old army fort, antique steam trains and a host of Western characters — gunfighters, etc. — acting out roles for the amusement of visitors. An interesting film show explains the history of Nevada and full details of the attractions are given on p.73.

Eight miles past Henderson US 93 and US 95 diverge. Take US 93 to Hoover Dam, 10 miles away.

The Hoover Dam, and Lake Mead Nevada/Arizona

The Hoover Dam, built in the 1930s to tame the Colorado River, which periodically brought disastrous floods to the surrounding countryside on its wild 1400-mile descent from the Rocky Mountains to the Pacific, is rightly considered to be one of America's seven wonders of civil engineering. The horseshoe-shaped dam wall rises 726ft high, and is 660ft thick at the base, tapering to a mere 45ft at the crest. The cost when it was completed in 1935 was $175,000,000.

Boulder City, built to house construction workers now has a thriving craft centre where pottery, leatherware and Mexican goods are on sale. The dam was in fact originally known as the Boulder Dam, but soon came to be known as the Hoover Dam after the then President of the USA, Herbert J. Hoover.

Parking places on both sides of

the Black Canyon provide vantage points for viewing the dam, but for those who are interested, guided tours operate daily at frequent intervals. A lift takes you down almost to the level of the river, and then you go inside the dam, through part of the complex network of tunnels bored into the cliffs to house the massive generators. In the Exhibition Hall, models of the course of the Colorado River and of the generators explain the history and workings of the dam.

Lake Mead, one of the world's largest man-made lakes, more than 115 miles long, is capable of storing two years' average flow from the river. The water provides hydro-electric power, irrigates parched desert land in the south-west of America and in Mexico as well as providing water for many cities in California and Nevada. Dry, sandy mountains, sweep right down to the shores of the lake. Except in high summer when temperatures rise above 100°F, this is fine walking country, provided you stick to the tracks. Pumas, deer, mountain sheep, wild asses and golden eagles inhabit the Sierra Madre, and in spring the hillsides are covered in wild flowers. At Boulder Beach, on the west side of the lake there is safe bathing, camping and restaurant facilities, North of the beach, Lake Mead Marina offers boat tours.

Leave Hoover Dam on US 93 and drive for 60 miles to Kingman. This is a mostly desert route, crossing rocky country and rolling hills.

Kingman, Arizona

The Mohave Museum of History and Arts is at 400 West Beale Street. Exhibits trace the history and development of north-west Arizona.

From Kingman take Interstate 40 to the Mohave Mountains exit. From there, State Route 95 takes you to Lake Havasu City, 10 miles away.

Lake Havasu City and Lake Havasu, Arizona/California

The city, set in the Chemehuevi Valley, was founded in 1964 as a speculative venture and is now a

Looking down on the Black Canyon and Lake Mead. The sparkling white rim of the Hoover Dam is just visible at the end of the gorge. The dam provides irrigation for thousands of acres of desert.

resort centre for Lake Havasu, formed by the building of the Parker Dam. The dam lies just south of the city, on State Route 95. One of its more bizarre attractions, and one that may well give visitors from London a surprise, is the granite bridge which now spans a channel of the Colorado River. It is London Bridge which, because maintenance was becoming too expensive, was sold to the McCulloch Corporation in 1969 for $2,460,000. This was $60,000 more than the agreed price, and the difference, a sentimental gesture, represented in thousands the age of the chairman of the McCulloch Corporation. Dismantled piece by piece, this historic bridge, designed by John Rennie in 1831, was transported to Arizona and re-erected in the desert. Part of the river was diverted by a channel specially excavated to allow water to flow under the bridge in a realistic manner. The cost of shipping the 10,000 tons of granite to the USA was $5,000,000.

An English village, with London bus, taxi and pub now stands beside the bridge, and every hour, a recording of the chimes of Big Ben booms out over the lake. Long before it became one of the most popular holiday centres in Arizona, the Indians named this beautiful place 'havasu', meaning 'land of the blue-green water.' A fisherman's paradise, the magnificent lake has a picturesque shoreline over 45 miles in length. Its rocky, red cliffs are rich in gemstones: agate, jasper, turquoise, are all to be found here. Boat tours from the marina take visitors to explore Topock Gorge, 8 miles north of the city and accessible only by boat or footpath. The gorge is part of the Lake Havasu National Wildlife Refuge and, in addition to its spectacular scenery and fascinating petroglyphs — ancient rock-carvings incised by the original Indian inhabitants — shelters many species of birds: falcons, loons, herons, cormorants among them. Perhaps the most sought-after resident, the Harris

Hawk is one of America's rarest birds of prey.

Drive south on State Route 95, passing the Buckskin Mountain/ Colorado River State Park. At Parker, join State Route 62 and drive 12 miles to Vidal Junction. Pick up US 95 and follow it for 40 miles to reach Interstate 40 at Needles.
Twelve miles further on, turn off on to northbound US 95, for 40 miles to Searchlight, once a bustling mining centre but now a sleepy town, from where an unclassified road leads east to Lake Mohave.

Lake Mohave Nevada/Arizona
Extending southwards from the hub of Hoover Dam is Lake Mohave, a popular leisure centre. The cold waters of this lake are drawn from the depths of its sister, Lake Mead, and stocked with fish from the nearby Willow Beach National Fish Hatchery, so fishing is excellent, particularly for trout. Swimming, sailing and water-skiing are popular all year round, and there are caravan sites and overnight accommodation in the vicinity.
Return to US 95, and drive for 55 miles back through Henderson to Las Vegas.

Union Jacks and the Stars and Stripes decorate the parapet of London Bridge, re-erected in Arizona at Lake Havasu City

The New Orleans waterfront by night.
The illuminated smoke stacks of one of
the old riverboats pierce the darkened
sky. Cruises on the Mississippi are one
of the pleasantest ways to see the Old
South and explore the intricate network
of Louisiana's waterways

New Orleans

Born of old traditions and Mediterranean culture, New Orleans is the most fascinating city in the whole of the American South.

Founded by the French, sold to the Spanish, resold to the French and finally purchased by the United States, the city has preserved through all its ups and downs its own distinctive Creole heritage, derived from a heady mixture of French, Spanish and Negro culture.

Sustained and nourished for more than 250 years by the mighty Mississippi — Old Man River himself — New Orleans has grown into a city of superlatives. Where else can you eat such varied and exotic food, hear so much authentic jazz and attend so many joyous celebrations?

The gracious old houses, their delicate wrought-iron balconies festooned with flowers, and the stately plantation houses surrounded by trees draped with trailing Spanish moss, are the epitome of Southern elegance and leisure. In sharp contrast, but somehow not striking a discordant note, is the insistent music of the many jazz clubs and the flamboyant extravagance of carnival time on Mardi Gras.

81

New Orleans

Walk up one of America's widest thoroughfares, Canal Street, which in the mile-long stretch leading to the Mississippi cuts straight through the heart of New Orleans, and on each side you will hear its heartbeat throbbing to a totally different rhythm.

The left side, the French Quarter, drums to a syncopated jazz beat, while the right, the area around the massive World Trade Center on the banks of the river, sounds more like the familiar pulse of a bustling commercial city. It is this contrast that makes New Orleans such a fascinating place, for though the rapid growth in the number of high-rise buildings and sky-scraper hotels is constantly changing the skyline, it is miraculously not intruding on the fundamental appeal of the city.

Jazz, food and festivals are the three most important components of its character, and they are famed for playing better jazz, serving finer food and throwing better parties in New Orleans than anywhere else in the world. While the French Quarter is not the only place where you will find good restaurants, or see colourful parades, or listen to the hottest jazz, it does provide the right mood and setting for them, and in the French Quarter you can trace the very roots of the city. Within its seventy blocks, bounded by Canal Street, Rampart Street, Esplanade Avenue and the river, the Vieux Carré (the original name of the French Quarter, meaning 'old square') has a touch of early Soho, a soupçon of the Paris Left Bank and, in Bourbon Street (named after the French royal dynasty, not the American whisky), the coarse clamour of Hamburg's Reeperbahn.

Beyond the strip clubs and the porno-graphic bookshops, Bourbon Street is the gateway to a fairyland, where dainty gingerbread cottages nestle close to nineteenth-century stucco villas, whose façades are embellished with delicate iron-lace balconies, while the narrow streets they line are full of laughter and music. Many are still private houses, and even the hotels, with names like the Marie Antoinette, the Maison Dupuy, and the Bourbon Orleans, hide unobtrusively behind stylish façades.

While the music is aimed at the crowds jostling outside, the three-piece band playing in a smoke-filled bar, the trumpeter bewailing the blues from an

One of the three bands that 'blow up a storm' at the Maison Bourbon. The sound of jazz pours out from almost every bar around Bourbon Street

upstairs window, or the Dixieland group in the doorway of a café, are as much expressing a genuine cultural need as trying to earn an honest living. These people live to play as happily as they play to live. An art form that the American South can truly claim as its own, jazz is an echo of New Orleans' early struggles. It found expression among the rough elements who frequented the brothels of the infamous Storyville area which flourished in the French Quarter for twenty years until the Government forced it to close down in 1917.

Said to be Negro slang for sexual intercourse, jazz developed from a mixture of African music, voodoo ritual chants, worksongs and the spirituals taught to the Negroes by Methodist missionaries. It finally gained respectability when it was first played for dances, picnics, church socials, parades and even funerals. Even today, no funeral of a jazz musician would be complete without a band in attendance, probably playing 'When the Saints Go Marching In', at the end of the ceremony.

Trumpeters, trombonists, clarinettists, saxophonists and drummers emerged out of the shadowy streets in those early days to make music for no better reason than to 'make yer tap ·yer feet', as Louis Armstrong put it. Buddy Bolden, Nick LaRocca, Jelly Roll Morton, like Armstrong, were the true exponents of jazz, and the traditions they created thrive today.

You can still see their like at Preservation Hall (see p.95) in St Peter Street. A crumbling small hall, this mecca of jazz is crowded every night, for passers-by are soon ensnared by the clarity of the sound emerging from the shabby doorway. There are very few seats available, but the audience will stand for hours or squat on the floor, responding only to the people crushed against them if any movement in the crowd threatens their space. It has been like that for fifty years, and the only concession to the present is that the familiar blue haze of smoke is missing. Anyone who dares to light up is firmly told by one of the players to stop or leave.

Several top-line jazz clubs flourish in the French Quarter. At his club in Bourbon Street, trumpeter Al Hirt every night blows hot and cool into the smoke-filled room, and whatever the familiar tune, 'Strangers in the Night' or 'Sugar Lips' sounds fresher and clearer than if it had come out of the most sophisticated hi-fi set-up. Another great virtuoso, clarinettist Pete Fountain, for years drew the crowds to his club in Bourbon Street, but in 1977 when the Hilton Hotel opened on the riverside, Fountain moved to his own place on the third floor of the hotel.

A serious sociological study of jazz is being made at Tulane University, one of three major universities in New Orleans. In its archives are already thousands of taped interviews with the great exponents of jazz, together with a collection of recordings, sheet music, programmes and

On Chartres Street, graceful wrought-iron balconies and flower-filled patios typify the ambience of the New Orleans French Quarter

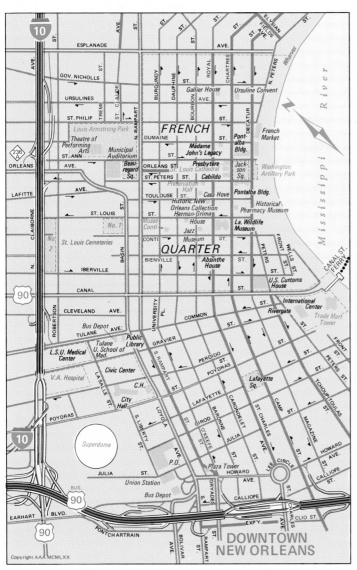

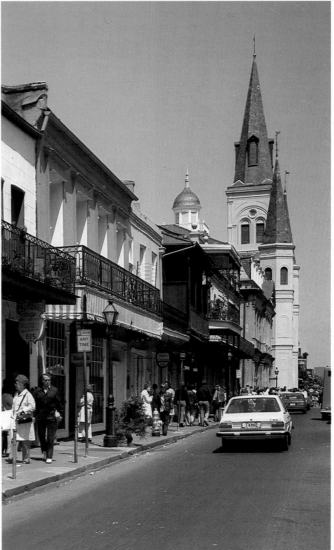

posters. At the edge of the Vieux Carré, a large park (see p.86), where the city's prestigious Theater for the Performing Arts can draw an audience of 2300 to popular musical events, has been named after Louis Armstrong.

According to the aficionados, jazz and food don't very often mix. So at the serious jazz emporia, only drinks are available, while in many New Orleans restaurants, particularly those in hotels, music comes a poor second to the noble pursuit of eating.

New Orleans food is part of its heritage, and because the city derives from three cultures, its distinctive cuisine is based on the culinary traditions of the French, Spanish and Cajun (French Canadian) settlers. The native food is Creole, a subtle blend of the delicate flavours of French cooking with the fiery, spicy tastes of Spanish dishes.

The Creoles are themselves such a mixture — products of the seventeenth- and eighteenth-century Spanish and French communities who first settled in New Orleans. The success of the food they created reflects how well they have melded together. (A pineapple is the symbol of Creole hospitality.)

Cajun food is distinctively different, and less piquant than Creole cuisine. The Cajuns brought their culture to New Orleans from Acadia in eastern Canada

when they fled from British rule, and, like the Creoles, were French-speaking people. Both communities relied heavily on seafood, because it was available in such abundance in the marshes and bayous around the city and in the Gulf of Mexico. Oysters, trout, redfish, shrimps and crabs are excellent and look out for crayfish (called 'crawfish' in New Orleans) on the menu, though they are in season for only a few months in the spring and early summer. Generally smaller than the European variety, the crawfish, a type of small freshwater lobster, is usually boiled, or can be made into a delicious pie. Oysters, easily available in bars and at snack counters, are among the cheapest seafood. They are nearly always opened in front of your very eyes, and are eaten raw with brown bread and a mustard or piquant sauce, or fried, baked, poached, or even encased in a pastry.

This convenient 'larder' on the doorstep led the French settlers to create many tasty new dishes. Moreover, the ingredients were cheap and wholesome. Little was wasted, and what went back into the stock pot became the basis for some of today's much sought after specialities — gumbo soup, jambalaya, courtbouillon, muffalotta, beignets (see 'What Does it Mean' on p.88), and above all the ubiquitous po'-boy, a sandwich filled to

overflowing, which was once the only meal of the day for the city's 'poor boys'.

Some of the drinks are more familiar to European palates — café au lait is very popular — but typically Creole is café brûlot, a festive drink of coffee with spices, orange peel and flaming brandy, prepared with stylish ceremony in the fashionable New Orleans restaurants. The silver brûlot bowl is brought to the table and, as the lights are lowered, a flame is lit and the spices, sugar and orange rind are dropped into the bowl. Then the cognac is slowly heated, set alight and gently stirred to mix the ingredients. After that comes the strong black coffee, which, mixed with the ingredients in the bowl, is topped with a little more brandy and flamed once again. The process is repeated twice more before this stunningly aromatic concoction is poured into the cups.

The three main native alcoholic drinks are Ramos Gin Fizz, a smooth mixture of cream, gin and orange-flower water; Sazerac, a blend of rye whisky and bitters; and the Hurricane, a red, fiery libation served in a tall 29-ounce hand-blown crested glass and said to have been invented by Pat O'Brien, founder of a famous bar in St Peter Street. Sazerac, named after an elegant Regency-style restaurant at the Fairmont Hotel in

City Walks

FRENCH QUARTER
The abundance of sights and sounds in the Vieux Carré — the old French Quarter of New Orleans — can only be appreciated if you are prepared to leave your car and wander around on foot.
A good starting point is Jackson Square, named after the victor of the Battle of New Orleans (1815), General Andrew Jackson, whose statue graces the centre. On the St Peter and St Ann Street sides of the square, Pontalba Buildings, the oldest apartment houses in America, display the graceful wrought-iron balconies so characteristic of the New Orleans style. The Cabildo and the Presbytère, on either side of the cathedral, now form part of the Louisiana State Museum. St Louis Cathedral dates from 1794

and is the second building on this site, the previous one having fallen victim to fire. Walk along Chartres Street and turn left into Dumaine Street, where Madame John's Legacy stands, a fine example of a raised plantation cottage, named after the heroine of a Creole short story by George Cable. Turn left into Royal Street. St Anthony's Garden, behind the cathedral, was a favourite duelling ground in the 19th century. Another left turn, down Pirates' Alley, brings you into the French Quarter's artists' colony, then turn right and right again to return to Royal Street. On your left is New Orleans' first 'skyscraper', a modest four storeys high, erected only as far as the third storey in 1811 because of fears that the

subsoil would not support a taller building. The last storey was added 65 years later. Look for the initials 'YLM' in the ironwork; this is the monogram of Yves Le Monnier, its first owner. Walk down Royal Street to Bienville Street, past the French Quarter's most exclusive restaurants and antique shops. On the corner of Bienville and Bourbon Streets, you could call in at the Old Absinthe House, birthplace of a now illegal drink called absinthe frappé, before turning right into the hurly-burly of Bourbon Street. Turn left into Conti Street to tour the Musée Conti Wax Museum, then right into Dauphine Street and right again into St Louis Street, past the early 19th-century Hermann-Grima House, which has a lovely courtyard. Take the next left back into Bourbon Street. Turn right on Toulouse Street and notice the Lion Gate, named after two small lions perched high above the pavement. Pass the Casa Hove, another very old building, with fine period furnishings, which houses a museum of perfumery.
A left turn brings you back into Royal Street. Gallier House is the former home of the 19th-century architect

James Gallier, and in the next-door house is an exhibition that portrays New Orleans' changing lifestyle. Go back down Royal Street to Ursulines Avenue and turn left. On the corner of the avenue and Chartres Street stands the Ursuline Convent, the first nunnery in Louisiana, which dates back to 1734. Carry on as far as Decatur Street, turn right, and then left down Dumaine Street to reach the old French Market, and so back to Jackson Square.

GARDEN DISTRICT
Apart from the numerous antique shops and galleries, on Magazine Street, the Garden District, which lies between St Charles Avenue and the Mississippi, is worth exploring for its architectural splendours. This route merely highlights the more interesting houses, some of which, though privately owned and occupied, can be viewed during the Spring Fiesta (see p. 89). The interior layout and furnishings of many of the homes are often even more rewarding than the exteriors. From the Louise S. McGehee School, an interesting Renaissance-style building, walk from St Charles Avenue down 1st Street and cross

Prytania Street to view the oldest house in the Garden District at 2340 Prytania Street on the corner of 1st Street. A raised cottage with square columns rising to a Greek cornice, it dates from 1838 and is colloquially known, after its first owner, as Toby's Corner.
Turn right into Coliseum Street and right into 3rd Street, where no. 1415 is a good example of the more ornate antebellum (pre-Civil War) design. Turn left to return to Prytania Street and, as you cross 4th Street, admire the cornstalk design of the wrought-iron fence. Turn left down Washington Avenue, left into Coliseum Street, right down 3rd Street and left into Chestnut Street — a route lined with a wealth of 19th-century houses. At 1st Street, turn right to admire no. 1236, which was built in 1847, and no. 1239, built in 1840 — both Greek Revival houses open for viewing during the Spring Fiesta. Still further along, at no. 1134, Jefferson Davis, President of the Confederacy during the Civil War, died in 1889. At the next turning you have a chance to admire the antique shops of Magazine Street before taking any convenient right turn back to St Charles Avenue.

The façades of many of the older buildings in the Vieux Carré are decorated with white lacy ironwork, a design particularly associated with New Orleans

University Place, originated in its hotel bar. So did Ramos Gin Fizz. In fact, New Orleans claims to have invented the world's first cocktail. When entertaining his guests for dinner one night, a local pharmacist, Antoine Peychaud, made up a concoction of brandy and bitters, and served it in an egg-cup called a *coquetier*. As its popularity spread, the drink soon became known, thanks to American pronunciation, as a cocktail. In the Caribbean Room of the Pontchartrain Hotel — one of New Orlean's finest temples of good living — which specializes in Creole and French cuisine, you can sample another of the city's culinary triumphs — the hotel's world-famous speciality, the 'Mile High Pecan Pie'; A glorified gateau, of pecan nuts, ice-cream, toasted meringue and bittersweet chocolate sauce, the gargantuan slice stands a foot high and only falls over when divided up at your table. Like most left-overs in American restaurants, the remains can be taken home in a 'doggy bag', although the pie's delicate consistency would hardly allow it to survive the confines of a handbag or pocket for long.

The Pontchartrain, like many other fashionable hotels and restaurants in the area, stands in the Garden District, which rivals the French Quarter in architectural interest and historic importance. Situated beyond the central business area across the great divide of Canal Street, the Garden District developed as a direct result of conflicting influences from the city's three nations — French, Spanish and American — who each, at some stage in its history, ruled New Orleans. Each

had grandiose designs on this swampy patch of land in the bend of the river.

The mighty Mississippi, the longest river in the United States at 2300 miles, offered the seventeenth-century French settlers an invaluable trade route through vast tracts of the new territories. For nearly two centuries, however, trade remained pretty well one-way, for until the arrival of steam-power in the early nineteenth century, boats could not sail upstream against the strong current. Nevertheless, with the Gulf of Mexico as the gateway, trappers and merchants from the North converged on it to trade with the newcomers.

In 1717, the man who was to coordinate their efforts and ambitions, the Sieur de Bienville, arrived from Canada. He was an adventurer who, acting for the Regent of France, the Duc d'Orléans, decided that the five-mile strip of swamp which lay between Lake Pontchartrain and a twenty-five-mile stretch of river was the ideal spot for the building of a great port.

The entire territory of Louisiana had already been claimed by French explorers and settlers and had been named after Louis XIV. A year after de Bienville arrived he set eighty hardy sailors to clear the river bank and began to build his city on the site now occupied by the French Quarter. Louisiana enjoyed French rule until 1762, when Louis XV ceded the entire province to his cousin, King Charles III of Spain. Nobody worried much about it, but when, a few years later, a Spanish commissioner arrived to impose Spanish rule, the locals professed to know nothing about their new masters and, in due course, drove him

and his party out. Eventually twenty-five Spanish warships landed in the bend of the river and, with the help of 3000 soldiers, imposed control. Spanish settlers intermarried with the French, and in time their descendants became known as Creoles, 'children of the colony', and a tough, proud race of people they were, soon developing a distinctive, indigenous culture.

Meanwhile, New Orleans changed hands once again. Spain sold the territory back to France in 1801, but Napoleon, in a famous deal called the Louisiana Purchase, sold it to the United States two years later for $15 million.

The American takeover was strongly resented by the Creoles, who had by that time twice seen their city destroyed by fire and had rebuilt it. The French Quarter was now a wholly Creole settlement, and the link with French rule had become tenuous. The Americans, recognizing the gulf that separated them from the Creoles, left them to it and built their own community next door, on the other side of what is now Canal Street, ensuring thereby that if the two factions could not live together, they could at least live side by side.

In 1812, Louisiana was admitted to the Union, but the troubles of New Orleans were not by any means over. In 1783, after Britain had lost the War of Independence, she had ceded to the newly formed Union all her territories east of the Mississippi

New Orleans

Parks

New Orleans has four major parks, all of which offer more than landscaped grounds and vast expanses of lawns. Most varied, and one of the country's largest municipal parks is the 1500-acre **City** Park, once part of a plantation, which cuts a swathe a mile wide through the northern end of the city. It houses the New Orleans Museum of Art, two sports stadiums, three golf courses, a riding academy, tennis courts, boating lagoons, and many attractions for children, including a children's storyland of larger-than-life papier-mâché figures of such characters as Humpty Dumpty, Jack and the Beanstalk, and Mother Goose. There is also a miniature train. Other unusual diversions are an 18ft-sundial, a floral clock, and Suicide Oak, one of a group of duelling oaks where old scores were once settled at dawn.

Audubon Park, named after the naturalist and painter who illustrated *The Birds of America,* is situated in a bend of the river in the university section of the city. Its main attractions are the zoo and the Odenheimer Aquarium. It also has a golf course, swimming pool and tennis courts. Overlooking the Mississippi is a 40-acre landscaped area which gives excellent views of the river. Winding lagoons, fountains, statues and avenues of oak trees make Audubon, formerly the plantation of Etienne de Bore, who founded his fortune on his invention of a method of granulating sugar, one of the most popular beauty spots in New Orleans. Electric lighting was first successfully demonstrated in Audubon Park in 1884-5 at the World Industrial and Cotton Exposition.

For a riot of colour in formal flower gardens, the **Longue Vue Gardens** at 7 Bamboo Road, off Metairie Road, cover eight acres. The grounds are laid out in Spanish garden themes and include a canal garden, a walled garden and a wild garden. Inside the modern house are exhibitions of decorative arts and daily film shows. Tel. 488 1875 or 5488 for information.

Louis Armstrong Park is really the back lawn of two of New Orleans' most sought-after amenities: the Municipal Auditorium Cultural Attraction Center, and the lavish, 2300-seat Theater for the Performing Arts, which has an impressive entrance with fountains, and 10,000 sq ft of hydraulically operated stage area. This is the heart of New Orleans' cultural life. The New Orleans Philharmonic and the New Orleans Symphony Orchestra both hold concerts here. For information, tel. 524 0404. The Municipal Auditorium also holds concerts, tel. 525 3942.

and south of the Canadian border. In 1812, however, war broke out between the countries once again, because of trouble on the north-western border with Canada, and the British sailed into the Gulf of Mexico to seize New Orleans and take control of the Mississippi. General Andrew Jackson, commanding a force of Creoles, Negro slaves and Indians, routed the invaders at the Battle of New Orleans in January 1815. The one irony of his victory was that Britain and America had signed a peace treaty some months earlier, but the news had not got through.

For a time, Old Man River, around which there had been so much conflict, was left in peace to keep on rolling along. This was the dawn of the era of the great riverboats — steamships known as side-wheelers or stern-wheelers, many owned by the rich cotton or sugar planters whose black slaves toiled in the fields. The increasing river traffic brought greater prosperity to New Orleans, and despite the ravages of the American Civil War (1861-5), the city was set to become a port second only to New York in wealth. Even today, New York is the only American port that handles more foreign ships than New Orleans.

Having triumphed over so much adversity and achieved so much prosperity, is it any wonder that New Orleans likes to celebrate? The city's calendar (see p.89) particularly in the first half of the year, is crammed with festivals. No matter what time of year, something colourful, exciting and impressive is going on somewhere in New Orleans. The best-known of its festivals, Mardi Gras, is more religious than historical in origin and significance. Matched in size and gaiety only by the Carnival in Rio de Janeiro, Mardi Gras is not so much a festival as a way of life. It goes on for several weeks, building up to its glorious climax on the last Tuesday before Lent — Fat Tuesday, or, in French, *le mardi gras,* known as Shrove Tuesday to the British — when the main carnival parades are held. Traditionally, Mardi Gras was a day of gluttony immediately before the onset of 40 days of self-denial for Lent. As an excuse for a festival it was too good for New Orleans to miss.

The celebrations are organized by the 'mystick krewes', secret societies similar to Masonic groups. The oldest and most exclusive is the Krewe of Comus, which organized the first Carnival Day Parade in 1857. Wildly enthusiastic crowds flocked into the streets of the French Quarter to watch as masked riders and costumed ladies in open carriages tossed fruit and sweets to the crowds. Since those days the festivities have grown and grown, and now more than $1 million worth of beads, trinkets and special traditional medallions are thrown to the Carnival crowds each year. While Mardi Gras has sometimes been known to turn into pitched battles between krewes, it has become the one occasion in the American social calendar when it is safe to go out into the streets even in drag without risk of either immediate arrest or a beating up. The ritual elements of the Mardi Gras are always jealously guarded, and there is a strict code of secrecy about who does what, where and when. From Twelfth Night onwards, krewes organize balls and parades for almost every day. About ninety large-scale dances are held, but most of these are private functions.

The colourful parades through the city streets that are such an exciting feature of the Mardi Gras carnival in New Orleans were begun early in the 19th century. Each 'Krewe' organizes its own parade and most of them take place in the last 11 days of the celebrations

86

On Mardi Gras itself, about fifty parades with floats, fancy dress, music, singing and dancing revellers wind through the streets bringing expected and well-planned chaos to traffic and business life. The marchers vie with each other for attention, spending millions of dollars between them in an attempt to outshine their rivals. Famous showbiz personalities often head the parades. Bob Hope and Danny Kaye were early candidates, and visitors have included royal and political figures from all over the world. Though the celebrations are said to be funded solely by members of the krewes, the benefits help the city to attract tourists and commerce. But be warned: the 36,000 hotel rooms the city expect to have available by the mid-1980s may still not be enough to ensure accommodation without early booking. If you want to join the mêlée, remember that like Easter, on which its date depends, Mardi Gras is a movable feast. In 1982 it is on 23 February; in 1983 on 5 February; in 1984 on 6 March. The weather is usually at its most equable at that time of year, with temperatures comfortably around 60°F and with rainfall at about the lowest level of the year.

You might expect that once the flags had been taken down, the costumes put away for another year, and the streets cleared of their heaps of litter, New Orleans would be happy to relax and stay at home. Not at all. No sooner is Easter over than the Spring Fiesta tours (see p.89, Carnival Calendar) begin. In June and July come the food festivals, and other celebrations follow thick and fast.

The distinctive character of its people, its jazz and its festivals is not the only factor that sets New Orleans apart from any other American city. Its architecture, too, is uniquely elegant, deriving from French and Spanish traditions and modified to suit the marshy terrain on which the old city was built. St Louis Cathedral, with its three steeples, stands in the heart of the French Quarter, in Jackson Square. One of more than 1000 churches in New Orleans, it dates back to 1727 when the site was first selected for a place of worship. The first church on the site was among the 856 buildings destroyed in the first great fire of New Orleans, on Good Friday 1788. Approximately four-fifths of the city's residential area went up in flames. The new church, completed six years later, nearly suffered the same fate, for another disastrous fire swept through the city destroying 200 buildings. But the church survived, and sixteen days later was dedicated as a cathedral on Christmas Eve 1794. The secluded garden of the cathedral was notorious in time gone by as the site of sword duels to the death, but it was also the centre of the French Quarter's community life. The cathedral is flanked on one side by the Cabildo (see p.94) — the seat of Government when the Spaniards

New Orleans

See p. 84 for the precise method of preparation.

What does it Mean?

English may be the official language of New Orleans, but the city has preserved many colourful words and phrases from its intricate history that will certainly puzzle European visitors, and possibly fellow Americans too. Those expressions most commonly heard are listed here.

GENERAL

Banquette: pavement. In the early years, New Orleans needed planked, raised pavements to keep pedestrians clear of the muddy streets.

Bayou: river or creek. Generally used to describe the marshes or streams that result from the overflow of a river.

Cajun: name given to the Acadians, a group of French-speaking people who migrated from eastern Canada in the mid 18th century to settle in south and central Louisiana.

Creole: descendant of the original French and Spanish settlers of south Louisiana. Often used to describe their style of cooking, crafts, architecture or language.

Doubloons: Coin-like trinkets traditionally thrown to the crowds by the masked revellers at Mardi Gras parades. The value of these doubloons increases the longer they are kept.

Levee: embankment or dike holding river or marshes at bay. Whenever the Mississippi rises more than 15ft, a levee keeps New Orleans from being flooded.

Lovebugs: swarms of termite-like insects that descend on New Orleans in spring and autumn. They stick to your skin and excrete a type of caustic acid that can strip the polish off a car.

Picayune: once a Spanish coin of small value, its present day meaning is 'insignificant.'

Pirogue: small canoe made out of a long log and used on the bayous.

FOOD

Beignet: square doughnut, without a hole in the middle, covered in powdered sugar. The perfect accompaniment to a cup of *café au lait.*

Café brûlot: a mixture of coffee, spices, orange peel and brandy. See p. 84 for the precise method of preparation.

Courtbouillon: a highly seasoned, white-wine sauce in which redfish are cooked.

Crawfish: the local name for crayfish, also familiarly called 'crawdads'. Loved and revered throughout Louisiana, but only available in spring and early summer.

Gumbo: nourishing soup made of seafood, chicken and vegetables, thickened with okra. Very popular in New Orleans and very Creole.

Jambalaya: Creole dish of rice, shrimp, crab, oyster, sausage, chicken or game, all cooked together in the manner of an Italian *risotto.* Also the name sometimes given to the city's efforts to promote cultural events.

Muffalotta: Italian sandwich of bread flavoured with sesame seeds and cold meats, topped with an olive salad.

Papillote: greaseproof paper envelope in which food is wrapped before cooking to retain the flavour.

Po'-boy, or *poorboy:* French-loaf sandwich, overfilled with meat or cheese. Po'-boys survive more on their reputation for being a meal in themselves than on their flavour.

Praline: a very sweet 'sweet', made of pecan nuts browned in sugar.

controlled New Orleans, and scene of the formal transfer of the province from Spain to France and from France to the Union — and on the other by the Presbytère, once used as a court chamber, but now the home of the Louisiana State Museum (see p.94).

Once a parade ground for both the French and Spanish armies, and originally called the Place d'Armes, Jackson Square was renamed after General Andrew Jackson in 1848. His statue, at the centre of the square, depicts him seated on a prancing horse. The whole statue is in fact balanced on the two back legs of the horse, without any other form of support — a sculpturally difficult feat, and this is supposedly the first successful attempt at it ever made. The major draw for visitors to the square is the spontaneous parade of human eccentricities displayed by its habitués. Children and animals are the principal performers. A clown appears, offering balloon toys which he makes in front of a Pied-Piper crowd of youngsters and then throws into the forest of outstretched arms. A wet dog, and his indulgent master, perform a kind of extravagant charade, each pretending to be annoyed with the other, while other regulars of the square gather round to offer encouragement and sweets. The *joie de vivre* of the crowd is infectious, and strangers are soon made to feel at home.

Within a stone's throw is the French Market, once a collection of open-air stalls, and now, with its early nineteenth-century stucco houses restored, a thriving clutch of small shops and restaurants, where you can watch pralines and beignets being made and see craftsmen at work on pottery and cane.

Old cannon in Jackson Square are a reminder of the origins of this delightful city park, which started life as a military parade ground

Carnival Calendar

Whatever the time of year, New Orleans is usually either holding a festival, preparing for one, or recovering from the last one. While actual dates vary from one year to the next, here is a rough seasonal guide to the most colourful festivals in the New Orleans calendar of events.

January 6th to February or March: Mardi Gras celebrations (see p. 86-7), with processions and parades culminating on the Mardi Gras itself in the most Tuesday before Lent.

Mid March: St Patrick's Day parades in the two main parishes of New Orleans. Colourful, boisterous, fun.

Mid April: Crawfish Festival in St Bernard Parish to coincide with the height of the crawfish (crayfish) season. Lots of succulent morsels of the favourite crustacean delicacy of New Orleans.

Late April to early May: Jazz and Heritage Festival, which covers two weekends of jazz jollifications involving more than 1000 performers from soloists to big bands. Louisiana shows off its crafts and foods simultaneously at the Heritage Fair in the Fairground.

Late April to early May: Spring Fiesta. Visits to private homes in the French Quarter and Garden District of New Orleans are arranged, and the hosts and hostesses dress themselves in 18th- and 19th-century costumes. There are also tours of plantation houses and romantic, candlelight parades in the evenings.

Late June to early July: Food Festival. The best food that Louisiana can provide is available in specially erected food-tasting booths.

Mid July: France-Louisiana Festival. A bit of everything happens in the city over two weekends. a jazz parade, Cajun music festival, golf, tennis and cycling tournaments, and the ever popular opportunities for tasting food in the best of New Orleans' restaurants. The festival, coinciding with Bastille day (14 July), also includes formal commemorative ceremonies.

Mid July: Louisiana Oyster Festival. Another gargantuan feast, this time in praise of the ubiquitous oyster, at Galliano in Lafourche Parish.

Late July: International Tarpon Rodeo. Another joyful excuse for a celebration, at Grand Isle in Jefferson Parish.

Early August: Jefferson Parish Seafood Festival.

Mid August: Blessing of the Fleet, that is, the fishing fleet, at Grand Isle, Jefferson Parish.

Late August: Jefferson Parish Redfish Rodeo.

Early October: Gumbo Festival. Gumbo is the all-in-one soup, usually based on a mixture of chicken and fish, which New Orleans has made all its own. This jamoree takes place in Jefferson Parish.

Early October: Spanish Heritage and Cultural Festival, at Chalmette in St Bernard Parish.

Late October: Bouillabaisse Festival, at Larose in Lafourche Parish.

Mid November: Crafts Festival, in St Tammany Parish.

Early December: Louisiana Orange Festival, at Burns in Plaquemines Parish.

At the Café du Monde, which is open 24 hours a day, you can eat the beignets, sip *café au lait* and enjoy the passing scene. Or you can buy one of the pavement-artist canvases hanging on the ornate, iron-lace fences, or wander along the bank of the Mississippi on the wooden-planked embankment promenade called Moonwalk, after a former mayor, Moon Landrieu, sit on the benches and dream of the vanished world of Mark Twain, conjuring up the ghosts of Tom Sawyer and Huckleberry Finn as the sedate paddle steamers pass by taking boatloads of tourists up river.

Five miles across town, another stretch of water offers a variety of different sights and sounds. The twenty-three-mile-wide Lake Pontchartrain, named after Louis XIV's Minister of the Marine, provides a five-mile lakefront stretch of facilities and amusements, including a marina, picnic and recreational area, an amusement park and delightful seafood restaurants standing on stilts above the water. The lake also boasts the world's longest road bridge over water, stretching a phenomenal twenty-four miles. Driving across the lake is like skimming over the water in a hydrofoil. One eight-mile stretch of the causeway is totally out of sight of land — an eerie experience, compounded by the fact that the bridge is so close to the water that the roadway has to hump occasionally like a fairground big-dipper to allow small boats to pass under it. Elaborate safety regulations are enforced to help keep the traffic moving. Despite its length, the bridge tolls are no more expensive than for more conventional road bridges in America. The bridge has another distinction — it is seventeen yards longer in one direction than in the other — due, it appears, to a

need to have started and finished the second span from a different anchorage from the first. It was completed in 1969 to open up an easy route to the Louisiana hinterland, where magnificent mansions on massive plantations are open to the public.

The state park of Fontainebleau, once part of a plantation, is only five miles east of the causeway, and Fairview Park is just three miles to the west.

Another recent engineering marvel in New Orleans is the Superdome (see p.94). Standing on fifty-one acres of a former freight yard, it has a dome so vast that it balloons above the rooftops like the hull of an enormous airship, still anchored on the ground. Standing 273ft high, the 27-storey 'world's largest steel-constructed hall unobstructed by posts' is kept air conditioned at a comfortable 72°F all the year round 'to stop clouds forming under the roof', as one cynic put it. It seats 95,000 people. To help control the crowds, the designers have had to

Side-wheelers and stern-wheelers still steam up and down the Mississippi, no longer filled with poker-playing gamblers in ruffled shirts and bootlace ties, but packed with sightseeing tourists

New Orleans

develop new ideas such as mobile stands which adjust the seating capacity, and giant TV monitors that are lowered from the roof to bring the action right in front of spectators who otherwise would not be able to see what was going on in the arena far below. Just in case the place ever has empty seats, they have covered all the seating in a special material so that on home screens the empty seats look occupied. When the stadium empties, the crowds have to negotiate sloping exit ramps which are carpeted in a cleverly

lined pattern to give an optical illusion of a flight of steps. It stops many people from running down to the exits. For the privileged few, luxury abounds on the executive floors where there are eight sumptuous suites consisting of dressing rooms, private lounges, offices and a large reception area for entertaining VIPs. There are also sixty-four plush box suites. The pivot of Poydras Plaza, one of the newest shopping complexes in the city, the Superdome is also made conveniently accessible to guests of the Hyatt Regency Hotel, which is linked by a special walkway to the stadium.

It doesn't really pay to drive round the old streets in the downtown area of New Orleans, although it is worthwhile hiring a car for tours out of the city (see pp.96-101), and there are very efficient freeways to help you get out of town. Like San Francisco, New Orleans still clings to its surviving streetcar line, which runs through the Garden District. While there is no longer a line on Desire Parkway (made famous by Tenessee Williams' play, *A Streetcar named Desire*), the existing route between Carondelet Street at the junction with Canal Street, and Carrollton Way, has now been safeguarded as a 'historic treasure'. Despite the wooden seats and the swaying, noisy ride, the streetcar, powered by an overhead trolley (but don't refer to it as a trolley car) is one of the cheapest rides in the world. It is also the oldest continuously operating street

Superdome, New Orleans' enormous stadium, seen from the Hyatt Hotel walkway

railway in the world. Its history goes back to when it was a horse-drawn street railway in 1835. Later it was powered by steam, and in 1893 the electric car was introduced on 225 miles of New Orleans' highways. Along the route, the architectural styles of the restored former homes of planters and bootleggers varies from Victorian turrets and cupolas with vast, dark-panelled rooms, to the cottage-style buildings built above ground to guard against floods.

With their covered porches and roofs overhanging the ornately decorated balconies for which New Orleans is famous, these mansions are surrounded by beautifully maintained gardens with lawns and a variety of trees and other greenery. Lining the streets are oaks, magnolias, and palms. Apart from the choice of famous restaurants in the Garden District, there is a plethora of museums and, as the streetcar leaves the Garden District for the university area, a concentration of student bohemia.

Three of New Orleans' colleges are located in this district — Loyola, Tulane and St Mary's Dominican College. Tulane began in 1834 as a medical college and now specializes in engineering, social sciences, art and architecture. It also claims to be the oldest college of commerce in the United States. In 1911, Loyola University was formed from a

The last working streetcar line runs along St Charles Avenue through the old American Quarter of the city. The 'Streetcar named Desire' no longer runs

The old street sign and lamp (left) help maintain Royal Street's charm. The city's more exotic past (above) is shown at the Voodoo Museum

Old shop signs in Royal Street

One of the most popular nightspots in New Orleans is the jazz club run by the famous trumpeter Al Hirt. Bourbon Street is the hub of the city's nightlife

A slightly macabre sight, the old cemeteries, with Creole and Cajun tombs raised above the marshy ground

The world's longest bridge is the 23¾-mile causeway on Lake Pontchartrain

merger with a Jesuit college. Today it is the largest Catholic university in the American South.

The whole of the uptown section of New Orleans provides numerous points of interest for the tourist. There are always good reasons for walking the streets, and if you want to savour one of New Orleans' finest features, spend some time in the section which follows the bend of the river along Magazine Street (see p.95). Originally the street was a centre for upholstery and furniture-making. Now there are often more antique bargains to be found in Magazine Street than in the select reaches of the French Quarter — particularly Royal Street where some of the most high-priced shops can be found.

But Royal Street is not just a shoppers' delight. Its lovingly preserved houses with their iron filigree balconies covered in flowers, are some of the finest examples of nineteenth-century architecture in the city. The Greater New Orleans Visitors and Convention Bureau, which has the task of promoting the city for its visitors, conveniently occupies a beautiful building like that; dating back to 1826, it was once a legion hall. Nearby, elegant Pontalba Buildings are believed to be the oldest apartment houses in America. Built in 1849, these handsome red-brick flats were for many years the most desirable residences for the New Orleans gentry, and some are still occupied. Part of the

building is an offshoot of the Louisiana State Museum and includes a historical 'puppetorium' with automated marionettes portraying historical events in New Orleans. It has the largest collection of puppets and dolls in the States.

Rather different kinds of dolls are assembled at the Voodoo Museum in Bourbon Street (see p.94). Voodoo rituals are part of New Orleans' folklore and their impact on the black community was particularly strong.

For a touch of the real macabre, New Orleans even offers tours of two of its oldest cemeteries. Creole and Cajun dead are entombed above ground in imposing tombs in various styles of decorative stonework — above ground because of the waterlogged land, which sometimes caused bodies buried conventionally to float to the surface. Though drainage techniques have much improved now, burials in crypts and raised tombs are still widespread. You can find Cemetery 1 on Basin Street, between St Louis and Toulouse Streets, and Cemetery 2 between North Claiborne and Bienville Streets. You would probably be wise not to wander through these cemeteries alone, for they are notorious hunting-grounds for muggers — even in daylight. It is best to go in a guided party.

For an active day out, the marshlands and bayous are ideal for the fisherman or the hunter (see p.94). In many stretches of brackish water, the extraordinary alchemy of salt water from the Gulf of Mexico and the fresh water from the Mississippi produce a rich harvest of fish, many of which land on the tables of New Orleans' select restaurants. All kinds of waterfowl and game inhabit the marshlands, — geese, doves, quail, snipe, woodcock and deer.

For the less energetic, the whole area can be surveyed reed-high on an hour's flight in a Cessna from New Orleans Lakefront airport (internal flights), on the shores of Lake Pontchartrain. Charter flights are, of course, not cheap, but they give an unparalleled view of the Crescent City, as New Orleans is known — because of its position in the bend of the river.

New Orleans

Particularly impressive from the air are the two majestic bridges across the Mississippi — the Huey Long, (named after a well-known and controversial political figure) which carries the main US 90 Federal road, and the tracks of the Southern Pacific railroad to the suburb of Jefferson; and the Greater New Orleans Bridge whose 1575ft cantilever span, is one of the longest in the United States.

Sometimes the Lakefront flights have to be curtailed to avoid traffic from New Orleans International Airport (see p.94), On the other hand, if conditions are favourable, the flight might last ten minutes or so longer than scheduled — the reason being that the pilot might want to offer his passengers a little *lagniappe* (pronounced 'lanyap'). You will hear this word used frequently in the city. A Cajun term, it means that indefinable touch of goodwill, that elusive bit of something extra, which the people of New Orleans like to offer each other, and extend wholeheartedly to strangers. *Lagniappe* can take all kinds of tangible forms. You might find that the waiter shelling your dozen oysters gives you thirteen or fourteen as a matter of course; a bartender may pour you a drink on the house, or a shopkeeper may sometimes slip a small gift in with your purchase. *Lagniappe* is part of the soul of New Orleans.

The Greater New Orleans Bridge, spanning the Mississippi River

New Orleans Directory

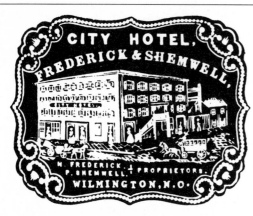

Hotels and Restaurants

The hotels and restaurants listed here are either recommended by the American Automobile Association (AAA) or have been selected because they are of interest to tourists. As a rough guide to cost, they have been classified as either expensive, moderate or reasonable. Hotels all have private bathrooms and colour television.

Hotels

BEST WESTERN FRENCH MARKET INN: 501 Decatur St, tel. 561 5621, freephone 800 528 1234. 36 rooms. Pay parking. Near Jackson Square at the heart of the French Quarter. Motel, moderate.

BIENVILLE HOUSE MOTOR HOTEL: 320 Decatur St, tel. 529 2345, freephone 800 535 9595. 82 rooms. Free parking. Restaurant, swimming pool. Motor inn, French Quarter, moderate.

DE LA POSTE MOTOR HOTEL: 316 Chartres St, tel. 581 1200. 100 rooms. Free parking. Restaurant, swimming pool and patio. An attractively modernized building in the French Quarter. Motor inn, moderate.

FAIRMONT HOTEL: University Pl., tel. 529 7111, freephone 800 527 4727. 730 rooms. Three restaurants, swimming pool, tennis courts. Luxury hotel, on the edge of the French Quarter. Expensive.

HOLIDAY INN — AIRPORT: 2929 Williams Blvd, tel. 467 5611, freephone 800 238 8000. 306 rooms. Free parking. Restaurant and coffee shop, swimming pool, putting green. Motor inn, near airport (transport to and from), reasonable.

HOWARD JOHNSON'S, THE DOWNTOWN: 330 Loyola Ave, tel. 581 1600, freephone 800 535 7830. 300 rooms. Free parking. Restaurant, swimming pool. Between the Superdome and the French Quarter, moderate.

HOWARD JOHNSON'S MOTOR LODGE — AIRPORT: 6401 Veterans' Blvd, tel. 885 5700. 240 rooms. Restaurant, swimming pool. Motor hotel, near airport (transport to and from), reasonable.

HYATT REGENCY: 500 Poydras Plaza, tel. 561 1234, freephone 800 228 9000. 1200 rooms. Pay valet parking. Restaurants and coffee shop, swimming pool. Luxury hotel in business district, near Superdome and French Quarter, expensive.

LAMOTHE HOUSE: 621 Esplanade Ave, tel. 947 1161/2. 13 rooms. Free parking. An old house with period furnishings, converted into a small, intimate hotel on the edge of the French Quarter. Closed July-August. Reasonable.

LE RICHELIEU MOTOR HOTEL: 1234 Chartres St, tel. 529 2492. 88 rooms. Free parking. Restaurant, swimming pool and courtyard. An old building,

well modernized, in the heart of the French Quarter. Moderate.

NEW ORLEANS AIRPORT HILTON INN: 901 Airline Highway, tel. 721 3471, freephone 800 452 8703. 290 rooms. Free parking. Restaurants and coffee shop, swimming pool, tennis courts, putting green. Motor hotel, opposite airport entrance (transport to and from), moderately expensive.

PLACE D'ARMES HOTEL: 625 St Ann St, tel. 524 4531. 72 rooms. Pay parking. Restaurant, swimming pool. Many rooms in this charming old hotel overlook an attractive, shady courtyard. Near Jackson Square in the heart of the French Quarter. Moderate.

PRINCE CONTI HOTEL: 830 Conti St, tel. 529 4172, freephone 800 535 9111. 50 rooms. Free valet parking. French Quarter, moderately expensive.

PROVINCIAL MOTOR HOTEL: 1024 Chartres St, tel. 581 4995. 100 rooms. Free parking. Restaurant.

SQUARETOE'S
CONTINUOUS LUNCH
ALL NIGHT! ALL DAY!
—
SNAPPER SOUP
All Hot.
—
SHEEP'S TONGUES
AND
GOOSE'S LIVER
All Cold.
—
All Temperaments
Suited.

Swimming pool and patio. Family-run establishment in the heart of the French Quarter, specializing in Creole cooking. Many rooms overlook a quiet courtyard. Reasonable.

ROYAL ORLEANS HOTEL: Royal and St Louis Sts, tel. 529 5333, freephone 800 223 5757. 386 rooms. Pay valet garage. Restaurants, swimming pool. The Rib Room restaurant is famous. French Quarter, expensive.

ROYAL SONESTA HOTEL: 300 Bourbon St, tel. 586 0300. 485 rooms. Pay garage parking. Restaurants and coffee shop, swimming pool. French Quarter, expensive.

SHERATON INN — INTERNATIONAL AIRPORT: 2150 Veterans' Blvd, tel. 467 3111, freephone 800 325 3535. 253 rooms. Free parking. Restaurant, swimming pool and sauna. Near airport (transport to and from), moderate.

VIEUX CARRE MOTOR LODGE: 920 N. Rampart St, tel. 524 0461. 100 rooms. Free parking. Restaurant, swimming pool and courtyard. Motor inn, French Quarter, reasonable.

WARWICK HOTEL: 1315 Gravier St, tel. 586 0100. 176 rooms. Free garage parking. Restaurant, sauna. Near the French Quarter and the Superdome. Moderate.

Restaurants

Note: Many of New Orleans' more expensive restaurants impose a rigorous dress code; men are expected to wear a jacket and tie. It is advisable to check when booking.

Restaurants often do not admit to being closed. Instead they simply say 'Sunday dark'. This does not mean candlelit suppers, simply that Sunday, or whichever day, is a day off.

THE ANDREW JACKSON: 221 Royal St, tel. 529 2603. Since the Sevin Brothers opened it in 1964, the restaurant has earned a reputation for fine food in elegant surroundings. The decor is distinguished by a lavender marble fireplace, which came from the Paris Opera House, a life-sized sculpture of Andrew Jackson by Enrique Alferez, and crystal chandeliers. Authentic New Orleans cuisine — house specialities include veal King Ferdinand VII — sliced braised veal covered with crabmeat and Béarnaise sauce — and Chateaubriand steak. Expensive.

ANTOINE'S: 713 St Louis St, tel. 581 4422. Very well known restaurant, established in 1840 and still run by the same family. Menu is entirely in French, but includes Creole dishes. Many widely acclaimed specialities, including oysters Rockefeller

and pompano en papillote. Excellent wine cellar. Closed Sundays. French Quarter, expensive.

ARNAUD'S: 813 Rue Bienville, tel. 523 5433. Founded by Count Arnaud Cazenave in 1918 and recently restored to its former splendour. The menu features some of the Count's own specialities such as shrimp Arnaud and oysters Bienville. Closed for lunch at weekends. French Quarter, moderate.

THE BON TON: 401 Magazine St, tel. 524 3386. Creole restaurant; local seafood is a speciality and the menu features old Cajun family recipes. Popular for business lunches. Closed weekends. Moderate.

BOURBON ORLEANS HOTEL: Bourbon and Orleans Sts, tel. 523 5251. **MAURICE'S RESTAURANT** serves excellent traditional or New Orleans breakfasts; salads and snacks at lunchtime; continental cuisine in the evening. French Quarter, moderate.

BRENNAN'S: 417 Royal St, tel. 525 9711. World-famous for 'Breakfast at Brennan's', served from 8am to 2.30pm. French and Creole specialities include gourmet egg dishes, quail and crabs, with delicious crêpes to follow. Dinner also served. The early 19th-century house features 10 elegant dining rooms and a lush tropical-style patio where cocktails are served. French Quarter, moderate.

BROUSSARD'S: 819 Conti St, tel. 581 3866. Fine Creole and traditional New Orleans cuisine in attractive surroundings recently refurbished. Open for dinner only, but also breakfast at weekends, 9am to 3pm. French Quarter, moderate.

H.C. BRUNING: 1870 Orpheum Ave, tel. 282 9395. One of Lake Ponchartrain's oldest lakeside restaurants with a huge, mahogany bar. Marvellous value for simple seafood dishes like boiled crab. Friendly service. Closed Wednesdays. Reasonable.

CAFE DU MONDE: French Market — 800 Decatur St, tel. 561 9235. Open-air pavement café serving coffee, milk, chocolate and hot beignets. Open 24 hours. French Quarter, reasonable.

CASTILLO'S MEXICAN RESTAURANT: 620 Conti St, tel. 581 9602. Popular and exotic Mexican dishes served in this colourful restaurant with a friendly atmosphere. French Quarter, reasonable.

COMMANDER'S PALACE: Washington Ave and Coliseum St, tel. 899 8221. Fine old restaurant in the Garden District, run by the Brennan family. Creole dishes served; a particular speciality is crabmeat imperial. Live jazz at weekend brunch. Valet parking in evenings. Moderate.

THE COURT OF TWO SISTERS: 613 Royal St, tel. 522 7261. One of the city's better-known restaurants, with a large courtyard. Wide choice of dishes. Live jazz at brunch, 9am-3pm daily. Also open for dinner. French Quarter, moderate.

FAIRMONT HOTEL: University Place, tel. 529 7111. The BLUE ROOM offers dinner, dancing and night-club entertainment, sometimes featuring well-known stars, while the SAZERAC is open for lunch on weekdays and dinner every night. Both expensive. BAILEYS serves a wide choice of good sandwiches, salads and fresh local seafoods 24 hours a day. Valet parking.

FELIX'S: 739 Iberville St, tel. 522 4440/522 0324. Local seafood is the speciality here, including oysters, shrimps and gumbo. Steaks are also served, and there is an extensive à la carte menu. French Quarter, reasonable.

GALATOIRE'S: 209 Bourbon St, tel. 525 2021. A long-established family restaurant. The emphasis is on Creole-French cuisine; specialities include trout Marguery and shrimp remoulade. Excellent coffee. No reservations; advisable to eat early or be prepared to wait. Closed Monday. French Quarter, moderate.

LA BOUCHERIE/GUMBO POT: 330 Chartres St, tel. 522 6672. Cafe with upstairs disco and games room. Creole and Cajun food, hot sandwiches, salad bar. French Quarter, reasonable.

LERUTH'S: 636 Franklin St, Gretna, tel. 372 4914. Reached by a 15-minute drive from downtown New Orleans. Outstanding French cuisine which has won many awards.

Chef-owner Warren LeRuth makes the most of local seafood, and the sauces are excellent. Bread and ice-cream are home-made. Extensive wine list. Closed Sunday and Monday. Free parking. Expensive.

THE OLD SPAGHETTI FACTORY: 330 St Charles Ave, tel. 561 1068. As famous for its decor as for its food, this restaurant is packed with unusual antiques ranging from a preacher's pulpit to an old tramcar. Spaghetti is served with a choice of 7 freshly-made sauces. Reasonable.

ORIGINAL PAPA JOE'S CAFE: 600 Bourbon St, tel. 529 5576. Steaks, seafood and snacks are served in addition to all the traditional drinks of New Orleans. Live entertainment nightly. French Quarter, reasonable.

T. PITTARI'S: 4200 S. Claiborne Ave, tel. 891 2801. Open since 1895, this seafood speciality restaurant is also famed for its Montana wild game skillet, a mixture of Buffalo, elk and venison. Moderate.

PONTCHARTRAIN HOTEL — CARIBBEAN ROOM: 2031 St Charles Ave, tel. 524 0581. De luxe restaurant in one of the city's top hotels. Fish and seafood are specialities. Expensive.

RUTH'S CHRIS STEAK HOUSES: 3633 Veterans Blvd, Metairie, tel. 888 3600; 501 Gretna Blvd, Gretna, tel. 367 1100; 711 N. Broad St, tel. 482 9278. Several types of steak are served with generous salads or vegetables. Moderate.

TCHOUPITOULAS PLANTATION RESTAURANT: 6535 River Rd, Westbank in Avondale, tel. 436 1277. 30 minutes' drive from downtown New Orleans. Leisurely dining in a delightful country plantation house. Grounds cover 12 acres, featuring fine old oak trees, native flowering shrubs and peacocks. You can begin your meal with a specially created 'Jezebel' cocktail. Closed for lunch on Saturday. Moderate.

THE VIEUX CARRE RESTAURANT: 241 Bourbon St, tel. 524 0114. Gourmet French and Creole cuisine in one of the city's oldest dining rooms, built in 1831. French Quarter, moderate.

Transport

MOISANT INTERNATIONAL AIRPORT: New Orleans (Moisant) airport lies about 12 miles west of the city in Kenner. Airline Highway (US 61) runs past the airport directly into the city centre. The Orleans Transportation Service, tel. 581 7222, runs a limousine service between the airport and central hotels, and there is an express bus service run by the Louisiana Transit Company to and from their terminal near the Civic Center on Tulane Avenue. About 14 major airlines operate from Moisant; it is the main transfer point for Mexico, Central and South America.

TAXIS: Cruising taxis are easy to find in the downtown area and the French Quarter; elsewhere, it is best to telephone. The largest companies are: Checker, tel. 943 2411; Ed's, tel. 522 0241; United, tel. 522 9771; Yellow, tel. 525 3311.

BUSES: New Orleans Public Service runs cheap, efficient and frequent bus services within the city limits. Their information desk is at 317 Baronne, or phone 586 2192 (New Orleans Tourist Office) for information. A treat not to be missed is the one remaining streetcar line, whose charming, antiquated, wooden-seated vehicles rattle and clatter along St Charles Avenue. Correct fare is required on all buses.

TRAINS: The Union Passenger Terminal is at 1001 Loyola Ave. Information about train services can be obtained from AMTRAK National Information Center, tel. freephone 800 874 2800.

CAR HIRE: The Yellow Pages of the telephone directory have a complete list of car-rental agencies, but the larger firms with offices in New Orleans are: Airways, tel. 466 9321; Avis Rent-a-Car, tel. 523 4317; Budget Rent-a-Car, tel. 525 9417; Dollar Rent-a-Car, tel. 721 6288; Hertz, tel. 568 1645 and National Car Rental, tel. 525 0416.

Touring Information

SIGHTSEEING: Riverboat cruises on the Mississippi are one of the major attractions of New Orleans. Cruises leave either from the Canal St Docks or from Toulouse St Wharf near Jackson Square. Details can be obtained from the Visitor Information Center (see below). On dry land, a Peggy Wilson's Guided Trolley Tour offers an easy and entertaining way to see the principal sights. Tel. 895 0412, or 866 1689.

AAA: The AAA has no office in New Orleans itself, but the AAA Central Gulf Division office in the suburb of Metairie offers a helpful service to motorists. They are at 3445 N. Causeway Blvd, Metairie, tel. 837 1080. Open in office hours.

VISITOR INFORMATION CENTER: 344 Royal St, New Orleans, tel. 522 8772 (cultural events information, tel. 522 2787) has brochures, booklets, guides and information on all tourist attractions in and around the city. Open daily in office hours.

CLIMATE: The weather in New Orleans is subtropical. Winds from the Gulf of Mexico make the air humid, but temper the effects of the fierce sunlight. The average high temperature in July and August is just over 90° and the average low temperature in December, January and February is 45°. Snow and frost are very rare, but the annual rainfall is around 54 inches.

Museums

THE CABILDO: Jackson Sq., tel. 581 4321. This historic building has been, in its time, a French police station and guardhouse, the council chamber under Spanish rule, the city hall and the state supreme court. Now owned by the Louisiana State Museum, the late 18th-century building houses permanent displays whose exhibits include Napoleon's death mask and the founding stone of the colony set up here in the 17th century. An art exhibition now occupies the room where the Louisiana Purchase was signed in 1803, whilst other rooms are devoted to illustrating the history, culture and trade of the area. Closed Monday.

CABRINI DOLL MUSEUM: 1218 Burgundy St, tel. 586 5204. Dolls from all over the world may be seen here. Some are on loan from other leading doll collections. Children's books and art are also on display in this former Creole cottage. Open weekday afternoons and all day Saturday.

HISTORIC NEW ORLEANS COLLECTION: 533 Royal St, tel. 523 7146. An extensive collection of paintings, prints and documents relating to the history of Louisiana can be seen in 18th-century Merieult House, one of the very few buildings in the French Quarter to escape the disastrous fire of 1794. Other public galleries feature temporary exhibitions, mainly on cultural and historical subjects. Closed Sunday and Monday.

HISTORICAL PHARMACY MUSEUM: 514 Chartres St. A drug store dating from the 1820s is the home of this unusual collection illustrating the early history of medicine. Voodoo potions are on display along with many more orthodox remedies. Closed Monday.

MUSEE CONTI WAX MUSEUM: 917 Conti St, tel. 525 2605. The history and legends of New Orleans and Louisiana are told in period tableaux featuring beautifully costumed life-size wax figures. The Haunted Dungeon depicts well-known horror stories.

NEW ORLEANS MUSEUM OF ART: Lelong Ave in City Park, tel. 488 2631. The varied permanent collection ranges from works dating back to the pre-Christian era to recent African and Far Eastern art. The museum is housed in a fine neo-classical building, and the collection is arranged to show the development of art over the centuries. Major international exhibitions also take place on a temporary basis. Admission free on Thursday; closed Monday.

PRESBYTERE: Jackson Sq., tel. 581 4321. Originally intended as a home for the cathedral priests, this building was completed in 1813 and was intended as a courthouse. It belongs to the Louisiana State Museum, and its exhibits include a very early submarine, built by the Confederate Navy and launched in 1861. Visitors can also see displays of Mardi Gras and other costumes, toys, jewels and portraits. Closed Monday.

SUN OAK: FAUBOURG MARIGNY COLLECTION: 2020 Burgundy St, tel. 945 0322. The Faubourg Marigny was the first Creole suburb of New Orleans, and the two restored buildings which make up the collection are Creole cottages dating from 1836 and 1870. The houses are furnished with fine French, Creole and Acadian antiques, and are set amid patios and gardens dominated by the ancient Sun Oak. Open by appointment Monday, Wednesday and Friday 9-11am, Tuesday and Thursday 2-5pm, and Monday to Friday 7-9pm.

VOODOO MUSEUM: 739 Bourbon St, tel. 523 2906. This is the country's only voodoo museum. The history of this strange cult is told by the collection of ritual objects such as drums, grisgris and a real voodoo altar. Visitors can have readings done by psychics, and there is a gift shop where dolls, potions etc. can be bought.

Sport

SUPERDOME: Poydras St, tel. 587 3663. Aptly named, this gigantic circular building with seating for 95,000 spectators, is the venue for basketball, baseball, and American football (the Saints). The Superdome is said to have the largest diameter (680ft) of any building in the world. Completely windowless, its temperature and humidity are controlled by a computerised system using 9000 tons of equipment. Theatrical and musical entertainments, if they are on a sufficiently large scale, are also held here. There are guided tours of the building (see the phone number above for information).

HORSE-RACING: There are two tracks, Fair Grounds, off Gentilly Blvd, and Jefferson Downs, off Interstate 10 near Lake Pontchartrain. Fair Grounds is open from November to March, Jefferson Downs from April to September.

FISHING: The Louisiana salt marshes and bayous (creeks) offer superb fishing. Several firms organize fishing trips and hire tackle and bait. A Visitor Information Center booklet (see above) gives details.

New Orleans is well provided with golf courses, tennis courts and facilities for horse riding. Information is available from the Visitor Information Center. For children, the New Orleans Recreation Dept (NORD), tel. 586 4461, sponsors various events at playgrounds in the city.

Shops

FRENCH QUARTER: Chartres, Royal and St Ann Sts are all full of shops specializing in antiques, interesting and original gifts, handicrafts, Creole delicacies, clothes and everything a visitor might wish to buy. It is best simply to stroll around and choose, but the Visitor Information Center booklet gives an exhaustive list of individual shops. The French Market, down by the Mississippi, has colourful and exotic fruit and vegetable stalls. Its attractive 160-year-old buildings house small shops, restaurants, cafés and coffee-stalls as well. Not far away, off Decatur St, the Flea Market, open on Saturday and Sunday, presents the usual colourful assortment of bric-à-brac, and more than 100 local craftsmen's stalls with pottery, jewellery, leatherwork and weaving.

RIVERBEND: Take the St Charles Ave streetcar past Audubon Park to Carrollton Ave. The Riverbend shopping area is a small Victorian enclave, between the avenue and the Mississippi where, on Dante, Dublin and Hampson Sts, are shops specializing in all manner of gifts and luxury goods. There are also a number of pleasant restaurants.

UPTOWN SQUARE: Off Broadway and Perrier, Uptown Sq. is a fashionable modern precinct built in traditional style around courtyards and plazas.

FAT CITY: This is an extensive shopping area bordered by N. Causeway, Veterans' Blvd, Division St and W. Esplanade.

DEPARTMENT STORES: Godchaux, 828 Canal St, Maison Blanche, 901 Canal St, and D.H. Holmes Company, 819 Canal St, are the three most fashionable old-established New Orleans department stores. All are central, and near the French Quarter.

DESTREHAM: For something a little different, and further out, the Destreham Plantation House, about 10 miles past the airport on River Rd, is a fine 18th-century house where the visitor can combine historical interest with shopping for gifts and antiques.

Nightlife

AL HIRT'S: 501 Bourbon St, tel. 525 6167. Trumpet virtuoso Al Hirt — the 'king of Bourbon Street' — and his jazz band entertain here most weekday evenings.

BEVERLY DINNER PLAYHOUSE: 217 Labarre Rd, tel. 837 4022. This old mansion was a de luxe casino and supper club that attracted famous names in the 1940s. Restored and re-opened several years ago it once again stages productions featuring Broadway and Hollywood stars, and offers an elegant setting for dining and drinking. Closed Monday; noon buffet and matinee, Sunday.

BLUE ROOM: Fairmont Hotel, University Pl, tel. 529 7111. Opulent surroundings of blue and gold, complete with crystal chandeliers, provide the setting for entertainment by world-famous stars in this old favourite among New Orleans nightspots. The dinner menu includes Creole and continental dishes, or you can come just for the show (cover charge payable).

DUKE'S PLACE: Monteleone Hotel, 214 Royal St, tel. 581 1567. Traditional Dixieland jazz is played here by the Dukes of Dixieland, a long-established New Orleans band. The venue is the hotel's rooftop lounge, offering breathtaking views over the Mississippi and the French Quarter.

THE NATCHEZ: Toulouse St Wharf, tel. 586 8777. A dinner cruise on this old stern-wheeler riverboat makes an unusual evening out. Closed Monday, special moonlight dance cruise, Saturday.

OLD ABSINTHE HOUSE: 400 Bourbon St; 240 Bourbon St. The site of the original bar is no. 240, but all the old fixtures and fittings, including the original marble-based fountains, used to drip water into absinthe (now an illegal drink), are now installed at no.400. They were moved in the 1920s, the Prohibition era, when the bar, which had been operating as a speakeasy, was closed. This bar also offers live entertainment in the form of progressive jazz and rhythm-and-blues.

PAT O'BRIENS: 718 St Peter St, tel. 525 4823. This world-famous bar occupies a building that was the first Spanish theatre in the USA. Customers have a choice of 3 bars: an attractive patio, the main bar at the entrance, or a large lounge where there is often raucous entertainment in the form of live piano music. Pat O'Briens is well known for its 'Hurricane'

cocktail, an exotic, rum-based drink served in huge, hand-blown glasses.

LE PETIT THEATRE DU VIEUX CARRE: 616 St Peter St, tel. 522 2081. Set in the heart of the French Quarter, this is one of the oldest non-professional theatres in the USA. The standard is very high, and the theatre is well worth a visit if a production is being staged while you are staying in New Orleans. Members have priority booking but some seats are always set aside for tourists.

PRESERVATION HALL: 726 St Peter St. A treat for those who like their jazz with no frills and much as it was in its early days. Some of the performers are the old-time greats who have played at Preservation Hall for decades, and the atmosphere is unchanged, as is the entrance fee, still only $1 at the time of writing. Accommodation is basic — a few wooden chairs or benches and no tables or drinks.

TULANE UNIVERSITY THEATRE: Phoenix Theatre, 9 McAlister Drive (Tulane Campus), tel. 865 6204. Student productions of a high standard are staged here.

Places of interest

BEAUREGARD HOUSE: 1113 Chartres St, tel. 523 7257. Built in 1826 by Joseph Le Carpentier, a wealthy New Orleans auctioneer, this fine Creole house with its Doric columns and twin staircase was later the home of

General Beauregard. Known as 'the Great Creole' he was a confederate general in the Civil War, and spent the winter of 1866-7 here following the Union victory. The house was later the home of Frances Parkinson Keyes, who wrote many novels about the New Orleans region. Closed Sunday.

CASA HOVE: 723 Toulouse St. tel. 525 7827. One of the oldest houses in the French Quarter, Casa Hove was originally built in the 1720s, though it later suffered extensive fire damage. It is a fine example of early Spanish architecture, and is furnished with priceless antiques. The ground floor is occupied by a *parfumerie* but the upper floors may be toured. Closed Sunday.

CHALMETTE NATIONAL HISTORICAL PARK: Arabi, tel. 271 2412. This was the site of the Battle of New Orleans in January 1815, when a hurriedly assembled and inexperienced American army under General Andrew Jackson defeated the British. Ramparts and cannons can still be seen on the battlefield, and a visitor centre has been established in the Beauregard Plantation House on the site.

THE 1850 HOUSE: 523 St Ann St. Restored to look just as it did 130 years ago, this typical New Orleans house is furnished with fine antiques that include a great tester canopied bed, authentic utensils and toys of the period. The slave quarters can be seen on the fourth floor. Closed Monday.

HERMANN-GRIMA HOUSE: 820 St Louis St, tel. 525 5661. This 3-storey mansion, complete with courtyards and stables (now a shop) was built in 1831. Demonstrations of Creole cooking take place in the restored kitchen on alternate Thursdays. Closed Sunday morning and all day Wednesday.

INTERNATIONAL TRADE MART: 2 Canal St. This is the centre of the maritime industry in New Orleans, and most international consulates are also housed in the skyscraper. On the 31st floor is an observation deck that offers panoramic views of the city and its busy docks. The Louisiana Maritime Museum's collection of charts, model ships and other items connected with New Orleans' shipping history is on the

same floor (closed Sunday). There is a revolving cocktail bar — the 'Top of the Mart' — on the 33rd floor.

JACKSON BARRACKS: 6400 St Claude Ave. These fine old white-columned brick buildings were constructed in the 1830s for troops stationed at the river forts. The Louisiana National Guard now has its headquarters here, and the old powder magazine has been imaginatively converted into a museum. Closed Monday.

LOOM ROOM: 623 Royal St, tel. 522 7101. Local weavers can often be seen at work in the demonstrations that take place here, and examples of the weaver's craft are on display to the public.

MADAME JOHN'S LEGACY: 632 Dumaine St, tel. 581 4321. Sometimes claimed to be the oldest building on the Mississippi, the present building was probably not built until 1789 — after the great fire — replacing an earlier house of which this is a faithful replica. The house is a fine example of a Creole planter's cottage and is furnished with 18th- and 19th-century antiques. Closed Monday.

NEW ORLEANS SPRING FIESTA HOUSE: 826 St Ann St, tel. 581 1367. Bequeathed to the New Orleans Spring Fiesta Association in 1977, this house is thought to date from the late 1830s though the second storey was not added until 1850. It is a typical town house of the period, and has a delightful courtyard. Open Monday and Thursday 11am-4pm.

OLD URSULINE CONVENT: 1114 Chartres St. This was the first convent established in Louisiana, completed soon after the founding of New Orleans. The sisters were at that time the only teachers and nurses in the city, establishing several schools and an orphanage. After the nuns moved out in 1824, the state legislative met in this building. The charming courtyard, with its herb garden, is reached through an unusual brick gateway.

RIVERGATE EXHIBITION CENTER: 4 Canal St. Next to the International Trade Mart is this huge modern building where some of New Orleans' many conventions, trade fairs and exhibitions take place. It is also used in the Mardi Gras celebrations every year.

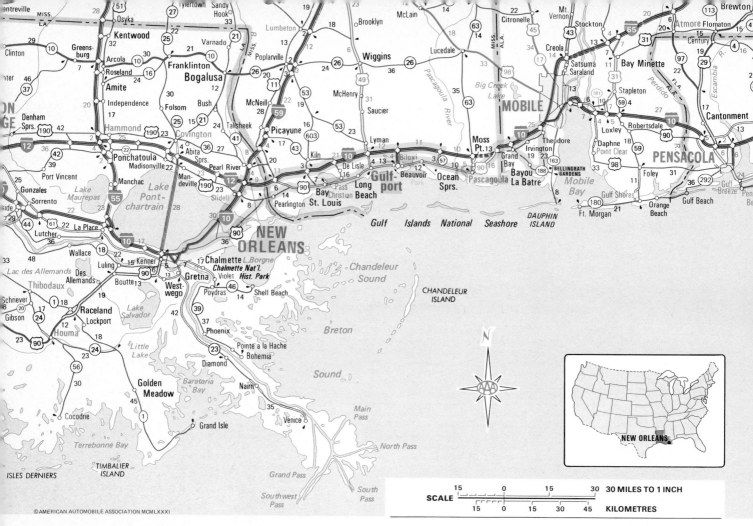

SCALE

15   0   15   30   **30 MILES TO 1 INCH**

15   0   15   30   45   **KILOMETRES**

Mobile and the Mississippi Gulf

2 days — approx 300 miles

New Orleans - Gulfport - Biloxi - Ocean Springs - Pascagoula -Mobile - Bellingrath Gardens - New Orleans.

East of New Orleans is the resort area of Mississippi's sparkling Gulf Coast. For miles you spin along the historic Old Spanish Trail beside white palm-fringed beaches. One of the longest man-made beaches in the world extends along the scenic seawall and beach parkway for 27 miles from Pass Christian to Biloxi. A string of islands — part of the Gulf Island National Seashore Park — follows the coastline, and there are regular trips to Ship Island from Gulfport or Biloxi. The Alabama seaport of Mobile, the end of the outward trail, is a city full of interest and best seen from February to April when it is ablaze with king-sized azaleas.

Follow the Old Spanish Trail — US 90 — east across the mouth of Lake Pontchartrain, then cross the Pearl River and drive on to Pearlington. Continue east for 25 miles and cross a scenic causeway to reach Pass Christian, then drive by dazzling white beaches for another 11 miles to Gulfport.

Gulfport, Mississippi

As well as being an important seaport, shipping fish, timber and cotton, Gulfport is a popular holiday resort which boasts miles of fine beaches, scenic drives and boulevards. The annual Mississippi Deep Sea Fishing Rodeo attracts competitors from all over the States and is held here for three days in early July.

Ship Island may be reached from Gulfport on the *Pan American Clipper*. Twelve miles south of the town, the island guards the entrance to Biloxi Bay and has a stormy history of capture and recapture. Fort Massachusetts, ruined but still standing, was captured by Confederate (southern) troops in 1861 during the Civil War. They named it Fort Twiggs, in honour of a Confederate general. Later the same year, when Union troops retook it, they gave it the name of Fort Massachusetts. It provided a vital link in the northern naval blockade of the southern states, and many Confederates were imprisoned there. Boat trips operate daily between April and September.

Continue east along US 90 for 11½ miles to Beauvoir.

Beauvoir, Mississippi

Visitors interested in Civil War history will not want to miss a visit to the home of Jefferson Davis. The former Confederate president spent the last 12 years of his life here, after he was released from prison in the north. He wrote *The Rise and Fall of the Confederate Government* whilst living here, using the small white cottage in the grounds as his library and study. Many of the books he used can still be seen in the cottage. The elegant house itself was built in 1853, and still contains its original furnishings. After Jefferson's death, a hospital for Confederate veterans was set up here. This is now an Old South museum, and the whole 50-acre estate has been turned into a Confederate shrine which the public may visit. It is open daily.

Drive on for 5½ miles along US 90 to Biloxi.

Biloxi, Mississippi

Perched on a narrow peninsula, bordered by the Mississippi Sound, Biloxi Bay and Back Bay, this delightful resort city offers old world charm and a consistently mild climate. Biloxi, with its tall trees trailing Spanish moss, and its streets perfumed by magnolia and camellia blossom, is one of the prettiest towns in the Gulf. Beach Boulevard offers a breathtakingly beautiful drive along the coast.

'Biloxi' means 'first people', and the original site, dating from 1699, was across the bay. In 1719 the French captured the settlement from the warlike Biloxi Indians and moved its location. It was the capital of the French territory of Louisiana until 1923, when New Orleans took over the role.

Biloxi is known for its shrimp- and oyster-fishing industries. Every June the shrimp fleet is blessed in a colourful ceremony which attracts many visitors. A good introduction to Biloxi is provided by the Shrimp Tour Train, which provides guided tours by open trolley. A tape recording outlines the history and events of the city and beach. The tours depart from Biloxi Lighthouse, on US 90 at the foot of Porter Avenue. The trip takes just over an hour, and there are four trips daily between April and September.

The lighthouse itself is of interest; it was built in 1848, and its lens was removed and buried by a Biloxi citizen during the Civil War so that the lighthouse should be of no help to the approaching Union forces. For 62 years after the war, the lighthouse was operated by a mother and daughter team.

Visitors to Biloxi may be interested in taking one of the 1½-hour harbour tours, which leave the small craft harbour at the foot of Main Street. On these sightseeing and trawling expeditions aboard the *Sailfish*, fish are caught, displayed and identified by experts.

Cross Back Bay and drive for about 3 miles along US 90 to Ocean Springs.

Ocean Springs, Mississippi

This attractive Gulf resort has recently acquired a reputation as an artists' and craftsmen's colony. Established in 1699 by d'Iberville, who built Fort Maurepas on this site, it was the first permanent European settlement in the Mississippi Valley. You can enjoy good Creole food and seafood here at Trilby's restaurant.

Continue east for 19 miles on US 90 to Pascagoula.

Pascagoula, Mississippi

Founded in 1718, this town and the river on which it stands take their name from the Pascagoula Indians, who lived here long before that. Legend has it that the tribe came to a tragic end when they chose to commit mass suicide by walking hand-in-hand into the Pascagoula River, rather than to

suffer an ignominious defeat at the hands of the fierce Biloxi tribe. To this day, it is said that their death chant can be heard by the river on still summer evenings, and the Pascagoula is still called the 'Singing River'.

On Krebs Lake, just off US 90, is the Old Spanish Fort. Although it was in fact built by the French, in 1718, it was later captured by the Spanish — hence its name. The fort is one of the oldest

structures still standing in the Mississippi Valley.

Drive north-east for 10 miles on US 90 and join Interstate 10 for the last 21 miles to Mobile.

Mobile, Alabama

Nestling on the west side of Mobile Bay, this world port is well protected by the 27-mile-long inlet that takes its name. Though eight miles across, the bay is protected at its mouth by Dauphin Island and the Gulf Shores peninsula.

Originally settled by the Mauvilla Indians, after whom it was named, Mobile was founded by a Frenchman, Sieur de Bienville, in 1702. The first permanent white settlement in Alabama, the city served as the capital of the French colonial empire until 1719. In 1763 the English took over, then in 1780 the Spanish gained possession. The United States seized the city in 1813, but peace still did not reign in this coveted port, and Confederate and Federal troops battled here during the 1860s. Finally, in 1865, the Federal forces besieged the surrounding forts and the Confederates surrendered.

Mobile still retains much of the atmosphere of the Old South. Pre-Civil War architecture is well represented and many of the city's historic buildings are open to visitors. Among them is Fort Condé, on Royal Street. Originally built in 1724, the fort

Gulfport's superb beaches stretch for miles. Glittering white sands palm trees and blue, blue sea and sky form a tropical paradise

was used successively by French, Spanish, British and American troops. It has been restored to look as it did in its French colonial days, and houses a museum illustrating the fort's history.

Fort Condé-Charlotte House, in Theatre Street, was built in 1822 and named after two forts in Mobile. It is worth a visit to see its 18th- and 19th-century European and American furnishings.

On North Joachim Street, in De Toni Square, is Richards-DAR House, an Italianate town house built around 1860. Elaborate ironwork and lavish period furnishings are particular attractions. There is a formal garden, and a guide service.

At 350 Oakleigh Place is the splendid Oakleigh Mansion, built by slaves in 1833. Period furnishings and antiques are supplemented by a display of Civil War relics.

Among interesting places of worship in Mobile is the Catholic Cathedral of the Immaculate Conception on Claiborne Street. One of the oldest churches in the city, it occupies the site used by the first settlers as a burial ground.

As at New Orleans, the early French settlers handed down the custom of celebrating Mardi Gras, and it is still a significant festival in Mobile. Celebrations begin as early as November, and a ball is

Steeped in the atmosphere of the Old South, Beauvoir, the home of Confederate President Jefferson Davis, is now a museum

The Mississippi Gulf

held every week until Ash Wednesday. The major festivities are confined to the two weeks before Lent, when there are evening parades by different mystic societies.

Mobile has a number of unusual and interesting museums, admission to all of which is free. On Government Street, the Museum of the City of Mobile, in a restored 1872 town house, has memorabilia portraying the history of the seaport, as well as a fascinating collection of horse-drawn carriages. Vehicles of a different kind are featured in the Phoenix Fire Museum on Claiborne Street, where the history of firefighting in Mobile is displayed.

The Fine Arts Museum of the South, on Museum Drive, has a collection of 19th- and 20th-century American art, southern decorative arts, African art and a contemporary crafts display. The museum is attractively situated on the south shore of the lake in Langan Park.

Beautiful parks and gardens are characteristic of the Mobile area, for many exotic plants thrive in the warm, humid Gulf climate. Bienville Square, named after the founder of Mobile, is known for its azaleas, and there is a specially planned azalea trail through the city's residential areas. It winds for 35 miles through streets lined with glorious blooms from February to May, and is marked out with signposts and pink lines.

The huge natural harbour that has made Mobile such a coveted site over the centuries is still responsible for much of what makes the city tick today. It is Alabama's only seaport, and its huge docks are owned and run by the state. One of the largest dry docks and shipbuilding centres on the Gulf, it was responsible for the construction, conversion and repair of many naval craft during the Second World War. Most of its other industries are associated with the busy docks, including petroleum refineries, paper mills, chemical works and food processing plants.

A number of places of interest lie just outside Mobile, or are easily reached on a day trip from the city. Leaving in an easterly direction, one of the first attractions you will reach — about two-and-a-half miles out on US 90 via the Bankhead Tunnel — is the USS *Alabama* Battleship Memorial. It is dedicated to the men of Alabama who served in the

Second World War. Visitors may tour the decks, turrets, berthing compartments, messes, captain's cabin, bridge and wardroom. A bonus is a visit to the torpedo rooms and the crew's quarters on the USS *Drum*, a submarine docked alongside.

Further along US 90, at Malbis, is the Greek Orthodox Malbis Memorial Church. A striking copy of a Byzantine church in Athens, its interior is adorned by lovely mosaics and murals. The furnishings include a hand-carved white marble pulpit and altar.

Further away from the city are two forts — Morgan and Gaines — that were constructed to guard the seaward end of Mobile Bay. Both were of great strategic importance in the Civil War. At Mobile Point, 21 miles west of Gulf Shores and on the east side of the bay, is Fort Morgan. This Confederate stronghold surrendered in 1864 after an 18-day siege following the Battle of Mobile Bay. It is now preserved as a historic site.

The other stronghold, Fort Gaines, stands on Dauphin Island, on the western side of the bay. Visited by the Spanish as early as the 16th century, this island was later settled by the French before they moved to the mainland. After 200 years of being devoted to military purposes, the island has now been developed as a resort, offering boating and fishing facilities and superb beaches. Until 1979 the island could be reached by a bridge, but this was destroyed by Hurricane Frederick in 1979, and a ferry service now operates while the bridge is being rebuilt.

From Mobile drive south on Interstate 10 and US 90 to Theodore, then take County Route 59 for a total of 20 miles to Bellingrath Gardens.

Bellingrath Gardens, Alabama

Once a tropical jungle, these 65-acre gardens are now a year-round blaze of landscaped colour. Azaleas (250,000 of them) flower from February to April, followed

by mountain laurel, dogwood and spirea. May sees the blooming of hydrangeas and gardenias and a host of annuals steals the scene in summer. Chrysanthemums come into their own from October to December, with camellias blooming from September right through to April. Giant live oaks heavy with bearded Spanish moss are an appropriate backdrop (see under New Iberia, p.100).

The brick and wrought-iron mansion contains the Bessie Morse Bellingrath collection of antique furniture, Dresden and Meissen porcelain, silver, crystal and oriental rugs. More porcelains — Boehm this time — are displayed in the gallery.

Continue south on County Route 59, then turn right on to State Route 188 and drive for about 20 miles to Interstate 10. Drive west on Interstate 10 for about 27 miles, then turn right on to State Route 57. After 3 miles, rejoin Interstate 10 and continue west for about 90 miles to New Orleans.

The landscaped acres of Bellingrath Gardens retain something of the primeval atmosphere of the jungle they once were. Paths and bridges make even the remote parts of the gardens easily accessible to visitors

The Blue Bayous
of Acadiana

2 days — 335 miles

New Orleans — Chalmette National Historical Park — Houma —
Thibodaux — New Iberia — Avery Island — St Martinville —
Lafayette — Baton Rouge — Plaquemine — New Orleans.

Lazy, lost bayous set the easy pace in Acadiana, west of New Orleans. A bayou is a stretch of water which has wandered away from, or been left behind by a slow-flowing main river — in this case the Mississippi. Filled with swamp grass and patrolled by alligators, the sleepy blue bayous meander from Lafayette down to the Gulf Coast. Highways tend to follow this sinuous trail. Dozens of little towns, each with its own festival, pepper the route, and a number of cities boast spectacular gardens and the stately, colonnaded, sugar-plantation mansions, so evocative of the Deep South. Sugar was as much the staple crop of Louisiana as cotton was in Georgia or tobacco in Virginia. Plantations were almost self-sufficient communities, with countless slaves supplying both skilled and unskilled labour. After 1865, when the Southern states lost the Civil War, and the slaves were freed, many of the great plantations fell into disrepair.

On the way out of downtown New Orleans, make a detour by taking State Route 46 for about 10 miles south-east to Chalmette National Historical Park.

Chalmette National Historical Park, Louisiana
The last significant struggle between the United States and Great Britain, known as the Battle of New Orleans (see p.86) took place on 8 January 1815 at Chalmette Battlefield. It enabled America to expand into the territories west of the Mississippi, and General Andrew Jackson, the American commander, became a national hero and ultimately President. Nearly 2000 British troops were casualties.

Information on the strategies of the battle is available at the visitors' centre at Beauregard

Plantation House. A tour of the battlefield includes Chalmette National Cemetery.

Retrace your path and join US 90, driving along it for about 46 miles east to Houma.

Houma, Louisiana
On the Intracoastal Canal, Houma is sustained by the shrimps and oysters taken from the waters of the Gulf. Local seafood-packing plants may be toured during mornings in summer, and tours of the US Sugarcane Experimental Station are also available by appointment.

Drive north-east on State Route 24 for about 12 miles to Thibodaux.

Beauregard Plantation House, a magnificent mansion, is now the Visitor Center at Chalmette Park

Thibodaux, Louisiana
This sugar-belt town is on peaceful Bayou Lafourche. It was the first trading post established between New Orleans and Bayou Teche, and was incorporated in 1838. A beautiful plantation, among many in the area, is Rienzi, which dates from 1796. It can be seen across the bayou, but is not open to the public.

West of Thibodaux is the heart of the Bayou Country where highways are very labyrinthine.

Take State Route 20 to Morgan City, 30 miles away, then follow US 90 for 29 miles to New Iberia.

New Iberia, Louisiana
This thriving town is the centre of the sugar-cane industry, and stands on the romantic Bayou Teche, which flows as its name suggests — it is Indian for 'snake'. The first French and Spanish settlers came here in the late 18th century, but the population was boosted in the 1830s when New Iberia became the terminus for steamboats travelling up the bayou from New Orleans. Yellow fever wiped out over a quarter of the population in 1839, but New Iberia went on to become a Confederate training centre in the Civil War and is now one of the chief towns in 'Cajun Country'. The present population are descendants of the Spanish, the French and the Acadians, or 'Cajuns' — French Canadian immigrants. Known as the 'sugar bowl of Louisiana', the area is famous for its stately old mansions, several of which are owned and maintained by the National Trust for Historical Preservation.

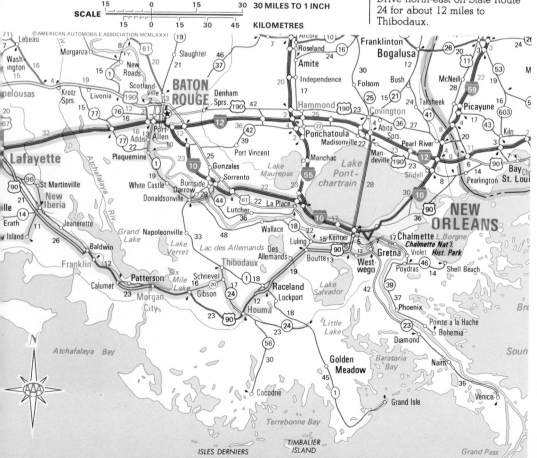

The Blue Bayous

In the heart of town, at 117 E. Main St, is Shadows-on-the-Teche, a beautifully preserved, vintage 1830 plantation mansion. The house was built for David Weeks, a wealthy planter, and its architecture and furnishings reflect the classical taste which was so fashionable in the mid 19th century. Moss-draped trees and a captivating garden of camellias, orchids, and other flowering shrubs, lead to a lawn which slopes down to the Bayou Teche.

Seven miles south of town are Live Oak Gardens, which are landscaped in the English manner and take their name from the live oak, an evergreen species native to America's west coast, and common in the Deep South. A marked trail takes in some of these huge, ancient oaks, as well as other delightful wooded areas, exotic flowering shrubs, fountains and a Japanese Tea House and Garden.

Just outside the town are two islands formed by salt domes which were elevated from the sea-level marshlands millions of years ago. You can watch salt being mined here. To the east of New Iberia, at 401 Main St, Loreauville, is the Heritage Museum, which depicts the history of the area around Bayou Teche. The outdoor museum is arranged like a village with different sections depicting Indian, Spanish, Acadian and early 20th-century American life.

Drive south for about 7 miles on State Route 329, over a toll bridge to Avery Island.

Avery Island, Louisiana

This island standss on an enormous salt dome, which in parts is within 12ft of the surface. The oldest rock-salt mine in the Western Hemisphere is to be found here. The dominant name on Avery Island is McIlhenny — the name of the man who used the fiery local peppers in his secret recipe for the manufacture of the now world-famous Tabasco sauce.

100

Luxuriant gardens surround Shadows-on-the-Teche, a handsome 19th-century plantation mansion on the banks of Bayou Teche at New Iberia, in the Louisiana 'sugar bowl' area

The company is still run by his descendants, who cultivate and harvest the peppers and make the sauce to the original recipe. Guided tours of the old, ivy-clad factory are available.

A legacy of Edward Avery McIlhenny is the Jungle Gardens and Bird Sanctuary, off State Route 329. Three hundred acres of landscaped gardens and exotic blooms may be enjoyed in winter and spring. The Chinese Garden has a Buddha that is almost 1000 years old. The bird sanctuary is famous for its colony of egrets. Enormous flocks of herons can be seen here in summer, and ducks and other migrating fowl appear in winter.

Avery Island is now the primary US producer of coypu fur, following the escape of some domestic animals which proceeded to overpopulate the bayous.

Return north on State Route 329 for 7 miles and follow signs for about another 7 miles to St Martinville.

St Martinville, Louisiana

One of the oldest and most charming places in Louisiana, this small town was settled in the 18th century by Acadians and French refugees. Many French aristocrats who fled their homeland during the Revolution settled here, and St Martinville — once nicknamed 'Le petit Paris' — became a centre of fashionable living and culture, where sumptuously dressed nobles attended balls and operas. In Main Street is the Musée du petit Paris, which takes its theme from these days of elegance. Housed in an 18th-century building that was once a men's college is an interesting collection illustrating the life of those early French

aristocratic refugees, together with Mardi Gras costumes, antiques, coats of arms and general memorabilia connected with the Bayou Teche region.

More coats of arms of the early French aristocracy, and records dating from 1760 to 1815, may be seen at the old Courthouse.

St Martinville is steeped in tributes to Longfellow's fictitious Indian princess Evangeline. Evangeline Oak, on the bayou at the end of Port Street, is claimed to be the most photographed tree in America. It was here that the princess is said to have met her lover, and where she docked her boat on completion of her long journey from Nova Scotia. The character of Evangeline is thought to have been modelled on Emmeline Labiche, whose grave can still be seen beside St Martin's Catholic Church. A life-size bronze statue of Evangeline in the churchyard was modelled on Dolores del Rio, who played the film role of the Indian princess. The statue was donated to the town in 1929 by the company who made the film.

St Martin's Church itself is the mother church of the Acadians, and one of the oldest in the state. It was established in 1765 and rebuilt in 1832. The original box pews can still be seen inside, and there is also a replica of the Grotto of Lourdes, and a baptismal font which was a gift from Louis XVI.

A visit to the Grand Encore Bluff, high above Red River, will enable you to capture the scene where Evangeline took her life on learning that her lover had married another.

To the north of the town, on State Route 31 is the Longfellow-Evangeline State Commemorative Area, a large and beautiful park on the banks of the Bayou Teche. Many Acadians settled in this region after they were driven out of Nova Scotia in the 1760s. The 18th-century building that is now the Acadian House Museum is said to ahve been the home of Louis Arceneaux, the 'Gabriel' of Longfellow's poen. Displays of Acadian life and exhibits of coats of arms of the early French aristocracy are on view in the museum and the *cuisine* (outdoor kitchen) and *magazin* (storehouse) may also be toured. The 'Cajun cabin' houses a gift shop, and there are camping facilities, picnicking areas, a restaurant and a pool in the grounds.

Take State Route 96 for about 4 miles and join US 90 for 11 miles to Lafayette.

Lafayette, Louisiana

This city — the undisputed centre of Acadiana — was founded by some of the first French exiles who arrived here from Nova Scotia in

the 18th century.

In February and March Lafayette is the scene of the Azalea Trail festivities, when plantation homes throughout the area are open to the public and thousands of azaleas burst into bloom.

The Lafayette Museum, on Lafayette Street, occupies a fine early 19th-century town house with square columns and two galleries. It contains period furnishings, Mardi Gras costumes and heirlooms. Other museums in the town include the Natural History Museum and Planetarium, and the Southwest Louisiana Art Center, which features a fine collection of 19th-century paintings and many works by local artists.

The 800-acre campus of the University of South-west Louisiana has a Maison Acadienne, which is dedicated to preserving French and Acadian traditions.

Lafayette is also the home of the Live Oak Society. Trees must be over 100 years old to qualify, and membership dues are 25 acorns a year!

One of the chief attractions of the Lafayette area is the Acadian Village and Tropical Garden. Situated three miles south of Lafayette off Interstate 10, the village is reached by following signs through Scott. Here, in a typical setting beside a sleepy bayou, an authentic Cajun village has been reconstructed to reflect the life of the early exiles. Visitors can stroll through the village and see the general store, the trading post, a blacksmith's shop and a number of 19th-century homes. The buildings contain furniture, clothes and tools that belonged to

An Acadian village, portraying the old Cajun way of life, has been reconstructed near Lafayette

be found in the area around St Francisville, north of Baton Rouge. The finest of them, set in magnificent formal gardens designed by the French landscape gardener, Le Notre, is Rosedown. The house, built in the neoclassical style, contains its original furnishings. Mount Hope Plantation, dating from 1817 and only five minutes' drive from Baton Rouge on Highland Road, is considered to be one of Louisiana's best restorations. This classic example of southern architecture and plantation life is exquisitely furnished in the Federal Sheraton and Empire styles. A similar house, built in the late 18th century, Magnolia Mound, can be seen on Nicholson Drive in Baton Rouge itself.

Drive south for about 10 miles on State Route 1 to Plaquemine.

Plaquemine, Louisiana
The Chapel of the Madonna, between Point Pleasant and Bayou Goula on State Route 168, is the most interesting feature of this small town. The tiny building contains an altar and five chairs, with just enough room to accommodate a priest and an acolyte during Mass. The congregation have to stay outside. An Italian immigrant built the chapel single-handed in the hope that the Virgin Mary would cure his desperately ill child.

On Martin Street, the Carriage House Museum is full of historical exhibits. Also of interest in Plaquemine is the City Hall. Built as a parish courthouse in 1849, the fine old building has served as the City Hall since 1906.

Continue south on State Route 1 for about 20 miles, cross the Intracoastal Canal toll-bridge and drive north-east to Interstate 10. Turn right on to the highway and drive for 36 miles to New Orleans.

Baton Rouge takes pride in its past. This historic site recalls the Indians who first settled here

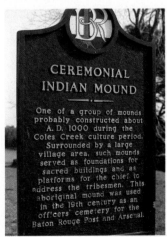

early settlers in the Bayou country. The chapel at New Hope in the centre is the hub of fund-raising activity for the Alleman Center for Louisiana's handicapped citizens. The Around-the-World Tropical Gardens are also a part of the Alleman Center. Different gardens are devoted to representative plants from various hot areas of the world — the semi-tropical US, Latin America, Asia, Africa and the Pacific Islands.

Drive east on Interstate 10 for 38 miles to Baton Rouge.

Baton Rouge, Louisiana
This gracious city of lakes, bayous, 19th-century mansions, winding drives and magnolias is the capital of Louisiana. Smaller and less internationally famous than New Orleans, it is nevertheless a vigorous commercial and retail centre. Its docks on the Mississippi can accommodate the largest ocean-going vessels, many of which carry local sugar cane to all parts of the world. The city has been possessed by a variety of European nations — English, French and Spanish influences still alive in the town are a fascinating reminder of its chequered past.

On State Capitol Avenue is America's tallest state capitol, rising 34 floors above pleasant formal gardens. An excellent introduction to Baton Rouge is to go up to the observation tower, which gives a dramatic view of the city and the Mississippi. Free tours of the first floor include the spot where Huey P. Long (Governor of Louisiana when this

building was constructed) was assassinated. Murals, statuary, bas-relief on huge brass doors and the magnificent Marble Hall, constructed with marble from all parts of the globe, are other star attractions. A sunken garden in the grounds contains the grave of Huey P. Long, and his statue stands beside it.

On Lafayette Street and North Boulevard is the Gothic-style Old State Capitol. Built in 1847 and resembling a Norman castle, it was burned by the Union Army, but was later repaired and restored. Of particular interest inside is a vast spiral staircase which winds up to a spectacular stained-glass dome with a prison skylight. Outside is a hand-wrought iron fence. At the base of the staircase is the Baton Rouge Tourist Information Center. Excellent exhibits of contemporary art may be seen in the old Senate and House chambers.

Reminiscent of *Gone with the Wind,* across the lake from the capitol, is the Governor's Mansion. Built in 1963 as a replica of a lavish plantation mansion, it is open for free tours by appointment.

The old Governor's Mansion Museum, built in 1930 by Huey P. Long, is now the Louisiana Arts and Science Center, exhibiting art, natural history and anthropology. Furnished with fine antiques, each room is dedicated to the memorabilia of a particular Louisiana governor. Adjacent to the museum, also on North Boulevard, is a planetarium. Housed in a magnificent old railway station beside the river is the Riverside Museum. A part of

The Governor's Mansion at Baton Rouge was not built until 1963, but is a faithful copy of traditional Southern architecture

the Arts and Science Center, this museum has fine art exhibits, a genuine mummy and a graphic three-dimensional display which illustrates the channel changes of the Mississippi. You may also savour Creole cuisine in the restaurant. A 1918 steam engine and other vintage railway relics are on display next to the museum.

On the heights overlooking the river is Southern University — the nation's largest predominantly Black university. Three miles south of the town is the Louisiana State University campus. In the base of the Memorial Tower at the centre of the campus is an information centre and the Anglo-American Art Museum which includes portrait and silver collections. Foster Hall contains the Museum of Natural Science, which has life-size dioramas of Louisiana wildlife scenes and many other natural history displays. The Geoscience Museum, also on the campus, exhibits archaeological finds from the historic Bayou Jasmin Site as well as Indian folklore relics.

On Thomas Rock is the fascinating Baton Rouge Zoo. Over 500 animals from six continents live in natural settings in this 140-acre wooded expanse with its picturesque walkways. Trains and trams are available for those who prefer not to walk.

Numerous splendid colonnaded southern plantation homes are to

Between the Atlantic Ocean and Biscayne Bay stretches the ten-mile-long island of Miami Beach, where luxury hotels stand shoulder to shoulder

Miami

Miami is, for many European tourists, their first encounter with America. The warmth of the welcome, the heat of the sun and the convenience of America's lifestyle often come as a surprise, and always make an impact on the holidaymaker.

Miami is not, of course, Blackpool, Benidorm, or even Nice. Miami is essentially an American resort, much favoured by sun-seeking Americans from the north in mid-winter, and overrun by British and other Europeans when the sub-tropical climate is at its fiercest in mid-summer. As a tourist resort, Miami developed quite recently. The fierce

Seminole Indians, the alligator-infested swamps of the Everglades, the danger of hurricanes and the remoteness of the Florida peninsula from America's centres of commerce, all held development back until the twentieth century. However, Florida's superb climate and a stunning coastline of golden beaches, azure seas, and a ribbon of dazzling islands, finally assured its place as a holiday paradise.

'See it like a Native' urge the Miami tourist promoters, as their slogan for welcoming visitors. But the truth is that Miami offers such a choice of entertainment, and activities geared to the holidaymaker, that no native could ever be expected to see the place in quite the same way as the tourist is invited to see it.

As most tourists fly into Miami just to soak up the Florida sun on the first beach they can find, many of them are surprised to discover that Miami itself has virtually no beach, but Miami Beach, the narrow, ten-mile-long island just off the coast, which is linked to the mainland by five causeways, has a magnificent beach — thanks to the United States Army Corps of Engineers. Towards the end of the 1970s, a whole army of soldiers laboured for two years to deposit 13,500,000 cubic yards of crisp white sand on the beach, in order to repair the ravages of seventy years of folly, during which hotels and houses were built too close to the coastline. At a cost of more than £30,000,000, they rolled back the Atlantic, and in place of the pathetic ribbon of desert waste, an unbroken highway of shimmering sand, nine-and-a-half

miles long and 100 yards wide, now stretches away towards the horizon. Although parts of the beach in the height of the season can become crowded, there is enough sand for everyone to have all the freedom and space he needs.

Some stretches of beach are still, as in parts of Europe, controlled by the major hotels that line the front, and are reserved for residents, but most of the new beach is accessible from the road and freely available. Some beaches are more secluded than others, some have more facilities, such as sunshades, refreshment kiosks, public conveniences (called 'restrooms' or 'comfort stations'). All parts have an undiluted, unrationed supply of sunshine, balmy winds and warm, docile waters (see the box on p.107 for details of beaches).

In comparison, the city of Miami has only

Downtown Miami's waterfront marina is transformed by night into a dazzling display of green and gold

two modest stretches of sand, far down in the south-east corner of the town. Attached to the parks, they concentrate more on recreational provisions, such as boating and swimming. Miami's inhabitants prefer the beaches to be found on Key Biscayne, the most easily accessible of the numerous islands — or 'keys', as they are known — dotted around the Florida peninsula. The only way on and off Key Biscayne is the Rickenbacker Causeway, a four-mile link from the mainland to this idyllic pleasure island. First discovered in 1497 by the explorer John Cabot, the island was left to its own devices (and they included several Indian uprisings) until 1902 when a New York businessman, William James Matheson, bought an estate, built a house on it, and established an extensive coconut-palm plantation. He lived there with his family until 1947 when, with the opening of the $10,000,000 bridge, he lost his privacy and packed his bags. Now everything on the island is geared for holiday and leisure. The two-mile-long coastline is split into seven beach areas, including a secluded stretch for nude bathing. Swimming, water sports of all kinds, fishing, cycling, and golf are just some of the activities available, but there are also several colossal spectator attractions. Among them, Planet Ocean displays all manner of underwater phenomena (see p.114). Another dramatic, aquatic diversion on Key Biscayne is the Seaquarium, a sixty-acre park with a spectacular killer-whale show in which daring performers ride on the backs of Lolita and Hugo, two four-ton whales. Porpoises, dolphins and sharks also help to while away an entertaining two hours. Then there are the delights of Bill Bagg's Cape Florida State Recreation Area. Named after a former editor of the *Miami News,* an avid conservationist, it is situated on 900 acres on the south tip of Key Biscayne. Other public attractions are a zoo with 1200 animals and a marine stadium which can hold 6500 people during regattas and other water shows.

Despite this concentration of entertainment on Key Biscayne it is in Miami and Miami Beach that the serious business of amusing the tourist is relentlessly pursued. And like a gigantic holiday camp, the city and its rival beach resort do the job very thoroughly. In truth, neither has anything special to offer apart from the sunshine and the beaches. All along the southern Florida coastline — known as the Gold Coast (see the Motor Tour on pp.115-7) — golden beaches fringe wealthy communities like Fort Lauderdale and Palm Beach, while hotels of shining opulence and splendour vie for the custom of holidaymakers. Offshore, the magnificent Overseas Highway linking the Florida Keys, is beckoning, too.

The most southerly part of the United States, Key West, is only ninety miles from Cuba, and has become, in the last twenty years, a kind of transit station for Latin-American refugees. Miami's population of 350,000 still reflects the desperate political consequences of Fidel Castro's regime in Cuba. Since he came to power, more than 200,000 Cubans have found refuge in Miami. Dade County, the Metropolitan area of Miami and Miami Beach had a population of 1,600,000 at the end of 1980 and the total Latin population was around 700,000. Unfortunately, among the Cuban refugees are a number of ex-criminals released and expelled by Castro to reduce his 'overheads'. This has

Aquatic stars such as Flipper, the performing dolphin, can be seen at Miami's spectacular Seaquarium

understandably led to anxiety about the rising crime rate in the city, and over the last few years, Miami's immigration problems have been aggravated by the infiltration of drug smugglers from Central American countries — notably Colombia. There are areas of the city mostly the poorer quarters, and especially the 'Liberty City' area, where it is definitely inadvisable for tourists to go, even in daylight. However, most of the Cubans, Haitians and other Latin-American newcomers fit well into the community. Hard-working and clannish to the point of being insular, the Cubans have settled in a few streets centred on 8th

Street in the south-east section of town — known as Little Havana — and turned the area within a few years into a thriving community of restaurants, shops and offices. Here you can experience the strident and colourful atmosphere of the Caribbean — and sample dishes that you would never find on a restaurant menu at home. Here your nostrils are constantly assailed by the exotic aromas of Cuban delicacies, one of the most lingering being pork yucca con mojo — meat in a savoury sauce, heavy with garlic and sharpened with bitter orange juice, banana and fresh black Cuban coffee. More than half the population of Dade County — the administrative area of Miami — was born in a Latin country. The most bilingual city in the States, Miami even sells America's ubiquitous snack — the hot dog — under the Spanish name of

Miami

perro caliente, a literal translation.

It was the Indians, however, who were the original inhabitants of Florida, and all around Miami are remains of their settlements. Miami itself is just a fledgling: when America celebrated its bicentennial in 1976, Miami was only eighty years old, and it has gone to almost neurotic lengths to ensure that every step in the city's development is recorded and

permanently marked. Dozens of plaques to mark the most notable events have been placed all over the city by the Historical Association of Southern Florida in a campaign to push Miami into the pages of history. Its oldest souvenir is, however, not a local one. The Cloisters of the Monastery of St Bernard, known as the Spanish Monastery, were built by King Alphonso of Spain in 1141 in the province

of Segovia. The monastery's 35,000 stones were shipped over to America in 11,000 crates in 1925. Millionaire newspaper tycoon and inveterate art collector William Randolph Hearst, intended to re-erect it in the grounds of Hearst Castle in California (see p.61). The monastery never reached its destination because the protective hay in the crates was considered to be an animal-health hazard, and the whole consignment was impounded. It remained in Department of Agriculture custody until nearly forty years later, when, in 1964, two South Florida businessmen, having acquired the crates from the Hearst estate, erected the ancient building at 16711 W. Dixie Highway on North Miami Beach. Now it makes a haunting setting for concerts and other musical events.

Miami's earliest recorded event is commemorated in Bayfront Park at the foot of Flagler Street. There a plaque marks the spot where the Tequesta Indians first set up a village — regarded as the first Miami settlement. But it was another Indian tribe, the Calusa, who are said to have given the city its name when they called the river on which Miami now stands, Mayami. Centuries later, the Seminole Indians, encouraged and protected by the Spanish, who owned Florida, settled in the area. The Seminoles had been driven south by the advancing tide of white settlers; a belligerent tribe, they caused so

much trouble by guerilla-style raids across the Florida border that in 1817 and 1818, General Andrew Jackson (see New Orleans) marched into Florida to subdue them. In 1819, by the Continental Treaty, Spain ceded the territory to America, and at the same time relinquished its claim to the Pacific coastlands north of San Francisco. Peace came slowly to Florida, however. In 1836, the American army had to march south once again to quell an uprising. The soldiers established their base at Fort Dallas at the mouth of the Miami River in 1836. When, a few years later, the garrison was recalled, several soldiers stayed behind to chance their luck in wresting a livelihood from the mangroves and swamps of the sub-tropical jungle. What they lacked was efficient means of communication with the markets of the north. Surprisingly, it was a woman who eventually made that link possible, and thereby assured Miami's future. Julia Tuttle, widow of a wealthy Cleveland merchant, and daughter of a

member of Florida's State legislature, had, during her father's lifetime, so enjoyed visiting his homestead eight miles north of the river that in 1890, after his death, she took her two children to live in Florida. At first she set up home in the old Fort Dallas barracks, then she bought 600 acres of land on which to plant orange groves.

Railway and oil magnate Henry Flagler was at that time slowly inching his railway track down the east coast of Florida, but in 1895, when most of the state's crops were destroyed in an unexpected sharp frost, he suddenly abandoned his plans to cut his way right through to the tip of the peninsula. Dismayed, Julia Tuttle sent him a sprig of frost-free orange blossom, picked on her estate the same week, to prove to him that southern Florida enjoyed a much better climate. Hurricanes and tidal waves yes, these Miami had to endure in plenty and when the boats called from Cuba, there was disease, too. But frost, she said, never.

A Guide to Miami's Beaches

With such magnificent beaches all around Miami, sand, sea and sun are certainly not in short supply. While downtown Miami has almost no beaches, there are numerous attractive stretches on Key Biscayne and on Miami Beach. Here is what they offer:

KEY BISCAYNE
Bear's Cut: Two lifeguards patrol the 120-yard beach, where pine trees provide excellent shade, but strong currents make swimming difficult and dangerous. Bike trails and jogging paths wind through the woods behind the beach, but there are no other facilities.
Crandon Park Beach: To serve this four-mile stretch of beach are three food stands, shady palms, 75 barbecue grills, benches for picnickers and three large car parks. Thatched huts can be rented by the day, week, month or even annually. Shower facilities and special ramps to help the disabled get to the water's edge are also provided.
Hobie Beach: Marvellous sandy beaches each side of the Rickenbacker Causeway, but the water is too shallow for good bathing.
Virginia Beach: Soft sand and lots of privacy. Safe for swimming, with three lifeguards on duty. Closed weekdays. Snackbars are too far away to be absolutely convenient, but there are lots of parking spaces.
Virginia Key South: A 'natural' beach, where it is

White sands and azure sky are an all-year-round feature of Miami Beach

possible to drive straight on to the sand.
Virginia Key North: Ideal for naturists, although there are often as many dressed spectators as naked sunbathers. No lifeguards.

MIAMI BEACH
Pier Park: Some of the smoothest waves are to be found here. Ideal for surfers. Free fishing, roller skating and skateboarding on the municipal pier. Toilets and snack bars.
Lummus Park: Smooth, sandy beach and clear water. Huts and palm trees provide shade. Toilets nearby, and a lifeguard on duty.
21st-Street Beach: Where the young congregate. Snackbar selling hamburgers and beer next to car park. Lifeguard and seagulls hover.

35th-Street Beach: Good place for shell hunting. Municipal parking. Lifeguard. Sailboats provide free show in front of Fontainebleau Hilton Hotel.
46th-Street Beach: Good beach is mainly for guests of the Fontainebleau Hilton, the Doral-on-the-Ocean and Eden Roc hotels. Some of the hotels rent boats to non-guests, who can also hire sun chairs, swim in the hotel pool and drink in their outside bars. Toilets are outside too.
53rd and 64th-Street Beach: Two relatively uncrowded beaches, patrolled by lifeguards, away from hotels and shops. Considered to be secluded and discreet. Toilets.
72nd-74th-Street Beach: Good swimming. Municipal parking and plenty of huts for shade.

North Shore Open Space Park: A 'heart' trail for keeping fit consists of 20 stations on the beach, each several hundred feet apart, explaining what exercises to take and when. Toilets adapted for the handicapped.
Surfside: At 93rd Street, the beach's smooth, white sands are perfect for strolling and swimming in uncrowded conditions. Public parking across the street.
Bal Harbour: Colourful shells are found in abundance just a few yards north of Surfside Beach. Palm trees are plentiful. Exercise course.
Haulover Beach Park: Part of the park, this one-and-a-half-mile beach is full of young people who surf, throw frisbees, and fish off the pier. Bait and tackle shop, snack bar, paved walkway for joggers. Palm trees shade the

beach. Barbecue grills available.
Sunny Isles: This two-mile beach is mostly used by guests of the luxury hotels alongside 192nd Street and Sunny Isles Boulevard. But the beach is open to the public.

COPING WITH THE SUN
The Florida sun, especially in summer, is fierce and needs to be treated with respect. Below are a few tips to help you cope with the heat and the sunshine.
1. Invest in a sunhat with a wide brim.
2. Buy a good brand of suntan lotion — and remember to use it after every dip in the sea.
3. Start with half-an-hour's sunbathing — and avoid the hottest part of the day. Build up your sun-tanning periods slowly.
4. Keep tender skin covered in the open and even in overcast conditions. The sun's harmful rays pierce through clouds almost as effectively as when the sky is clear.
5. If you are feeling very hot, don't succumb to the temptation of drinking large quantities of ice-cold drinks quickly. It may give you stomach cramp, or you may even faint. Sip a cool drink slowly until you cool down.
6. Be careful how much alcohol you drink in the heat of the day. Do not rush into the sea immediately after eating a heavy meal — allow two or three hours to elapse before swimming.

Miami

Her gesture did the trick. Flagler's curiosity was aroused and he travelled down to Miami to meet her. A few days later he returned home, convinced that he should spend millions investing in the little village of Miami. In her gratitude, she gave him some of her land. He, in turn, kept his word; nine months after the railroad route had been surveyed, the last section of the track was completed, and on 15 April 1896 the first wood-burning locomotive, carrying a load of building material, chugged into Miami, followed a week later by the first passenger train.

Flagler soon started building a large hotel, clearing streets, and laying water pipes and electric cables; as word went out that there was money to be made in Miami, more and more people converged on the town. The boom was short-lived. By the autumn of 1899, a yellow-fever epidemic brought over in a cattle boat from Cuba, and two enormous fires which destroyed the heart of the city, ruined Miami's immediate prospects of prosperity. For several years the city stagnated. In 1906, by which time a port was being developed, another blow struck the city. A hurricane hit the peninsula and 200 men, working on the railroad across the islands to Key West, were swept into the sea. But the rail-link was nonetheless completed the year before another great Miami landmark was reached — the opening of a two-mile-long wooden bridge between Miami and Miami Beach.

As a sop to the speculators' vanity, the streets of Miami were named after some of them, with the result that several streets carried the same name. To avoid confusion, the city fathers adopted a system already favoured by many American cities — of identifying the streets with numbers as well, but having laid out the entire city in the usual square grid pattern of intersecting streets and avenues, there was still mathematical confusion. The solution was to divide the downtown area according to the points of the compass. The visitor must establish whether the road he wants is in the north-west, north-east, south-west or south-east district, as the number of every road is prefaced with the appropriate initials.

By 1920, Miami was growing fast. Her population was four-and-a-half times greater than it had been ten years earlier. Houses were quickly erected for the new arrivals, and alongside Miami grew the satellite cities of Coral Gables, Hialea and Hollywood. Plots of land that were bought one year could be sold a year later for ten times the original price. Then, once again, a hurricane with winds reaching 138 miles an hour wreaked havoc in Miami. With a death toll of more than 200, and damage estimated at millions of dollars, it must have seemed to many hopeless to start again. But start again they did — this time using modern building materials and designs more suitable to the volatile climatic extremes. Next time a hurricane struck, the city rode the impact better. And though a twenty-foot wall of water overwhelmed the Florida Keys in June 1935, killing nearly 400 workers on a train taking them from the disaster area, the only permanent effect was on the railroad itself. So exposed was it that there was no way the engineers felt it could ever be completely protected against the weather, and three

years later, the Overseas Highway — one of the longest over-water roads in the world — opened on the route that had carried the railway track. For an increasingly automobile-conscious economy, the change was welcomed. Now the affluent holidaymakers could leave their winter homes and drive all the way to Key West. Since 1928 when Pan American Airways first set up a small airfield five miles from Miami on the site of what became, thirty years later, the $26,000,000, 2800-acre Miami International Airport, the tourists have also been flying down to the sun in increasing numbers.

Among the early arrivals there had been several unwelcome guests. In the 1930s, Chicago gangster Al Capone built a lavish home on Palm Island off MacArthur Causeway, and though unpopular, he defied for years all attempts to winkle him out. The first real tourists arrived in Miami at the turn of the century and became known as 'swells' because of their affluence. For a while the city flourished as a gambling centre, attracting unwelcome attention from the Mafia and notorious gangland figures. Eventually gambling was abolished in Miami, but the real-estate boom encouraged the sharp practices of get-rich-quick land speculators.

It is in the winter that Miami has its main holiday season, when temperatures hover around the seventies, the ocean is seldom cooler than 68°F, the air is as pure as nectar, and the atmosphere clean and dry. Thanks to aggressive promotions by airlines, in particular the cut-price fares of Laker, Air Florida and the more enterprising package-tour operators, some of whom have set up in business in Miami, the city is leading the way in the British tourist trade. In 1980, more than 100,000 Britons came to Miami Beach and some 20,000 or more every year expect to catch their first glimpse of the States when they look out of their aircraft window at the Florida coastline. Already there are nearly 500 hotels, 300 motels, and 3000 restaurants in Dade County and $100,000,000 is earmarked to bring older properties up to international hotel standards. In 1980 Miami Beach threw a two-day party, complete with Beefeater Guards, a Shakespearean troupe, jousters and jesters, just to inaugurate the building of a miniature version of Big Ben on the front lawn of the Miami Beach Tourist and Convention Centre on 17th Street.

Summer is when the majority of British tourists converge on Miami, when the heat can often be intolerable and, to paraphrase the famous Noel Coward song — 'only mad dogs and Englishmen go out in the Miami sun.' The British have a repu-

Tourists first came to Florida in the inter-war years. This elegant hotel at Boca Raton is typical of the period

Cycle and Walking Tours

Opportunities for walking and cycling are, like swimming, numerous in the Miami area. Information on the extensive cycling paths and suggested walking routes in Miami, Miami Beach, Coconut Grove and Coral Gables can be obtained from Dade County Parks Department, tel. 579 2672. Several conducted group tours are also available. Jim Ingram runs 'Ride a Bicycle, Inc', from 1286 N.E. 191st St., on North Miami Beach. He hires out the bikes, fitting them, when requested, with the more staid upright handlebars, handlebar bags and seat covers. Setting off from any conveniently located hotel, he first gives his group a short summary on safety and

traffic law, and later points out important landmarks on the route. An example of a 20-mile route is one that crosses Indian Creek via a footbridge, goes north to Pine Tree Park, on to La Gorce Island — a private cluster of multi-million-dollar estates — then along North Bay Road, stopping off at various viewpoints, and west across the Venetian Causeway to downtown Miami via Bayshore Drive. After taking the bike paths laid down in 1976 when the 35-acre Bicentennial Park was built on Biscayne Boulevard to commemorate America's anniversary, the group moves on further south along Biscayne Boulevard to Bayfront Park and to a

dockside restaurant for lunch before returning to Miami Beach for a tour of the Art Deco district.
This last area can be better appreciated on a walking tour. The Miami Design Preservation League, at 1630 Euclid Avenue, Miami Beach, tel. 672 2014, can suggest various routes which will highlight good examples of distinctive 1930s architecture. One tour covers most of Ocean Drive, where the hotels stand shoulder to shoulder, turns west on 14th Street, then goes south down the west side of Collins Avenue, crossing to the east side after the Marlin Hotel to continue south. Other routes follow Ocean Drive, Collins and Washington Avenues.

tation for needing to frequent the Miami hospitals soon after arrival with scorched skin and sunstroke (see the box on p.107 for advice on sun protection). In Miami Beach you can see the American survivors of many years of such reckless over-exposure — their wrinkled faces turned firmly away from direct sunshine, they are now happy to sit out the day in the shade. Many of them came from New York to enjoy retirement under the shady palms. Once affluent, they have since become the victims of inflation and social change, eking out an impoverished existence in a world that has rapidly passed them by.

Like so much of the architecture on Miami Beach, they are what is left of the city's once glorious era of splendour. Between the wars, a battery of buildings with fussy, fluted façades grew up near

the beach — creating a distinctive style later to become known as Art Deco. After World War II, the architectural self-indulgence of the 1930s went out of fashion and the buildings quickly fell into decay. But fashions change, and by the late 1960s, Miami Beach's 800 or so surviving Art Deco buildings, many of them concentrated in a square-mile area, were being enthusiastically revived and restored. Many of the surviving buildings are still hotels and grandiose apartment blocks. All are distinguished by the angular lines of their façades. The elegant sweeping lines of balconies, cornices and gables are said to have expressed the unspoken need in the 1930s for a fast, sophisticated life, in keeping with the jazz age. An ambitious programme of restoration was launched by the Miami

Design Preservation League, a ginger-group of architects, artists and local business people, in the late 1970s, and many of the run-down hotels are now being refurbished inside and out. There is much to preserve: flamboyant courtyards with statues and central fountains and figurines, and lots of bakelite, stainless steel, porcelain-enamelled metals and aluminium decorations often lit by fluorescent and neon lighting.

Bounded by Meridian Avenue to the west, and lying between 8th and 21st Streets, the Art Deco district has been entered in America's historical area register — the first district built in the twentieth century to make the history books. Like the hotels and apartment houses in the district, the shops and restaurants still clinging to the looks and

Horses for Courses

In a city so geared to outdoor holiday pursuits, it is not suprising that horses play a big part in Miami's sporting activities. Horse-racing is one of the most popular attractions, and there are two main race tracks.

HIALEAH PARK, at E.21st St. and E.4th Ave. in Hialeah, is in one of the world's most beautiful settings — a park with formal gardens and coconut palms, Australian pines and, among other tropical birds, a huge flock of flamingoes, covering the park lake in a riot of colour. There is also a museum crammed with racing memorabilia.
CALDER RACE TRACK on 27th Ave, between Miami Gardens Dr. and Hallandale Blvd, has a 10-storey stand with seating for 13,500. The mile-long course is artificially turfed to allow for all-weather

racing, but it is only open between 14 May and 10 November.
To see parts of the city and its environs from a saddle is another popular activity, and the list below gives details of riding centres and schools in the Greater Miami area. As a rough guide, prices have been classified as expensive, moderate or reasonable.

ACTION ACRES: 13700 N.W. 97th Ave, tel. 821 0947. Trail riding, Western and English saddle, summer camp for children, private tuition. Moderate.
CIMARRON ACRES STABLES: 11850 S.W. 64th St, tel. 271 3812. Show instruction, mainly for horse owners. Expensive.
CORAL GABLES RIDING ACADEMY: 6000 S.W. 123 Ave, tel. 271 2251. Private tuition, English saddle. Moderate.

COUNTRY GENTLEMAN STABLES: 15500 Quail Roost Dr, tel. 233 6615. Trail riding, English and Western saddle, group instruction. Reasonable.

EXECUTIVE TRAINING CENTRE: 6201 S.W. 122nd

Ave, tel. 274 3923. English saddle, private tuition. Expensive.
GOLDEN EAGLES RANCH: 41 S.W. 122nd Ave, tel. 221 4312. Trail riding, Western saddle. Moderate.
HUNTING HORN STABLE: 12200 Miller Rd, tel. 223

3133. Private tuition, English and Western saddle, group instruction. Expensive.

QUAIL ROOST RANCH: 15400 Quail Roost Rd, tel. 253 3308. Private tuition, trail rides, English and Western saddle. Moderate.

Fish and chips — that peculiarly un-American speciality — is becoming increasingly popular, thanks to Arthur Treacher's chain of fast-food restaurants. In Miami, with its large British tourist population, the quality of the fish and chips is particularly vulnerable to criticism. The average portion is modestly priced, but has certain peculiarities the British might find hard to swallow — for instance five-inch long chips cut like railway sleepers, and batter which, though dry and tasty, is iron-hard. You can also sample Hush-Puppies — deep-fried rolls of onion flavoured cornmeal, the sort used for stuffing poultry. The staff, in brown 'Andy Capp' caps and tight-fitting brown jeans look more like latter-day members of the Dead End Kids gang than waiters, but are wonderfully cheerful and helpful.

If the visitor tires of sunbathing and sampling local delicacies, opportunities for shopping abound. Bal Harbour, for example, claims to be one of the world's most expensive shopping complexes. So select is this 600ft-long, three-storey repository of the finest merchandise of internationally renowned shops such as Cartier's, Neiman-Marcus, Saks Fifth Avenue, Gucci, Guy Laroche, Ted Lapidus and about fifty others, that it has attracted wealthy people from America, Canada and South America in particular, to buy property in the village of Bal Harbour. Now the community supports six luxury hotels, and thirty-six blocks of

The distinctive façades (left) of the 1930s hotels in the Art Deco district of Miami Beach, now designated historic monuments

Stucco-walled houses are reminders that Florida's history stretches back to the days of the Spanish Conquistadores

likes of fashions thirty or forty years ago are now all the rage again. Washington Avenue, for instance, the main artery of the Art Deco district, is full of small, old-fashioned shops, and eating places. The best known is The Famous Restaurant which lives up to its name by offering traditional Jewish fare as it has done for more than fifty years to a predominantly Jewish community. Older still is Joe's Stone Crab Restaurant, which claims to be the oldest eating house in Miami Beach, established in 1913 in Biscayne Street. A eulogy was once written about its stone crabs by the famous American short-story writer Damon Runyon. Joe's is only open between October and April when the stone crabs, a larger and harder species of crustaceans than are found elsewhere in the States, are in season. Collected by owner Joe Weiss and his staff in his own boats and from his own private fishing ground off the coast, 1000lbs of stone crabs are consumed every day by a

fanatical coterie of gourmets who crowd out the restaurant from mid-morning for lunch and from 5pm for dinner. As only the meat of the claws is edible, the body is put back in the sea and regenerates itself. The business of eating them is a ritual demanding patience and a technique more elaborate than that for dealing with undressed crabs or lobsters in their shell. A paper bib is ceremoniously tied round your neck by the waiter, who is quickly on first-name terms. The dish of a dozen boiled crabs (they are always caught the same day, and cannot be successfully frozen) is brought to the table in a steel plate with a steel side-plate, and shells are cracked with a mallet. A dish of melted butter helps to mess up the fingers. One of Miami's most fashionable and delightful places to eat is Food Among the Flowers (see the Miami Directory). The restaurant, on N.E. 36th Street, is filled with fragrant blooms, and there is a flower shop adjacent to the dining room.

luxury flats. Past the line of Rolls Royces and Mercedes Benzes parked in the driveway of the shopping precinct, is a palm-lined courtyard with over 100 flowering orange trees, bushes, shrubs and fountains. A bevy of attractive attendants in tropical white uniforms can show you the way to your favourite temple of extravagance. Bal Harbour's motto — 'There is nothing like a little something from Bal Harbour' nicely understates the fact that you can pay anything between $10 (£4), and $100,000 (£40,000) for the privilege of buying a little something at Bal Harbour.

Of course it has its competitors, too. Just off South Dixie Highway at S.W. 136th Street, the Falls, described as the largest environmental shopping, dining and entertainment complex in the United States, is laid out around a waterfall, and wooden bridges lead from one shopping area to another. The decor resembles a rustic village surrounded by a tropical rain forest. There are more than fifty speciality shops, boutiques and restaurants set in frontages of split cedar and rough-sawn timber. Omni, on Biscayne Boulevard, is massive, with 165 stores, 21 restaurants, 6 cinemas, an amusement centre and a crèche, as well as a 20-storey, 556-roomed luxury hotel on the site. Of special interest to British tourists is Pompano Fashion Square thirty miles north of Miami Beach, because it is owned, implausible though it seems, by the British Coal Industry's Pension Fund. Its American subsidiary, Pan American Properties, bought the shopping area with its 100 shops for about £15,000,000 early in 1980, as an investment. Although West Flagler Street, Washington Avenue, in Miami Beach, and Collins Avenue, which runs the length of the island, are all full of small quaint shops, high-class boutiques, and modest one-man businesses (one of the smallest of them proclaiming that it has the 'largest selection of swimwear in the world'), the shops in Coconut Grove and Coral Gables cater for more specialized tastes, and are worth sampling.

Coconut Grove, lying in the south-west of the city, is a popular haunt of artists. Its classy Mayfair shopping centre, built like a fairground castle, looks out of place, for its papier-mâché appearance contrasts sharply with the Greenwich Village or

Thirty acres of formal gardens surround the Vizcaya-Dade County Art Museum

Chelsea atmosphere in the streets. Inside the three-storey building are elegant, wrought-iron winding staircases, brick walkways, mahogany ceilings, sculptures, plant pots overflowing with lush tropical foliage, fountains, reflecting pools and waterfalls in unlikely nooks and crannies. The forty-seven shops are high-class and generally expensive. The Grove itself is not. Site of the first permanent Miami settlement, it has an attractive mixture of early twentieth-century farm houses, and Colonial ranch- and Tudor English-style cottages, many built from shipwreck timber. You can shop here for local pottery, hand-painted cloth and all manner of artwork.

Unlike Coconut Grove, Coral Gables, with a population of 42,000, is a city in its own right. Adjoining Miami to the south-west, it was built in Spanish-Colonial style. Aggressively proud of its independence and its attraction to big business since it was founded in the early part of

the century, it manages to retain a tolerable balance between the architectural disciplines of the modern buildings and its inheritance of a clutch of homesteads built out of the coral rock under its foundations. Look out for high archways, fountains, squares, miles of tree-lined boulevards, and a seemingly endless parade of shops along Miracle Mile, specializing in high fashion, art and Cuban and Haitian food. Coral Gables's municipal pride and joy is the Venetian Pool, promoted as 'the world's most beautiful swimming hole' — a claim hard to accept, but impossible to dispute. Built out of coral rock in the 1920s to represent a Venetian lagoon, with grottos, shady porticoes, and vine-covered loggias, it still encourages a 'flapper era' mood among the 200,000 visitors who arrive each year; many do not even come to swim, preferring to wander in the landscaped grounds. Despite its strong Spanish influence, the city is cosmopoli-

All Creatures Great and Small

Since hunting them was banned in the mid 1960s, alligators have multiplied so dramatically in southern Florida that people even claim to have seen them in the streets of Miami, but the stories you hear of people being chased by hungry alligators are probably apocryphal. The only unfamiliar creatures you are

likely to encounter on the beaches are sandflies. They bite like mosquitoes, and may need to be discouraged with a suitable repellent. Mosquitoes are very prevalent in the Everglades, and precautions should be taken against them. Poisonous snakes are rare in built-up areas, but you are likely to see harmless multi-

coloured lizards from time to time in the bushes. The most unwelcome — though quite harmless insect — is the cockroach. Large, hard-shelled and always too conspicuous, the palmetto bug, as it is called, appears unexpectedly and is unpleasant to dispose of. The best course is to ignore it and it will wander away.

Miami

tan. It accommodates a Chinese village, three French villages, (in differing regional styles) and even a Dutch-South African village. They are all situated between Le Jeune Road, which separates Miami from Coral Gables, and the main campus of the University of Miami.

The University's three campuses — the others are in downtown Miami and on Virginia Key, a small island to the north of Key Biscayne — accommodate 18,000 students in 150 buildings. Founded in 1926, it attracts sixty-four per cent of its student body from outside Florida and since 1926 has built up a strong musical tradition, forming its first symphony orchestra in its first year. Its school of music has seventy-two different ensembles, at least one of which performs on nearly every day of the year. The university's Gussman Concert Hall at the corner of Flagler Street and S.E. 2nd Avenue, has a forty-week season of music and theatre presentations. Other musical

The average visitor spends a total of 9 hours at Walt Disney World, Florida's version of the California Disneyland

events take place at the Dade County Auditorium, north of West Flagler Street, and at the Miami Beach Theater of the Performing Arts on Washington Avenue. There is a 2900-seat auditorium attracting Broadway shows, concerts by the Florida Philharmonic Orchestra during its October to May season, and guest appearances by vocalists, instrumentalists and pop stars. While Miami is not noted for its cultural life, it has a splendid range of museums, notably the Bass, the Lowe and the Vizcaya (see the Miami Directory).

Outside the city are several Indian villages worth exploring, and there are Indian artefacts at the Chiquita State Recreation Park, named after the fierce Calusa Indian chief who was hanged by an American army force in the late 1880s after he had been accused of the massacre of a pioneering white settlement. Lying thirty-five miles south-west of Miami, it covers 640 acres, and has camp and caravan sites.

The Tamiami Trail gives access, shortly before the '40-mile-bend', to Shark Valley, part of the Everglades National Park, where you can take a ninety-minute trip in open-air trams — truck-drawn,

canopy-covered trailers, each carrying sixty passengers. Other principal entrances to the Everglades are at Florida City, off US 1, and Everglades City, 100 miles from Miami on the north-west corner of the Everglades. Viewing this vast, swampy wilderness, awesome in its marshy mystery, is made easy these days, thanks to the loving care the National Parks Service bestows on these 1,500,000 acres of land and water, the largest sub-tropical wilderness in America, and the third largest of its national parks. Yet only seven per cent of this enormous expanse of mangrove swamps and prairies of sawgrass is under man's control, though its indigenous wildlife is carefully protected. There are several places for the tourist to start exploring the Everglades (see also the Motor Tour on p.118). Trails vary from a half-mile-walk near Florida City, on a raised boardwalk over sawgrass marshland (where you may get the occasional glimpse of an alligator basking in the water, and many brilliantly coloured birds flash in and out of the undergrowth), to the hundred-mile trip by canoe from Everglades City to the southernmost point at Flamingo in Florida

Bay. While airboat rides are not permitted in the park, because they cause too much disturbance to wildlife, many of the swamps outside the park are served by airboat operators. This is an exciting, if rather noisy, way to see the Everglades at close quarters; in these blunt-ended, flat-bottomed boats powered by aircraft engines and propellors, you can skim the water and penetrate the reed beds at speeds of up to forty miles an hour.

Much further north, Walt Disney World at Lake Buena Vista, west of Orlando, is an immense entertainment complex rivalling Disneyland in California, which, since it opened in 1971, has drawn more and more tourists away from Miami. This is also where Walt Disney's greatest dream, the Experimental Prototype Community of Tomorrow (EPCOT) is being turned into reality. The plan for the EPCOT centre includes Future World, a series of major exhibitions foreshadowing the future, and the World Showcase, an international exhibition concentrating on

Hundreds of exotic birds fly free, and even ride bicycles, at Parrot Jungle

the cultures, traditions and accomplishments of mankind. The whole project will cost eventually close on £300,000,000.

From Miami you can travel south across the sea to the Bahamas, the Caribbean, and South America from the largest cruise port in the world. Miami's port, into which the first passenger liner sailed as recently as 1927, is planned to grow to twice its present size, taking in Dodge, Lummus and Sam's islands to make a total dockside area of 600 acres. Since the beginning of the 1980s, around 1,500,000 passengers have sailed every year on the port's twenty-one cruise ships, but you can also take more modest day-long cruises from Haulover Beach on Miami Beach. Some of these take in the island of Indian Creek Village and Country Club, where a house can cost £500,000, and also call at several tiny islands along the South Florida coast.

Further south still, the entire area around Key Largo is peppered with small islands. About twenty-five of these keys form the Biscayne National Monument, but because no scheduled ferry services go there, it is necessary to hire a boat to roam about this quasi-Caribbean about ten miles from the Florida coast.

Miami Directory

Hotels

Unless otherwise indicated, all the hotels listed are on the seafront at Miami Beach and have rooms with private bathrooms and colour televisions. As a rough guide to cost, hotels and restaurants have been classified as either expensive, moderate or reasonable.

DI LIDO HOTEL: 155 Lincoln Rd, tel. 538 0611. 351 rooms, night club, coffee shop, swimming pools, refrigerators in all rooms. Moderate.

DORAL-ON-THE-OCEAN HOTEL: 4833 Collins Ave, tel. 532 3600. 425 rooms,

sports courts, refrigerators in all rooms, cocktail lounges, rooftop dining room. Expensive.

EDEN ROC: 4525 Collins Ave, tel. 327 8337. 350 rooms, solarium, dance lessons from resident instructors, famous-name cabaret, unique views of beach. Expensive.

FONTAINEBLEAU HILTON: 4441 Collins Ave, tel. 327 8367. 1200 rooms, Jacuzzi baths, golf course, tennis courts, bowling alleys, pool tables, cocktail lounges, two nightclubs. Expensive.

RALEIGH HOTEL: 1777 Collins Ave, tel. 531 0792. 126 rooms, swimming pool, coffee shop, beach huts for use of residents. Reasonable.

SHERATON BEACH RESORT: 19400 Collins Ave, tel. 325 3535. 498 rooms, many with private terraces. Swimming pools, tennis courts. Moderate.

WELWORTH HOTEL: 7326 Collins Ave, tel. 861 2426. 35 rooms with refrigerators, and a number of apartments at budget rates. Reasonable.

HADDON HALL HOTEL: 1500 Collins Ave, tel. 531 1251. 126 rooms, across the street from the beach. No TV in rooms. Reasonable.

KONOVER HOTEL: 5445 Collins Ave, tel. 327 0555. 465 rooms, all with refrigerators and king-size beds. 2 swimming pools, sports and recreation rooms, famous-name cabaret and dancing. Expensive.

MARINA PARK HOTEL: 340 Biscayne Blvd, Miami, tel. 371 4400. 210 rooms. Bar, restaurant and lobby on three levels make an attractive garden terrace. Near marina and port area, moderate.

Restaurants

Eating places in Miami range from gourmet restaurants to sandwich shops, with some of the finest Cuban and Kosher restaurants to be found anywhere in the world. Specialities from the Gold Coast include seafood such as Florida lobster or crewfish, Everglades frogs' legs or stone crabs from south Florida.

EMBERS: 245 22nd St, tel. 538 4345 . Seafood such as Maine lobster and Icelandic flounder is a speciality, though if you order prime ribs of beef, chicken, duck or pheasant you will be able to watch it being grilled over hickory charcoal while you wait. Open evenings only. Moderate.

FAMOUS RESTAURANT: 671 Washington Ave, tel. 531 3981. The enormous menu features Jewish-American, Romanian, Hungarian, Ukrainian and Polish specialities. Open evenings only. Moderate.

FORGE RESTAURANT: 432 Arthur Godfrey Rd, tel. 538 8533. Crystal chandeliers that once hung in the White House adorn this high-class steak house. Live music nightly. Open evenings only. Expensive.

JOE'S STONE CRAB RESTAURANT: 227 Biscayne St, tel. 673 0365. As the name suggests, this is a seafood restaurant, specializing in stone crabs. Be prepared to wait for a table. Moderate.

PIETRO'S RESTAURANT: 1233 Lincoln Rd, tel. 673 8722. Up-market Italian cooking, with speciality Saltimbocca and linguine with clam sauce. Moderate.

PUMPERNIK'S: 6700 Collins Ave, tel. 866 0242. A full delicatessen menu is available at Pumpernik's with interesting meats and cheeses and imaginative sweets. You can even go here for breakfast. Reasonable.

RONEY PUB: 2305 Collins Ave, tel. 532 3353. New York cut sirloin cooked on the open-hearthed charcoal fire, varied seafood dishes and a stunning array of sweets. Open evenings only. Moderate.

SONNY'S ITALIAN RESTAURANT AND PIZZERIA: 247 23rd St, tel. 538 1196. Pizzas are the speciality, but the large menu lists almost every Italian dish ever thought of. Open evenings only. Moderate.

WOLFIE'S: 195 Lincoln Rd, tel. 538 0326, and 2038 Collins Ave, tel. 538 6626 Delicatessen menu served at both locations concentrating on imaginative soups, pastries, well-stuffed sandwiches and good coffee. Reasonable.

Transport

MIAMI INTERNATIONAL AIRPORT: Le Jeune Road and N.W. 36th St. This is one of the world's busiest airports. There are direct flights from Britain and all major American cities, and over 750 flights weekly from 48 Latin-American cities. CAR HIRE: Rental rates can vary considerably between agencies and depending on the season. The major companies are: Airways, 3590 N.W. 36th St, tel. 635 6444; Avis, 244 N.E. 1st St, tel. 377 2531; Dollar, 300 Biscayne Blvd, Miami Beach, tel. 358 2541; Hertz, 666 Biscayne Blvd, tel. 377 4601; National, Miami International Airport, tel. 526 5645.

BUSES: The Metro Transit Agency serves downtown Miami and links with routes to Miami Beach and Coral Gables. A special shuttle bus covers the city centre in a continuous loop throughout the day, stopping at major shopping streets.

TAXIS: Taxis are plentiful and it is usually possible to hail one in the street or pick one up at the entrance of a major hotel. The major companies are: Diamond Cab Company, tel. 545 7575, and Yellow Cab Company, tel. 634 4444. Others are listed in the telephone directory.

Touring Information

AAA: The office of the East Florida Division of the AAA is at 4300 Biscayne Blvd, tel. 573 5611. Open during office hours, Monday to Friday.

METROPOLITAN DADE COUNTY DEPT OF TOURISM, 24 W. Flagler St, Miami, tel. 579 4694.

MIAMI BEACH VISITOR AND CONVENTION AUTHORITY, 555 17th St, Miami Beach, tel. 673 7070.

Places of Interest

CRANDON PARK ZOO: 4000 Crandon Blvd, Key Biscayne, tel. 361 2515. Over 1200 animals, including Bengal tigers, live at this well-equipped zoo. Children are welcome at the 'petting zoo'.

METROZOO: S.W. 152nd St. Many of the animals kept here roam in locations that look like film-sets — temple ruins and Asian jungles, for example. Already covering a 260-acre site, Metrozoo is destined to become the largest zoo in America.

MONKEY JUNGLE: 14805 S.W. 216th St, Goulds (22 miles south off US 1), tel. 235 1611. Orang-utans, gibbons and chimpanzees run free and swing through the trees above your head. South American monkeys can be seen in their natural habitat — an Amazonian rain forest.

SEAQUARIUM: Rickenbacker Causeway, tel. 361 5703. This is the world's largest tropical marine aquarium. Killer whales, sharks, sea lions, seals and dolphins perform here daily.

Museums and Galleries

BACARDI ART GALLERY: 2100 Biscayne Blvd. This gallery exhibits work by local, national and international artists.

BASS MUSEUM: Collins Ave at 21st and 22nd Sts. Displays Renaissance, Baroque, Rococo and modern painting as well as sculpture, tapestries and artists' prints.

GROVE HOUSE: 3496 Main Hwy, tel. 445 5633. A non-profit co-operative for artists and craftsmen, exhibiting the work of award-winning Florida artists.

LOWE ART MUSEUM: 1301 Miller Dr, tel. 284 3535. Fast gaining a reputation as one of the south's finest galleries, this museum is part of the University of Miami at Coral Gables. It specializes in Indian tribal art, oriental porcelain and bronze.

MIAMI WAX MUSEUM: 13899 Biscayne Blvd, tel. 945

Parks and Gardens

BAYFRONT PARK: Biscayne Bay, N.E. 5th St to S.E. 2nd St. Open-air concerts and special events take place in this pleasant park lined with royal and coconut palms.

FAIRCHILD TROPICAL GARDENS: 10901 Old Cutler Rd. Billed as the 'largest tropical botanical garden in America,' this is 83 acres of tropical and sub-tropical plants and trees set amidst lakes and rolling greenery.

GARDEN OF OUR LORD: St James Lutheran Church, 110 Phonetia, Coral Gables. Here are grown many beautiful and

3641. More than 40 scenes in wax depict America's past and present. Life-size statues of Columbus and ex-president Carter are among the exhibits.

MUSEUM OF SCIENCE: 3280 South Miami Ave, tel. 845 4242. This well equipped museum has a space planetarium, observatory, exhibits on gem cutting and the wild life and past cultures and wildlife of Florida. Among its live exhibits are an iguana, a tarantula spider and a baby alligator.

PLANET OCEAN: 3979 Rickenbacker Causeway, Key Biscayne, tel. 361 9455. The story of the world's oceans is told in seven multi-media theatres and with the aid of over 100 fascinating exhibits, including a real iceberg (see main text for more details).

VIZCAYA-DADE COUNTY MUSEUM: 3251 S. Miami Ave, tel. 845 3531. A beautiful Italianate villa boasting Renaissance, Baroque, Rococo and Neo-classical rooms, and superb gardens studded with pools, fountains and sculptures, make up this palatial estate. Works of art spanning 18 centuries are on show.

exotic plants which are mentioned in the Bible.

JAPANESE GARDEN: Watson Park, MacArthur Causeway. This oriental paradise features a pagoda, rock gardens, lanterns and a lagoon with a waterfall.

ORCHID JUNGLE: 26715 S.W. 157th Ave, Homestead, 25 miles south of Miami. Jungle trails wind through colourful displays of orchids.

REDLAND FRUIT AND SPICE PARK: Off US 1 at the intersection of Coconut Palm Dr and Redland Rd, Homestead, tel. 247 5727. Contains more than 250 species of fruit, nut and spice-producing plants.

Sport

GOLF: More than 35 golf courses are open to the public in Miami. Three of the best are Crooked Creek: 9950 S.W. 104th St, tel. 274 8308, Kendale Lakes: 6041 Kendale Lakes Dr, tel. 279 3130 and championship course Key Biscayne, Crandon Blvd, tel. 361 9129.

TENNIS: Many of the larger hotels have their own tennis courts, but public facilities exist throughout the county. Three of the best are Flamingo Park: (13 clay courts) 1245 Michigan Ave, tel. 673 7761, Morningside Park: N.E. 55th Terr. at Biscayne Bay and Tamiami: 11201 S.W. 24th St, tel. 223 7076.

Theatres

COCONUT GROVE PLAYHOUSE: 3500 Main Hwy, tel. 442 4000. This is the base of Miami's resident repertory company, The Players, who perform anything from classical plays to experimental theatre.

DADE COUNTY AUDITORIUM: 2901 West Flagler St, tel. 642 9061. All-year-round theatrical and cultural events.

THE GUSSMAN CULTURAL CENTER: 174 East Flagler St, tel. 358 3430. Dramas and musicals of all kinds.

THE MIAMI BEACH CENTER OF THE PERFORMING ARTS: 1700 Washington Ave, tel. 673 8300. Pre- and post-Broadway shows stop here as well as other touring plays and musicals.

Miami Gold Coast Tour

2 days — 158 miles

Miami — Hollywood — Dania — Pompano Beach — Boca Raton —
West Palm Beach — Palm Beach — Fort Lauderdale — Miami.

Sun, sea and sand — Florida's Gold Coast offers many such beaches

The Gold Coast is the pride of Florida: its dazzling sands are lined by opulent hotels, each struggling to outdo all the others in sheer luxury and magnificence. Homes of the famous are strewn along Palm Beach, and shopping and nightlife are among the best in the country. Fort Lauderdale is a thriving resort offering a host of water sports to attract the younger set. Lapped by the warm waters of the Gulf Stream, the palm-fringed beaches of the Atlantic coast will long linger in the memory.

Drive north through Miami on the North-South Expressway (Interstate 95) for 10 miles to a multiple junction. Here, continue on Interstate 95 for about 7 miles to Hollywood.

Hollywood, Florida
Palm-lined ocean beaches are the striking feature of this popular resort and residential city. Whilst lacking the notoriety of its Californian namesake, this Hollywood still has plenty of entertainment to offer. Music at the municipal bandstand in Young Circle Park, and the Theater Under the Stars are free.

Off US 441 is the Okalee Village Seminole Indian Reservation, where you may see a display of Seminole arts and crafts.

Continue north on Interstate 95 for 2 miles, then turn right at the interchange and drive for a mile on State Route 822. Then head north on US 1 and drive for about a mile to Dania.

Dania, Florida
This attractive winter resort has a fine ocean beach and is renowned for its antique shops. You may rent fishing tackle from the pier,

SCALE

10   0   10   **15.8 MILES TO 1 INCH**

10   0   10   **KILOMETRES**

Miami's Gold Coast

Jai Alai, a fast and furious version of the old Basque game, pelota

or watch jai alai (a fast version of handball) at the front on Dania Beach Boulevard.

Take S.W. 48th Street (State Route 818), which skirts the south side of the Fort Lauderdale and Hollywood International Airport, and rejoin Interstate 95. Continue north on this road for 13 miles to Pompano Beach.

Pompano Beach, Florida

Named after a delicious local fish, this is another swinging resort with a fabulous beach, excellent shopping, exciting night life, tropical cuisine and accommodation to suit any pocket.

If you fancy a bet, harness racing is featured from late November to early April and horse racing operates between late May and late July. For those who prefer more active pursuits, there are 10 golf courses, a number of tennis courts and facilities for water-skiing, scuba-diving and other water sports.

For an unusual outing, visit Krakatoa, a theme park whose attractions include a 60ft volcano. Also in Pompano Beach are the Tradewinds Park Botanical Gardens. Visitors come here not only for the plant life, but also for the small zoo, which is especially popular with children.

Return to Interstate 95 via Copans Road and drive north for 7 miles, then turn right on to State Route 798 and drive for 2 miles to Boca Raton.

Boca Raton, Florida

Early Spanish seamen called the area around this opulent town *boca de ratones,* which means 'mouth of rats'. It refers to the pointed rocks surrounding the inlet, which resemble the sharp teeth of rodents. During the 17th century many pirates were attracted to this inlet, and the notorious gangster Al Capone once had his headquarters on nearby Deerfield Island Park — formerly called Capone Island. The island is now popular with ornithologists and hikers.

Continue north from Boca Raton on US 1 for about 3 miles, then head west towards Interstate 95 on State Route 794. Drive north on Interstate 95 for 27 miles to West Palm Beach.

West Palm Beach, Florida

Bordering Lake Worth and noted for its 50,000 palm trees, this bustling commercial and industrial centre is still an attractive resort, even if it is now somewhat overshadowed by its exclusive neighbour, Palm Beach. Lake Mangonia and Clear Lake are in the centre of the city.

Dreher Park and Zoo, at 1301 Summit Boulevard, will appeal to children, and you can picnic in the grounds. A science museum and a planetarium are located in the park.

The best known local tourist attraction is nearly 17 miles away on US 98, 441 and State Route 80. This is a 640-acre fenced game reserve called Lion Country Safari, where African animals such as lions, rhinos, elephants, giraffes and zebras roam freely. Landscaped barriers separate natural enemies. You

An unusually quiet moment at Palm Beach, with the surf breaking on the warm sand

may drive through the reserve, but car windows must be kept closed because the animals can be dangerous. Children must be accompanied by an adult other than the driver and must not be left alone in the back of a four-door car. Patrol vehicles are always on duty in case of breakdowns. An animal nursery, a zoo and a reptile display are outside the reserve, and other animals may be seen by taking the tram, boat or jeep rides that are included in the admission fee.

Return southwards from downtown West Palm Beach on Interstate 95 for 2 miles. At the interchange head eastwards on State Route 704 and cross Lake Worth on Royal Palm Bridge to Palm Beach.

Palm Beach, Florida

Now one of Florida's most fashionable resorts, Palm Beach owes its existence to a man called Henry Morrison Flagler. This 19th-century multimillionaire railway pioneer, oil magnate and hotel-owner might be said to have put Florida on the map by building the railway line along Florida's 'Gold Coast' (see pp. 107-8). Realizing the potential of what was then a barren offshore island that the locals were only too glad to sell, he bought the land and developed it. His careful planning has allowed Palm Beach to retain its quiet charm and tropical beauty even into our own brash era. The palms that are such a characteristic feature of the resort are imports — albeit accidental ones. The coconuts from which they grew were part of the cargo of a Spanish ship that was wrecked here in 1878.

Palm Beach carries all the signs of an exclusive resort — from the expensive shops bearing the names of Gucci, Dior and St

William Lauderdale, who built a fort on the site in 1838. Now this lively resort is both a magnet for the younger set — with a burgeoning nightlife to complement the water sport activities of the day — and a popular retirement haven for the wealthy. A prime residential spot, at first sight it does not seem like a resort — more a nest for the rich, with its strikingly beautiful homes offset by canals and waterways — particularly lavish to the east of US 1.

The city is also a commercial centre, and Port Everglades, two miles to the south, has one of the deepest harbours in the country. As well as handling millions of tons of cargo, three modern terminals provide facilities for Caribbean-bound luxury liners.

A must for every visitor is a cruise on the *Jungle Queen.* Trips start from the Bahia Mar Yacht Centre on State Route A1A and cruise for three hours down New River past luxurious homes and downtown Fort Lauderdale. Alligator wrestling and animal shows are a distraction to be sampled at an Indian village en route. There are three cruises a day, and the last of them features dinner and entertainment. The *Paddlewheel Queen* is another cruise boat offering a similar service along the Intracoastal waterway.

An alternative way of seeing the sights is by Voyager Sightseeing Train. Ninety-minute tours of old and new Fort Lauderdale are available. The starting point is opposite the north entrance of the Bahia-Mar Yacht Basin.

If steam is your passion, then visit the Gold Coast Railroad Station and Museum. The era of Flagler's famous railway is vividly recalled at this historical depot.

Items connected with the railway are on display, and visitors can even ride on a steam train.

One mile east of US 1, at 1701 S.E. 17th Street, is Ocean World, where performing sea lions and porpoises can be seen. The moat contains sharks, reef fishes and large sea-turtles. Cable-car and boat rides are available.

Just north of Bahia-Mar is the International Swimming Hall of Fame. This commemorates the achievements of famous swimmers including Johnny Weismuller, Buster Crabbe and Esther Williams. Nearby are the Hall of Fame pools, which are open to the public daily.

At Sunrise Boulevard is the Hugh Taylor Birch State Recreational Area. This 180-acre park has something for all the family, including a miniature railway which follows a scenic three-mile route. Another park, south of Fort Lauderdale, is the 243-acre John Lloyd Beach Recreation Area. This is still being developed, and offers picnicking, swimming and boating, as well as skin- and scuba-diving facilities.

In Holiday Park is the modern War Memorial Auditorium, where concerts, plays, operas, sports and exhibitions take place.

Take State Route A1A south out of Fort Lauderdale and join US 1. Drive southwards for 3 miles, then turn east along Dania Beach Boulevard. Drive southwards down the 9 miles of this scenic highway and continue south along Harding Avenue and Collins Avenue (still part of State Route A1A) for another 11 miles. At 5th Street, near the southern end of Collins Avenue drive westwards across US 41, and continue over causeways for 4 miles on the return to downtown Miami.

The palm trees at Palm Beach came, it is said, from coconuts washed up from the wreck of a Spanish galleon

Laurent, which line elegant Worth Avenue, to the opulent Mediterranean mansions along Ocean Boulevard. Nearly 50 miles of sparkling white beaches offer fishing, scuba-diving and water sports, while in the harbour you may gaze at sleek, opulent yachts.

On Coconut Row stands a white marble palace called Whitehall — another of Henry Flagler's contributions to his development of Palm Beach. The elegantly furnished house, built by Flagler for his third bride in 1902, is now the Henry Morrison Flagler Museum. Early photographs of the area are on display, and the tycoon's private railway carriage can be seen in the grounds.

Just off Royal Palm Way, in the Four Arts Plaza, is the Society of

the Four Arts, which consists of a library, an art museum, an auditorium and gardens.

Drive south along State Route A1A for about 40 miles past Atlantic Ocean beaches and views of the glittering sea to Fort Lauderdale.

Fort Lauderdale, Florida

Rivers, bays, inlets, lagoons and canals make up over ten per cent of this city of islands. Over 165 miles of waterways allow the boat to compete with the motor car as the main means of transport. With numerous moorings for boats of all sizes, the city claims to be the country's largest yacht basin. In addition, it has six miles of splendid sandy beaches which allow safe bathing.

The city is named after Major

Paintings from all over the world are displayed in the magnificent Henry M. Flagler Museum

The Everglades and the Florida Keys

3 days — 402 miles

Miami — Coral Gables — Goulds — Homestead — Everglades
National Park — Flamingo — Key Largo — Islamorada — Layton —
Big Pine Key — Key West — Miami.

Spectacular scenery that is like no other in the USA makes this tour of the southern tip of Florida a 'must'. The route leads through several sub-tropical towns, each of which has something to offer the tourist, and into the Everglades National Park. One of the world's wild places, this is a land of mysterious forests, mangrove swamps and creeks where alligators roam.

Take US 1 through South Miami and proceed southwards to Coral Gables.

Coral Gables, Florida
This elegant city, which adjoins Miami, is mainly the result of careful planning in the 1920s, when the Miami area was becoming a fashionable resort. Modern industry and new building are carefully controlled so that they do not intrude on the handsome townscape of spacious plazas and parkways, landscaped gardens, tasteful mansions and a shopping boulevard — all representative of the lavish lifestyle enjoyed by residents of Coral Gables in the 1920s. Several buildings lend the city a Mediterranean air, such as the Spanish-style city hall and the Venetian Pool, a public swimming pool, complete with lagoons and grottoes.

Also of interest is the ethnic architecture of the Chinese, Dutch and French villages between Le Jeune Road and the University of Miami. In the 83-acre Fairchild Tropical Gardens, plants such as orchids, bromeliads and tropical fern thrive in settings that include a rain forest, palm glades and a rare plant house. Also well worth a visit is the Lowe Art Museum on the university campus (see p.114).

The Chamber of Commerce, at 50 Aragon Avenue, provides tour maps.

Leave Coral Gables and continue south on US 1 for 8 miles to enter Goulds.

Monkey Jungle — 'where humans are caged and monkeys run wild'

Goulds, Florida
Three miles west of US 1, at 14805 S.W. 216th Street, is Monkey Jungle, a novel zoo park where the monkeys run wild in a natural jungle habitat, whilst the spectators are in cages. Many species can be seen here, including marmosets, gibbons, orang-utans and gorillas. There is even a rain forest featuring South American monkeys in their natural habitat.

Still on US 1, drive for 12 miles from Goulds to Homestead.

Homestead, Florida
Situated just two miles north of this town on US 1 is a fascinating structure known as the Coral Castle. It was built and furnished by a Latvian immigrant, Edward Leedskalnin, who worked single-handed from 1920 to 1930, using only primitive tools. The castle is constructed entirely of huge blocks of hand-hewn coral — some weighing 30 tons.

Also north of Homestead, on Newton road (26715 S.W. 157th Ave), is Orchid Jungle, where large and small orchids from all over the world can be seen growing on live oaks in an approximation of their natural habitats. Every female visitor receives an orchid as a souvenir.

From Homestead drive on along US 1 for about 2 miles, then turn right at Florida City, taking State Route 27 to enter the Everglades National Park.

Everglades National Park, Florida
The largest remaining sub-tropical wilderness in the States, the Everglades National Park comprises 1,500,000 acres of land and water. Most of it is essentially a slow-moving freshwater river, 50 miles wide and only a few inches deep, fed by Lake Okeechobee. The Indian name for the area is Pa-hay-okee, which means 'river of grass'. Much of the region is a labyrinth of mangrove-studded waterways and sawgrass marsh relieved here and there by slightly higher ridges, 'hummocks' and 'bayheads', as the forested islands are called, and prairies. Nowhere does the land rise to more than 10ft above sea level, and during the rainy season in summer, all but the very driest spots can become swampland. Midges and mosquitoes thrive in the damp conditions and insect repellent is a

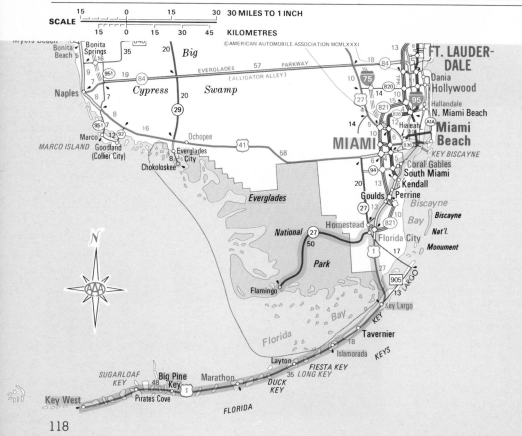

High speed airboats (above) skim over the waters of the Everglades. (Left) the Miccosukee Indian Reservation on the Tamiami Trail

must, especially from May to November.

You will not see the Everglades on a fast drive through the Park; even a slow drive will not do. To appreciate this natural wonderland, you must be prepared to spend some time here. The Everglades offer an astonishing variety of plant and animal life — a subtle blend of North American and West Indian, much of it unchanged for thousands of years. A few hours spent exploring one or two of the many marked nature trails (often on raised boardwalks), with or without the benefit of a Park Ranger, will reward you handsomely with sights of the most spectacular wildlife, such as alligators, raccoons, panthers, mink, sea cows and sea turtles. Among 300 varieties of birds found here are egrets, herons and roseate spoonbills. Plant life includes palm and mahogany trees, and numerous mangroves, with tangled branches and great,

arched roots rising from the water. The 'prop roots', as they are called, provide shelter for wildlife and also trap debris, such as grass and dead leaves, which decomposes and eventually provides food for the tree.

If you want to explore the depths of the mangrove swamps and visit the remote villages of the Seminole Indians — who lived here before the first white men came — you will have to travel by boat.

There are displays and a film at the Parachute Key Visitor Center, at the park entrance. Naturalists are also on duty here to answer questions.

Proceed on State Route 27 through the Park for about 40 miles to Flamingo.

Flamingo, Florida
This town on the southern tip of the Florida peninsula offers restaurant facilities and accommodation to explorers of the Everglades National Park. The Visitor Center and Museum is staffed by Park Service naturalists, and is conveniently located near the restaurant and gift shop. There are frequent excursion boat trips

from Flamingo Marina or, if you prefer to go it alone, you can hire anything from a canoe to a fully equipped cruising houseboat. A cruise from here to Everglades City, on the north-western edge of the Park, reveals a new dimension of the Everglades.

From Flamingo, return along the same route (State Route 27) for 50 miles to Florida City. Drive southwards on US 1 for 21 miles into Key Largo, crossing Jewfish Creek Bridge, where ospreys' nests can be seen on top of the telegraph poles.

Key Largo, Florida
The largest in the chain of 45 islands known as the Florida Keys, Key Largo is known for the John Pennekamp Coral Reef State Park, which lies two-and-a-quarter miles to the north-east of Key Largo town, off US 1. This unique undersea state park covers 150 square miles of protected ocean waters. Divers, snorkelers, swimmers and non-swimmers are kept fascinated for hours in this coral wonderland. Sail-and-snorkel, scuba-diving or snorkel tours can all be arranged, and for those who prefer to keep dry, a

two-and-a-half-hour tour in a
glass-bottomed boat offers an
excellent view of the seabed with
its hosts of colourful sea creatures,
coral creations and plant life. An
underwater bronze statue is a
feature of the park, and there are
also shipwrecks to be seen. Over
the centuries numerous ships,
ranging from Spanish galleons to
20th-century tankers, have met
with disaster on the Florida Keys.
Relics from some of the wrecks
can be seen in McKee's Museum
of Sunken Treasure on Plantation
Key, a little further south-west.

The visitors' centre features
aquariums, films and information
about the park and its
development.
    Drive south-westwards for 9
    miles to reach the historic island
    of Islamorada.

Islamorada, Florida

The name of this attractive fishing
resort and the island on which it
stands is a Spanish word meaning
'purple isle', so named because of
the island's hue when viewed from
a distance. It was given this name
by an early Spanish explorer, and
is the oldest inhabited site in the
Keys. Photographers and
underwater explorers will find
much of interest in the wreck of
the galleon *Herrera* which can be
found two-and-a-half miles off
Whale Harbour Bridge.
Islamorada town is the third
largest in the Keys and is an
excellent shopping centre, full of
good motels and restaurants.
    Just over one mile north of
Islamorada is the Theater of the
Sea, which features playful
performances by marine creatures

such as sharks, porpoises and sea
lions.
    From Islamorada continue for 15
    miles on US 1 into Layton,
    situated on Long Key.

Layton, Florida

Sea World's Shark Institute is a
research station here which, as
well as its serious scientific study of
marine life, offers displays of many
species of shark, including the
bull, lemon, grey and tiger shark,
in outdoor lagoons. Rays and
sawfish may also be seen. Visitors
may stand on a specially built
elevated platform to watch the
sharks being fed. Other attractions
include indoor aquariums,
Caribbean tide pools and a
tropical reef tank.
    Continue southwards on US 1
    for 38 miles to Big Pine Key.

*The haunting wilderness of the
Florida Keys, a chain of 45
remote and beautiful islands
which stretch southwards to the
Caribbean and Cuba*

*Ernest Hemingway, one of the
outstanding figures of 20th-
century literature, was one of the
many famous people who made
their homes on Key West*

Big Pine Key, Florida

This is the only island in the Keys
where the Florida Key whitetail
deer is found. These small animals
are very shy and seldom seen
except in the early morning or at
dusk. The area has been
designated a wildlife sanctuary for
their protection, and there is also
a bird refuge here, where the
great white heron is among the

The Florida Everglades

Audubon House (1851), home of the naturalist John James Audubon

species protected. Two miles north of US 1, on State Route 940, there is a visitor centre which offers information on the deer sanctuary. The final destination on this tour is Key West, which lies 30 miles south-west of Big Pine Key on US 1.

Key West, Florida

This is the most southerly point in the continental United States, just a 90-mile swim away from Cuba. Bahamian, Caribbean and Yankee influences combine to form a unique culture apparent in the architecture and cuisine — which features such delights as turtle steak, conch chowder, hot *bollos* (small loaves) and key lime pie.

Since the island was discovered in the 16th century, the population of Key West has turned its hand to

a variety of industries. Before the building of a lighthouse reduced the number of shipwrecks in the area, the people of Key West were notorious for plundering wrecked ships as a means of earning their livelihood. Sponge-diving and cigar-manufacturing took over, then the town became an important naval base, and it is now largely given over to the business of catering for tourists.

It is not surprising that the relaxed, individualistic atmosphere of Key West has attracted artists, writers and statesmen to this tranquil slip of sand and sea. Ernest Hemingway was probably the most famous devotee. He lived here during his most productive period when he completed such classics as *To Have and Have Not, For Whom the Bell Tolls, Green Hills of Africa,* and one of his greatest short stories, *The Snows of Kilimanjaro.* Among others who have been attracted to Key West are World War II president Harry S. Truman, naturalist John James Audubon, playwright Tennessee Williams, novelist John Dos Passos and poet Robert Frost.

Visitors to Key West will find themselves well looked after at the Chamber of Commerce in Mallory Square, where plenty of maps and brochures are available. A good introduction to the 'sights' is to take a 90-minute guided tour in the Conch Tour Train. There are frequent departures every day, and the 14-mile tour takes in both Old and New Key West. Those who prefer a walking tour can

follow a well-marked and carefully planned route through Old Town, called the Pelican Path.

Among the many places of interest to be seen in the city is the Ernest Hemingway Home and Museum. Situated at 907 Whitehead Street, this Spanish colonial-style mansion was owned by the Nobel-Prize-winning author from 1931 until his death in 1961. Some of Hemingway's possessions are on display, and the house is open to visitors.

Audubon House and Gardens on Whitehead and Greene Streets, is where John James Audubon lived while painting the wildlife of the Florida Keys in 1832. His restored house is furnished with 18th- and 19th-century pieces. The main attraction is a rare, complete set of Audubon's series of engravings *The Birds of America.* The collection includes illustrations of 1065 birds and is said to have cost £20,000 to produce.

All kinds of exhibits relating to Key West and the Florida Keys, as well as an extensive art collection, can be found in the Martello Gallery and Museum on South Roosevelt Boulevard. Housed in the remains of a Civil War fort, the gallery and museum is open to the public daily.

A fine way to see the spectacular coral reef is by taking the two-hour guided cruise in *Fireball,* a glass-bottomed sightseeing boat. The return journey is made via the same route along the Overseas Highway (US 1) into Miami.

121

The imposing white dome of the Capitol Building — seat of the United States Government — dominates Washington DC. The building is crowned by a 19ft-high statue symbolizing freedom, the work of sculptor Thomas Crawford

122

Washington

Washington is not the oldest, the largest, or even the prettiest of the world's capitals, but it is certainly among the friendliest. As host to diplomats from all over the world it knows how to make visitors feel welcome. Carved out of the states of Maryland and Virginia, the District of Columbia, which gives Washington its D.C., draws much of its style from its Southern location. Though cosmopolitan and sophisticated, it is a city where you can still hear people address each other with a polite 'Sir' or 'Ma'am' in a soft Southern drawl.

As befits a great capital city, Washington is characterized by stately avenues, streets and squares, interspersed with well-planned parks — it is one of the most open cities in the world. The glorious past, high-flying politics, gleaming white buildings and glittering international occasions are only part of the story. The sombre side exists and the city lives uneasily with a disparate population. There are certain areas, away from the centre, where tourists should not venture.

Any city that offers itself so generously for inspection — Washington's numerous public buildings and parks can be visited free of charge — must rank high on any tourist itinerary. Most of what any visitor will want to see is conveniently accessible in the north-west section of the city. Then there are the charms of Georgetown with its Bohemian artiness, and the more studied elegance of Alexandria, a city in its own right only eight miles from the city. Beyond Washington, in Virginia and Maryland, is much else to give the British tourist a feeling of belonging. Here is where Britain and the Colonies separated 200 years ago. The city and the countryside are packed with evidence of the Revolution and American Independence.

The white marble columns of the Lincoln Memorial, mirrored in the Reflecting Pool, surround the massive figure (inset) of America's 16th president

America's imposing capital stands on three waterways — the Potomac River, which separates the city, on the east bank, from the state of Virginia on the west bank, the Anacostia, which skirts the southern extremes of the Maryland area of the city, and Rock Creek, which winds north for twelve miles.

The standard route into Washington from Dulles International Airport is along the magnificent new George Washington Memorial Parkway — a broad tree-lined dual carriageway, which curves through the lush, green Virginia countryside.

If one conveniently forgets the official boundaries of the District of Columbia, the sixty-nine square miles of self-contained administrative area from which Washington derives its D.C., there are thirty-three parklands in Washington, another eighty in Maryland and nearly fifty in Virginia. The greenery encompasses not only the great estates that were once plantations all around the city, but also the elegant and well-manicured lawns of Arlington National Cemetery, the 121-acre Ladybird Johnson Park on the west side of the Potomac River, Theodore Roosevelt Island in the middle of the river, and, separated by a tidal basin on the east bank, the two vast expanses of the Potomac Park.

Washington is the seat of the most powerful government in the Western world. It is therefore hardly surprising that politics and the business of politics occupies a pre-eminent place in the life of the city. Nearly half its population of nearly 730,000 is employed by, or connected with government — a vast concentration of civil servants, legislators, congressmen, senators and foreign diplomats. Dominating the city centre, the domed Capitol building (see the Washington Directory for details of this and other public buildings) stands majestically on Capitol Hill, looking down the broad, green Mall to Washington's two most famous landmarks, the Washington Monument and the Lincoln Memorial. Between the Capitol and the White House, the official residence of the president, lies what is popularly called the Federal Triangle, where most of the government buildings are to be found. Pennsylvania Avenue, or 'Avenue of the President', as it is sometimes known because it is the route followed by the inaugural parade of each new president, forms the north side of the triangle and Constitution Avenue the south side. Linking them is 15th Street N.W. Outside this triangle, on the east bank of the Potomac River is the Department of State and on the opposite bank, near Arlington National Cemetery, is the Pentagon, a massive five-sided building housing a complex of satellite offices. This is the home of the Department of Defense, built during World War II and looking appropriately forbidding. Wherever you look in downtown Washington, civic pride is self-evident. The streets are wide, well manicured, and lined with impressive monuments, statues and museums which not only testify to the importance of the capital, but document the real significance of the country's past. Over and over again in Washington, one is reminded of that famous victory at Yorktown in 1781 when raw colonial troops overthrew the army of General Cornwallis and so brought the American War of Independence (the Revolutionary War) to an end 200 years ago.

In the years immediately following the War of Independence, the newly formed Congress had set up a temporary home in Philadelphia, and for seven years its members debated as to where they should establish the monument to their great victory, the nation's capital. The Northerners, naturally, wanted it in their part of the world and the Southerners in theirs. Eventually a compromise was reached and the states of Maryland and Virginia agreed to give up a part of their territories for the proposed new capital city and its administrative area. The site chosen was a low-lying marsh on the banks of the Potomac River. When George Washington first surveyed it in 1791, he wrote in his diary, 'I derived no great satisfaction from the review.' Nevertheless he immediately commissioned a brilliant French engineer, Major Pierre Charles L'Enfant, to design the plan of the city. L'Enfant produced a magnificent scheme, which envisaged the Capitol building and an Executive Mansion at the centre of a network of streets, squares and parks, intersected by broad diagonal avenues named after the different states in the Union. Washington was to have rivalled Paris in elegance and grandeur. His original plans can be seen in the Library of Congress, and although Congress rejected his scheme on the grounds of cost, most of his plans were finally carried out, although the work took more than a century to complete. There were other problems too. Virginia, angered by the slow progress of the work, claimed back its share of the territory, just over thirty square miles on the west bank of the Potomac. This enabled the flourishing port of Alexandria to retain its separate identity, which it does to this day. For decades after that, Washington remained a mud-track. Few people wanted to live there, and those who did move to the city were only interested in

Piercing the darkened skyline, the soaring 555ft-high Washington Monument is said to be the tallest stone structure in the world

Washington

patronizing the many saloons. As a capital, Washington fell far short of the expectations and ideals of the nation's new leaders.

But the building of the Capitol, to provide a new home for Congress, went on. The cornerstone was laid in 1793, and seven years later, in the year after Washington died, the north wing was finished, allowing the sessions to be transferred from Philadelphia. The birth pangs of the Capitol, however, were by no means over. In 1812, as a result of trade and boundary disputes, Congress declared war on Britain. America did not think that the British would trouble to attack Washington, since the city was still regarded as insignificant, and so they did not take any measures to safeguard it. British troops entered the city in 1814 and burnt the President's house, the partially finished Capitol, and many public buildings. If it had not been for a torrential thunderstorm, the whole city would have been destroyed by fire.

Though blackened by the flames, the walls of the President's house survived. When the mansion was reconstructed after the end of the war (1815) the walls were repainted white, and it came to be called the White House, although the name was not in fact made official until the first decade of this century when President Theodore Roosevelt was in office.

The new White House signalled a new beginning for Washington. Slowly the seeds of prosperity were being sown. Increasingly, trade links were being developed through the already existing ports of Alexandria and Georgetown. Despite the devastation of the American Civil War (1861-5), Washington emerged

largely unscathed. Twice it escaped capture by the Confederate (Southern) forces only because the besieging army did not strike quickly enough, and the Union armies had time to recoup. After 1865, Washington got down to fulfilling the vision of its first President — to build a clean and thriving capital. In the 1870s, thanks to the energy of 'Boss' Shepherd, the chief of works appointed by President Grant, the unpaved, muddy streets were transformed. In three years Shepherd had paving and main services laid, had provided street lights, and established some of the parks that Pierre L'Enfant had

Washington's most popular tourist attraction, The White House, receives more than 1,500,000 visitors a year

originally envisaged. It was another turning point. And as the years went on the transformation culminated at the turn of the century in the design of an aesthetically pleasing administrative centre. Today, the White House, at 1600 Pennsylvania Avenue, sparkles in its pristine coat of white paint. It dominates the majestic buildings that line the avenue, and it forms the apex of a triangle

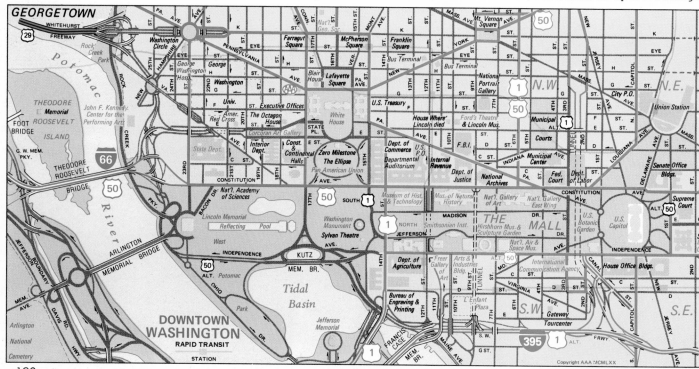

Town Walks

Washington and its neighbourhoods provide contrasting settings for sightseeing walks. In Washington itself, the route covers a concentrated area of impressive buildings and famous administrative offices. In Georgetown, the walk is pretty, passing through streets of quaint old houses, many of them with stories to tell. The Alexandria walk goes from shady cobbled streets and 18th-century houses to a modern shopping complex. The Washington Directory (pp.133-5) or the main city text, gives information on features not detailed here.

WASHINGTON: the length of time this walk takes depends on the number of places you decide to visit en route. Start at the White House, walk around the Ellipse to the south side and cross Constitution Avenue to the Washington Monument. Due west is the Reflecting Pool and the Lincoln Memorial; east, at the head of the Mall, the Capitol. Cross the Mall diagonally south-east to the Bureau of Engraving and Printing at 14th and C Streets S.W. This is where 3000 trusted citizens design, engrave and print more than $12,000,000 in treasury notes. You can see them at work on weekdays between 8am and 11.30am and between 12.30pm and 2.00pm.

Go east along D Street, turn left at 12th Street, cross Independence Avenue, and on Jefferson Drive visit the Freer Gallery of Art, the first of several Smithsonian Institution buildings in the area. Almost next door is the Arts and Industries building, next to it the Hirshhorn, and across the Mall, north of Madison Drive, is the National Gallery of Art at 6th Street.

You can take a rest from Smithsonian buildings for a while by touring the National Archives on the opposite side of Constitution Avenue at 8th Street, then go north-west on Pennsylvania Avenue, crossing over at 9th Street to see the J. Edgar Hoover building, home of the FBI (see main text for details).

Proceed up 9th Street and turn left on to E Street and right at 10th Street to Ford's Theater where President Lincoln was fatally wounded. Across the road is the house where he died. Walking south down 10th Street and across Constitution Avenue again, look in on the Museum of Natural History and then go west past the Museum of History and Technology — both Smithsonian buildings. Cross over and walk up 14th Street to E Street and turn left to return to the White House.

GEORGETOWN: A delightful half-hour walk through the charming old-world streets of Georgetown should start at its most vaunted landmark — the Old Stone House, at 3051, M Street N.W. Built in 1765, it is thought to be the oldest house still standing in Georgetown. First owned by a cabinet-maker who worked in the ground-floor rooms, it is partly still furnished in late 18th-century style, and is open daily.

Turn left down M Street, right on 30th Street, and walk down to the Chesapeake and Ohio canal, where at 1050, the Duvall Foundry, built in 1856, is part of Georgetown's industrial heritage. After the Civil War, it became a veterinary hospital, a stable, a stonecutter's shop, and artists' studios. Now it is a restaurant and part of a shopping mall. You can walk for miles along the canal, past the restored locks and lockhouses, and a variety of delightful old canalside homes. Masses of wild flowers grow along the towpath. For a short walk, however, turn right along the canal towpath and right again into 31st Street. At the corner of M Street at 3118 is the first Mayor's House, built in the 18th century. Further along M Street is the City Tavern, at 3206. Opened in the early part of the 19th century it served as a popular tavern for many years and in 1962 became the home of a social club.

ALEXANDRIA: Covering about 18 blocks, this pleasant one-hour stroll starts at the Alexandria Tourist Council headquarters in King Street at the corner of Fairfax Street. Going east, turn left into Lee Street, walk to the corner of Cameron Street, then turn left to stroll along this charming old shopping street. At the corner of Royal Street is Gadsby's Tavern, one part of which was built in 1770 and the other in 1792. Further along Cameron Street is George Washington's reconstructed town house. Continue to Washington Street and turn left to visit the George Washington Bi-Centennial Center at the corner of Prince Street. Here paintings and antiques help the audio-visual commentary to tell the story of the American Revolution. Walk east along Prince Street for some way, passing several interesting 18th- and 19th-century houses until you reach Union Street where you turn left to King Street where you will find the artists' studios and shops of the Torpedo Factory (see p.133). All around here is the Waterfront area, where you can walk along the banks of the Potomac River. The neat grid system of Alexandria's streets makes it a simple matter to return to your starting point whenever you feel inclined. Wolfe, Duke, Prince, King, Cameron and Queen Streets all run west-east and are intersected by, starting from the riverside, Union, Lee, Fairfax, Royal, Pitt, St Asaph, Washington and Columbus Streets.

that has the Capitol at one corner and the Lincoln Memorial at the other.

Washington probably has more public monuments than any other American city. Two of the most famous, the Washington Monument and the Lincoln Memorial, stand in West Potomac Park, separated by the 2000ft long Reflecting Pool and the oval Rainbow Pool. The whole city may be said to be George Washington's monument, but Abraham Lincoln too, as befits the man who was responsible for ending the slave system, has several memorials in the city. The best known is Ford's Theater, on 10th Street N.W., where Lincoln was shot on 14 April 1865 while watching a play. John Wilkes Booth, the assassin, was an actor who knew almost every line of the play, *Our American Cousin,* and thus was able to choose his moment carefully. However, while trying to escape he fell and broke his leg. The box in which Lincoln was shot is preserved, and there is a museum in the basement although the theatre is now functioning as a playhouse. Petersen House, opposite, is the building to which the fatally wounded president was taken,

and this too is a museum. Visitors can see the room on the first floor in which Lincoln died the day after the attack, and there are other rooms devoted to his relics. Of the many early statesmen honoured in the capital, Thomas Jefferson, author of the Declaration of Independence, and third president of the Union, is probably the most famous. His circular, domed memorial stands in East Potomac Park, looking across the waters of the Tidal Basin to the memorials of his two fellow statesmen Washington and Lincoln.

You cannot go into Franklin D. Roosevelt's rather modest white marble monument on Pennsylvania Avenue — he was president for twelve years until just before the end of World War II — because it is not big enough, but the entire population of the city could crowd on to the eighty-eight-acre memorial island which commemorates Theodore Roosevelt whose administration lasted from 1901 to 1909. On the island is a massive granite monument which includes a seventeen-foot bronze statue of Roosevelt, matched by four towering slabs immortalizing his ideas on nature, manhood, youth and the

state. The island can be reached on foot from the carpark off the George Washington Memorial Parkway, which is reached by driving across the Theodore Roosevelt Bridge, one of seven bridges

Ford's Theater has been restored to look much as it did when President Lincoln was fatally wounded here in 1865

across the Potomac, linking the District of Columbia and Virginia.

President John F. Kennedy is commemorated by the superb John F. Kennedy Center for the Performing Arts, which opened in 1971 on the banks of the Potomac at the junction of Rock Creek Parkway and New Hampshire Avenue. Woodrow Wilson, president from 1913 to 1921 rates an out-of-town bridge named after him — it is part of the Capital Beltway skirting the city. So does Francis Scott Key, the man who wrote the words to the 'Star Spangled Banner'. They had to knock his house down to put up the bridge. A better known composer to lovers of military brass band music, is Philip Sousa, the king of marches, who is also immortalized in a bridge spanning the Anacostia River.

Conscious always of their strong links with Britain, Washingtonians point with pride at the symbolic significance of Winston Churchill's statue outside the British Embassy. He has one foot on American soil and one on British. The

Embassy at the top of Massachusetts Avenue is in 'Embassy Row' where most of the 132 nations represented in Washington have their accredited staff. Perhaps the most far-reaching memorial in Washington is to an obscure English scientist called James Smithson (1765-1829), an illegitimate son of the Duke of Northumberland. The museums administered by the institution that bears his name between them contain more than 70,000,000 catalogued items. No other city has a treasure trove of the size and scope of the Smithsonian Institution museums. It could be said that the English, in the name of James Smithson, made amends for pillaging Washington in 1814, because the philanthropist bequeathed to the United States his entire fortune of some $500,000, to create a foundation 'For the increase and diffusion of knowledge among men.' The United States Congress accepted the gift and the Smithsonian Institute was established in 1846. The original, ornate building, a charming Gothic fantasy with towers and

An eternal flame burns on President Kennedy's simple grave at Arlington

Parks & Gardens

With more than 30 major parklands in Washington, and so many more outside the District of Columbia, tourists aiming to spend part of their holidays in the open air have an enormous choice. Each park mentioned here has been chosen because it has something special to offer the visitor.

Anacostia Park: On the 750 acres of Anacostia Park, which lies on both sides of the Anacostia River, once stood a large Indian village named Nacotchtank, surrounded by superb tracts of untamed marshlands. Today some of the park is still wild and unkempt, and this has helped to attract all kinds and colours of birds. Striking green and blue heron, all types of geese and ducks, and songbirds may be seen in the bird sanctuary. The park also offers all kinds of recreational facilities such as swimming, tennis, and water sports. You can hire boats to explore the marshlands and the small tributaries that reach almost to **Kenilworth Aquatic Gardens.**

Though developed separately as a private garden by a former government clerk in the 1880s and later by his daughter, Kenilworth is a part of Anacostia Park often neglected by visitors. In its 14 acres of ponds are more than 100,000 plants, including rare flowering plants, as well as frogs and turtles. The park has been under National Park Service

protection since 1938. In Lovers Lane is the entrance to **Dumbarton Oaks Park**, its 27 acres described as America's smallest national wilderness park. Part of the former 50-acre Georgetown estate of the American diplomat Robert Woods Bliss, it has some of the most beautiful formal gardens in America. The park itself is best seen between April and late June when it is a riot of colourful blooms.

It is worth making a special trip to Washington in the spring just to motor along Ohio Drive, which follows the river and around the 700-acre **Potomac Park.** It is then that 3000 Japanese cherry trees burst into bloom and for 10 days provide a breathtaking mauve, pink and white halo over the area, and later a thick carpet of blossom.

Twelve varieties of the trees, originally a gift from Japan to the United States, were planted in 1912 and since 1927 a cherry blossom festival has been held every year. Another 3800 trees were sent to the United States in 1965, after America had sent cuttings from its trees back to Japan to help it restock the nurseries that had been devastated during the war.

Following the banks of the 12-mile-long Rock Creek, **Rock Creek Park** is a mile wide at some places — encompassing 1754 acres of natural woodlands. There are two riding stables, tennis courts, picnic areas, a golf course and an athletics field. In the park can be seen a reconstructed Civil-War fort. Outside the city limits, Maryland can lure the nature

lover to the **Chesapeake and Ohio Canal National Historical Park** which follows the Maryland side of the Potomac River from Georgetown to Cumberland along a 184-mile canal. On the Virginia side of the river, **Great Falls Park** offers spectacular views of the Great Falls of the Potomac River, the highest fall being 35ft and the Mather Gorge one mile long. Unfortunately there is no direct link communicating between the two parks.

Other parks worth seeking out are **Gambrill State Park** on Catoctin Mountain, near the city of Frederick in Maryland, the **Fort Ward Museum and Park** in Alexandria, and the **Bull Run Occoquan Regional Park**, where 25 miles of the shore around a reservoir providing

water to most of Northern Virginia are open for fishing and boating. Stretching out behind the reservoir are 5000 acres of woods and meadows, divided into four separate recreational parks.

The National Park Service is the authority responsible for all this lush greenery, and they arrange and publish an elaborate monthly programme of events in several of the parks in and around Washington.

Festivals

CHERRY BLOSSOM FESTIVAL: Tidal Basin. This spectacular season lasts for a week every spring — but nobody can forecast exactly *which* week — it all depends on when the blossoms decide to bloom. About 650 pink-blossomed Japanese cherry trees circle the Tidal Basin, others line the paths of East Potomac Park. The white-blossomed variety may be seen at Kenwood in Maryland, reached via Wisconsin Ave and Route 191.

PAGEANT OF PEACE: Each year this charming Christmas festival runs for the last two weeks of December, starting with the illumination of the 40ft Colorado blue spruce National Christmas Tree by the president himself. He then broadcasts his Christmas greetings for world peace, and choirs sing madrigals and Christmas carols. Live reindeer can be seen around the tree.

The Metro

Washington's most recent addition to the public transport system, the Metro underground, doesn't attempt to rival New York's subway or London's Tube in complexity or frequency of service, but it is immensely clean and airy — a great relief in the height of the summer when temperatures above ground are often around 90°F and can reach more than 100°F.

So far, only 38 miles out of the planned 101-mile network is operational. Three lines, Red, Blue and Orange, serve stations from the National Airport in the south to Silver Spring in the north, and from Ballston in the west to New Carrollton in the east.

Two of the lines meet at Metro Center — a unique station with direct access to a large department store at F and 12th Streets. The store paid for the construction of the station facilities — an investment which has paid off in the numbers of passengers who need look no further for freshly baked bread, sweets, newspapers, magazines and books, clothes and gifts than the counters they pass on their way to and from the station. At street level, stations are identified by the letter M perched on a column. Inside, they are decorated in brown and cream. Once underground you may need to consult colour-coded maps near the station entrance to determine the line you want, or whether it will be necessary to change lines, and to read off the correct fare. The 'farecard' machine needs some study, too. If you are unfamiliar with its inflexible computer-like efficiency you could end up either losing your money or with the wrong ticket. The machine will swallow nickels (5 cents), dimes (10 cents), quarters (25 cents), half-dollars (50 cents), $1 and $5 notes, and will deliver the right ticket with your change. Notes must be fed into the machine the right way up — a diagram explains which this is. To avoid the paraphernalia of buying a ticket every time you travel, you can usefully buy a ticket up to $20 if you wish, and the automatic barrier will return the ticket to you until you have used up the journeys you have paid for. You can also change to a bus by using a transfer ticket obtainable from a machine at the barrier.

pinnacles in the style of a medieval castle, stands in the southern part of the Mall. No less than seven museums (see the Washington Directory for details) connected with the Institution line the western part of the Mall. Altogether, there are thirteen Smithsonian museums, twelve of them in Washington and the thirteenth, the Cooper-Hewitt Museum, in New York.

By far the largest national monument associated with Washington is the Arlington National Cemetery, established in 1864 on the south bank of the Potomac. It covers more than 600 acres and contains the graves of many famous American public figures, as well as the graves of countless thousands of members of the armed services — anyone who has served in the US armed forces has the right to be buried here. The graves of John F. Kennedy, the thirty-fifth president, murdered in Dallas on 22 November 1963, and his brother Robert, murdered in Los Angeles on 6 June 1968 are both here. The central feature of John Kennedy's tomb is an eternal flame. Perhaps the best known Arlington monument is the United States Marine Corps Memorial which stands just outside the north end of the cemetery. It is an impressive group of four bronze figures raising the American flag on Mount Suribachi on the Japanese island of Iwo Jima in 1945. The sculpture was inspired by a famous Press photograph, and was the largest ever to be cast as a single piece. The figures are more than five times life size and the whole work is 78ft high.

Do not miss the National Archives in Constitution Avenue between 7th and 9th Streets N.W. where, if your political tastes border on the macabre, you can while away an hour or so listening to a selection of the choicest Watergate tapes — that scandal of the Nixon administration — expletives unexpurgated. Watergate is a name that still brings a slight shudder over Americans when they hear it. The actual building where the burglary took

This imposing building is the home of the US National Archives, a huge collection of documents which includes the Declaration of Independence

Washington

place, and which started the scandal, is a vast complex of shops and offices and, big though it is, looks too ordinary to have been the touchstone that led to the downfall of a president. Some cities might have wanted to change its notorious name, but Washington has never had any inhibitions about exposing its wrinkles or its smiles. Another macabre experience is to spend 75 minutes at the J. Edgar Hoover Building, between 9th and 10th Streets on Pennsylvania Avenue. This is an ugly tan block named after the legendary former head of the FBI. An arsenal of villany and an absolute 'must' for students of the American gangster culture, it is packed with photographs and biographies of some of the most notorious Hollywood-style crooks and their firearms. It also has a board of photographs of the ten most wanted men displayed at the desk where the man who hunted them sat for more than a generation.

Hillwood (see the Washington Directory) at 4155 Linnean Avenue N.W., is the 40-room Colonial mansion built out of the fortunes of a world-famous cereal company, founded by the father of Marjorie Merriweather Post, who lived there until she died in 1973. The company is now the giant conglomerate General Foods Corporation. Marjorie Merriweather Post, wife of a former ambassador to Russia between the wars, later added immeasurably to her family fortune by encouraging and backing an unknown 'boffin' to preserve food by freezing it. His name was Birdseye.

In downtown Washington, as befits the capital of the Western World, restaurants, hotels and shops cater for virtually all nations, customs and tastes. Many of the best restaurants are on or near Connecticut Avenue, or Wisconsin Avenue N.W. Some restaurants offer more than you may expect. At La Niçoise on Wisconsin Avenue, for example, service comes not only with a smile but speedily — on roller skates. At the Big Cheese on M Street

I.M. Pei designed the spectacular East Building of the National Gallery of Art, a seven-storey structure composed of interlocking triangular sections

N.W., the cheese dishes include a daunting delicacy of deep-fried camembert with strawberry jam. Some of the best fast-food bargains are the museum restaurants, for example the Terrace Café of the Air and Space Museum. Inexpensive and clean, it is excellent value for Washington's army of sightseers.

Some of the major hotels are to be found on upper Connecticut Avenue and around lower 16th Street. There are more than 30,000 hotel rooms in the city, ranging from the 1200 in the Washington Hilton at

Connecticut Avenue and Columbia Road N.W., to the select 170 rooms in the Fairfax Hotel on Massachusetts Avenue, N.W. Some hotels, such as the One Washington Circle at 23rd and K Streets N.W. have been adapted into apartment hotels with the usual hotel services, but in addition provide a fully equipped kitchen in most rooms without charging luxury hotel prices for these facilities. These hotels are becoming increasingly popular with visiting diplomats and tourists.

Many of the most famous department stores like Garfinkle's, Hecht's, and

The White House

The railings surrounding the 18-acre grounds of the White House are fortunately not the nearest a tourist can get to the seat of power in Washington. The White House is open to the public for two hours a day all year round from Tuesdays to Saturdays. An extra 45 minutes is allocated in the height of the season between June and August, but then the tours have to be booked in advance for specific times and you have to collect the ticket yourself from a booth on the Ellipse at Constitution Avenue. At other times of the year, you can take your turn and wait in a queue (there are seats) at the East Gate on East Executive Avenue.

The tour takes in the State Dining Room and the Red, Blue, Green and East Rooms on the ground and first floors. Unfortunately, the Oval office is not included, but there are enough glimpses into the current president's life to remind you that you are not in a museum. The furnishings include antiques and original pieces acquired by previous occupants of the hot seat, many dating back to the early 19th century. The elegant lines of the White House are a hotchpotch: James Hoban's original design, chosen for the presidential mansion in 1792, was never completely realized because many of its occupants kept changing it, particularly in the early years. As every president except George Washington has lived here, there could have been as many as 40 different sets of ideas applied to the design of the place, but President Truman was the last president to undertake major changes. He had the interior renovated between 1948 and 1952.

If you prefer to watch from afar, much of the White House grounds are within sight of the railings. The gardens contain 80 varieties of trees, among them two maples, planted by President Jimmy Carter, an enormous elm from which Betty Ford, wife of President Gerald Ford, planted a seedling in 1975, and there are notable oaks, walnuts, sequoias, birches, elms and maples about — all planted at the personal request of one president or another. Among several gardens are the Rose Garden, overlooked by the Oval Office, where many press conferences are held, and the Children's Garden, which contains a 'climbable' apple tree, the delight of many young visitors.

Woodward and Lothrop (which has its own underground station inside the store, delivering thousands of commuters past the tempting counters every day) are concentrated on F Street. But other big stores, such as Bloomingdale's, have opened in suburban centres like Tyson's Corner in the last few years, and other famous American department stores, such as I. Magnin, Neiman-Marcus and Saks Fifth Avenue, have branches in Washington.

Like many major American cities, notably New York's Manhattan and Miami, the streets are identified by numbers and

Visitors to the Smithsonian Institution Air and Space Museum can enter the Skylab Orbital Workshop (inset), and see space rockets and moon rock samples

letters in a grid system of horizontal and vertical streets. Streets running north and south are numbered in sequence, but in both directions. Streets running from east to west are distinguished by the letters of the alphabet. Each of the four sections of the city is identified by its geographical position — North-west, North-east, South-west and South-east, and the abreviations (N.W., N.E., S.W., S.E.) are added to the number of the street to avoid confusion. The visitor must bear this system in mind when looking for an address. The basic grid is also overlaid by the great avenues radiating out from the Capitol. Apart from Independence and Constitution Avenues, these bear the names of American States. Simple though the system is, there are traps for tourists. Watch out for I Street which is sometimes spelt out as the word 'Eye'. As there are at least two I (eye)

Streets as well as two 1st Streets it is easy to confuse them.

Washington's pavements are wide and generally not overcrowded, but pedestrians have more than their usual rights in the road, too. They can cross on certain junctions diagonally on specially marked lines. Whenever this right is exercised it effectively stops the roar of traffic in all directions at that junction for anything up to a minute. It pays always to walk safely. Safe walking is not just about road safety. There are areas of the city which the locals advise the tourist to avoid and it is not too difficult to detect the atmosphere in those streets in which it is sometimes not wise to linger. A busy thoroughfare where traffic flows smoothly at one end can turn into a sinister, sleazy neighbourhood at the other. In the evening, when fewer people are about,

Washington

and the shadows are too numerous to avoid, it is best to turn back into the lighted busy streets.

The National Visitor Center at Union Station on Massachusetts Avenue is even more eager than the average hotel desk clerk to show where everything is and how to go about seeing it all. There are information kiosks dotted about the downtown area of the city, where advice is dispensed with enthusiasm and courtesy. But nothing need really stop you from exploring the city — and the countryside around Washington — using the numerous transport options. Inter-city coach and train seats are best reserved in advance. The busy air shuttle service between Washington and New York, on the other hand, copes with walk-on passengers without problems. And because Washington's domestic airport, the National, is virtually in the heart of the city it provides an efficient air bus service for city-to-city commuting. Domestic flights are casual, quick and uncomplicated. The airport is so close to the city centre — just across the river — that at any time of day you can look into the sky and see these wide-bodied monsters climb steeply over the roof-tops. The point has not escaped the city fathers, and for years the controversy has raged over the risks to the city that these flights represent. One of the arguments for

A grey squirrel forms part of the autumn scene in Georgetown, the elegant residential suburb where many of Washington's diplomats have their homes

keeping the airport is that it is convenient for the nation's leaders when they need to jet in and out of the city without delay.

If you want to hire a car, the airport is the place to choose one of the giant international chains, or there are about 400 other firms in the city's Yellow Pages. Driving in the city is not difficult, particularly if you avoid the rush-hour. There are, of course, many confusing multi-junctions; below the Pentagon, on the edge of Arlington National Cemetery is a seven-interchange 'Spaghetti Junction' that locals have nicknamed 'The Mixing Bowl.' Parking requires the usual caution; Washington D.C. likes to keep its roads clear for moving traffic and the police are quite ruthless about towing away illegally parked cars at a moment's notice, usually denying the culprit a clue to its whereabouts. Any of twenty or more car compounds might need to be visited (phoning them is not likely to elicit any information) before the car is traced.

Taxis are relatively pricey — inside the city centre they work on a fixed tariff — but they are easy to hail or call. Apart from their convenience, they are often slower and it is best to go by bus or take the Metro Underground (see p.129). The red, white and blue buses are part of the Metro system, and are only crowded with office-bound commuters in rush-hours. While the correct fare is necessary as is the custom in most American cities, bus tokens can be bought at vending kiosks and — strangely enough — at banks. More accessible to the tourist are the Tourmobiles — open-sided buses whose routes link the tourist-area attractions,

while a cheerful guide on board describes what is what. Most of the public buildings offer free tours, sometimes mixing drama, spectacle and entertainment which would be hard for a commercial entrepreneur to match.

Outside the city limits, a unique cultural draw for inhabitants of Washington is Wolf Trap, a 117-acre farm park in suburban Vienna, Virginia. Wolf Trap was the first national park for the performing arts to be established in America. The park is open all year round, and the Filene Center from mid June to early September. Here, in the summer months, a wide-ranging programme of music, dance and drama is staged in a naturalistic open-air theatre. Though some of the auditorium is under cover, the theatre is open-sided, and the amphitheatre is a gentle, grass-covered hillside. People of all ages, carrying blankets to lie under the stars, converge on this unique concert platform to enjoy a range of opera, ballet, symphony music, jazz and drama.

To buy an expensive *objet d'art,* probably cheaper than anywhere else, the antique shops and art galleries in Alexandria and Georgetown can offer a dazzling choice. Both communities, coincidentally, founded by Scottish merchants long before Washington itself had taken more than a muddy footstep towards progress, are, each in its own way, a treasure house of good living and provide a feast of taste and entertainment. Georgetown was a town in its own right until 1871 when it lost its charter and became part of the City of Washington.

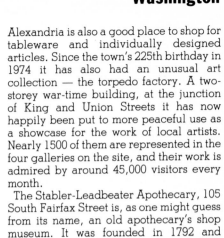

The John F. Kennedy Center for the Performing Arts, seen from the Potomac River; in the background Watergate

For years neglected and unwanted by the growing giant across the Rock Creek it benefited from the 1950s trend to preserve the past which brought new life and vigour to the areas centred around Wisconsin Avenue and M Street. It is now populated and patronized by a fashionable coterie from the Washington diplomatic corps as well as by tourists and visitors. Here you can buy china and glassware, oriental and Mexican fabrics, eat in chic, bohemian restaurants and visit the Old Stone House, built in 1765 at 3051 M Street North-west, and the oldest house in Georgetown.

Trendy to the point of being aloof, Alexandria is proud of its independence. Nonetheless it contributes 108,000 to the population of over three million in Washington's Greater Metropolitan area. Apart from its range of high-priced shops and residential properties it is renowned for its local delicacy, the soft-shell crab — a crustacean with a special flavour.

Alexandria is also a good place to shop for tableware and individually designed articles. Since the town's 225th birthday in 1974 it has also had an unusual art collection — the torpedo factory. A two-storey war-time building, at the junction of King and Union Streets it has now happily been put to more peaceful use as a showcase for the work of local artists. Nearly 1500 of them are represented in the four galleries on the site, and their work is admired by around 45,000 visitors every month.

The Stabler-Leadbeater Apothecary, 105 South Fairfax Street is, as one might guess from its name, an old apothecary's shop museum. It was founded in 1792 and remained in business as a shop until 1933. Antique equipment, jars, remedies and prescriptions make this unusual museum a fascinating place to visit. Among the most cherished relics is a note written by Mrs Washington to order castor oil. George Washington was among the many distinguished patrons of Gadsby's Tavern at Royal and Cameron Streets. Fellow diners included John Adams, Thomas Jefferson and the Marquis de Lafayette, who came from France to take part in the American Revolution and became a lifelong friend of the Washington family. The tavern is partly a museum, partly a functioning eating house where visitors can sample the traditional Colonial dishes that Washington and his compatriots often enjoyed. Alexandria residents, though cherishing their independence from the Federal Capital have retained the custom of celebrating Washington's birthday here every year on 22 February.

Washington Directory

Climate

Washington has four very distinct seasons. Spring, made beautiful by pink cherry blossom, is mild, with warm days and cooler evenings. Autumn is equally mild and pleasant. In summer the temperature can soar into the 90s, with a humidity to match, but in winter snow is fairly common, often playing havoc with the traffic.

Transport

AIRPORTS: Washington is served by three airports. Most international flights come into Dulles, however, 25 miles west of Washington, near Chantilly, Virginia. The Baltimore — Washington International Airport is 34 miles north-east of the city, off the Baltimore — Washington Parkway, and the National Airport, for internal flights, lies just across the Potomac River from the city centre and is much used by American senators and congressmen commuting between their home towns and Washington.

BUSES: The Metro bus system covers the entire District of Columbia — that is, the area occupied by the city of Washington itself, and the metropolitan area including parts of Maryland and Northern Virginia. Metro express buses operate during rush hours and have limited stops. Correct fare is needed as no change is given.

CAR HIRE: Of the many car hire firms that operate in Washington the largest, with offices in the city, in the suburbs, and at the airports are: Americar Rental Systems, 2600 Jefferson Davis Hwy, Arlington, tel. 684 7500; Avis, 1722 M St N.W., tel. 467 6585; Dollar Rent-a-Car Systems, 2400 Jefferson Davis Hwy, Arlington, tel. 979 4200; Hertz, 1622 L St N.W., tel. 800 654 3131; National, 12th and K Sts N.W., tel. 842 1000.

TAXIS: District of Columbia taxis charge by the zone and are relatively expensive. The major companies are: Capitol, tel. 546 2400. Eastern Imperial, tel. 829 4222 and Yellow, tel. 544 1212.

TRAINS: Union Station is at 1st Street and Massachusetts Avenue N.E., near the city centre. Rail connections with all parts of the States are good, and the Metroliner takes passengers to New York swiftly — journey time is approximately three hours.

Touring Information

AAA: The Potomac Division of the AAA has offices at 1730 Pennsylvania Ave N.W., Suite 300, tel. 393 3300. Other offices are in Alexandria and Falls Church, Virginia, and in Wheaton, Maryland. Open office hours, Monday to Friday; Washington office, Saturday.

NATIONAL VISITOR CENTER: Union Station, Massachusetts Ave at E St N.E., tel. 523 5300. The office is open from 9 am to 5.30 pm Monday to Friday. There are also kiosks at the Lincoln Memorial, Washington Monument, the Ellipse, Jefferson Memorial, Lafayette Park, the Museums of Air and Space, Natural History, History and Technology and the National Gallery of Art.

Museums & Galleries

ANACOSTIA NEIGHBOURHOOD MUSEUM: (Smithsonian)
2405 Martin Luther King Ave S.E., tel. 628 4422. Located in a converted cinema in the Anacostia section of Washington, this is a museum and research centre dealing with Afro-American history.

ARTS AND INDUSTRIES BUILDING: (Smithsonian)
900 Jefferson Dr. S.W., tel. 357 2700. Houses exhibits originally displayed at the 1876 Centennial exhibition in Philadelphia.

FORD'S THEATER: 511 10th St, N.W., tel. 347 4833.
These premises mark the spot where Lincoln was shot by John Wilkes Booth on 14 April 1865, and have been restored to 19th-century appearance. During the day, mini-plays depict life as it was in the middle of last century, and tell the story of Lincoln's life and the history of the Civil War (see also Theatres). Also here is the Lincoln Museum.

FREER GALLERY OF ART:
(Smithsonian) 12th St and Jefferson Drive S.W., tel. 357 2700. This gallery houses one of the world's finest collections of oriental art, amassed by Detroit industrialist Charles L. Freer. Also here are over 1000 of the works of Freer's friend, the painter James McNeill Whistler, and other American artists.

HILLWOOD MUSEUM: 4155
Linnean Ave, N.W., tel. 686 5807. China used by Catherine the Great can be seen in this mansion, once owned by Marjorie Merriweather Post, the daughter of the founder of the Postum Cereal Company. Also on display is an array of bejewelled Easter eggs made by Carl Fabergé for the Russian imperial court.

HIRSHHORN MUSEUM AND SCULPTURE GARDEN:
(Smithsonian) Independence Ave and 8th St S.W., tel. 357 2700. The distinctive circular building houses an art collection that reflects the change in style in painting and sculpture from the late 19th century to the present. The works of artists such as Edgar Degas, Henri Matisse and Pablo Picasso are here.

MUSEUM OF AFRICAN ART: (Smithsonian) 316-31 A St N.E., tel. 287 3490.
Exhibits reflect the rich and colourful history of Africa, and her influence, as a country, on modern art.

NATIONAL AIR AND SPACE MUSEUM: (Smithsonian)
Independence Ave, between 4th and 7th Sts S.W., tel. 357 2700. Dedicated to the history of flight, this is the largest of the Smithsonian museums, with exhibits such as the Wright brothers' plane and the Apollo-Soyuz spacecraft.

NATIONAL GALLERY OF ART: 6th St at Constitution Ave N.W., tel. 737 4215.
Here is one of the world's finest collections of European and American paintings, sculpture and graphic arts. The National Gallery is the only American museum which owns a painting by Leonardo da Vinci, his beautiful portrait of Ginevra de' Benci. The gallery is administered by the Smithsonian, but the basis of its collection was the gift by Andrew Mellon (1855-1937) of his outstanding collection of works of art. Other collections were soon added, and there are now more than 30,000 items.
The new East Building, incorporates a soaring white tower, tapering almost to a point, and was opened as recently as 1978. Designed by the New York architects I. M. Pei and Partners, it is one of the most striking of Washington's buildings.

NATIONAL MUSEUM OF AMERICAN ART:
(Smithsonian) 8th and G Sts N.W., tel. 628 4422. American works of art from the 18th century to the present day are housed here. Two special galleries help the young to explore the sensory aspects of art.

NATIONAL MUSEUM OF AMERICAN HISTORY:
(Smithsonian), Constitution Ave at 12th and 14th Sts N.W. tel. 357 2700. Highlights of this museum range from the domestic — for example, George Washington's false teeth, his uniform and tent, and the gowns of numerous 'First Ladies' — to inventions such as Bell's telephone, Edison's light bulb and Whitney's model of the original cotton gin. Other exhibits embrace art, stamps, ceramics and many other subjects representing the history of invention.

NATIONAL MUSEUM OF NATURAL HISTORY:
(Smithsonian) Constitution Ave at 10th St N.W., tel. 357 2700. The fascinating array of 60,000,000 exhibits ranges from a mounted African bush elephant to the Hope Diamond.

NATIONAL PORTRAIT GALLERY: (Smithsonian) 8th and F St N.W., tel. 357 2700.
Visitors can trace the history of America through the portraits in this gallery. Paintings of more than 500 people who helped shape its development in the political, scientific, literary, artistic or military spheres can be seen on display here.

RENWICK GALLERY:
(Smithsonian) Pennsylvania Ave at 17th St N.W., tel. 357 2700. The principal rooms in this gallery have been restored and refurnished in 19th-century style. On show are changing exhibits of contemporary and historic American crafts.

SMITHSONIAN INSTITUTION BUILDING:
The Castle, 1000 Jefferson Drive S.W., tel. 357 2700. Established in 1846 with funds bequeathed by James Smithson (see p.128), an English scientist, this is the administration building of the largest museum complex in the world. More than 70 million objects and specimens exist in the Smithsonian's 12 Washington museums and zoo. The arts, history, technology, natural history, aviation, industry, biology and many other subjects are represented and scholars use the huge reference departments as research centres. The individual museums are listed alphabetically.

WASHINGTON DOLLS' HOUSE AND TOY MUSEUM:
5236 44th St N.W., tel. 244 0024. The lifetime collection of Flora Gill Jacobs, author and well-known authority on miniature antiques, is housed here. It includes antique toys and games and a wide-ranging collection of delightful old, authentically-furnished dolls' houses.

WOODROW WILSON HOUSE: 2340 S St N.W., tel. 673 4034.
The home of ex-president Woodrow Wilson who was one of the principal founders of the League of Nations after World War I, has been restored, and retains its original furniture and memorabilia.

Places of Interest

THE CAPITOL: Capitol Hill, between Constitution and Independence Aves. Probably America's greatest monument, the 188-year-old Capitol is the home of the US Government — the Senate is in one wing and the House of Representatives in the other. The building's imposing beauty is complemented by the graceful 131-acre park in which it is set. The great dome is decorated with a fresco, and it stands above the great Rotunda circular hall, which is filled with numerous works of art. It is here that honoured Americans lie in state. Within the Capitol are further ornate frescoes in the corridors of the Senate wing, the original Supreme Court chambers and in the Statuary Hall, where famous figures, cast in bronze, represent each State.

FEDERAL BUREAU OF INVESTIGATION: E St, between 9th and 10th Sts N.W., tel. 324 3447.
Guided tours show devotees of American television detective series what the FBI is really like, with fire-arm demonstrations, a visit to 'rogues' gallery', tours of the laboratories, and a brief history of the Bureau.

FOLGER SHAKESPEARE LIBRARY: 201 East Capitol St S.E., tel. 546 4800.
One of the world's finest collections of Reinaissance books and manuscripts has been amassed here. Tours by appointment only.

THE LIBRARY OF CONGRESS: 1st St between E, E. Capitol St and Independence Ave, tel. 287 5000.
The world's largest and richest library is contained in this beautiful Italian Renaissance-style structure. Originally designed as a research base for the Congress, the Library's 76,000,000 items include motion pictures, music, maps, manuscripts and photographs. Among the exhibits are one of the three existing copies of the Gutenberg Bible and the oldest existing film — Thomas Edison's three-second *Sneeze*. dating from the 1890s.
Lectures and concerts take place regularly in the Coolidge Auditorium.

JEFFERSON MEMORIAL:
East Potomac Park. A domed colonnaded building commemorates Thomas Jefferson (1743-1826), author of the Declaration of Independence, founder of the Democratic Party and third president of the United States. The memorial was completed in 1939, and incorporates some of Jefferson's own architectural ideas. Extracts from his speeches and writings decorate the interior, which contains a bronze statue of him.

LINCOLN MEMORIAL: West
Potomac Park. This dignified classical building, clad in white marble, commemorates President Abraham Lincoln who was assassinated in 1865 (see Ford's Theater). Its design was inspired by the Parthenon in Athens and the 36 columns surrounding the outside represent the number of states in the Union at the time of his presidency. The interior is dominated by the massive, seated figure of Lincoln, and the walls are inscribed with his famous Gettysburg Address and his Second Inauguration Address.

NATIONAL ARCHIVES:
Constitution Ave, between 7th and 9th Sts N.W., tel. 523 3000. All major American historical records are on file in this handsome building, designed with flair by John Russell Pope. Its treasures include the Declaration of Independence and the Bill of Rights, which are kept in helium-filled glass and bronze cases to protect them.

ROOSEVELT MEMORIAL:
The memorial to Theodore Roosevelt, president from 1901 to 1909, stands on Roosevelt Island in the Potomac River. The island can be reached via Theodore Roosevelt Bridge. Nearly two miles of footpaths wind through picturesque woods and marshland, the highlight of which is a statuary garden centring on President Roosevelt's statue. Rangers are on hand to give guided tours of the island.

TREASURY DEPARTMENT EXHIBIT HALL: 15th and Pennsylvania Ave, N.W., tel. 566 5221. Real and counterfeit money is on display here, as well as solid gold bars and uncirculated coins.

WASHINGTON CATHEDRAL: Winconsin, Massachusetts and Woodley Aves N.W. A prime example of Gothic architecture, this cathedral, begun in 1907, was one of the last to be built in the style, and is still not completed. Its central tower is the highest point in Washington. The cathedral contains some remarkable stained glass windows, including one depicting the space age and incorporating a piece of moon rock.

WASHINGTON MONUMENT: on the Mall at 15th St. This huge, white marble obelisk, completed in 1884, soars 555ft into the sky and was erected to commemorate George Washington, first president of the Union. It dominates the Mall, a two-mile grand avenue of green leading from the Lincoln Memorial to the Capitol. From the top (reached by lift) there is a splendid view of the city.

Theatres

ARENA STAGE AND THE KREEGER THEATER: 6th and M St, S.W., tel. 488 3300. Original and classical plays are staged in spring, autumn and winter.

FORD'S THEATER: 511 10th St, N.W., tel. 347 4833. The theatre, scene of President Lincoln's assassination was for many years a museum. It now stages plays once more, and the museum has been rehoused in the basement.

FOLGER LIBRARY'S ELIZABETHAN THEATER: 201 E Capitol St, S.E., tel. 546 4800. Although staging contemporary plays, this Elizabethan-style theatre specializes in Shakespearian productions.

JOHN F KENNEDY CENTER FOR THE PERFORMING ARTS: Rock Creek Parkway and New Hampshire Ave N.W., tel. 254 3600. This magnificent arts complex includes an opera house and concert hall, the Eisenhower Theater and new Terrace Theater. It is also the home of the National Symphony Orchestra.

NATIONAL THEATER: 1321 E St, N.W., tel. 628 3393, puts on major productions all the year round.

OLNEY THEATER: rt 108, Olney, Md., tel. 924 3400, presents summertime productions featuring college student players, as well as well-known actors. About an hour's drive from the City.

WOLF TRAP FARM PARK FOR THE PERFORMING ARTS: rt 7 near Vienna, Va — accessible via Dulles Airport access highway, tel. 703 938 3800. Symphony music, pop concerts, ballet and musicals are presented here in beautiful outdoor surroundings.

Sport

GOLF: Courses in the vicinity include **East Potomac Park**, Hains Point, tel. 554 9813, and **Rock Creek Park**, Military Road N.W., tel. 723 9832.

SWIMMING: There are no beaches for swimming in Washington, but the District of Columbia Department of Recreation operates 41 swimming pools in the area, to which admission is free. One of the best is **Capitol East Natatorium**, 635 North Carolina Ave, S.E.

TENNIS: There are 49 hard surface courts in and around the city, of which several are floodlit for evening play. A free permit to use these courts may be obtained from DC Department of Recreation, 3149 16th St N.W. tel. 673 7646.

The hotels and restaurants listed here are either recommended by the American Automobile Association (AAA) or have been selected because they are of interest to tourists. As a rough guide to cost, they have been classified as either expensive, moderate or reasonable. Unless otherwise stated, hotels all have private bathrooms and colour television.

Hotels

ALLEN LEE HOTEL: 2224 F St N.W., tel. 331 1224, 100 rooms. All rooms air conditioned, only half with private bathrooms. Near Kennedy Center and George Washington University. Reasonable.

HARRINGTON HOTEL: 11th and E Sts N.W., tel. 628 8140. 600 rooms, cafeteria, garage, phones in every room, air conditioning. Within walking distance of White House, Mall and Capitol. Reasonable.

HOTEL WASHINGTON: 15th and Pennsylvania Ave N.W., tel. 638 5900. 370 rooms. Rooftop restaurant. Central, moderate.

LOMBARDY TOWERS: 2019 Eye St N.W., tel. 828 2600, 127 apartments. Desks in all rooms, walk-in closets, kitchenettes, laundry facilities. Moderate.

THE MADISON: 15th and M Sts N.W., tel. 826 1600. 374 rooms. Saunas, refrigerators in rooms. Expensive.

PARK CENTRAL HOTEL: 705 18th St N.W., tel. 393 4700. 250 rooms. Roof garden and restaurant. Central. Moderate.

QUALITY INN — CAPITOL HILL: 415 New Jersey Ave N.W., tel. 638 1616. 350 rooms. Sauna, gymnasium, swimming pool, restaurant, cocktail lounge. Moderately expensive.

WATERGATE HOTEL: 2650 Virginia Ave N.W., tel. 965 2300. 238 rooms, swimming pool, health club, restaurant, cocktail lounge, shopping mall. Expensive.

Restaurants

Thanks to the increase in the number of excellent restaurants which have opened in Washington in recent years, it is not only possible to eat well in pleasant surroundings, but also to experience a wide and tempting variety of authentic dishes from Asia and Latin America — Europe, too, if you are missing the cooking from nearer home.

THE BREAD OVEN: 1220 19th St N.W., tel. 466 4264. This busy, bright, French-style restaurant is open for breakfast (smell that fresh French bread!) lunch, tea and dinner. Lunch is especially good, with a choice of five main dishes. Specialities include veau Niçoise and lamb couscous.

CAFE RONDO: 1900 Q St, corner of Connecticut Ave, tel. 232 1885. Enjoy an al fresco lunch or dinner under striped awnings in this busy area of town. Soups, egg dishes (lots of quiches) and salads are available, or linger longer over the original beef Rondo — meat and vegetables in wine sauce. Reasonable.

EL CARIBE: 1828 Columbia Rd N.W., tel. 234 6969. A small lantern-lit restaurant with wooden walls and a beamed ceiling. It specialises in Latin-American, Spanish and Mexican cuisine, with seafood, poultry and meat served in traditional style, together with beans and rice. It deserves the awards it has won. Reasonable.

THE DELLY ON CAPITOL HILL: 332 Pennsylvania Ave S.E., tel. 547 8668. Close to the Capitol (and a favourite of the staff) this modern-looking restaurant serves old fashioned food, such as thick sandwiches on rye bread, hot pastrami and corned beef and home-made chicken soup. There are some superbly rich desserts, too, such as creamy cheesecake. Reasonable.

IRON GATE INN: 1734 N St N.W., tel. 737 1370. Originally a coachhouse, this is one of Washington's most charming restaurants. It is set in attractive grounds, where you can eat al fresco, and specializes in Middle Eastern cuisine. There are daily specials or a combination platter with a taste of everything; don't miss the humus (chick pea dip with sesame paste) or the memorable sweets. Moderate.

K STREET SALOON AND STEAKERY: 1511 K St N.W., tel. 659 8170. You can dine in style on steaks (prime rib is popular) or roast beef at this intimate, elegant Victorian-style restaurant. Choosing a main course entitles you to as many trips to the splendid salad bar as you can manage. Pleasant service and bargain prices — especially at lunchtime. Moderate.

MARTIN'S TAVERN: 1264 Wisconsin Ave N.W., tel. FE3 7370. Here is down-to-earth food and lots of it, served by witty waiters in the mid-30s movie surroundings of this dark-walled tavern. Try the roast duck if the cabbage and corned beef 'special' doesn't appeal. Reasonable.

MIKADO: 4707 Wisconsin Ave N.W., tel. 244 1740. Small and serene, like the waitresses in their traditional costumes, Mikado is a delightfully authentic Japanese restaurant. Feast on a ten-course dinner, or simply sample familiar sukiyaki or try less familiar sashimi (raw fish) or donburi (shrimps, eggs or meat on rice). Leave room for one of the tempting desserts. Moderately expensive.

PIER 7: 7th St and Main Ave S.W., tel. 554 2500. Super seafood restaurant on the water-front with a warm and convivial atmosphere. There is a wide assortment of meat and poultry, but don't miss the mouthwatering delights of the shrimps, lobsters, clams, oysters and crabs, as well as the tempting accompanying sauces. Reasonable/moderate.

TABARD INN: 1739 N St N.W., tel. 785 1277. This peaceful, simply-decorated restaurant on downtown's doorstep provides efficiently served food that tastes as good as it looks. Continental breakfasts (with extras if desired) start at 7am. There is a lot to excite the palate, and the dressed, cold chicken is especially good. Moderate.

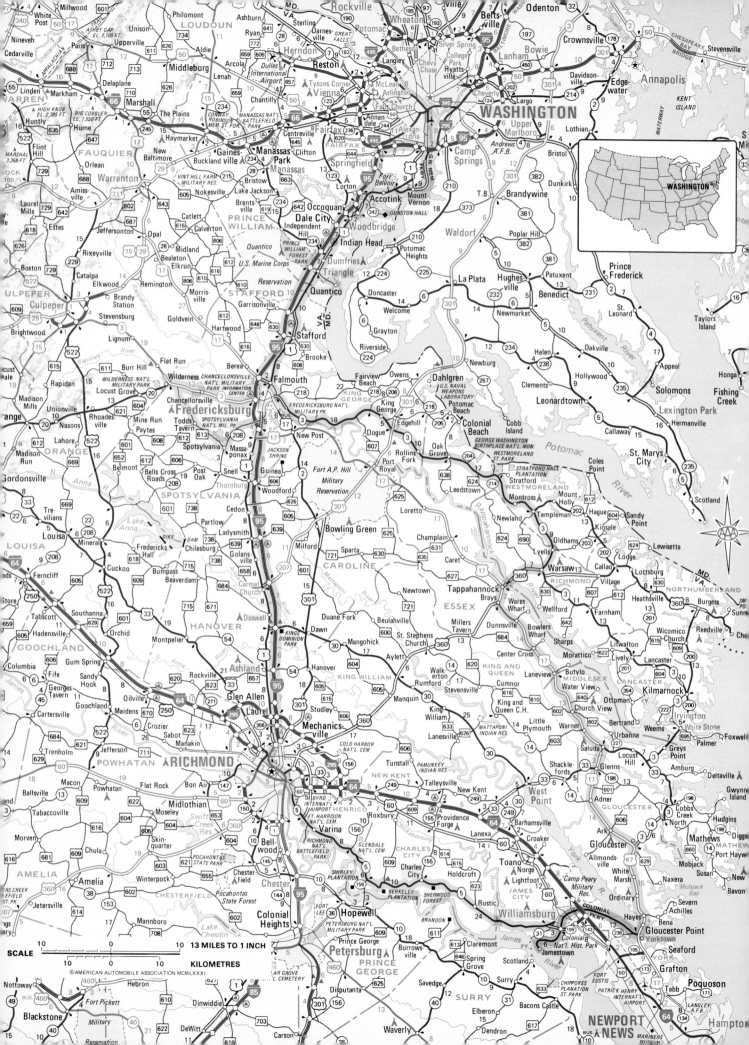

Mount Vernon and Colonial Virginia

3 days — 312 miles

Washington — Mount Vernon — Fort Belvoir — Accotink (Pohick Church) — Gunston Hall — Triangle — Quantico — Chancellorsville — Wilderness — Spotsylvania — Doswell — Ashland — Richmond — Richmond National Battlefield Park — Charles City — Williamsburg — Jamestown — Yorktown — Stratford — George Washington Birthplace National Monument — Washington

America's colonial heritage is nowhere more apparent than in the three Colonial cities of Jamestown, Williamsburg and Yorktown — all conveniently linked by the Colonial Parkway. Indeed throughout this tour, history is the keynote, with visits to some of the great plantation houses which were the homes and birthplaces of many of America's most famous statesmen, among them George Washington, Patrick Henry and Robert E. Lee.
> Leave Washington on the George Washington Memorial Parkway via Alexandria. After 9 miles enter Mount Vernon.

Mount Vernon, Virginia
George Washington's father, Augustine, brought his family to Little Hunting Creek Plantation, as the Mount Vernon estate was then called, in 1735. On his death in 1743 the property, which had been given to his eldest son, Lawrence, was renamed Mount Vernon in honour of the British admiral Lord Edward Vernon, under whose command Lawrence Washington had served in the Caribbean in 1739. Two years after Lawrence's death in 1752, his widow gave up her interest in the estate to George Washington. Apart from his service as American Commander in the War of Independence (1776-81) and his term as President (1789-97), George Washington and his wife, Martha, made their home at Mount Vernon until his death in 1799. He and his wife, who died in 1802, lie buried in a mausoleum at the foot of the hill.

The white-painted house, a superb example of colonial architecture, stands in a delightful park, overlooking the thickly wooded valley of the Potomac River and the Maryland hills. Since 1858, when the estate was purchased from a descendant of the Washington family by the Mount Vernon Ladies' Association, it has been preserved as a national monument. Estate records have enabled the buildings and the grounds to be restored authentically, and many of the original items of furniture,

Mount Vernon, now a national monument, was the home of the Washington family. George Washington and his wife, Martha, are buried on the estate

including the bed in which Washington died, have been returned to the house. It is not known whether he employed an architect when he began to enlarge the mansion, but contemporary accounts confirm that he personally directed much of the work, including the construction of the elegant colonnaded piazza that runs along the east front, where he and his wife loved to sit and look out over the river valley.

In colonial times, a Virginia estate had to be as nearly self-sufficient as possible. Thus, Mount Vernon was organized like a small village, with its spinning house, storehouse, smokehouse, washhouse and stables fanning out along two wide avenues on either side of the house. The kitchen, as in many plantation houses of the time, was in a separate building, to keep the smells and heat of cooking away from the main house. All these buildings have been restored and contain the authentic utensils of the period. The kitchen gardens and the formal flower gardens have been stocked with plants that are either mentioned in the estate records or are known to have been common in 18th-century Virginia. Packets

of seeds, on sale at the greenhouse shop, make an attractive souvenir. A tour of the house and grounds will take at least an hour.
> Proceed on Mt Vernon Highway to US 1 which leads south to Fort Belvoir.

Fort Belvoir, Virginia
This US Army post was once the site of Belvoir (1741), the plantation home of Colonel William Fairfax, a close friend of George Washington. The base is now the home of the Engineer School, Mobility Equipment Research and Development Center, Computer Systems Command, Davison Army Air Field, De Witt Army Hospital, the 15th Combat Support Hospital and the Naval Nuclear Power Unit. Certain unrestricted areas are open to the public. The US Army Engineer Museum on Belvoir Rd at 16th Street covers the 200-year history of the Army Corps of Engineers.
> Continue southwards on US 1 for a couple of miles to Accotink. About 2 miles south-west of the town, still on US 1, is Pohick Church.

Pohick Church, Virginia
Pohick Church was built in 1773, on a site selected by George Washington, to serve as the parish church of Mount Vernon, Gunston Hall (see below) and Belvoir. George Washington served here as vestryman for 27 years. The interior has been restored since the Civil War when the fittings were ripped out so that the building could be used as a stable for the Federal troops' horses. The old stone baptismal font was found many years after the war. It was serving as a trough in a farmyard.
> Leave Pohick Church on US 1 and turn off east on State Route 242 to Gunston Hall.

Gunston Hall, Virginia
This 18th-century mansion beside the Potomac River was built by George Mason, a member of one of Virginia's oldest families. An outstanding Revolutionary patriot, Mason wrote the Virginia Declaration of Rights in 1776 and later helped to frame the American Constitution (1787) and the Bill of Rights (1791). The mansion, built in the Georgian style, is surrounded by pleasant gardens and is open to the public.
> Return to US 1 and continue southwards for approximately 16 miles into Triangle.

Triangle, Virginia
The main attraction here is the 18,571-acre forest around Quantico Creek, known as the Prince-William Forest Park. Wildlife flourishes among the pines and hardwood and you may see white-tailed deer, red and grey foxes, beavers, woodchucks and flying squirrels. There is a rich variety of birdlife in the forest. Information, lectures, exhibitions and audio-visual shows are available most weekends at the Turkey Run Ridge Nature Center.
> From Triangle turn left on to an unclassified road into Quantico.

Quantico, Virginia
At the entrance of the Marine Corps Development and Education Command can be seen a replica of the statue depicting the soldiers of the US Marine Corps raising their flag on Mount Suribachi at Iwo Jima. This was one of the most terrible battles of World War II, fought in the Pacific during the last months of the war, in February-March 1945. The original stands in Arlington National Cemetery. Quantico is one of the largest Marine Corps posts in the country.

The Marine Corps Aviation Museum, situated off US 1 and

Colonial Virginia

Interstate 95, contains examples of the planes, weapons and equipment used in World War II. There is also an exhibition which traces the development of aviation technology from its beginnings to the present day.

Return to the US 1 at Triangle and proceed southwards for 18 miles into Falmouth. From Falmouth join Interstate 95 and after 4 miles turn right on to State Route 3 for Chancellorsville.

Chancellorsville, Virginia
In 1863 one of the most important battles of the Civil War took place at Chancellorsville. The battle resulted in a brilliant victory for the Confederacy, whose forces were commanded by General Robert E. Lee and General 'Stonewall' Jackson. More than 30,000 men were killed.

The battlefield and those of Spotsylvania Court House and Wilderness (see below) form part of the Fredericksburg and Spotsylvania National Military Park, established in 1927. Trench remains and gunpits are well preserved, as are several historic sites such as the Jackson Shrine, commemorating the death of General Jackson at Guiney's Station in May 1863. The visitors' centre on the Chancellorsville battlefield offers slide shows and has a small museum. Detailed maps of the battlefields, explaining strategy and troop movements, are on show at the visitors' centre on Lafayette Boulevard (US 1) in Fredericksburg.

Continue for 13 miles along State Route 3 and enter Wilderness.

Wilderness, Virginia
Wilderness, in the Fredericksburg and Spotsylvania National Park, was the site where the Supreme Commander of the Northern Armies, General Ulysses S. Grant, opened his final offensive against General Robert E. Lee's Confederate Army on 5 May 1864. The battle ended in a victory for neither side, but after it, the way to Richmond, capital of the Confederate States, lay open to Grant.

From Wilderness take Local Route 613 and proceed for approximately 12 miles to Spotsylvania.

Spotsylvania, Virginia
One of the fiercest campaigns of the Civil War was fought around Spotsylvania Court House between 8 and 21 May 1864. The climax of the fighting, known as the Battle of 'Bloody Angle', took place on 12 May and resulted in a bitter defeat for Lee's Confederate army.

Leave Spotsylvania on Local Route 208 and continue for 6 miles. Turn right on to Interstate 95 for approximately 30 miles into Doswell and Kings Dominion.

Doswell, Virginia
If you feel that you have seen enough of battlefields, Kings Dominion offers some present-day refreshment in the form of a 1,300-acre multi-attraction amusement park. You can stroll down International Street with its sidewalk cafés, quaint buildings and replica of the Eiffel Tower, or explore the wonders of Candy Apple Grove, a turn-of-the-century amusement park featuring 36 thrilling rides. Other themes include Happy Land, inhabited by cartoon characters, where you can take miniature rides and watch puppet and dolphin shows; Old Virginia; a Broadway review called New York, New York; the Lost World with its underwater Atlantis and Time Shaft where you can experience a gravity-defying spin through the centuries, and finally a safari park where you travel by monorail through a wildlife preserve inhabited by nearly 100 species, including rare animals such as the white rhino.

Continue on Interstate 95 for 6 miles into Ashland.

Ashland, Virginia
Approximately nine miles north-west of the town is Scotchtown which was from 1771 to 1777 the home of Patrick Henry, a lawyer of great eloquence who played a significant role in the American War of Independence. His fiery speech in favour of arming the Virginia Militia, delivered in 1775, contained the stirring battlecry, 'then give me liberty or give me death.' In 1776 he became the first governor of the newly formed state of Virginia.

Ashland was also the childhood home of Dolley Payne, who, after her marriage to James Madison, president of the United States from 1809 to 1817, became a brilliant political hostess.

Leave Ashland on Interstate 95 and continue south for 15 miles into Richmond.

Richmond, Virginia
Richmond today combines the atmosphere of a gracious cultural centre with the industrial drive of one of the world's greatest tobacco markets. It has been the capital city of Virginia since 1779 and was built in 1737 close to the site of a pioneer settlement called 'None Such', built by Captain John Smith on a tract of land he bought in 1609 from the Indian chief, Powhatan. Powhatan's daughter, Pocahontas, married the English settler, John Rolfe, and died in England in 1617.

After the southern states seceded from the Union, Richmond became (1861-5) the capital of the Confederate States of America. Many unsuccessful attempts were made to capture the city, which was ultimately taken by General Ulysses S. Grant, who had forced the Confederacy's downfall at the siege of Petersburg, after which General Lee's army surrendered,

on 9 April 1865. Most of the city was destroyed in a fire started by the retreating Confederate troops.

In downtown Richmond, the old commercial centre, around James River, has recently been restored. Here can be seen the old cobbled streets, lined with tobacco warehouses, many now converted to restaurants and shops. Victorian and Edwardian town houses can be seen in the Fan District, which lies to the west of the Capitol.

The Capitol building on Capitol Square was designed in 1788 by Thomas Jefferson on the lines of the Maison Carrée, a Roman temple at Nîmes in southern France. One of the outstanding figures of American history, Jefferson not only drafted the American Declaration of Independence and became the country's third president in 1801, but also found time to work as a designer of buildings and inventor of machinery.

There are dozens of museums in Richmond. The most unusual, perhaps, is the Poe Museum and Richmond's Oldest House. The Old Stone House, as it is called, was built between 1685 and 1688, a curious structure of unhewn river stones. A converted carriage-house is now the Edgar Allan Poe Museum and contains a series of illustrations by James Carling, inspired by Poe's famous poem, The Raven. Poe, the master of tales of mystery and the unexplained, lived for a short time in Richmond in the 1830s. He died in poverty in Baltimore in 1849 at the age of forty.

The Valentine Museum in Clay Street portrays the life and history of Richmond. It is a magnificent 19th-century house, furnished in period, with fascinating displays of costumes, textiles, silver and china.

The Museum of the Confederacy stands in the grounds of the Confederate White House, a

mansion built in 1817, and the official residence of Jefferson Davis, president of the short-lived Confederacy, from 1861-5. In the museum are many Civil-War relics.

The Virginia Museum of Fine Arts on Grove Avenue, one of the largest in the south, has a superb collection of objects created by Fabergé, jeweller to the Court of the Tsars, including five of his famous jewelled Easter eggs.

St John's Church, an elegant 18th-century structure, crowned with a graceful three-storey tower, was built in 1741. This is where Patrick Henry made his great speech on liberty (see Ashland).

Take State Route 5 and drive 7 miles south on to a small road to the right leading to Richmond National Battlefield Park.

Richmond National Battlefield Park, Virginia
Although seven 'on-to-Richmond' offensives were mounted by the Union forces during the Civil War, the Confederate capital resisted them all, until the seige of Petersburg in 1865 finally forced General Lee to abandon defence of the city.

The Richmond National Battlefield Park includes several Civil War sites. Seven Pines, also known as Fair Oaks, was fought in May 1862; the Seven Days Battles were a series of clashes that took place in the last week of June 1862; and the Battle of Cold Harbor took place in May 1864. The number of dead at Cold Harbor — more than 7000 in 30 minutes' fighting — was horrific. It was a victory — the last — for General Lee and the

Generals Robert E. Lee and 'Stonewall' Jackson commanded the Southern forces at the Battle of Chancellorsville, which took place in 1863

Exact replicas of the ships that brought the first settlers to Virginia, moored on the James River

Confederates. The main visitors' centre and museum is at Chimborazo Park just outside Richmond and there is another at Fort Harrison.

| Return to State Route 5 and drive 24 miles south-east to Charles City.

Charles City, Virginia

Some of the most historic houses in Virginia are to be found around Charles City. Berkeley Plantation, standing in wooded grounds on the Richmond side of the city, was the ancestral house of the Harrison family, two of whose members, William Henry and his grandson, Benjamin, became presidents of the United States. The land on which Berkeley stands was granted to the Berkeley Company in 1619 by King James I. The present mansion, an elegant, three-storey brick house, was built in 1726. In 1781, towards the end of the War of Independence, Benedict Arnold, an American commander in the pay of the British, led troops to plunder the estate, and Union forces occupied it during the Civil War. The house has been restored and furnished with period pieces and is open daily from 8am to 5pm.

Nearby, the Shirley Plantation has been owned and occupied by the Hill Carter family, who still live there, for more than two centuries. Shirley was the family home of Ann Hill Carter, mother of Robert E. Lee. Founded in 1613, the present house dates from 1723. Family portraits spanning nine generations and a magnificent walnut staircase, which appears to have no visible means of support, rising the full height of the house, are among the many interesting items.

At Shirley, visitors can see something of how a James-River

estate was run, as the plantation still produces corn, barley, wheat and soya. Among the original dependencies, restored to their 18th-century state, are a kitchen, smokehouse, dovecot and stables.

East of Charles City is Sherwood Forest, the plantation home of President John Tyler. Built in 1703, the restored, 300ft-long frame house contains many original pieces.

| Drive south-east for 24 miles on State Route 5 (through James River plantation country) to Williamsburg and the 'Historic Triangle' of Virginia.

Williamsburg, Virginia

Williamsburg, Jamestown and Yorktown form the 'Historic Triangle' of Virginia: British America was established at Jamestown, enjoyed its golden age at Williamsburg and ended at Yorktown in 1781 with the surrender of General Cornwallis. In 1699, the capital of the settlers' colony moved from low-lying Jamestown, whose atmosphere was considered unhealthy, to Middle Plantation, renamed Williamsburg in honour of King William III. It remained Virginia's capital until 1780, when Richmond became the seat of the state government.

Colonial Williamsburg is a mile-long area, restored down to the last detail to its appearance in the 18th century. Restoration work was started in 1926 by John D. Rockefeller Jr, and involved many years of research to establish not only the design and furnishing of the buildings, but also the layout of the gardens. No traffic, other than horse-drawn carriages, is allowed in the streets in daylight hours, and the guides and craftsmen all wear 18th-century dress.

Among the public buildings are the State Capitol of 1705 which has been reconstructed on the original foundations. Rare portraits of Washington, and Presidents Jefferson, Madison and

Monroe are displayed here. The most magnificent building is the Governor's Palace, which was used by royal governors from 1720 to 1775. The whole complex has been splendidly reconstructed.

Diverse craft shops, where revived arts, trades and crafts are practised, using 18th-century tools and methods of production, include a bootmaker's, gunsmith's, basketmaker's, silversmith's, printer's and apothecary's shops, a flour mill, a brickfield and a post office.

Raleigh Tavern, in Duke of Gloucester Street, became a centre of social and political life before the Revolution. George Washington, Patrick Henry, Thomas Jefferson and Edmund Pendleton are among the luminaries who made history in this tavern.

Authentic colonial food is served at three restored 18th-century inns, Christiana Campbell's Tavern, the King's Arms Tavern

and Chowning's Tavern. The Williamsburg Inn is a luxury hotel that runs two colonial houses, authentically furnished (but with bathrooms), as an annexe for visitors. Tickets for Colonial Williamsburg can be obtained from the Information Center on Colonial Parkway.

Six miles south-east, via the 18th-century County Road, is the beautiful Carter's Grove plantation, once owned by Robert, nicknamed 'King', Carter, whose plantation of more than 300,000 acres was worked by 1000 slaves. The mansion, built in 1750-3 by Carter Burwell, is furnished in a fascinating mixture of styles.

| Drive 3 miles on State Route 199 to the Colonial Parkway and head south for 6 miles to Jamestown.

Jamestown, Virginia

In December, 1606, three small ships, financed by the Virginia Company, set sail from London

The Raleigh Tavern in colonial Williamsburg, site of many historic meetings in the early days of the colony of Virginia

Colonial Virginia

for America. The *Susan Constant,* the *Godspeed* and the *Discovery* reached Virginia in May 1607, and the 104 settlers made their way up the James River, where they discovered a favourable site and built a fort. This eventually grew into Jamestown, the first permanent English colony in the New World. The early years of the colony were harsh, but in 1612 John Rolfe (who later married the Indian princess, Pocahontas) discovered a new way to cure tobacco and the success of the colony was established. Almost nothing now remains of colonial Jamestown — the old church tower is the only standing ruin.

Jamestown Festival Park, however, created in 1957 for the 350th anniversary of the town, is a fascinating reconstruction of the early settlement. It is at the entrance to the causeway leading to Jamestown, and consists of the triangular fort first built by the settlers, a 17th-century pottery, and Powhatan's Lodge, a typical Indian ceremonial lodge. On the river ride full-scale replicas of the three tiny ships on which the first settlers made their journey. You can actually board the *Susan Constant* and view the cramped quarters which housed the brave families.

Drive 18 miles along the Colonial Freeway east to Yorktown.

Yorktown, Virginia
One of the four official ports licensed to ship tobacco from the Colony of Virginia, Yorktown was founded in 1691. It flourished until the War of Independence when it was blockaded by the British, and it was here that General Cornwallis surrendered in 1781 to the combined French and American forces led by George Washington. Cornwallis and the defeated British army marched out of Yorktown to the tune 'The World Turned Upside Down.'

The Yorktown Victory Centre, two miles west of the town, shows a film of the 1781 battle, and visitors can tour the battlefield. The National Park Visitor Center, east of Main Street, has information about the historic buildings in the town. Of special interest is Moore House, where British, French and American representatives met to draw up papers formalizing the surrender of the British in October 1781.

Take US 17 and drive north through White Marsh for about 50 miles, then cross the Rappahannock River on US 360. After 7 miles, join State Route 3 and drive for about 17 miles to State Route 214 for Stratford.

Stratford, Virginia
Stratford Hall Plantation is a fascinating restoration of a working colonial plantation. Methods of the 18th and 19th centuries are still practised, and visitors may wander over more than 1500 acres of woods, meadows and gardens.

Stratford Hall, built in 1725 by Thomas Lee, was the birthplace (1807) of Robert E. Lee. The house is one of the finest examples of Jacobean architecture in the United States and contains many original exhibits, among them a spinning and weaving room. There is also a working water mill.

Return to State Route 3 and drive for about 4 miles. Turn right on State Route 204 for George Washington Birthplace National Monument.

George Washington Birthplace National Monument, Virginia
George Washington was born here in 1732. The original house, built by Augustine Washington between 1722 and 1726, was destroyed by fire on Christmas Day, 1779. Excavations have revealed as many as five original foundations, and the present house is a reconstructed 18th-century plantation house, built of handmade bricks, and is furnished with antiques of the period of Washington's boyhood.

The Colonial Living Farm has livestock and plants which were common varieties in George Washington's day. Crops are raised by methods used during the colonial period. The grounds cover more than 538 acres and include a cemetery containing the graves of more than 30 members of the Washington family, among them George Washington's father, grandfather and great grandfather.

Return to State Route 3 and drive for 36 miles north-west to Falmouth. From Falmouth take Interstate 95 back to Washington.

The Governor's Palace in Williamsburg, symbol of British colonial rule

Annapolis and Chesapeake Bay

1 day — 82 miles

Washington DC — Annapolis/Chesapeake Bay

Leave Washington on the Baltimore-Washington Parkway. 8 miles from the city take US 50 east, then after 2 miles turn south on to State Route 202. After 5 miles turn west on to State Route 214 at Largo. The route crosses the Patuxent river. Continue on State Route 214, State Route 2 and State Route 450 into Annapolis.

Annapolis, Maryland

Established in 1649 by a group of Puritan families from Virginia, the historic town of Annapolis is set on the western shore of Chesapeake Bay, at the mouth of the River Severn, and has been the capital of Maryland since 1694. One of the oldest cities in the USA, it was named after Princess Anne, later Queen Anne of England. Annapolis boasts the only remaining 18th-century waterfront on the Atlantic coast, and still retains many fine buildings from its colonial days. The downtown area of Annapolis is a Registered Historic District.

Perhaps its most famous building is State House, where the American Revolution came to its official end in 1784. The building served as Capitol of the United States from 26 November 1783 to 13 August 1784, and is the oldest state capitol in continuous legislative use. In the Old Senate Chamber, Washington resigned his commission as Commander-in-Chief of the Continental Army. It is still in use as the local parliament building and is open for free guided tours daily. Look carefully at the unusual dome, which is wooden and was constructed entirely without nails.

William Paca House and garden, at 186 Prince George St, is a mid 18th-century estate which features a Chippendale bridge and a 'wilderness garden'. The house itself has been carefully restored and is furnished in period style. The property was once owned by a governor of Maryland who was a signatory to the Declaration of Independence.

St Anne's Church, at Church Circle, has a beautiful memorial window which won first prize for ecclesiastical art at the Chicago World Fair in 1893. The present church is the third on the site, and dates from 1859.

The US Naval Academy, which stands on the site of Old Fort Severn and covers more than 300 acres on the south side of the Severn River, has a museum displaying battle flags, ship models, portraits, weapons and the souvenirs of Navy-trained astronauts. Dress parades are held in Worden Field on Wednesday afternoons in spring and autumn.

Information on guided walking tours of Annapolis is available at the Old Treasury Building on State Circle. For an excellent introduction to the whole area, park the car and take a leisurely seven-and-a-half-hour tour cruising Chesapeake Bay on the *Annapolis*. It will give a different perspective on landmarks like the US Naval Academy building, the 19th-century lighthouse, and the Chesapeake Maritime Museum in the restored fishing village of St Michael's, across the bay, where passengers are sensibly allowed three hours for lunch. This is your chance to taste fresh oysters, crabs, clams and even terrapin, as never before. Chesapeake Bay, America's largest estuary, is a seafood gourmet's paradise, and a place where both work and relaxation centre around the water. The cruising season lasts way into October, when one of the largest floating exhibitions in the States, the 'In the Water Boat Show', is held here. Cruises are on Saturdays and Sundays between May and September.
Return to Washington on US 50.

The Blackwater National Wildlife Refuge looks out over Chesapeake Bay, America's largest estuary

This unusual, six-sided lighthouse at Chesapeake is raised on stilts

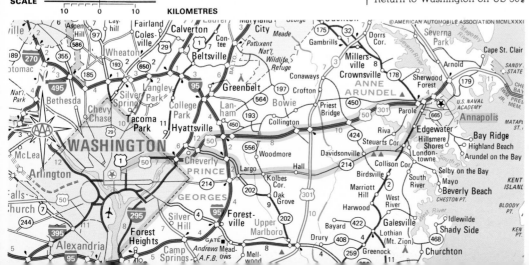

SCALE — 8 MILES TO 1 INCH — KILOMETRES

©AMERICAN AUTOMOBILE ASSOCIATION MCMLXXXI

The Three States Historic Tour

2 days — 121 miles

This short tour passes through three states — Maryland, West Virginia and Virginia, in the heart of George Washington Country. Here is the stuff that American country music is made of — long country roads, the breathtaking scenery of the Blue Ridge Mountains and the sleepy Shenandoah River — with generous helpings of American history thrown in. On this journey you can visit the spot where John Brown's ill-fated raid on Harper's Ferry took place, see an Old Colonial town virtually unchanged by the passage of time, and learn more than you had ever hoped to know about the Civil War.

Leave Washington centre on Wisconsin Ave to join State Route 355, turning off at the first exit on to Interstate 270. Continue on Interstate 270 through Rockville to exit 8, where you should turn on to State Route 75 and continue to New Market.

Washington DC — New Market — Frederick — Burkittsville — Harper's Ferry — Leesburg — Chantilly — Falls Church — Washington

---

New Market, Maryland

Founded in 1793, New Market became an important stopping-off point for travellers on their way west in search of a home in Ohio in the late 18th century. In the old part of the village you can still see the original plot laid out by New Market's founders.

Today, visitors to New Market are not after a change of horse and fresh supplies. Instead they come here to hunt for bargains in the village's many antique and craft shops. There are almost 40 of these, and New Market has been called 'the Antiques Capital of Maryland'.

Leave New Market on Interstate 40 and continue for 9 miles into Frederick.

Frederick, Maryland

The town's historic interest dates from 1863, when it was used by the Union Army as its headquarters. In the following year General Early of the Confederate Army levied a $200,000 ransom on the city. The debt incurred by the city to pay the ransom was not cleared until October 1951, 87 years later.

A specially designated National Historic District in Frederick includes Barbara Frietchie House, a reconstruction of the original building, which was demolished during the re-coursing of Carroll Creek. The house contains many articles of historic interest. John Greenleaf Whittier's Civil War poem *Barbara Frietchie*, which tells how the old woman courageously defied General 'Stonewall' Jackson and his army, is said to be based on happenings at this house.

Mount Olivet Cemetery, at the south end of Market Street, contains the graves of many famous townspeople including those of Barbara Freitchie and Francis Scott Key, who wrote the words of 'The Star-Spangled Banner'.

The Rose Hill Manor Children's Museum, at 1611 Market Street, was the home of Maryland's first governor, Thomas Johnson. The life of a typical 19th-century family is now depicted by varied exhibits in the house and garden.

To find out more about the fascinating town of Frederick, pay

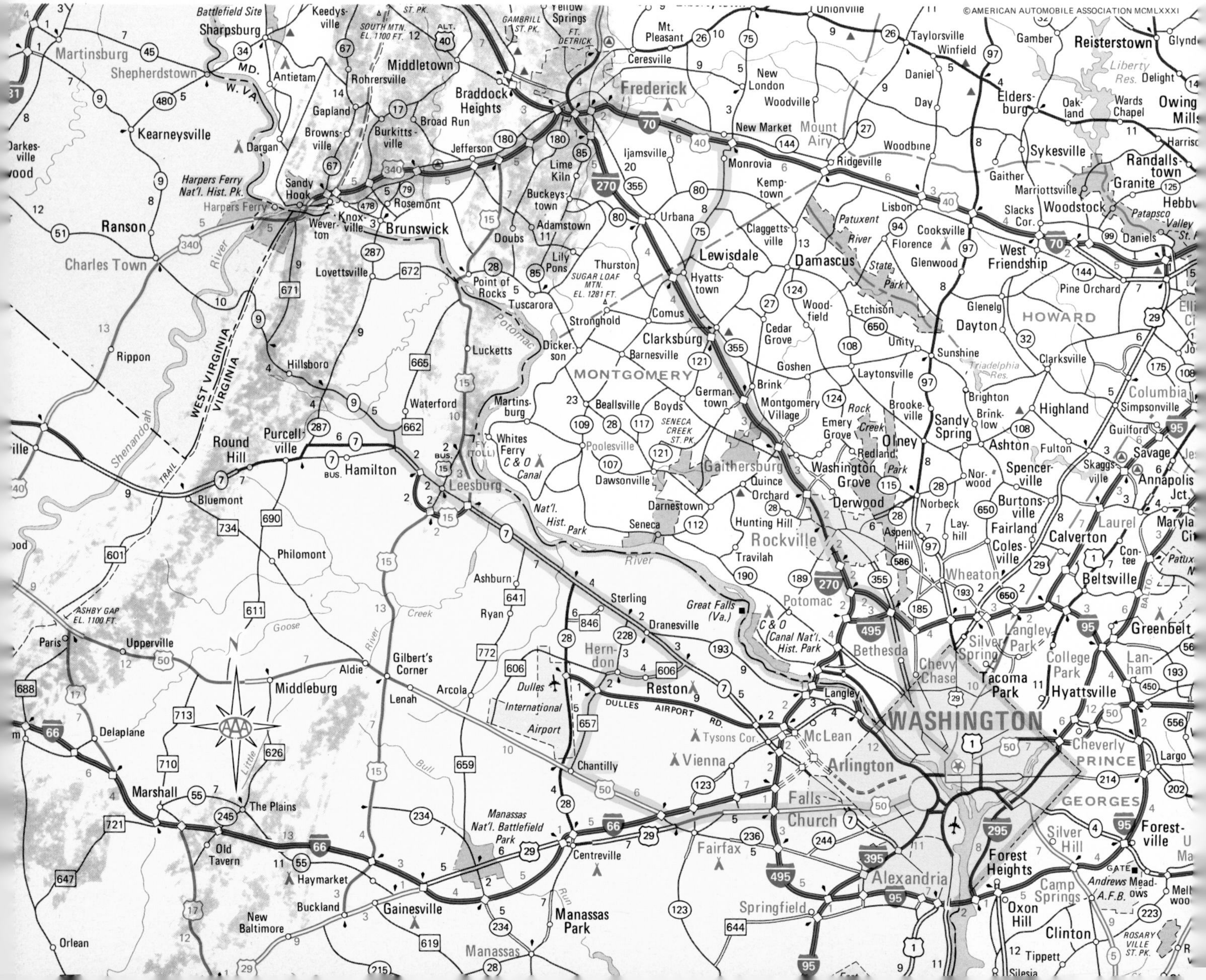

The main street at New Market. Many of the old wooden houses have a new lease of life as antique and craft shops

a visit to the information centre at 19 E Church Street. The centre offers guided walking tours of the Historic District.

Eight miles south, via Interstate 270 and State Route 640 (Urbana exit), is Sugarloaf Mountain. Rising an impressive 1281ft above the surrounding countryside, this is a popular picnicking and hiking area within a private estate.

| Leave Frederick on US 340 and at the fifth exit (State Route 17), turn right for Burkittsville.

Burkittsville, Maryland
One mile west of this small village is Gathland State Park, which covers 135 acres and has notable connections with the Civil War. It was the estate of George Townsend, the famous Civil War journalist, who raised a monument to war correspondents on the ridge of South Mountain here. Mementoes of Townsend and various Civil War artefacts are on display in the visitor centre. The Appalachian Trail, a well-known long-distance mountain trail running 2000 miles from Maine to Georgia, goes through the park.

| Return to US 340 and continue for 10 miles to Harper's Ferry.

Harper's Ferry, West Virginia
Situated at the majestic confluence of the Shenandoah and Potomac Rivers, the town of Harper's Ferry boasts a very special link with American history. It was here on 16 October 1859 that John Brown's historic raid against slavery took place. Harper's Ferry was the site of the Federal arsenal and armoury. Brown, a militant anti-slavery campaigner, planned to raid the arsenal and give the arms to Southern slaves, inciting them to rebel against the slave-owners. The raid was a failure: Brown surrendered after 10 of his 18 men had been killed, and he and the rest of his force were convicted of treason and hanged. But his failure was one of the most 'successful' in history, for he gave the anti-slavery movement its first martyr and a stirring battle-song which, like John Brown's soul, still 'goes marching on'.

Harper's Ferry is now a National Historical Park, consisting of four separate areas: downtown has been restored to look almost as it did in 1859, and there are three tracts of lovely countryside

nearby. The area is a tranquil place of outstanding natural beauty, of which Thomas Jefferson once said 'The scene is worth a voyage across the Atlantic.'

A set of stone steps leads up from the High Street to Harper House, which dates from 1782 and is furnished in typical mid-19th-century style.

The old brick armoury, known as John Brown's Fort, in Old Arsenal Square, was the scene of Brown's capture in 1895. The arsenal itself was destroyed during the Civil War, when the Federal troops who were garrisoned here were obliged to abandon the town before an approaching force of Virginians. They destroyed the arsenal before they left, and it was never rebuilt.

In Shenandoah Street is the one-time home of the Armoury's chief gunsmith, the Master Armourer's House. It now houses an interesting museum of the gunsmith's craft.

To complete the historical tour of Harper's Ferry, a trip to the Visitor Center on Shenandoah Street is well worth while. Exhibits and audio-visual programmes are offered here, as well as suggestions for walking tours.

| Leave Harper's Ferry on US 340, driving eastwards back into Virginia. Turn right on to County Route 671 and follow it to State Route 9. Follow State Route 9 to State Route 7 and take this road into Leesburg.

Leesburg, Virginia
One of the oldest towns in northern Virginia, Leesburg was named after land-owner Francis 'Lightfoot' Lee who was one of the signers of the Declaration of Independence. Leesburg officially became a town in 1758, and many attractive Old Colonial homes and buildings can still be seen.

The area surrounding Leesburg is particularly noted for breeding fine racehorses, and the race meets and hunt clubs of Leesburg, Middleburg and other local communities are famous throughout the States.

Near Leesburg is the 1200-acre estate of Westmoreland Davis, a former governor of Virginia. The house is set amid lovely gardens. Nature trails are a feature of the park, where there is also an extensive and fascinating collection

of antique, horse-drawn carriages.

A visit to the 19th-century stately mansion of Oatlands is well worth the six-mile trip south on US 15. Built in 1800 and restored in the early years of this century, it is a fine example of Federal-style architecture, and is furnished in grand style. The formal gardens retain their original design and the surrounding grounds are the setting for point-to-point races, a horse show and other equestrian events.

| Continue on State Route 7 out of Leesburg for 9 miles then, at the first interchange, turn right on to State Route 28. After about 5 miles turn left on to Local Route 606 to reach Herndon. From Herndon take Local Route 657 to Chantilly, 5 miles south.

Chantilly, Virginia
Virginia is world-famous for its tobacco plantations, and a particularly fine one can be visited at Chantilly. Sully Plantation dates back to 1794, when the mansion was built by Richard Bland Lee. Sully Plantation remained in the Lee family until 1842, when it was sold to Jacob Haight, an industrious Quaker farmer who turned it into a model farm that attracted the attention of famous agrarian reformers. Today the mansion is of interest not only for its historical connections but also for its architecture, which combines characteristic Virginian features, such as the massive twin

chimneys, with elements of the architectural styles that Richard Bland Lee saw in the town houses of Philadelphia, where he attended Congress. The Lees furnished their home in style, and the original flooring and panelling can still be seen there, with fine antiques of the Federal period.

| Drive south from Chantilly on US 50 for 16 miles into Falls Church.

Falls Church, Virginia
The Falls Church, from which the town takes its name, is situated on US 29 and 211 at East Fairfax Street, south of Broad Street. It was erected in 1733 and served as a recruiting station during the Revolution. The church was used as a Federal hospital in the early years of the Civil War, and later as a stable. The building has now been restored to its 18th-century appearance, including the recent erection of galleries which were shown on the original plan.

The fountains and gardens of the National Memorial Park, two miles west of Falls Church, are particularly notable. The sculpture at the entrance to the park is dedicated to four Army chaplains who selflessly gave their lifejackets to soldiers on the troopship *Dorchester* when it was torpedoed near Greenland in 1943. Swedish sculptor Carl Milles designed the Fountain of Faith, which consists of 38 separate figures.

| Continue on US 50 back to Washington.

Shenandoah River, famed in song, flows through spectacular hill country, south-west of Harper's Ferry, where it joins the Potomac

*Manhattan in winter, seen from the Empire State Building.
Rank upon rank of skyscrapers, lit by the evening sun, stretch
away to the distant horizon*

New York

New York is a way of life. To be a part of its scene, even fleetingly as a holidaymaker or visitor, is an opportunity to take advantage of a prolific culture — a vast arena of museums, theatres, and shops — unmatched anywhere in the world.

Always a cosmopolitan city, in 1653 New York — or New Amsterdam, as it was then known to the early Dutch settlers — had 800 inhabitants who spoke eighteen different tongues. Today, almost half of the city's population are foreigners, either by birth or parentage. There are twenty-two radio stations broadcasting in sixteen different languages and eleven daily newspapers written in six. It is appropriate, then, that New York should play host to the United Nations. More than 7000 officials from 140 nations work in its towering headquarters on the banks of the East River.

New York has the busiest harbour in the world, clearing more than 26,000 vessels a year and shipping forty per cent of US foreign trade. Almost every main industry registered in the USA is represented here, and the 35,000 manufacturing plants within the city limits produce more than 300 different kinds of goods.

New York lends itself to staggering statistics of all kinds. But they tell only a fraction of the city's real story. For New York is about people. And whatever one might think about its brashness, its pace, its gusto, its rude vitality, New York is a great place to make friends.

It is easy enough for the first-time visitor to think Manhattan is all there is to New York. Most of New York's world-famous landmarks — 5th Avenue, Broadway, the Empire State Building and Greenwich Village — are to be found there. But in fact Manhattan is the smallest of the five boroughs that make up New York, even though to the stranger it seems to be the sum total of what makes the city the most exciting in the world. This has more than a little to do with Manhattan's familiar forest of skyscrapers, clinging together as though they had been dropped into place by giant cranes, that cast an eerie twilight over many of the glamorous avenues and dwarf the bustle in the city streets. The small patch of sky that the gigantic buildings grudgingly reveal is the only reminder that they are not part of some Leviathan shopping arcade. Looking up, the eye is dazzled by the reflection from these shining façades of glass and concrete sweeping up starkly on each side.

In common with the centres of many major cities Manhattan's population of 1,700,000 has, according to the official US census, been dwindling as more and more of its inhabitants move out into the suburbs. Yet the pressure on its twenty-two square miles of space is still growing with the development of new mid- and lower-Manhattan office accommodation.

This was one of the reasons that New York spawned the skyscraper — high-density living as had never been attempted before on such a scale. At the

turn of the century, when the first high-rise buildings poked tentative fingers above the roofline, the architects and builders were trying to overcome enormous problems with the kind of material available to them at the time. Fortunately, the area was not prone to earthquakes, and foundations could be solidly set, but the effects of wind and temperature were still largely unknown on excessively high buildings — most of them using pre-cast iron sections for the first time.

One of the earliest skyscrapers was the twenty-storey Flatiron building, named because of its wedge shape — a common enough household gadget of that period. Its shape was governed by the space between Broadway and 5th Avenue, and it was completed in 1902. But apartment houses, high though they too needed to be built because of the premium on space, never matched the grandiose ideas of the giant business corporations which in the 1920s seemed determined to outdo each other in the race for the sky.

Woolworth's was one of the first contestants. With its fussy, tiered façade the building rose sixty floors on a site on Broadway as early as 1912. The 1048ft-high art-deco-style Chrysler building at 42nd Street and Lexington Avenue, which really set off an unprecedented boom in high-rise buildings, did not emerge from all its scaffolding until 1930 — just a year before the most famous of them all, the Empire State Building, opened. This 102-storey milestone remained for over

New York's waterfront is dominated by the exciting architecture of the Lower Manhattan skyline; on the left, the twin towers of the World Trade Center

forty years the world's tallest office building — 1472ft from its base on 5th Avenue and 34th Street to the top of its 222ft TV transmitter mast. With 2,000,000 sq. ft of office space for 20,000 people, its famous observatories on the eighty-sixth floor and on the top floor, 1250ft above the ground, are open daily from 9.30 am until 11.30 pm. In the day, they give breath-taking fifty-mile views over four states, and at night they provide an incomparable panorama of the lights of New York.

But since it was completed in 1975, the twin-towered World Trade Center has offered the highest viewpoints over New York from the 110th floor where there is an open promenade 1302ft up. Standing on sixteen acres in Church Street, between Vesey and Liberty Streets, it has 9,000,000 sq. ft of office space and a landscaped plaza.

The difference between the two buildings is not only in style. It is also in the concept of how Manhattan's architecture should adapt to the modern techniques and materials now available. A dramatic change in design had already come in the late forties when the Rockefeller Center, the gigantic cluster of fourteen buildings created to provide a cohesive commercial hub on twenty-two acres of mid-Manhattan, began to expand with a new generation of skyscrapers.

146

In February 1946, within six months of the end of the Second World War, excavations started for a thirty-three-storey slab of glass and aluminium. When the Rockefeller Center was first mooted in October 1928, the idea was to build a new Metropolitan Opera House on the site, which was owned by Columbia University. Unfortunately, this Opera House was never built, but financier and philanthropist John D. Rockefeller, recognizing the potential of a valuable site in the hub of Manhattan, decided to develop it himself as an office and entertainment complex.

More than 220 buildings had to be knocked down to make room on the original twelve-acre site, and the 75,000 men who worked there, together with the 150,000 others manufacturing and assembling the materials, completed many of these colossi in less time than it takes today to erect a large house with all the latest techniques. The fastest feat was performed on the thirty-six-storey No.1 Rockefeller Plaza. Construction began in September 1936, and the building was opened seven months later. Nearly thirty-three years later, building work on the fifty-four-storey Exxon skyscraper of 2,100,000 sq. ft was started in January 1969, and was not finished for another two years and nine months, yet it was 100,000 sq. ft less than the RCA building on 49th Street nearby which, rising to seventy storeys, was completed in under eighteen months and opened in May 1933.

The last of the nineteen buildings in the present Rockefeller Center was finished in Spring 1973. A forty-five-storey skyscraper, the Celanese building took over two years to build. Four in the complex are mere tiddlers of six floors, the tallest rising to a mere ninety-two ft, but the pride of the collection is the 850ft-high RCA building. It has impressive murals and frescoes in the main lobby and a seventy-nine-foot mosaic depicting Thought in the loggia entrance. Woven into the design of the buildings are majestic pools and fountains, and trees set in plazas that complement the clean, sweeping lines of the architecture. Many of the buildings, though occupied by companies, can be visited on guided tours. Between most of the buildings are underground shopping malls. Apart from its commercial significance, the Rockefeller Center is also the home of the Radio City Music Hall, the world's largest indoor theatre. At the Center is also the headquarters of the National Broadcasting Company's radio and television network, with seven television and two radio studios. Attached to the fifty-one-storey

The Statue of Liberty, given by France in 1886 to commemorate the American Revolution 100 years earlier, stands out at night against the backdrop of the World Trade Center

New York

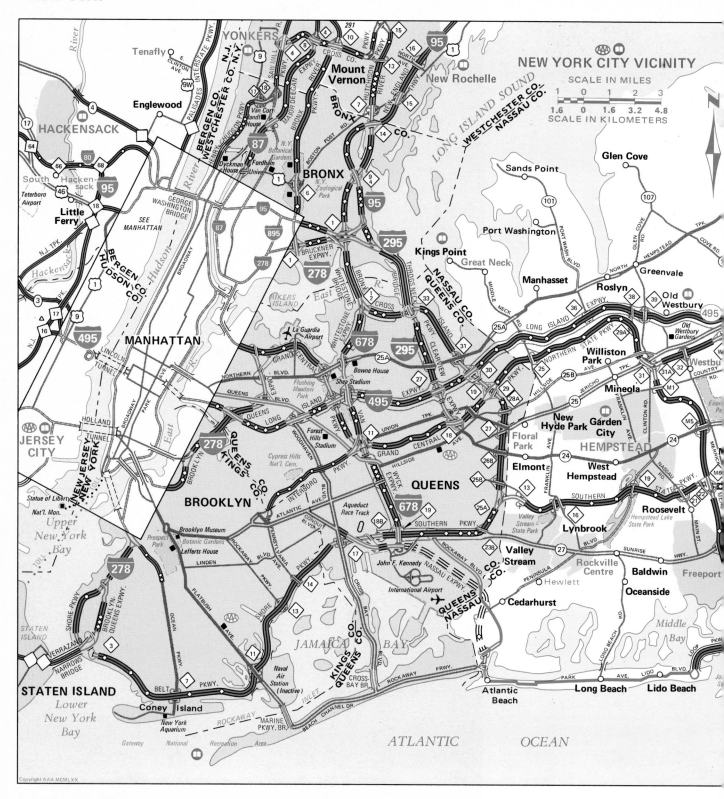

Copyright AAA MCMLXX

McGraw-Hill building is a small hall where visitors can hear a potted history of New York City.

There are also restaurants, a small film theatre and several exhibitions. Every winter, an outdoor restaurant on the Lower Plaza is turned into a 120ft-long and 59ft-wide ice-skating pond. Since it opened on Christmas Day in 1936 it has

attracted about 100,000 skaters a year and hundreds of thousands more come to watch. There are thirty-four other restaurants in the complex. Tours of this city within a city are every forty-five minutes from Monday to Saturday between 9.45 am and 4.45 pm. They start from the guided-tour lounge at 30 Rockefeller Plaza. The highlight of the

tour is a view of the city from the observation level atop the RCA Building.

John D. Rockefeller's interest in expensive Manhattan real estate, and his philanthropy, also helped the United Nations to find a prime eighteen-acre site for its headquarters along the banks of the East River. He offered about £3,500,000 to buy land in this run-down area of

148

slaughterhouses and light industry, and New York City chipped in with additional land. Since the four main buildings, dominated by the thirty-nine-storey glass and marble Secretariat Tower, opened in 1952, the UN headquarters has had nearly 7000 diplomats and secretariat personnel from 140 nations working there at any one time. They staff the linguistic, economic, editoral, social, legal, statistical and administrative functions of this vast organization. With over 20,000 employees throughout the world, the UN head-quarters draws in another 3000 when the General Assembly meets in the vaulted General Assembly building. With the low-rise rectangular Conference building and the Dag Hammarskjöld Library, named after the UN's second Secretary General who was killed in a plane crash in 1961, the UN complex attracts nearly 1,000,000 visitors a year. One of the more popular draws is the Foucault Pendulum near the main entrance, which gives visual proof of the earth's rotation. There is a chunk of moon rock and a model of Sputnik I, and, in the basement, the unique United Nations Post Office where tourists from all over the world can send mail stamped with the United Nations' own issue. A US postage stamp is not accepted here.

Chagall's stained glass window, sculptor Barbara Hepworth's bronze effigy of Dag Hammarskjöld and paintings by Temayo, Salvador Dali and Rouault are other attractions on guided tours. Visitors can also wander into the boutiques selling gifts from all over the world, including Chinese silver brooches, Delft cufflinks and enamelled Russian dolls. Although prices are high, shopping at the UN has the advantage of being free of the New York sales tax — a kind of VAT which is automatically added to bills for all goods and services.

The UN headquarters also provides a constant spectacle for passers-by outside in the street. They can watch a procession of cars with flags fluttering, to-ing and fro-ing through the gates, while the UN's own police force stands guard and, with unfailing courtesy, directs the traffic and

The flags of 12 nations flutter outside the United Nations headquarters, aptly located in this most cosmopolitan city

visitors. New York has absorbed this international community, apparently unaffected by the pressures of the political activity it brings to the city. Unlike the political industry in Washington, the United Nations minds its own business.

Though some might say the UN headquarters is a kind of Tower of Babel, its multi-national character fits a city with such an old established polyglot tradition as New York. The Dutch, attracted by the potential of New York's deep water harbour, founded the first colony in the mid seventeenth century by buying Manhattan from the Algonquin Indians for twenty-four dollars' worth of beads, buttons and other trinkets. They then established a thriving trading port which attracted merchants and settlers from all

over Europe. The negotiations were conducted by Peter Minuit, an enter-prising seventeenth-century Rockefeller who was a merchant explorer and later became the first governor of New Amsterdam — the first name for New York. Though the adventurous Portuguese and Italians had visited the attractive cluster of islands more than a century before — Florentine navigator Giovanni da Verrazano arrived in 1524 — the Dutch established themselves in 1609 when Henry Hudson, after whom one of New York's rivers was named, sailed as far as Albany to establish trading posts on behalf of his Dutch East India Company. The first permanent settlement was founded later by Adrian Block, another Dutch trader.

By 1653 the number of settlers had swelled to 800, with no fewer than 300 houses clustered around the southern tip of Manhattan. The British, who also had ambitions in that area, reacted to these colonial manoeuvres promptly by sending two warships up river under the command of the Duke of York, brother of Charles II of England. The Dutch, led by their unpopular governor Peter Stuyvesant (whose name has since gained un-expected popularity on a brand of cigarettes), capitulated without a fight and the English, flushed by their victory, immediately renamed their prize New York in honour of their commander. Under British rule, the colony prospered, and although not much of the Dutch presence of that period remains today, a few anglicized versions of Dutch place names survive. The Bowery, for instance, home for many of New York's homeless and destitute, is an echo of the Dutch farms known three centuries ago as the 'Bouweries'.

Another farmhouse that, though built nearly a century later, still reflects the influence of the Dutch colonies, is Dyckman House at Broadway and West 204th Street. Particularly notable Dutch features are the sweeping low-pitched roof extending over porches which are supported by plain box columns to create a charming veranda effect. The walls are

The City Within a City

Rockefeller Center — the city within a city — comprises 19 buildings, 15 of them standing more than 10 storeys high. The tallest of them, the 70-storey RCA building, was one of the first to be completed. Excavations began on the first four buildings in July 1931 and the RCA was the third to open, in May 1933.

The complex now has a daily population of 240,000 — the size of many big cities — of which more than half are

visitors. There are 388 lifts which, in the course of a year, soar a million miles up and plunge a million miles down. The fastest travels at 1400ft per minute — about 15 miles per hour — and takes 37 seconds non-stop to reach the 65th floor of the RCA building.

In addition there are 67 escalators, more than 48,700 windows, and about 900 people are employed to clean the 15,000,000 sq ft of buildings inside and out.

Each winter, the Rockefeller Center attracts thousands of skaters to its outdoor rink

How to Find Your Way in Manhattan

Finding your way around New York is the easiest thing in the world, provided that you can do simple sums in your head and memorize a magic formula.

Streets run east-west and avenues run north-south. Usually, when giving an address, Americans will not only state the number or the name of the building, and the street or avenue, but also specify the nearest intersection — for example: 357 5th Avenue at 72nd

Street, so that you know precisely where the building is and do not have to travel the whole length of the avenue to find the number you want. Streets also have a west and east side, with 5th Avenue marking the dividing line between west and east.

There are two systems to help you pinpoint an address exactly, one for the street system and another for the avenues. House numbers on streets go in blocks of 100 between intersections with the

avenues. It is assumed that there are 100 numbers in each block, regardless of whether there are in fact 100 buildings. If the address you want is, for example, the old Victorian brownstone house at 41 E. 72nd Street, a glance at the table below shows you that 41 must be in the block between 5th Avenue and Park Avenue. If, on the other hand, the address is 41 W. 72nd Street, the house will be between 5th and 6th Avenues.

The formula for locating an address on the avenues running north-south is more complicated, but it does work. For example, the Downing Square Restaurant is at 500 Lexington Avenue. To find out which block that is, proceed as follows:
A. Cancel the last figure of the number.
B. Divide your answer by 2.

C. Find the key number of your avenue in the table below, and add or subtract that number to the result of step B.
Thus, for 500 Lexington Avenue, A = 50, B = 25, C = 25 + 22 = 47. The Downing Square Restaurant is therefore near 47th Street on

Lexington Avenue. Exceptions to this formula are marked with an asterisk, but you can still pinpoint the address by leaving out step B. To find the apartment house at 11 Riverside Drive, for example: A = 1, C = 1 + 73 = 74. 11 Riverside Drive is near 74th Street.

East-West Numbered Streets

Addresses begin at the streets listed below.

East Side		West Side	
1	5th Ave.	1	5th Ave.
101	Park Ave.	101	6th Ave. (Ave. of the Americas)
201	3rd Ave.	201	7th Ave.
301	2nd Ave.	301	8th Ave.
401	1st Ave.	401	9th Ave.
501	York or Ave. A	501	10th Ave.
601	Ave. B	601	11th Ave.

North-South Avenues

*On streets or address numbers preceded by an asterisk, omit Step B from the computation.

Ave. A, B, C, D	3	10th Ave.	13
1st Ave.	3	11th Ave.	15
2nd Ave.	3	Amsterdam	59
3rd Ave.	10	Columbus	59
4th Ave.	8	Lexington	22
5th Ave.:		Madison	27
1-200	13	Park	34
201-400	16	West End	59
401-600	18	*Central Park West	60
601-775	20	*Riverside Dr.:	
*776-1286	Deduct 18	*1-567	73
Ave. of the Americas	Deduct 12	*Above 567	78
7th Ave.:		Broadway:	
1-1800	12	1-754 are below 8th St.	
Above 1800	20	754-858	Deduct 29
8th Ave.	9	858-958	Deduct 25
9th Ave.	13	Above 1000	Deduct 31

of brick and fieldstones and clapboard. The interior has been restored and furnished in period style and still contains many of the original belongings of the Dyckman family.

Most of the Georgian-style buildings the British built during their rule have now gone, but St Paul's Chapel, built in 1776 at the corner of Broadway and Fulton Street, is a surviving example of Britain's style. Ten years later, during the War of Independence, New York was badly damaged by fires as British troops drove George Washington and his army out. By 1783, it was all over for the British in New York. Two years later, Congress started a five-year temporary stay in New York; George Washington was inaugurated in New York, before Congress moved to the temporary capital of Philadelphia.

The late eighteenth- and nineteenth-century styles of architecture naturally have been preserved on a much larger scale numbers, despite the relentless obsession of the late 19th-century developers to tear things down and start again. Among the souvenirs is the Morris-Jumel Mansion, named after its early occupants, Roger Morris and Stephen Jumel. Morris settled in New York in 1775. Later, this two-storey colonnaded building was occupied by George Washington and even by the British as their campaign headquarters. It was also used as a tavern and a coach staging post. Thirty-four years later, dilapidated and crumbling, it was bought by a fashionable Frenchman, Stephen Jumel, who refurbished it without much regard for its period, though the priceless French furnishings he and his wife imported are still on show at the

house in Edgcombe Avenue and West 160th Street.

Another relic of colonial times is the massive Gracie Mansion on East End Avenue and 88th Street in the Carl Schurz Park. This large white-framed building, dating back to 1799, is the official residence of New York mayors.

Hamilton Grange, on 142nd Street, east of Convent Avenue, is a more modest example of early 19th-century architecture and has recently been restored, but the jewel of New York's architectural heritage is the Fraunces Tavern on Pearl Street at Broad Street. Named after a French innkeeper who bought it in 1762, the three-storey building was once a lively tavern, and is famous as the place where Washington said farewell to his troops in 1783. The interior was almost completely destroyed by fire in 1837. Since then it has been gradually reconstructed, and today it still serves food and drink.

In the nineteenth century, New York's population increased rapidly, as more and more settlers arrived, drawn by the promises of the New World. In twenty years the population doubled, reaching 120,000 by 1820. By 1880 it was over 1,000,000 and the incredible building boom was under way. At first there were the Victorian-style brownstone town houses which were built in the middle of the nineteenth century. Much admired and treasured where they can still be found throughout New York, brownstone is the term used for the soft brown porous sandstone quarried in Vermont and New York State. In a typical brownstone house it is set off by ornate timberwork on doors and windows. So popular are these

American architectural souvenirs that owning a brownstone has become a mark of distinction and achievement.

One of the favoured neighbourhoods for brownstone residences is Murray Hill. While not purely nineteenth-century in its architectural design, Murray Hill — a chunk of mid-Manhattan eight blocks wide between 34th and 42nd Street, and about seven blocks from Fifth Avenue to the East River — has been allowed to blend naturally into the pattern of New York's modern architecture. Elegant boutiques and department stores nestle in carriage houses (mews), beside grand mansions and a few modern high-rise buildings.

The brownstone revival, though fairly recent, has also helped to focus attention on several early examples of apartment houses saved from the path of the bulldozers. Overlooking the United Nations complex is a small square of apartment houses called Tudor City, hidden behind 42nd Street up several flights of steps. It is centred on a neat square and affords a glimpse of the way the professional people lived as America's affluence gathered momentum. Towering over it on one side is the twenty-one-storey Tudor Hotel, opened in 1930 when the Empire State building, ten minutes' walk away, was still under construction. The 500-room hotel, still flourishing, is something of an anachronism, but the popularity of the 1930s era, and the proximity of the United Nations headquarters, has given it an unexpected new lease of life. The rooms are ornate, perhaps over-furnished, with dark, solid and very reliable suites. The lobby, as busy as a railway terminal when

The stark, uncompromising lines of today's soaring skyscrapers contrast strongly with the flamboyant, art-deco style of the famous Chrysler Building, characteristic of the 1930s

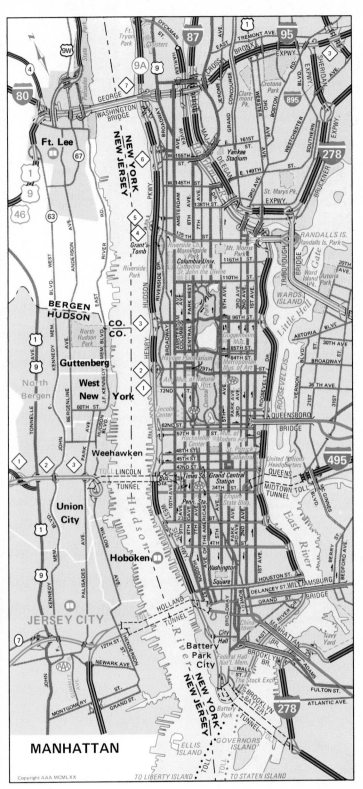

MANHATTAN

Copyright AAA MCMLXX

the coachloads of tourists arrive for the night, has a cheerful, decadent air, probably more genuine New York than most of the 100,000 hotel rooms the city has available. Not surprisingly, it is much in demand by UN delegates — even though the official United Nations Plaza Hotel, opposite the headquarters, is even closer, craning over Tudor City like a giant giraffe. Nearby, the bustling mix of business and bohemia that is 42nd Street runs right across world-famous avenues. Going east to west, the first recognizable name is Park Avenue, where some of the major office buildings, with stunning architectural features, stand in its mid-town section. Further north it is lined with expensive apartment houses. The next major avenue is Madison Avenue, famous for its numerous advertising agencies. In its lower reaches it has an array of stately old mansions; in the north unusual shops and stores. Next in line is 5th Avenue, where New York's Easter Parade is held. It is also the hinge of Manhattan's road pattern (see highlight for an explanation of how it works), for this is where east and

151

New York

west divide. It houses the finest department stores offering exquisite and expensive merchandise. Magnificent hotels with splendid façades stretch as far as 50th Street in the north. It then becomes an exclusive residential street.

A block along is the Avenue of the Americas. By rights, it should still be called 6th Avenue — and few New Yorkers have taken to its more pompous name. Since the early sixties it has gradually rivalled its more illustrious eastern neighbour for architectural splendour.

Seventh Avenue shows the first sign of New York's West Side Story. Unlike London and many European capitals where west is synonymous with affluence and sophistication, in New York and several other American cities the reverse generally applies. Seventh Avenue's main claim to tourist fame is that right in the heart of it Times Square has been created by the intersection of Broadway, which runs at an acute angle into it from the north. Broadway sweeps on to the east across all the west-side avenues and by the time it reaches 23rd Street at Madison Square Park, it intersects 5th Avenue before going on, across Union Square, right down to 10th Avenue, when it swerves sharply to make straight for Battery Park, at the very tip of Manhattan Island. Broadway is like an actor without make-up in the daytime, and a glittering star at night. Then, in sections as bright as Las Vegas Strip, it is a teeming, solid mass of people. The noise, the callous display of indifference of the crowds around, can make a stranger feel very lonely. It is all in stark contrast to so much of New York, which soon after dark empties of people and only the traffic with its innumerable cabs keeps the city teeming with life.

On Broadway you can indulge every whim. If you can find the space, you can roller-skate down the road in the face of traffic, play a guitar or tap dance, and even earn an indulgent round of applause for your efforts from the gathering crowd. Contrary to the impression given by the term, Broadway itself has only two theatres, although around the Times Square area there are at least thirty providing the finest and most lavish stage presentations in the world. The legitimate Broadway theatres differ from the off-Broadway theatres not because the latter are any further from Broadway, but because they are generally smaller and seats are marginally less expensive. The off-Broadway houses generally have fewer than 300 seats, but do not qualify as full Broadway theatres even when they are next door to a larger theatre right in the heart of theatreland.

In addition, there are another 230 or so theatres in New York which are defined as off-off-Broadway. This new category has emerged since the twenty off-Broadway theatres have become too respectable to

At night, the brash and brilliant world of neon advertising dominates the bustling avenues around the Times Square district

attract their special following any more. So now it is left to the fringe, the makeshift playhouses, some in churches, lofts or basements to serve up the experimental offerings so beloved of the coterie of intellectuals and artists. You could stumble on shows with genuinely exciting new ideas on makeshift stages in garages where the audience have to walk round a perimeter of scaffolding and the 'gallery' is at the top of ladders.

The tourist may find the Broadway theatres very expensive, but over the last few years they have come within everybody's pocket through the TKTS ticket scheme. Two booths, one at Broadway and 47th Street and the other at 100 William Street, offer reduced rates for tickets to shows on the day of performance. Also

available, though not as often as at one time, are 'twofers' — two for the price of one — tickets sold by theatres for long-running shows. There are also ticket agencies all over the town.

New York boasts nearly fifty dance companies, three opera companies, free open-air Shakespeare in Central Park and twenty-two radio stations. The city's cultural resources are not merely confined to performances. New York has a veritable bounty of museums and art galleries, many with unassailable reputations for taste and artistic fervour.

Among the eighty or more art galleries is the Metropolitan Museum of Art on 5th Avenue and 82nd Street in Central Park, with its pre-eminent collection of Egyptian, Greek, Roman and near

Eastern art and antiquities, European and Oriental paintings and sculptures, and American decorative arts. The American collection alone covers 130,000 sq. ft, seven times more than when the original American wing was opened in 1924. It includes a glass-enclosed garden court, seventy feet high, containing a pool and statues; examples of early American glass and ceramics; and decorative objects of gold, silver and pewter. For differing perspectives on George Washington, the wing exhibits a series of portraits of America's first president by distinguished painters and Leutze's tour-de-force, *Washington Crossing the Delaware*, painted in 1851.

A branch of the museum is the Cloisters, in Fort Tryon Park, at 190th Street and Fort Washington Avenue, where collections include statues, paintings, tapestries and stained-glass windows of the medieval periods. Then there are the incomparable treasures of the Frick Collection at 5th Avenue and East 70th Street. These are European masters from the 14th to the 19th centuries, including Goyas, Vermeers, and works by Renoir and El Greco, the personal collection of steel magnate Henry Clay Frick.

The J. P. Morgan Library, at 36th Street and Madison Avenue, has two Gutenberg Bibles and rare porcelain from the private collection of a wealthy nineteenth-century banker.

The Museum of Modern Art at West 53rd Street is devoted to modern sculpture, design, paintings, drawings and prints, photography and film, and has daily showings of documentary films.

The halls of the Metropolitan Museum of Art (left), and the spiral ramp of the Guggenheim (right) display the contrast between 19th- and 20th-century ideas on art

The opportunities to hear good music in New York are almost endless. Foremost are the programmes at Carnegie Hall with its refined acoustics. One of four major concert halls, it is at 57th Street and 7th Avenue. The largest, used mainly for opera, is the City Center on 55th Street between 6th and 7th Avenue, while the Avery-Fisher Hall at Broadway and 65th Street in the Lincoln Center Plaza, is the only tailor-made concert hall built in the city since 1891. It is the home of the New York Philharmonic Orchestra, and part of the £80,000,000 complex known as the Lincoln Center for the Performing Arts.

Standing on a fourteen-acre site, between Columbus and Amsterdam Avenues, and 62nd to 66th Streets, this encompasses the Metropolitan Opera House, with its gigantic Chagall painting and splendid cut crystal chandeliers; the Juilliard School, one of the world's greatest academies of music, allowing students scope to perform in four auditoriums; the Library and Museum of the Performing Arts, which also has its own small auditorium for chamber music, concerts, dance recitals and other events; and the New York State Theater, which is where the New York City Ballet and the New York City Opera can be found.

The 'Lights' District

Almost exactly 100 years ago, Thomas Edison first put his incandescent electric lamp to the commercial test in an area of Manhattan which is now part of the Financial District. He chose a house in Pearl Street (which runs north and south between Wall Street and Dover Street) to install his experimental equipment, because it had the advantage of being in the heart of the financial community whose support he desperately needed. Short of funds, he acquired the run-down property at No. 257 for a song.

The one-square-mile segment he first 'lit up' is today a mixture of the Woolworth skyscraper of 1912, and the oldest public building still in use in Manhattan. St Paul's Chapel, completed in 1766, was said to have been inspired by London's St Martin's-in-the-Fields, which had been built earlier in the century.

Start this pleasant half-day walk at the junction of Fulton Street and Pearl Street. A little way south, on Pearl Street, is no. 257, where a plaque commemorates the electricity generating station Edison built to serve the area. Turn right into Maiden Lane. No. 90 is one of the few remaining buildings which used cast-iron instead of stonework for the ornate facades favoured in Edison's day. Further west on Maiden Lane is the Nevelson Plaza Park at the junction with William and Liberty Streets. Here are abstract sculptures by Louise Nevelson, one of America's foremost contemporary sculptors, after whom the park was named. Still on Maiden Lane, on the 15th floor of no. 50, is America's most comprehensive collection of fire-fighting equipment (tel. 530 6800 for information).

Return to William Street, turn right and right again

into Liberty Street. At no. 33 is the famous Federal Reserve Bank. Even in 1924 when the building had only just been completed it was one of the largest banks in the world. In the basement is a gold vault almost half the length of an American football field, secured by 121 triple-locked compartments. Visitors are admitted for 45-minute tours, but 10 days' notice is required (tel. 791 6130).

Cross Nassau Street to 65 Liberty Street — the headquarters of the New York Chamber of Commerce. The Great Hall, designed in 1901, has one of the finest interiors in New York (tel. 766 1300 to arrange a visit). Continue to Broadway and turn right. Four blocks north, on the left, you will see St Paul's Chapel, where George Washington regularly worshipped. Many beautiful original furnishings are still in place.

Continue walking north on Broadway past Barclay Street, on your left, to reach the Woolworth Building with

its carved spires and ornate foyer, at 233 Broadway. Affectionately called the 'Cathedral of Commerce' it is open daily. Cross Broadway to City Hall Park and walk north-east along Park Row. No. 38 is the earliest (1883) Queen Anne-style house built with a steel frame. It is now an apartment house.

Finally, cross the park on your left to visit City Hall

(open by appointment, tel. 0566 8681, Monday to Friday, 10 am to 3 pm). Completed in 1811, this magnificent French Renaissance and Federal-style building is regarded as New York's most treasured architectural legacy of the 19th century. The area under the central dome has twin spiral marble staircases. President Lincoln's funeral was held there.

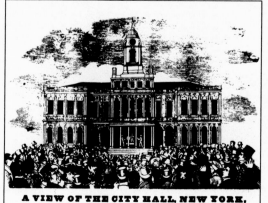

A VIEW OF THE CITY HALL, NEW YORK,

New York

The city's cultural tastes range far and wide. There are, for instance about twenty-one photographic exhibitions in New York. And Picasso's largest work is on a 20ft by 22ft curtain hanging between the bar and dining room at the Four Seasons Restaurant. Originally created in 1919 as a stage backdrop for the ballet *Le Tricorne* (the Three-Cornered Hat) by Diaghilev and Massin with music by De Falla, it depicts a Spanish village plaza in warm rose and ochre colours. One can see it from the Park Avenue entrance by looking through the glass foyer of the restaurant. Sometimes, it can be viewed at close quarters between mealtimes, when the management invite interested passers-by inside. You can, of course, see it at leisure if you decide to eat there, but the restaurant is expensive and exclusive.

Fashionable eating in New York is limitless. To eat well you don't have to go to Sardi's on West 44th Street between Broadway and 8th Avenue — patronized by many theatrical celebrities — or to Palm One or Palm Too on 2nd Avenue for a good steak, or to the Sea Fare of the Aegean on West 56th Street, for the best New York seafood in a Mediterranean decor.

You could try the more stylish bars like Knickers on 2nd Avenue between 47th and 48th Street. It comes straight out of a Damon Runyon short story — a 'set-'em-up, Joe' place, with dark polished wood bars and tankards of beer that only unfreezes in your mouth.

Right at the other end of the scale, you must sample the food of the last remaining automat in New York. On 3rd Avenue and 42nd Street, it dispenses coffee from a spout, and doughnuts from individual compartments as it has done for over thirty years. The automat belongs to the era when the fast-food industry was non-existent, when you could climb onto a bar stool in a drugstore for a quick cooked meal at any time of the day and most of the night.

Most of the drugstore food counters have gone now, and so have the automats. But a New York institution that is still very much alive is the breakfast bar. Brooking no barriers of class, money or dress, these bars cater for millions of New Yorkers every day. Customers can begin their day with freshly made orange juice, toast and coffee, eggs and hashbrowns (fried potatoes) or maybe five or six slices of Virginia ham, topped with cheese. Sometimes the breakfast bar is part of a delicatessen and delicatessens too are a

speciality of New York. One of the best examples is Reubens, which claims that its sandwiches are a national institution, and it is true that you can go to many places in the States and ask for a Reubens if you want a monumental meal tucked between two slices of bread. It may even have an unforgettable name such as Paul Newman — slices of turkey, bacon, lettuce or tomato with mayonnaise on white toast — or Robert Redford — Virginia ham, turkey with Swiss cheese, coleslaw and Russian dressing.

Despite this shameless piece of exploitation, Reubens is not really exceptional in a city with so many restaurants. It is just one of an amazing variety of eating places — some more given to gimmicks than others. More straightforward are the cheap 'fast-food' restaurant chains, who have stepped in in New York, as everywhere else, with their hamburgers and french fries with everything.

For the more discerning, individually cooked, reasonably priced meals in New York's ethnic restaurants are unmatched

Dozens of colourful banners are strewn across the crowded streets of Chinatown to celebrate festivals

A Walk in Greenwich Village

Greenwich Village is a sightseer's paradise — not just because the buildings are interesting and there are landmarks to visit, but because it is an ideal area for simply strolling about and allowing the buoyant atmosphere to carry you effortlessly along.

Below is a suggested hour's walk which can, of course, take much longer, depending on how long you want to linger en route.

From the foot of 5th Avenue at Washington Square, walk south across the park to W. 4th Street, and then turn right into La Guardia Place. Modern apartment buildings flank the east side of the street — a large Student Center belonging to New York University is on the west side. Turn right into Bleecker Street, passing the Other End, a lively, popular restaurant. At the corner of Thompson Street is Village Gate, a mecca for jazz and folk devotees. Continue on Bleecker Street, across 6th Avenue, then turn right on to Cornelia Street, which brings you back to W. 4th Street. Turn left and walk along it, past an interesting variety of small shops and cafés, until you reach 7th Avenue and turn right. Number 178 7th Avenue, between W. 11th and Perry Streets, is the Village Vanguard, a famous jazz club. Turn right on Perry Street, then right on Greenwich Avenue to 6th Avenue, passing on your way many more shops selling craft goods, clothing and jewellery. Turn left on 6th Avenue and walk along to W. 9th Street. Turn right down W. 9th Street and right into 5th Avenue to return to Washington Square. Off the north side of the square, in Washington Mews and Mac-Dougal Alley are New York's only remaining gaslamps.

for quality, variety and value for money. You will find them all over Manhattan, but in particular in overwhelming abundance in the ethnic areas which, more than in any other city in the United States, have adopted their national characteristics in appearance as well as behaviour. In Little Italy, an area bounded by Houston Street, Chrystie Street, Canal Street and Broadway, you can barely hear an American word spoken. Below Canal Street is Chinatown. Over 100 years old, it is so oriental that even the telephone booths are pagoda-shaped. Here you can enjoy a Dim Sum (Chinese dumplings) lunch at a Chinese tea parlour. Nom Wah at Doyer Street, and Hong Fat at Matt Street are just some of the hundreds of restaurants where you are served bigger portions than you could ever hope to eat for just a few dollars. Further east in the largely polyglot immigrant community of Lower East Side you can even eat at a Kosher Chinese Restaurant. It is Bernstein's in Essex Street. To the west lies SoHo, with its quaint shops and art galleries bounded by West Broadway, Canal, Lafayette and Houston Streets. Lying south of Houston Street, it has acquired its name simply by a convenient marriage of the first two letters of each of the words, South and Houston.

Further west is New York's world-renowned artists' colony, Greenwich Village. Like Chelsea in London, (but New York's own Chelsea isn't a bit like London's Chelsea!) or the Left Bank in Paris, Greenwich Village, extending west of Broadway to Hudson Street and south from 14th Street to Spring Street, is lined with fruit and vegetable pushcarts, food markets, art galleries, jewellery, fabrics, ceramics, dress and shoe shops, book and furnishing stores, coffee houses — and twenty-nine theatres. In Washington Square, at the foot of 5th Avenue, is the famous Washington Arch, built in 1893 to a design by Stanford White. To really savour Greenwich Village you need to turn off the main streets and saunter beside the quaint nineteenth-century houses (see the box at the top of this page for a suggested walk).

Near the southern tip of Manhattan is the Financial District, where Wall Street and two stock exchanges rule over the world's money markets. Originally, Wall Street traced the route of a wall erected in the seventeenth-century to keep the Indians out of New York. It was not a success — the Indians preferring to by-pass it by canoe — and anyway, the settlers kept pulling bits out of it for firewood. When it was pulled down in 1699, the path that was left grew into a street and, being close to the southern tip of Manhattan, it was a useful place for merchants to meet and do a spot of business. Eventually, the government started to take an interest in the financial deals, and the first stock exchange was established early in the nineteenth-century thus making Wall Street one of the world's leading financial centres.

Writers, artists and all New Yorkers enjoy the Bohemian atmosphere of Greenwich Village, with its old cobbled streets, colourful market stalls, coffee houses and shops

Right at the top end of Manhattan lies the dynamic Black community of Harlem, bounded on the east by the East and Harlem Rivers, on the south by 96th Street, on the north by 155th Street, and on the west by 5th and St Nicholas Avenues. For two centuries it grew slowly into a prosperous middle-class farming community, but early this century Black intellectuals, artists and entertainers started to gravitate to it. During the 1930s they created a new base there. Harlem has become a bastion of Black culture, and nowadays it is considered unwise for Whites to enter it. Nonetheless, like all other Manhattan communities, it has given New York a special vigour and flavour.

Not that New York's other four boroughs — Brooklyn, the Bronx, Queens and Staten Island — should be ignored. Each of them a large area where independent community life flourishes, they all lie just a bridge away from the centre of Manhattan, and are virtually cities in their own right. The best known is Brooklyn, where Coney Island —

Seen from the World Trade Center, the famous Brooklyn Bridge which, with its sister, the Manhattan Bridge, spans the East River. Inset, the view across Brooklyn Bridge to the Empire State Building

the Southend of New York, with its fairgrounds, candy floss and toffee apples, amusement arcades, and Nathan's famous hot-dog stand — draws the New Yorkers in their millions throughout the summer.

Yet there is so much else to see in Brooklyn — such as 520-acre Prospect Park, where you can climb Lookout Mountain to see the last powdery vestige of North America's glaciers. The park, laid out in the latter half of the nineteenth century, now includes a sixteen-acre lake. It is reached from Manhattan via the Manhattan Bridge and along Flatbush Avenue which runs through the park, or via Brooklyn Bridge, whose main claim to fame is that it has been sold more times by confidence tricksters than any other unattainable object. From its 1595ft-long span, 133ft above the East River, the $9,000,000 bridge, completed nearly 100 years ago, offers marvellous view of the Manhattan skyline. Several workers were seriously injured during its construction, and it has always been a favourite place for the suicidal.

Brooklyn also has the distinction of being reached by the longest underwater tunnel in America. It is the Brooklyn Battery Tunnel, which passes under the East River for two miles, connecting Brooklyn with Lower Manhattan. Linking Brooklyn with Staten Island is the 4260ft-long Verrazano Narrows Bridge, one of the longest suspension bridges in the world. The most recent of the sixty or so bridges that span the waterways of the New York area, it cost about £150,000,000 to put it up in 1964 and used about three times the amount of steel required to build the Empire State building, as well as 143,000 miles of cable strong enough to lift an ocean liner.

An attraction of a different kind in Brooklyn, and not to be missed, are the Botanic Gardens. The fifty-acre area, once an ash dump, has since 1910 provided a sharp and pleasing contrast to the concrete jungle of the streets around it.

Breukelen was among the earliest of five settlements the Dutch established, and the old buildings still clearly show the influence of the early Dutch settlers. Here you can see quaint cottages such as the Pieter Claassen Wyckoff house, built in the middle of the seventeenth century.

In comparison, the Bronx has a less dramatic history. The only borough attached to the mainland, not much of its forty-three square miles has anything of interest to tourists. Named after Jonas Bronck, a Danish immigrant who founded a 500-acre farm here in 1639, it is now home to more than 1,500,000 people.

The largest borough in land size is Queens. In its 121 square miles lie both Kennedy International Airport, with its thirty miles of runways, and the domestic airport of La Guardia, named after former New York mayor Fiorello La Guardia.

Staten Island, the sixty-square-mile island borough, also has a record-breaking bridge — the 1652ft Bayonne Bridge, which links it with the New Jersey mainland and is the longest steel arch bridge in the world. Originally called Staaten Eyland, in honour of the States General, the governing body of the Netherlands, it later became Richmond County, named after the Duke of Richmond. Staten Island became in the early part of this century a retreat for the wealthy, who encouraged the creation of fine parks, tennis courts (tennis was introduced to America on the Staten Island Cricket Club grounds) and golf courses. More recreational activities were gradually added, until more than 6,000,000 people were crossing the East River every year to enjoy the amenities of Staten Island. One of these is the Vanderbilt Mausoleum, believed to be the largest tomb in America, in the Staten Island Moravian Cemetery. Here the remains of William Vanderbilt have lain since his death in 1884. Considered the richest man in the world at the time, he built up a $200,000,000 fortune from his father's freight and passenger rail business. It originally only linked Staten Island with New York, but later the network developed into a mammoth transportation empire spreading out as far as the northern capital of Chicago.

Festivals

New Yorkers love to dress up in costume, and there are frequent opportunities for festivities throughout the year. National, religious and civic parades, festivals and celebrations take place almost every month all over the city. Below is a calendar of the more colourful events, but exact dates have been omitted as they can vary from year to year.

February: George Washington's Birthday.
March: Greek Independence Day.
April: Hans Christian Andersen Birthday ceremonies at the statue in Central Park; Pan American Day; Verrazano Day, to commemorate the Florentine navigator who first sighted the Hudson River in 1524.
May: Salute to Spring; I Am An American Day; St Joseph's Day; Loyalty Day; Armed Forces Day; Norwegian Constitution Day; National Maritime Day; Memorial Day.
June: Puerto Rican Day; Nationality Day USA; Blessing of the Fleet; San Juan's Day; Irish Feist; San Antonio.
July: Our Lady of Mount Carmel; Fourth of July fireworks.

August: St Stephen's Day.
September: Labor Day (first Monday in September) San Gennaro.
October: *Oktoberfest* in Yorkville; Ten-Ten Day Festival; Harvest Moon Ball; Columbus Day; Veteran's Day; Birthday observance of Statue of Liberty on Liberty Island; Hallowe'en.
November: Thanksgiving Day.

More information about when and where to see New York's many parades and celebrations can be obtained from the AAA or the New York Visitors' Bureau (see p.160 for addresses).

Staten Island's Todt Hill, rising 409ft above sea level, is the highest point on the East coast as far south as Key West, and is worth exploring. The borough now has a resident population of 355,000, who have the advantage of using the cheapest form of cross-river transport — the famous Staten Island Ferry. Offering the five-mile trip across New York Harbour for a fare of just a few cents per head, the ferry is one of the oldest in America — the first charter was issued in 1712. After the introduction of steam boats early in the nineteenth century, the trip could be made in around half an hour — only marginally longer than the journey takes today, when 20,000,000 passengers use the service every year. Many are commuters, but even more tourists take the trip to catch sight of the magnificent panorama of Manhattan's skyline from the boat, and of Liberty Island, where the 300ft-high Statue of Liberty has been raising her torch in welcome for almost 100 years. The figure itself is 151ft high and, standing on its 156ft pedestal, makes the tallest modern statue in the world. France paid for casting and erecting the statue to commemorate its support of the American Revolution. First, French sculptor Auguste Bartholdi was dispatched to New York to pick a site. On his return to France, he enlisted the help of Gustave Eiffel, the man whose name is on Paris's most famous landmark, to help design the statue. With an outer skin of copper sheeting and its inner skeleton made of steel, the 225-ton statue has the Torch of Freedom in her right hand, the Declaration of Independence in the other, and shackles to denote the defeat of tyranny at her feet. The statue was dedicated by President Cleveland on 28 October 1886. Inside visitors are carried by elevator to a spiral stairway leading to an observation platform in the statue's head. In her base is a museum of memorabilia of the early days of immigration, telling the story of how Ellis Island — a few hundred yards away and, like Liberty Island, straddling the approaches to the Hudson River — became the last stop for over 12,000,000 immigrants who converged on the United States around the turn of the century to find fame and fortune in the New World.

The cosmopolitan character of New York's population is largely due to the influx of European talent from the arts, sciences and crafts. Today, with the equivalent of more than 26,000 people on every one of its 340 square miles, New York City's metropolitan population of approximately 9,000,000 is fifty-three per cent of the total number of people who live in New York State — an area of 49,500 square miles!

With so many people about, it is a delight to walk in daylight in New York. Central Park is the place where office workers go to get away from the brooding shadows of the skyscrapers. In the 840 acres of woods and landscaped grounds — one-sixth of New York is parks and open spaces — are lakes, outdoor skating rinks, a swimming pool, the Delacorte outdoor Shakespearian theatre, and a small zoo. There is also a special children's zoo. All motor vehicles are barred from certain roads in Central Park in summer at certain times to make room for New York's many keen cyclists.

It is best not to hire a car for Manhattan sightseeing trips, if you want to avoid hours wasted in traffic jams. As a pedestrian, you can enjoy the neighbourhood much better. Another good way to get around Manhattan is to ride the subway — an experience rather less daunting than it may appear from the

Central Park provides a welcome refuge for New Yorkers. Here, an artist tries to capture the scene reflected in the lake

157

Transport

JOHN F. KENNEDY
INTERNATIONAL AIRPORT:
Queen's Borough, junction of
Van Wyck Expressway
(Interstate 678) and Belt
Parkway. Ten major terminals
serve passengers arriving in
New York from all over the
world. Bus services run to
and from the East Side
Airlines Terminal at 37th St
and 1st Ave, tel. 632 0500,
and along the Avenue of the
Americas (6th Ave). The bus
stops serving the airport can
be found at intervals all along
the avenue.

LA GUARDIA AIRPORT is
also in the Queen's District
and there is a bus service to
and from the East Side
Airlines Terminal.

TRAINS: New York has two
railway stations, both in
Manhattan. Grand Central
Station is at Park Ave and E.
42nd-44th Sts; Pennsylvania
Station is at 7th Avenue and
W. 33rd St. For information,
tel. AMTRAK 736 4545.

BUSES: There are 210 bus
lines in New York City. For
information, tel. 330 1234.
Exact fare is required on all
buses.

SUBWAY: The New York
underground system is cheap
and efficient, although
crowded during the morning
and evening rush hours, and
best avoided late at night.
Special tokens can be
bought, giving unlimited
travel on the 237-mile
network. Some stations are
served by both express and
local trains. Expresses stop at
a limited number of stations,
so it is important to know
whether your stop is one of
them. Stations all have good
maps and clear direction
signs.

TAXIS: Fares from either of
the two airports to central
Manhattan can be expensive,
especially at rush hour. As in
most large cities, taxis tend to
be an expensive way of
travel, but they are plentiful
and swift.

CAR HIRE: Manhattan is not
a good place for the tourist to
drive around. There is a lot
of traffic and parking is
almost impossible. The main
car-hire agencies are:
Airways, tel. 244 0440; Avis
Rent-a-Car, 217 E. 43rd St,
tel. 800 331 1212; Dollar
Rent-a-Car, tel. 800 569
8290; and Hertz Rent-a-Car,
tel. 654 3131. Others are
listed in the Yellow Pages of
the telephone directory.

Touring Information

AAA: The Automobile Club
of New York, 28 E. 78th St at
Madison Ave, tel. 586 1116,
has branches at the Hilton
Hotel, 7th Ave at 33rd St; at
the Lincoln Center, 1881
Broadway at W. 62nd St; at
1781 Flatbush Ave, Brooklyn;
at 186-06 Hillside Ave,
Jamaica, and at 729
Smithtown Bypass, Long
Island.
All are open during normal
office hours. As well as
getting helpful advice, maps
and brochures for touring,
the club offers a useful
service to anyone lost in New
York. Phone 594 0700 and
explain where you are and
where you want to get to, and
you will be given directions,
whether you are in a car or
travelling by public
transport.

NEW YORK CONVENTION
AND VISITORS' BUREAU:
2 Columbus Circle, tel. 397
8200. For information about
events, tel. 397 8222. The
Visitors' Bureau publishes a
number of helpful lists of
restaurants, events, shops
etc, as well as maps and
guides.

Parks and Gardens

BATTERY PARK: on the
southern tip of Manhattan
Island. In 1624 the first Dutch
settlers in the area built a fort
— hence the name of what is
now an attractive park
offering superb views of New
York Harbour and the Statue
of Liberty.

BROOKLYN BOTANIC
GARDEN: bordered by
Flatbush Ave, Empire Blvd,
Washington Ave and Eastern
Parkway. Many different
types of garden can be found
here, including a rose garden
with more than 700 varieties
of roses, and a garden of
fragrance for the blind.

CENTRAL PARK: bordered
by 59th and 110th Sts, 5th
Ave and Central Park West.
At the Plaza entrance on
Central Park South, you will
find horse-drawn carriages
for hire, an ideal way to tour
this 840-acre park. The
landscaped, wooded grounds
provide a pleasant refuge
from Manhattan's bustling
streets. Among the park's
attractions are lakes, a
swimming pool, skating rinks,
horse-riding, a zoo and an
open-air theatre — the
Delacorte Theater where
performances of Shakespeare
are given in summer. On no
account should tourists
wander in this, or any other
park, after dusk. In the
daytime, when plenty of
people are about, visitors
should be safe if they stay on
the frequented paths.

FLUSHING MEADOWS —
CORONA PARK: bordered
by Roosevelt Ave, Van Wyck
St, Union Turnpike and 111th
Sts. This is the most extensive
park in Queen's Borough, the
site of two world fairs, in
1939-40 and 1964-5. There
are miles of cycle paths, a
boating lake, putting green,
ice-rink, swimming pool, zoo,
pony rides and restaurants.

NEW YORK BOTANICAL
GARDENS: North-west Bronx
Park, Bronx Borough. This
230-acre garden boasts one
of the largest botanical
collections in the world.
Natural features in the park
include the Bronx River
gorge and waterfalls, and a
hemlock forest.

NEW YORK ZOOLOGICAL
PARK: bordered by Fordham
Rd and Southern Blvd, Bronx.
The Bronx Zoo, as it is
known, has a large collection
of animals, birds and reptiles.
Visitors can also take
monorail trips through a
safari park, and there are
animal rides and a
children's zoo.

WASHINGTON SQUARE
PARK: Greenwich Village.
All sorts of events take place
in this popular city park —
poetry readings, folk singing
and open-air art displays. In
one corner, chess and
draughts players meet during
the summer months and at weekends the square is thronged.

Shopping

The great department stores
of New York are world
famous, and 5th Avenue is
the centre of the shopping
world. Here, at 34th St, you
will find B. Altman & Co; at
39th St, Lord and Taylor,
and, best-known of all, Saks
Fifth Avenue, near the
Rockefeller Center at 50th
St. Also on 5th Ave, at 57th St,
is one of the world's most
famous jewellers, Tiffany's,
where you can see displays of
fabulous jewellery, and
sometimes find less expensive
gifts.

Back to department stores,
Bloomingdale's is on
Lexington Ave, at 59th St;
Macy's is at 34th St and
Broadway; Gimbels is on 6th
Avenue, at 33rd St, and its
offshoot, Gimbels East is on
Lexington Ave at 86th St.

If you are looking for
antiques, then the Manhattan
Art and Antique Center,
1050 2nd Ave at 56th St, is
an attractive, three-storey
arcade containing the shops
of more than 72 antique
dealers, jewellers and
craftsmen. Outdoor 'flea'
markets, offering a wide
assortment of bric-a-brac, are
at 6th Ave and 26th St open
Sundays and at 335 Canal St,
corner of Greene St (open
Saturdays and Sundays).

There are, of course, a host
of small shops and boutiques,
and to find out which of these
sells the sort of thing you are
looking for, it is easiest to
consult the New York Visitors'
Bureau, which has booklets
available.

Nightlife

New Yorkers are spoilt for
choice of entertainment, and
whether you are looking for
theatres, concerts, cinemas,
opera, ballet or nightclubs,

you are bound to find
something to interest you.
Calendars of events are
published by the Visitors'
Bureau, or you can simply
buy a copy of New York, the
New Yorker or Village Voice
magazines, all of which
contain lists of current shows,
events and concerts.
Nightclub tours are offered
by many of the sightseeing
tour companies.

Sightseeing

By far the quickest and
easiest way to find your feet
in such a vast city as New
York is to take one of the
many sightseeing bus tours
available. Gray Line is one of
the best known companies,
tel. 765 1600, and you can
also take boat trips around
Manhattan. Island Helicopters
run daily helicopter tours
from the heliport at 34th St
and East River.

Sport

Cycling, rowing, tennis and
horse-riding are all popular
sports that can be practised
in Central Park in the heart
of Manhattan. Cycles can be
hired from the Bicycle Club
of America, corner of 61st St
and Broadway, tel. 757 7957.
Rowing boats can be hired at
either of the lakes in Central
Park, and horses from the
Claremont Riding Academy
at 175 W. 89th St.

Spectator sports are also
available. Madison Square
Gardens, between 7th and
8th Aves and 31st and 33rd
Sts, tel. 564 4400, is the
place to go to watch the New
York Rangers play ice hockey
or the New York Knicks play
basketball. The Yankee
Stadium in the Bronx and
Shea Stadium in Queens are
home to baseball.

Museums

THE BROOKLYN MUSEUM:

Eastern Pkwy and Washington Ave, tel. 638 5000. This huge museum holds a superb collection of primitive and prehistoric art. An unusual and fascinating feature is a gallery devoted to the work of female artists from the 16th to the 20th century.

CHINESE MUSEUM: 8 Mott

St, Chinatown, tel. WO 4-1542. Exhibits include ancient Chinese coins, brightly-coloured costumes and beautiful antique chopsticks. Children will enjoy the push-button displays and educational quizzes.

THE CLOISTERS: Fort Tryon

Park, Fort Washington Ave and W. 190th St, tel. 923 3700. Probably the most unusual museum in the world, the Cloisters has been constructed from a number of medieval monasteries transported from the south of France and reassembled on a dramatic cliff, overlooking New York's Hudson River. Its treasures include the 15th-century tapestry *Hunt of the Unicorn*, medieval frescoes, precious stones, paintings and stained glass. In the Bonnefont Cloister is a herb garden planted with over 200 herbs known to have been used in western Europe before 1520, and in the Trie Cloister is a garden planted with the flowers and shrubs depicted in the *Unicorn* tapestries.

FIRE DEPARTMENT

MUSEUM: 104 Duane St, tel. 570 4230. This three-storey building is filled with all manner of antique fire-fighting equipment.

THE GUGGENHEIM

MUSEUM: 5th Ave, between E. 88th and E. 89th St, tel. 860 1313. Architect Frank Lloyd Wright (1867-1959) designed this controversial building referred to by its critics as the 'corkscrew' or the 'monstrous concrete mushroom'. In fact, the cream-coloured construction with its four-storey spiral cone is rather more reminiscent of a carousel, and its exterior arouses as much interest as the contemporary art displayed within its walls. Solomon R. Guggenheim, who commissioned Wright to design the museum, was a wealthy copper magnate fascinated by modern painting. His personal collection of the works of Kandinsky, Klee, Chagall, Delauney, Léger and others, forms the basis of the museum's exhibits. Other artists represented here include Picasso, Renoir, Cézanne, van Gogh, Degas and Toulouse-Lautrec. Visitors can take the lift to the top of the building then walk down, passing spectacular, naturally-lit paintings on the descent.

HAYDEN PLANETARIUM:

Central Park West and W. 81st St, tel. 873 8828. All you ever wanted to know about UFOs, meteorites, comets and space vehicles, will be revealed to you at the Hayden Planetarium. A 'sky show', in which constellations are projected onto the observatory ceiling, is a popular feature and the nightly 'Laserium' display, a kind of *son et lumière* with lasers, should not be missed.

METROPOLITAN MUSEUM

OF ART: 5th Ave at 82nd St, tel. 535 7710. This richly-endowed museum occupies a neo-Renaissance building of grey Indiana limestone, and consists of no fewer than 26 galleries, and 18 separate sections. Subjects covered include European sculpture, ceramics, glass, metalwork and decorative art, arms and armour, medieval art, musical instruments, Far-Eastern art, costume and primitive art. It also has an outstanding collection of American paintings, sculpture and design.

MUSEUM OF MODERN ART:

11 West 53rd St, tel. 956 6100. A popular meeting place, the Museum of Modern Art is housed in a light, airy geometric building designed by Phillip Goodwin and Edward Durell Stone. Its treasures include Vincent Van Gogh's masterpiece *Starry Night* and Monet's *Water Lilies*, and a popular attraction is the pleasant sculpture garden where works by Rodin, Renoir and Henry Moore are displayed.

THE MUSEUM OF NATURAL

HISTORY: Central Park West and W. 79th St, tel. 873 1300. One of the largest of its kind in the world, the Museum of Natural History began construction in 1874 and was the project of various architects over the years, thus resulting in a building of a curious mixture of architectural styles. Two sides of the structure resemble a medieval castle, while the others are more modern. More than 24,000 items are housed here and they include life-size dioramas of animals in their natural habitats, prehistoric monsters, oceanic birds and history of the development of complex human cultures.

COOPER HEWITT MUSEUM:

5th Ave at 91st St, tel. 860 6868. Part of Washington's Smithsonian Institution complex, and the only one of the 13 museums outside the capital, this museum of design is housed in a beautifully renovated Carnegie mansion. It provides visual information on the study of design, and is meant to serve as a working museum and reference centre for students. Included in the collection are 15th- to 20th-century drawings and prints, textiles, jewellery, wallpaper and hardware.

THE FRICK COLLECTION:

1 E. 70th St, tel. 288 0700. This luxurious mansion was designed in 1913 for Henry Clay Frick (1849-1919), a Pittsburgh industrialist, whose love of beautiful things is a legacy to the world. His collection of works of art from all parts of the globe includes Chinese porcelain, French bronzes from the 16th and 17th centuries, Swedish miniatures, and portraits and landscapes of the Dutch, French, Spanish and British schools. Each room of the mansion is exquisitely furnished with priceless pieces which set of the works of art and evoke the atmosphere of ages past.

Places of Interest

CITY HALL: At the end of

Brooklyn Bridge between Park Row and 250 Broadway, tel. 566 8681. Begun in 1803, this handsome building stands in a pleasant park, a constant reminder of the time before skyscrapers. The Mayor of New York and the city council have their offices here, and it was at City Hall that the body of Abraham Lincoln lay in state and was viewed by 120,000 grief-stricken New Yorkers after his assassination in 1865.

EMPIRE STATE BUILDING:

34th St and 5th Ave, tel. 736 3100. The shining spire of the Empire State Building, reaching 1472ft into the sky, makes it the third tallest building in the world. Its romantic Art Deco design attracts an average of 1,500,000 people a year, and some of them twice; once to view the layout of New York by day, and again in the evening to see the spectacle of the city's lights from the observatories on the 86th and 102nd floors.

FEDERAL HALL: At the

corner of Wall and Nassau Sts, tel. 264 4367. George Washington was sworn in as president on this site in 1789 and the present building, built of Massachusetts marble and reminiscent of a Doric temple, holds mementos of Washington. Documents concerning the Bill of Rights and citizens' rights to freedom of expression are on display.

LINCOLN CENTER:

Broadway and W. 66th St, tel. 877 1800. Comprising six buildings devoted to theatre, music and dance, the Lincoln Center can accommodate 13,747 spectators at a time within its Italian marble walls. Surrounded by the principal buildings of the Center is an attractive plaza with a black marble fountain. The Metropolitan Opera House, also part of the Center, is decorated with huge murals by the painter Marc Chagall, while the Avery Fisher Hall, home of the New York Philharmonic Orchestra, resembles a Greek temple. Other buildings are the New York State Theater, the Vivian Beaumont Theater, a branch of the New York Public Library, and the Juilliard School; a training ground for musicians, actors and dancers.

MADISON SQUARE

GARDEN: 4 Pennsylvania Plaza, W. 33rd St, between 7th and 8th Aves, tel. 564 4400. This enormous arena is the home of all New York's major events, such as world-class boxing, the National Horse Show, the Westminster Club Dog Show, rock concerts, circuses etc. It is the permanent base of the New York Knickerbockers basketball team and the New York Rangers ice hockey team.

NEW YORK STOCK

EXCHANGE: 20 Broad St, tel. 623 5167. This elegant building is composed of Corinthian columns and sculpted figures symbolizing commerce. A lone tree stands in front of the entrance to commemorate the buttonwood tree beneath which the first transaction took place in 1792. Today, visitors can view from a glass-enclosed gallery, while a guide attempts to explain some of the intricacies of high finance.

WORLD TRADE CENTER:

Bounded by West Church St, Liberty St and Vesey St, tel. 466 7397. Occupying a 16-acre site near the Hudson River, the World Trade Center exists to advance and expand international trade and has been called a 'United Nations of Commerce'. All international business services are concentrated in this 'central market', employing an estimated 50,000 people. The twin towers of the building, built to a new structural skyscraper design, make the World Trade Center the second tallest building in the world after the Sears Roebuck Building in Chicago. Numerous shops and restaurants are to be found within the Center.

YANKEE STADIUM: 161st St

and River Ave, The Bronx, tel. 293 6000. This famous stadium was built in 1923 and saw the heyday of American baseball heroes such as Babe Ruth and Joe Di Maggio. In 1974-75 it underwent renovation and now seats more than 54,000 people.

Around Long Island

2-3 days — 265 miles

New York City — Old Bethpage — Sayville — Shirley — Southampton — Bridgehampton — East Hampton — Amagansett — Montauk — Greenport — Cutchogue — Riverhead — Ridge — East Setauket — Setauket — Stony Brook — Centerport — Huntington — Oyster Bay — Kings Point — New York City.

Playground of the rich, Long Island is lined with the large estates and opulent homes of wealthy New York businessmen, many built in the 19th and early 20th centuries. Hedonism still rules here — as can be told by one look at Nassau County's fashionable North Shore, where the bays and harbours of Long Island Sound accommodate fleets of gleaming yachts and power boats. Many of the great mansions can be visited, and there are also a number of fascinating historic sites. The island is packed with excellent golf-courses, state parks, open-air art exhibitions and fascinating museums, and swimmers and fishers can take their pick from the pebbles of the north shore or the sands of the south.

Take Interstate 495 and State Route 495 to Old Bethpage (exit 48 on Round Swamp Road, one mile south of Long Island Expressway) approximately 22 miles away.

Old Bethpage, New York State

Old Bethpage takes the visitor back in time to the early 19th century. Twenty-five historic buildings from all over Long Island have been re-erected in this 200-acre valley. The village is an active farming community and realistically re-creates conditions of 150 years ago.

Tours begin at the reception buildings with an introductory film, to prepare you for a typical day in the life of a pre-Civil War community. As you explore the village you will encounter the blacksmith hammering at his anvil, the cobbler making shoes, the tailor with his needle and

thread, and farmworkers tilling the land.

Leave Old Bethpage on Round Swamp Road, passing through Bethpage State Park, then drive east for about ½ mile and south on Main Street, joining State Route 109 at Farmingdale. Pick up Sunrise Highway, State Route 27, and drive on for 10 miles before turning south on to Lakeland Avenue and heading coastwards for Sayville, about 4 miles away.

One of 25 traditional Long Island houses which have been brought to Old Bethpage and re-erected

Sayville, New York State

Between rounds on the West Sayville Golf Course (east on Montauk Highway) you can visit the Suffolk Marine Museum, with its extensive collection of model ships, paintings and mementoes of early seafaring days.

Leave on Montauk Highway for Shirley, 17 miles away.

Shirley, New York State

On a 127-acre site overlooking Great South Bay is the three-storey manor house and estate of St George, granted to William Tangier Smith by the British Crown in 1693. Furnishings from the early 1800s, paintings, and documents concerning the estate are on show.

Back on the Montauk Highway, drive along the coastal road past many bays and the Shinnecock Indian Reservation to reach Southampton, approximately 34 miles away.

Southampton, New York State

Largest and most famous of the Hamptons, a chain of seafaring towns that dominate Long Island's south shore for 35 miles, Southampton stages a number of annual events including a colourful Fourth of July parade, an open-air art sale in early July, and a September Indian pow-wow at nearby Shinnecock Indian Reservation. This involves a series of ceremonial dances to enact and celebrate the history and growth of the country in true Red Indian fashion.

The Elizabeth Morton National Wildlife Refuge, 5 miles north on North Sea Road then 5 miles east on Noyak Road, is an Atlantic Flyway feeding and resting place for all kinds of migrant birds. Visitors are asked to register in the booth near the car park.

Also in the area, to the north-west of the town, is one of the largest automobile museums in the world, the Long Island Automotive Museum, and ¾ mile south, the Old Halsey Homestead is to be found. This restored, two-storey house, a portion of which

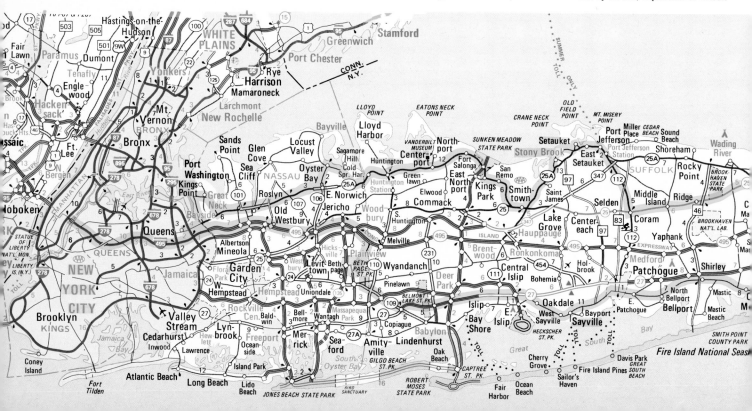

was built in 1648, is of interest for its 17th- and 18th-century furnishings and fascinating Colonial herb garden. At 25 Job Lane, displays of Renaissance and 19th-century American art make up the Parrish Art Museum and Arboretum. Southampton Historical Museum and Colonial Society, off Main Street at 17 Meeting House Lane, exhibits antiques dating from 1640, Indian art, whaling implements, an old fashioned, one-room school-house and a country store.

Follow the Montauk Highway and State Route 27 for 5 miles to Bridgehampton.

Bridgehampton, New York State
Visit Bridgehampton Historical Museum in Corwith House (1784) on Montauk and Corwith Avenue. The grounds hold the Hildreth-Simons Machine Shop, which contains working antique engines and farm machines, and the George W. Strong Wheelwright Shop, where old tools used to repair wagons are on show. Corwith House itself is a house of the Greek Revival, containing period furnishings from the late 18th century to the present day. A fascinating range of local crafts is on display here.

Continue on State Route 27 for 5 miles to East Hampton.

East Hampton, New York State
In this section of Long Island's south shore lie many handsome estates and fashionable summer holiday resorts. East Hampton is a charming rustic town which many writers and artists have made their home, though perhaps the town's greatest pride is the fact that John Howard Payne, composer of the

Montauk is famous for its 'cod ledge', one of the richest fishing areas in the world. Summer visitors flock here to enjoy the superb beaches and exhilarating sport of deep-sea fishing

song 'Home, Sweet Home' was born here in 1791. 'Home, Sweet Home' itself, John Howard Payne's birthplace and the inspiration for his famous song, is at 14 James Lane. See what there was to sing about by visiting the house, which still contains the 18th- and 19th-century furniture, china, glass, pewter and antiques collected in his lifetime.

Old Hook Mill, built in 1806 of oak and hickory wood brought from nearby Gardiners Island, is the only Dutch windmill in this area still in working order.

The Guild Hall, in beautiful, elm-lined Main Street, is a cultural centre which holds art exhibitions and theatre productions in July and August.

Just off the pretty village green,

which, with its duck-pond and circle of stately houses, resembles a rustic English scene, is the Mulford Farmhouse (circa 1660), furnished in 18th-century style.

The Main Street site of the Clinton Academy, the first academy to be chartered in the state, is now a museum exhibiting Indian relics and town history.

Rejoin State Route 27 and travel 4 miles to Amagansett.

Amagansett, New York State
The white sands of this seaside town were once trampled on by some unwelcome feet. A group of Nazi saboteurs came ashore here from a submarine during the Second World War, but they were captured before they could do any harm. Amagansett has a 250-year-

old Cape Cod house, popularly known as Miss Amelia's Cottage, and maintained as a museum by the town's historical society. Here, too, is East Hampton Town Marine Museum which depicts the history of whaling, commercial fishing, fish-farming and underwater archaeology. The garden makes an ideal picnic-place.

Drive along the Montauk Peninsula on State Route 27, which runs all the way along the coast to Montauk, 14 miles away. The countryside is spectacular — a succession of woodlands, rolling hills, cliffs and wonderful beaches. The sparkling freshwater lakes are summer homes for majestic migratory swans, just as the next point on the tour — Montauk — is itself a refuge for city-dwellers escaping from summer in New York.

Montauk, New York State
Montauk is reputedly the liveliest fishing village on Long Island. It is set on a ten-mile strip of land jutting into the sea and covered with acres of woodland, cliffs, white beaches and sand dunes. The 'cod ledge', off its banks, is one of the most famous fishing areas in the world. Deep-sea fishermen will have the chance to catch tuna, bluefish and other species. Other pastimes, such as surfing, bird-watching, swimming and sailing are equally well catered for here.

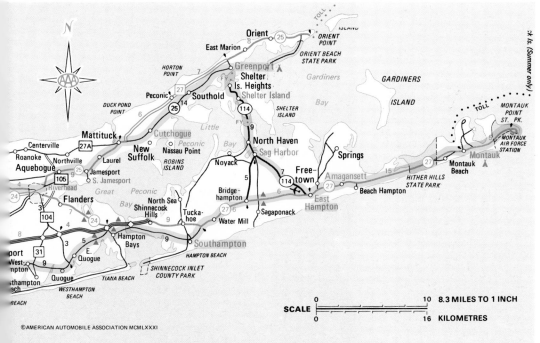

SCALE
10 — 8.3 MILES TO 1 INCH
16 — KILOMETRES

163

Long Island

Montauk lighthouse dominates the eastern headland of Long Island

Montauk Lighthouse, built in 1796 by order of President George Washington, is open to the public on weekend afternoons. From this point, at the end of the peninsula, it is possible to stand on a hill and view Block Island Sound in one direction, with the Atlantic stretching as far as the eye can see in another. It is easy to imagine the activities of the bootleggers who used these waters to smuggle their wares into Montauk at the time of Prohibition in the 1920s.

For family recreation, try Hither Hills and Montauk Point State Park. Caravans, trailers and tents are welcome at Hither Hills, where facilities are provided.

Retrace your steps to East Hampton and pick up State Route 114, passing through Sag Harbour and taking the car ferry over to Shelter Island, a yachting and golfing haven. A notable hotel here, small, friendly and reasonably priced, is Shelter Island Heights. All rooms overlook the harbour. On the far side of the island, take the ferry over to Greenport and the North Fork of Long Island.

Greenport, New York State
Known as the North Fork, this part of the island was famous for whaling and was the centre of Long Island's oyster industry at the turn of the century. Greenport, though no longer the major whaling port it once was, still retains its reputation for producing some of the best oysters in the world. So, do not leave this bustling dockside town without sampling them, especially if you are lucky enough to be here for the September Oyster Festival.

The Museum of Childhood, at 8 Broad Street, features a hand-carved Swiss model village and antique dolls.

Leave Greenport on State Route 25 and head back towards New York. In about 11 miles stop at Cutchogue.

Cutchogue, New York State
The name of this town is Indian for 'principal place'. If anyone is homesick for England, they can visit the Old House, built in 1649. Once the home of a sailing captain, it is considered to be the finest example of English architecture in the United States. Exposed sections inside the house show interesting features of construction methods.

From Cutchogue continue on State Route 25 for 12 miles into Riverhead.

Riverhead, New York State
Riverhead is the point where the North and South Forks of the island are joined together. It is set in a farming area, the most important crop being potatoes. New York State is known as one of the country's top potato-growing areas, almost entirely because of the excellent crops that are dug from the soil around Riverhead. Greenhouse products also thrive here, as do strawberries, peaches and cauliflowers. Put all these together with the succulent duck that Long Island is noted for, and you have a very pleasing menu for a local meal. Riverhead is the ideal place to eat it.

The Suffolk County Historical Society has its home here. Step inside to view the extensive collection of artefacts, lusterware and historical objects which tell the story of eastern Long Island's past. Legend has it that the pirate Captain Kidd once landed on this part of the island and buried his treasure here, confident that no-one would track it down amongst the thick woodlands and hilly, sheltered coves and inlets.

From Riverhead return to State Route 25, and pass Riverhead Racecourse for the 13-mile drive west to Ridge.

Ridge, New York State
The Brookhaven National Laboratory, on the William Floyd Parkway one mile north of State Route 495, exit 68, is an enormous, top-secret centre where research into the peaceful uses of atomic energy is carried out. It was established in 1946. Parts of the site can be visited, and displays include a model of a giant 'atom smasher', the first atomic reactor ever built for peace-time study and the decommissioned reactor's 'atomic pile'.

Leave Ridge on State Route 25 and drive straight on for 6 miles to Coram. From Coram head towards the coast in a north-westerly direction on State Route 112 then west on State Route 25A for about 9 miles to East Setauket.

East Setauket, New York State
On North Country Road, one mile north-east of Stony Brook station, is Sherwood-Jayne House, a typical 18th-century, English-style house with furnishings of the period and unusual painted walls.

Carry on up the unclassified road for about ¾ mile to Setauket.

Centerport: the baroque gateway to Eagle's Nest, now a museum of the collection made by millionaire globetrotter William K. Vanderbilt Jr

Setauket, New York State
The Caroline Church of Brookhaven, in the main street at Setauket Green, was built in 1729 and restored in 1937. Many features of the interior date from the early 18th century, and the church's most prized possession is a beautiful silver communion service given by Queen Caroline, wife of George IV of England.

Take State Route 25A and Ridgeway Avenue to Stony Brook, 2½ miles away.

Stony Brook, New York State
This residential community looks much the same as it did in the early 19th century. The shopping centre, though in reality very modern, has been modelled in the style of an old colonial village. A gristmill stands close by, and the post office is adorned by an all-American eagle that flaps its wings every hour on the hour.

Find time to visit the museum complex on Main Street, where a reconstructed blacksmith's forge, a carriage shed and a one-room school-house are among the 19 old buildings on display.

The local art gallery houses a permanent display of the paintings and memorabilia of the 19th-century painter William Sidney Mount (1807-1868). Mount made his home at Stony Brook, and began painting anecdotes of his rural surroundings. His works *Farmer Whetting his Scythe*, *Dancing on the Barn Floor* and *The Banjo Players* best illustrate the genre which he made famous. In the carriage museum on the

The opulent boating club at Huntington. Inset, the old farmhouse where the poet Walt Whitman, was born in 1819

south side of town are about 100 horse-drawn vehicles, some dating back to the late 17th century.

Return to State Route 25A for 7 miles to The Branch, then follow State Route 25 for 1½ miles. Rejoin State Route 25A just past Smithstown and travel north-west for about 11 miles to Centerport.

Centerport, New York State
On Little Neck Road in Centerport is a 43-acre estate which once belonged to William Vanderbilt, the son of the 19th-century financier and railway magnate, Cornelius Vanderbilt. This Spanish-Moroccan-style mansion is filled with fine antiques such as 17th-century Florentine carved walnut furniture, 13th-century Portuguese works of art, an enormous Aubusson tapestry and a magnificent organ. The house and beautifully kept gardens overlook Northport Bay. The

Vanderbilt Museum holds marine and wildlife specimens. Not to be missed is the planetarium, also in the mansion grounds, where hour-long shows are held.

Five miles from Centerport along State Route 25A lies the town of Huntington.

Huntington, New York State
Huntington has over 50 miles of coastline in its five harbours, and comprises a total of 17 communities. The town's main claim to fame is as the birthplace of Walt Whitman, the great American poet and journalist, often referred to as the 'good gray poet'. His boyhood home — a period style farmhouse — is now a historic site owned and maintained by New York State. Manuscripts, pictures and publications associated with Whitman are on display inside, and the house is well worth a visit.

The Heckscher Museum, in Heckscher Park at Prime Avenue and Main Street, contains a permanent collection of American and European paintings and sculpture, and holds a variety of special exhibitions.

From Huntington, pick up State Route 25A once more and follow it to the junction of Oyster Bay Cove Road. From here Sandy Hill Road will take you coastwards to Oyster Bay itself.

Oyster Bay, New York State
Originally, the hamlet of Oyster Bay was 'settled' by both the Dutch and English in the 17th century, and to this day there are two separate main streets, a block apart. Later the town became the headquarters of a detachment of British soldiers in the Revolutionary War.

Raynham Hall, at 20 West Main Street, was the farmhouse home of Samuel Townsend and his son Robert, who was an intelligence agent in New York City, and was one of the men responsible for the capture of the 18th-century British spy Major John André (see pp.167, 168) and the exposure of Benedict Arnold's treacherous plan to betray West Point.

Renowned as the summer home of Theodore Roosevelt, Oyster Bay's memorial to the president, the Roosevelt Bird Sanctuary and Trailside Museum, is at Cove Road. Examples of local flora and fauna such as would have pleased the conservationist president, are on show.

Sagamore Hill National History site (4 miles east via East Main Street and Cove Road) is named after Sagamore Mohannes, an early Indian chief who once owned this land. It was the home of Theodore Roosevelt until his death in 1919, and became known as the 'Summer White House'. The estate is furnished as it was when Roosevelt lived there with his family. Interesting exhibits are the gifts he received from foreign rulers, such as rugs from the Sultan of Turkey and elephant tusks from the Emperor of Ethiopia.

Leave Oyster Bay via State Route 106 to reach East Norwich, and transfer to State Route 25A which leads to Thomaston, about 10 miles away. From there, take Shore Road and Arrandale Hicks Lane coastwards to Kings Point, on Little Neck Bay.

Kings Point, New York State
This is the home of the United States Merchant Marine Academy. Founded during the First World War, it accommodates over 1000 midshipmen hoping to become officers and pursuing university degrees. The 75-acre grounds include the estate of the late Walter Chrysler.

Leave on Bayview Avenue and join State Route 25A at Greatneck Road. At exit 31 join Cross Island Parkway South, and at exit 30 switch to Long Island Expressway (Interstate 495) and head west for New York City.

The Hudson River

2 days — 265 miles

Manhattan — Yonkers — Tarrytown — Croton-on-Hudson — Garrison
— Beacon — Newburgh — Cornwall-on-the-Hudson — West Point —
Bear Mountain State Park — Stony Point — Tappan — Manhattan.

The Henry Hudson Parkway offers a dazzling view of the majestic George Washington Bridge, which links Manhattan and New Jersey

From its source, high in the Adirondack Mountains, the majestic Hudson River flows 315 miles through some of the most magnificent scenery in the States to reach its destination — New York Harbour. Along its banks tower the thickly wooded mountains of the Appalachian range and the spectacular cliffs of the Palisades, offset by fantastic neo-Gothic homes built by long-dead, wealthy merchants. One of America's great waterways, the Hudson opened up the West to the early pioneers and brought commerce to New York.

Take the Henry Hudson Parkway from Manhattan and drive 10 miles north to the Saw Mill River Parkway. After 9 miles turn right for Yonkers.

Yonkers, New York State

The largest city in suburban Westchester County, 'Yonkers' comes from the Dutch word *jonkheer*, meaning young nobility, and judging from the number of wealthy families who move to the tree-lined streets of Yonkers from New York, the city has its share of nobility, both young and old. Historic Yonkers Raceway has been celebrated for horse racing since 1894, and trotting races are held by night in the season. In August or September, the 'Yonkers Trot', one of the most fashionable trotting races, is held here.

In Trevor Park, the Hudson River Museum at 511 Warburton Avenue, includes a Victorian mansion called Glenview, which has exhibits of art, science and local history. There is a planetarium, and festivals, concerts, films, lectures and children's entertainments take place here.

Yonkers also boasts some of the state's biggest and best shopping centres, to cater for the millionaires, tycoons and celebrities who live in the area.

Continue north on US 9 for 10 miles to Tarrytown.

SCALE 5 0 5   **5.25 MILES TO 1 INCH**

5 0 5   **KILOMETRES**

Tarrytown, New York State

Tarrytown and North Tarrytown are deep in *Sleepy Hollow* country, made famous by the author Washington Irving (1783-1859) who is buried in the 17th-century Old Dutch Churchyard at North Tarrytown. The two towns sprawl along the east bank of the shimmering, three-mile-wide expanse of river, called here the Tappan Zee — a name coined by early Dutch settlers. According to Irving, 'Tarrytown' was reputedly given its name by its housewives, referring to their husbands' tendency to linger about the village tavern on market days.

Lyndhurst (635 S. Broadway) is a good example of Hudson Gothic. This incredibly flamboyant mansion was designed in 1838 by Alexander Jackson Davis and was later the home of railway tycoon Jay Gould. Period furniture representing the tastes of three successive owners, an art gallery and a collection of Tiffany objects are all on view in the house. The 67-acre estate offers spectacular views as well as outdoor concerts and festivals in warm weather. A rose garden and magnificent greenhouse are also open to the public.

Not least of the opulent estates to be found in Tarrytown is that occupied by the Rockefeller family at Pocantico Hills.

Patriots' Park (on US 9), contains the dividing line between the Tarrytowns, André Brook. Close to the brook, Major John André, a British spy, was captured during the War of

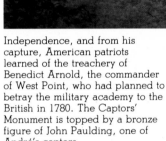

A working 18th-century gristmill and the original old oak dam at Philipsburg Manor, N. Tarrytown

Independence, and from his capture, American patriots learned of the treachery of Benedict Arnold, the commander of West Point, who had planned to betray the military academy to the British in 1780. The Captors' Monument is topped by a bronze figure of John Paulding, one of André's captors.

The Sunnyside Estate (W. Sunnyside Lane, off Broadway) was built to Washington Irving's own designs in 1835. He called the house his 'snuggery' and lived there for 24 years. Irving's own belongings, his books, manuscripts, household furnishings and some statues of his characters can be seen there. The house is surrounded by beautiful grounds. Washington Irving Memorial (W. Sunnyside Lane, at Broadway) is a tribute to the great author by Daniel Chester French, and shows a bust of Irving surrounded by figures of characters from his stories, including the reluctant hero of *The Legend of Sleepy Hollow*, Ichabod Crane.

Continue north on US 9 for 12 miles to Croton-on-Hudson.

Croton-on-Hudson, New York State

Just off US 9 is a restored 18th-century Dutch-English manor house, Van Cortlandt Manor, home of Pierre Van Cortlandt, a revolutionary patriot who became the first lieutenant governor of New York State. Only 20 acres of the original 86,000-acre estate remain. At the east end, the historic Ferry House and Ferry House Kitchen may be viewed. In the 18th century they supplied food and lodgings to travellers on the Albany Post Road. In the manor are portraits, furniture, porcelain and silver of the Van Cortlandt family, who counted fellow revolutionaries Benjamin

Dick's Hilltop Castle at Peekskill near Garrison is a dream-palace, modelled on the Alhambra at Granada in southern Spain

Franklin, Lafayette, Von Steuben and Rochambeau among their house guests. Spinning, weaving and dyeing demonstrations take place here in the summer months.

Continue north on US 9 for about 15 miles. Turn left on to State Route 403 and drive for 4 miles to Garrison.

Garrison, New York State

High above the Hudson Valley, Garrison boasts spectacular views, two remarkable mansions and an ecclesiastical centre.

Boscobel, north of the town on State Route 9D, is a glorious New York Federal-style villa, one of the finest in North America. It was built by S. M. Dyckman for his wife in 1806 and scheduled for demolition in 1960. A local restoration society managed to save it, and had it moved 15 miles north to its present site. It houses a collection of rare and beautiful antiques. The gardens are formal and offer magnificent southward vistas of the Hudson Valley. In the summer, splendid 'sound and light' presentations are held here, with an exciting historical narration.

Dick's Hilltop Castle is close by, an extraordinary near-replica of the Alhambra, built by a dreamer called Evans Dick, who unfortunately lost all his money on the stock market in 1911 and

167

Hudson River

never finished his fantasy.

Graymoor Christian Unity Center is on a mountain top just south of the junction of State Route 403 with US 9. It contains many chapels and shrines. The grounds give splendid views of the Hudson Valley below and picnicking is permitted.

Take State Route 9D and drive north for 4 miles to Cold Spring. Continue on State Route 9D through the beautiful Hudson Highlands State Park. Beacon is 6 miles north of Cold Spring.

Beacon, New York State
Set in noted skiing country, Beacon is a small town with Dutch connections, proud of its own heritage.

Each June on Beacon Day a grand parade is held, and the town is illuminated with a display of glorious fireworks to commemorate the day when fires were lit on high ground to warn Washington of the advance of British troops. This gave the town its name. The Madam Brett Homestead in Van Nydeck Avenue was built in 1709 and houses interesting period furnishings and historical exhibits. Notable architectural features are the hand-made scalloped roof shingles, hand-hewn beams, sloped dormers and an ancient kitchen fireplace.

Continue north for one mile on State Route 9D and cross the Hudson River at the next interchange. Drive south on US 9W at the first interchange, west of the river, to Newburgh.

Newburgh, New York State
Close to this riverside city are many reminders of George Washington's Revolutionary War successes. For more than a year, from 1 April 1782 to August 1783, Washington's headquarters were at the Jonathan Hasbrouck House, built in 1750, in Liberty Street. It is also called Washington's Headquarters State Historic Site. It was here that Washington created the order of the Purple Heart and disbanded the army after the successful conclusion of the War of Independence. Paintings, period furnishings and other fascinating relics are on display. The landscaped grounds contain a Tower of Victory and State Museum.

One mile north of Vails Gate on Temple Hill Road is the New Windsor Cantonment State Historic Site, which is a reconstruction of the Revolutionary army's winter camp on the original site. Guides wearing the uniforms of the Revolutionary army are on duty to explain the history. Here Washington dissuaded a group of his own officers from continuing with their plot for a coup against the newly formed Continental Congress. Another State Historic Site is the Knox Headquarters (1779-82), 4½ miles south-west on State Route 94. It was occupied by General Henry Knox, the heaviest man on Washington's payroll. A 50-acre farm and the John Ellison House, built in 1754, are here. Generals Green and Gates also occupied the building and Washington was a frequent visitor.

Continue southwards on US 9W then turn left at the first interchange on to State Route 218 to Cornwall-on-the-Hudson.

Cornwall-on-the-Hudson, New York State
The scenery west of this small town is reminiscent of the Alps, with distant views of the Scunemonk Mountains. The Hudson Valley narrows at this point, to run between the wooded hills of the Storm King State Park and the Hudson Highlands State Park.

Three-quarters of a mile south-west of State Route 128, on Mountain Road and the Boulevard, is a wildlife centre occupying 75 acres of woodlands. Interesting species of fish, mammals, reptiles and birds can be seen here and there are a number of nature trails.

Drive south on State Route 218 through the spectacular Storm King State Park for 6 miles to West Point.

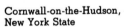

The Madam Brett Homestead is authentically furnished in early-18th-century American style

West Point Military Academy stands high above the Hudson River, affording superb views over the valley. Inset: officer cadets, the elite of the army, on parade

West Point, New York State
Training ground for some of the most famous of America's military leaders, West Point is the United States Military Academy. Its graduates include General MacArthur (1903), General Patton (1909) and General Eisenhower. Founded in 1802, the site on which this institution stands was first occupied as a military post during the American Revolution. In 1778, under the direction of Polish soldier Thaddeus Kosciuszko, a huge chain of defence was stretched across the Hudson River from West Point to Constitution Island to block the progress of the British fleet. In 1780, Benedict Arnold, officer in command of the post, turned traitor and attempted to betray it to the British.

Three chapels are open to the

public. The Cadet Chapel possesses one of the largest church organs in the world, containing over 18,000 pipes ranging in size from one smaller than a lead pencil to one 32ft long. It also has beautiful stained glass windows. The Old Cadet Chapel, built in 1836, is in the Post Cemetery. Its walls are hung with battle flags and marble shields from the Revolutionary period to commemorate the courageous American generals of the Revolutionary War. One had even been designated for Benedict Arnold until his treachery was revealed. The Chapel of the Most Holy Trinity is a Catholic chapel built in Norman Gothic style.

Fort Clinton is north and east of the Plain parade ground, and a monument to the great Polish soldier Thaddeus Kosciuszko is to be found on the east front. In 1778, Kosciuszko built a series of formidable defences against the British around West Point.

Trophy Point gives a bird's eye view of the Hudson River and features numerous relics of the American Revolutionary Wars. Links of the great chain stretched across the river to block the British Fleet are among the collection. Battle Monument is dedicated to men of the Regular Army who were killed in the American Civil War.

West Point Museum in Thayer Academic Hall contains a vast collection of weaponry.

Continue southwards for 6 miles, first on the scenic Old Storm King Highway (State Route 218), then, south of Highland Falls, on US 9W until you reach Bear Mountain State Park.

Bear Mountain State Park, New York State
This wonderful 5066-acre park has stupendous views over the river to the east and across the magnificent mountains to the west.

A visit to the summit of Bear Mountain (1305ft) along the George W. Perkins Memorial Drive is a must, and among the park's other attractions are five museums, tennis courts, an archery range, a zoo, a swimming pool, a boating lake, ice-skating rinks, ski slopes and pony jumps. Bear Mountain Inn is a charming old hostelry built in the style of a Swiss chalet and recently renovated at a cost of millions of

dollars. Excellent restaurant facilities and overnight accommodation are available here, and there are charming rustic lodges in the park for visitors making a longer stay.
Drive 6 miles south on US 9W through Jones Point to Stony Point.

Stony Point, New York State
Three-quarters of a mile north-east off US 9W is a rocky promontory overlooking the west bank of the Hudson River. Known as the Stony Point Battlefield State Historic Site, the 45 acres of land are preserved to commemorate the triumph of swashbuckling General 'Mad Anthony' Wayne (1745-96), who stormed a British post in 1779 and captured the garrison of 575 men.
Three miles south of Stony Point, turn right off US 9W on US 202. After 4 miles, turn south at the interchange and drive south on the Palisades Interstate Parkway for 12 miles. Turn south at the second interchange on to State Route 303 and drive for one mile to Tappan.

Tappan, New York State
This town, close to a picturesque lake, has the George Washington Masonic Shrine (DeWint House) on Livingston Avenue and Oak Tree Road. Built in 1700, George Washington occasionally used the house as army headquarters during the Revolutionary War. Four rooms are furnished in period style.
Drive north from Tappan on State Route 303, returning to the scenic Palisades Interstate Parkway and driving south for 14 miles. Return to Manhattan via the George Washington Bridge over the Hudson River.

New Yorkers are just a short drive away from the wooded hillsides and boating lakes of Bear Mountain State Park

Boston is forever associated with the famous Tea Party of 1773.
The brig, Beaver II, moored at Congress Street Bridge on Fort
Point Channel, is a full-scale replica of one of the ships
involved in that historic incident

Boston

Few cities can boast of having given birth to a
nation. Boston is among those that can. For it was
here, 350 years ago, that early Puritan settlers
started a community that 150 years later was to
lead to a rebellion and the War of Independence.
This was the scene of momentous events in
American history such as the Boston Tea Party and
the Battle of Bunker Hill, and the city revels in
remembering them and recreating them for its visitors.

Tradition lives on too, at Harvard, the world-
famous university on Boston's doorstep. Founded in
1636, it is the oldest university in the USA. Today
it is one of seventy-four colleges and universities in
and around Boston, and with a total student
population of more than 100,000 there is always
something new and exciting happening in the city.
Boston's colleges — notably Harvard and the
Massachusetts Institute of Technology — continue
to produce many of America's greatest intellects,
whether scientific, artistic or political. Having
fathered a revolution, Boston and its universities are
still the nursery-bed of some of the American
nation's greatest achievements.

The events leading up to the American War of Independence (in America usually called the 'Revolution', or the 'Revolutionary War') haunt the tourist in Boston. This is not really unexpected, as so much of what Boston is all about today has to do with what happened in and around the city 200 years ago.

Not that mementoes of battlefields are all that there is to Boston. The rich culture bequeathed over two centuries by men who had been drawn to the cause of freedom has helped to make Boston an intellectual and artistic jewel among American cities.

Nor should Britain's influence be discounted. All over Boston there are traces of her colonial legacy. In some ways the city is more conventionally British than the Lincolnshire town from which it borrowed its name. Yet in character and structure it is very North American, with a harsh, tough personality. It is not that there is less of a welcome for the stranger here than anywhere else in the States, but there is a noticeable reserve about many Bostonians. This may be due, in part, to the fact that Boston is really quite a small town. Unlike the great metropolis further down the coast, Boston, though only about 230 miles from New York, shares fewer of the 'Big Apple's' cosmopolitan characteristics than many American cities of similar size.

The Charles River, which separates the city from Charlestown and East Boston, two of its suburbs, also keeps it physically apart from the university city of Cambridge. Yet much of Boston's life-style is dominated by its illustrious neighbour on the northern bank. In turn, Cambridge, though it is administratively autonomous, is inextricably tied to Boston and, to all intents and purposes, is part of Boston's complex community life. Even more than its English namesake, Cambridge, Massachusetts exists for, and because of, its historic university. Coincidentally, its population of just over 100,000, swelled by more than 15,000 university students every year, is almost identical with that of Cambridge in England. Harvard's influence over Boston is very noticeable in its profusion of colleges, museums and art galleries, giving the city a generous cultural veneer it would otherwise not have had.

Boston is a judicious mixture of the old and the new. A centre for banking and finance, it is not only the capital of Massachusetts, but also the great commercial leader of New England. Its port, whose fifty miles of wharf serve over 100 shipping lines, is unequalled by any other city in New England.

Boston shows its age in numerous narrow streets and antiquated, stooped buildings, crouching under the shadow of motorways. More often, in the heart of the city centre — a bulge formed by the bend of the Charles River and the Fort Point Channel — traffic chaos in the narrow streets, built long before the motor-car, is much the same as many European cities have to endure. Boston also still makes use of mounted police in the streets — a reassuring homely touch. Wander through the history-laden area bounded by Cambridge Street as it smoothly describes almost half a circle, the

Looking across the Charles River from Cambridge to Boston. The wide, sheltered river estuary made Boston one of the wealthiest ports on the east coast

Fitzgerald Expressway to the east, Kneeland Street to the south and Commercial Street to the north, and you may come across one of the tall chestnut police horses tied to a lamp-post on the pavement. Indeed, parking in Boston is no easier for transport on four legs than four wheels. The higgledy-piggledy street layout, so different from the orderly grid system of most American cities, makes city driving a challenge that many people might find it best to resist.

Fortunately Boston offers countless good reasons for seeing the city on foot. The most rewarding walk is the one-and-a-half-mile Freedom Trail. Marked by a course of red bricks in the pavement, the Freedom Trail links sixteen historic sites in what is not so much a history lesson as an illuminating explanation of Boston's heritage.

It was in 1630 that the first colonists, led by John Winthrop, arrived in the Massachusetts Bay area, although the Pilgrim Fathers, in the *Mayflower,* had caught their first glimpse of New England ten years earlier. Most of the early settlers here were Puritans, attracted to the New World by the thought that there they would be able to practise their rigid puritanical religion without the hindrances they had experienced in England. The Pilgrim Fathers had landed, after a two-month crossing, at the tip of Cape Cod on 21 November 1620 and founded their settlement at what is now Plymouth. But their numbers were soon depleted by sickness and malnutrition, which so reduced their ranks that even the influx of new colonists over the next ten years could not swell their numbers much above 300.

The Massachusetts Bay colony got off to a better start. For one thing, there were more of them — nearly 1000 — and they were better equipped and financed. Settlements sprang up, often based on tightly knit family units, in the Boston area, and the numbers of colonists steadily increased. Differences in religious and political ideals were inevitable as the population grew, but most communities became self-governing, and for a time, life for the immigrant families seemed full of promise.

But by the start of the 1770s discontent with Britain was growing. The familiar cry of 'No taxation without representation' came to be heard among the colonists, because Britain insisted on its American colonies paying trade taxes on tea and other commodities, but would not allow them the right to vote.

Though the taxes did not amount to much, they were bitterly resented by the colonists, and in protest, a group of sixty or so patriots, disguised as Indians, crept on board three cargo ships at anchor on a raw December night in 1773 and unceremoniously threw 342 chests full of tea into Boston Harbour.

There had already been a major provocation nearly three years before the 'Boston Tea Party', as the incident became known. In what was later known as the Boston Massacre, British troops had fired into an unruly crowd which had attacked British sentries, killing five people. The Boston Tea Party brought confrontation almost to the stage of open warfare. It was to be another 16 months, though, before the conflict erupted irrevocably.

British troops were sent to keep order, but instead fanned the colonists' patriotic fervour. So, on 18 April, 1775, hearing that the colonists had stockpiled arms and ammunition at Concord, about 20 miles west of Boston, General Thomas Gage, the 56-year-old commander of the British forces in North America, sent 700 of his soldiers across the Charles River to seize the colonists' supplies. It turned out to be a fateful decision. As the column advanced towards Concord, Paul Revere rode ahead to warn of the troops' arrival. Revere, a 40-year-old blacksmith, silversmith and engraver, reached Lexington, about 6 miles east of Concord, about midnight to alert the local patriot leaders. He was captured, but his colleagues Samuel Prescott and William Dawes rode on to warn those in Concord.

By that time, battle had been joined between 100 militiamen, who came to be known as Minutemen, because they agreed to be ready to fight 'at a minute's

The 60th floor of the Hancock Tower, one of Boston's newest landmarks, offers panoramic views over the city

notice,' and the advancing Redcoats. It was on the approaches to the town, on Concord Bridge, that the first troops died. Under the statue of a Minuteman, the plaque recalls dramatically: 'On the opposite bank stood the American Militia. Here stood the invading army, and on this spot the first of the enemy fell, in the war of that revolution which gave independence to these United States'.

In a last desperate attempt to stem the tide of anger and hatred, the British officer in charge ordered a ceasefire, but his men ignored his order, and in the ensuing battle eight Americans died and ten were wounded. Soon, new forces of militia were on the road to harass the British column, and even after they had destroyed all the supplies they could find, the British were caught by cross-fire all

the way back to Boston. Before the day was out, they had suffered 273 casualties against only 95 American ones. News of the victory in that day's skirmishes soon spread to the other colonies, and the war developed into a unified struggle for independence.

Boston's role in these momentous events is marked by monuments and sites that have been carefully preserved. Many of them are on the Freedom Trail. The best place to begin the walk is on forty-eight-acre Boston Common, America's oldest public park, which dates from 1634. Adjoining the Common is the Public Garden, where a riot of colourful blooms surround a pond on which swan-shaped boats cruise. Boston's parks, known as the Emerald Necklace, include a wonderfully varied stretch of continuous parkland stretching several miles along both banks of the Charles River. On its 960 acres are six swimming pools, an eighteen-hole golf course, twelve tennis courts, two dance pavilions and two ice-skating arenas, with

Boston

excursion boats and concerts during the summer.

Boston Common's significance to the Freedom Trail is that it served as a military parade and training ground during the War of Independence. An important feature, in the middle of the Common, is the Soldier's Monument, signifying that from this spot Washington drove the British out of Boston on 17 March 1776.

Crossing the Common in a north-easterly direction to the junction of Park Street and Beacon Street you will reach the State House on Beacon Hill, one of Boston's major landmarks. Built in 1795, on land once owned by John Hancock, a former governor, it contains beneath its gilded dome (covered with £100,000 worth of gold leaf) the state archives, and statues, paintings and battle flags.

One of Boston's most historic neighbourhoods, Beacon Hill was home to Boston's first Black settlers, and later to eminent literary figures like Louisa May Alcott, of *Little Women* fame. The families who once owned some of the Federal and Greek Revival-style mansions on Beacon Hill were so select that they formed an exclusive group known today as the Brahmins.

Walk south-east down Park Street to the corner of Tremont Street to see Park Street Church. Built in 1809, it was once known as Brimstone Corner, because during the 1812 war with the British (see chapter on Washington D.C.), it was used as a gunpowder factory. It was also the place where William Lloyd Garrison caused a furore by first speaking against slavery in 1829.

Turn left up Tremont Street to the Granary Burying Ground, at the top of Bromfield Street. This is where the bodies of three of the signatories to the Declaration of Independence are buried. So are the victims of the Boston Massacre. Further along Tremont Street, at the junction with School Street, the King's Chapel, the second to be built on the site, was completed in 1754. It houses priceless silver and vestments sent by George III during British rule.

Turn into School Street, where a column marks the site of Boston's first public school. Founded in 1635, Boston Latin School was the first free school to be opened in America. It turned out several pupils with imperishable names, including Benjamin Franklin.

Continue along School Street to reach the Old Corner Book Store, built in 1712, which famous men of letters such as Ralph Waldo Emerson, Oliver Wendell Holmes and Henry Wadsworth Longfellow used as a meeting place. At Washington Street turn right and walk to the corner of Milk Street, passing a plaque marking Benjamin Franklin's birthplace. The Old South Meeting House stands on the corner. Though a predecessor stood here in 1669, the present building dates back to 1729, when it became the most important political and social venue in the city. The Boston Tea Party was organized from there, and so were protest meetings about the Boston Massacre.

Turn right into Washington Street, and walk to where State and Crown Streets intersect, to view the Old State House — on the site of the Town House. The building was erected in 1713, and became the debating chamber of royal governors and provincial delegates before the revo-

A plaque marks the site on Griffin's Wharf where the Boston Tea Party occurred in 1773

lution. Now it contains a museum of Boston history, and displays relics covering 200 years. There is even some tea left over from that tea party. It has witnessed more than its share of drama. The Boston Massacre occurred virtually outside its front door, and from the balcony facing State Street the Declaration of Independence was proclaimed. Here, too, in 1780, John Hancock was inaugurated as the Commonwealth's first governor.

On State Street, turn left to see the Boston Massacre site on Congress Street. It bears a monument, erected in 1888 by the Black community, to commemorate the events of 5 March 1770 when five people died from a volley intended to silence hecklers who had provoked the British troops with cries of 'Lobster-back' and 'Redcoat'. To their leader, a former slave called Crispus Attucks, is attributed the distinction of being the first American to die at the hands of the British.

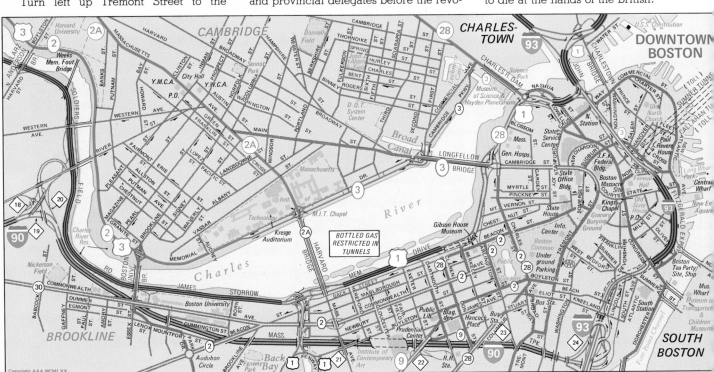

The Historic Neighborhoods Foundation, and Boston by Foot, are two non-profit-making organizations which arrange guided tours of Boston landmarks. The Historic Neighborhoods Foundation, 111 Atlantic Avenue, tel. 523 1860, is an educational body 'dedicated to increasing public awareness and appreciation of Boston's neighborhoods, architecture and urban design.' It offers tours of several areas at a small cost, which varies according to the length of the tour.

The Financial District tour, of commercial buildings constructed of sandstone, marble, granite and cast-iron, last an hour. The tour of the area destroyed by the fire of 1872 and rebuilt in different architectural styles, lasts 45 minutes. The Back Bay tour takes two hours. The walk round the North End, now largely an Italian neighbourhood and the oldest part of Boston, takes an hour.

The Waterfront tour takes you from the busy wharves, with their forest of cranes, to the colourful old market area, in an hour's walk, and the Beacon Hill walk lasts an hour and a half.

Boston by Foot, 77 North Washington Street, tel. 367 2345, was founded in 1976 to promote the city's historic sites and offers several interesting conducted tours. These include a 'Wednesday Brown Bag Mini-tour', where you bring sandwiches for lunch, and there are programmes of slide shows, as well as three one-day walks dealing with Boston's history, craftsmanship and folk art. Most of the walks are free to members, and charges vary for guests. There is a special children's tour of Beacon Hill, ending with a boat ride on the lake in the Public Garden, and on Sunday afternoons, children can go on an informative, historical 'Boston by Little Feet' walk (see p.176).

Guided Walking Tours

Walk north on Congress Street to Faneuil Hall Square at Merchants Row. Faneuil Hall was donated to the city by Peter Faneuil, a wealthy merchant, in 1742. Destroyed by fire in 1761, it was rebuilt two years later, and was used for so many political meetings that it became known as the 'Cradle of Liberty'.

Following the red-brick line, walk on for several blocks to view the oldest building in Boston, built with a wooden frame in 1676. It was owned by Paul Revere for thirty years until the end of the eighteenth century. Situated at 19 Old North Square, it was the house from which Revere set off on his fateful ride to warn the patriots at Lexington. The house has been restored and is still furnished in the period.

Continuing along the marked trail, you come to Salem Street, where, at the junction with Hull Street, is the oldest church building in Boston. Erected in 1723, Old North Church stood the test of time until the 1950s, when its steeple was blown over by a hurricane. On the night the British set off on their way to Concord, a lamp shone from the steeple as a pre-arranged signal to forewarn the patriots.

Almost opposite, Copps Hill Cemetery, between Charter and Hull Streets, was where the British aimed their guns across the Charles River at Bunker Hill in Charlestown — site of the first major battle of the American War of Independence on 17 June 1775.

Turn right along Hull Street, and left at Commercial Street to cross to Charlestown over the Charlestown Bridge. You may need to use public transport to reach Bunker Hill via Main Street, Park Street, Warren Street and Monument Avenue. The Bunker Hill Monument is a granite obelisk 22ft high, containing a 194-step spiral staircase. You can also see an audio-visual re-enactment of the Battle of Bunker Hill in a pavilion next to the USS frigate *Constitution* in Boston Harbour.

The final site on this version of the Freedom Trail (you can always cover the same ground in a different order), *Constitution,* known as 'Old Ironsides', is reached by making for the waterfront, at the side of the Boston Naval Shipyard. Launched in 1797, Old Ironsides came into its own in the war of 1812, and has been carefully restored several times. Its name is really a misnomer. It was built before the age of iron ships, but its oak timbers were said to be as strong as iron. This magnificent relic of a great naval heritage, with its forty-four guns, was built out of seasoned live oaks and red cedar timbers, bolted together and lined with

Where to Walk in Boston

There is so much that has to do with the past in Boston that the Freedom Trail (see main city text) only covers the obvious, essential landmarks. Many people enjoy seeing the less well-known sites, too, and the two walks described here are self-guided tours.

THE BLACK HERITAGE TRAIL explores the part played in the Black community in the events of the 18th and 19th centuries in Boston. Black slaves of African descent were first imported from the West Indies in 1638, and some of the places of interest mark their history. The tour is mainly in the Beacon Hill area and gives an opportunity to see some of Boston's finest architecture as well.

Start at Smith Court, just off Joy Street. No. 8 is a church built by free Black labour in 1806 and is one of the oldest church buildings for Black people in America. No. 7 is typical of the sort of homes occupied by Black families in the 19th century. On Joy Street, the Abiel Smith School, built in 1834 with money left by a White businessman, was for Black children, but when the Black community protested that their taxes also paid for schools from which their children were excluded, the Abiel Smith School became the issue over which the first integration battle was fought. In 1855 when integration was first introduced in America, the school was closed.

Turn right into Pinckney Street where, at nos. 5-7, is the home of Colonel George Middleton, a Black officer who led an all-Black army detachment in the Revolutionary War. The house, erected in the late 18th century, was probably one of the first to be built by Black labour. Further along Pinckney Street, at no. 86, the John J. Smith House was home to one of the most ardent advocates of school integration, and after segregation had been outlawed, John Smith was elected to the Massachusetts legislature.

Turn right up Anderson Street, pass Revere Street, and turn left into Phillips Street. At no. 66, the Lewis Hayden House commemorates a 19th-century American 'Scarlet Pimpernel', who helped numerous slaves to reach Canada and freedom via what became known as the 'underground railroad' escape route.

Now turn left into Cedar Street, right into Revere Street and right into Charles Street. The George Grant House at no. 108 is named after the inventor of the golf tee, a Black dentist. Walk down Charles Street, heading south, to the junction with Mount Vernon Street. Here, the Charles Street Meeting House, erected in 1807, was originally a church for Whites, but until the outbreak of World War II was used by the Black community as a meeting place in which they could express their social and political aspirations.

At Boston Common, turn left into Beacon Street and walk past Joy Street to Park Street. On Boston Common, take a look at the 54th Regiment Monument which commemorates the first Black division in the Civil War (1861-5) to fight on the Union side. The soldier who stopped the Confederates from capturing the regimental flag by wrapping it round his body, is specially honoured.

THE CAMBRIDGE HARVARD TRAIL starts at Cambridge Common. Go down Mason Street, passing Radcliffe College on the left. At Brattle Street, turn right to the Georgian-style home of the poet Longfellow. Now a National Historic Site, the house was his home from 1837, when he became a Harvard professor, until his death in 1882.

Return down Brattle Street to look at the Loeb Drama Center. At Boylston Street, turn right to see some of the typical University Houses — Eliot, Kirkland and John Hicks (at the corner of Boylston and South Streets.) Turn left on South Street and left on Dunster Street, then walk through Harvard Yard to the enormous library complex. The Harry Elkins Widener Memorial Library, at the heart of the collection, has a Gutenberg Bible, some Shakespeare folios and many other treasures.

Walk east to Quincy Street, where the Fogg Art Museum is situated, then turn left, and walk on to reach Kirkland Street. Turn right and left on Kirkland Street to see the Busch-Reisinger Museum, then on to Divinity Avenue, past the Peabody Museum, to the main University Museum. Continue to Oxford Street and turn left; cross over Cambridge Street, taking the overpass through Old Harvard Yard to Massachusetts Avenue. Turn right on the avenue and then left on to Garden Street to return to the Common.

Boston

copper — the work of the versatile Paul Revere. Next to the ship is a museum which tells its history.

Though not on the officially marked Trail, one very important landmark of the period is well worth a visit. The Boston Tea Party ship and museum at the Congress Street Bridge, on the Fort Point Channel, dispenses eighteenth-century drama with twentieth-century technique. You can inspect documents and a tea chest reputed to have been among those thrown overboard; you can even throw a tea chest yourself from the deck of the 110ft full-sized working replica of one of the three original Tea Party brigantines.

Another way to see these landmarks is to take an organized guided tour. If you have a young family, the children can enjoy a 'Boston by Little Feet' tour. Aimed at children between six and twelve, it not only includes many of the sites on the Freedom Trail, but also allows the youngsters to measure doorways, touch and discuss the texture of various building features and, of course, ask many question. (See p.175 for more walking tours.)

Even without a planned route, Boston's charming old side streets, often intimate, ornate and picturesque, can provide a sightseeing tour in themselves. For instance, returning from the Boston Tea Party ship, you can cut through streets with pretty-sounding names like Water

When Paul Revere bought this timber-frame house, now a museum, in 1770, it was already more than 100 years old

Street, Milk Street and Battery Street, to stroll among the flourishing, aromatic stalls and shops in Quincy Market.

For nearly 125 years the market has flourished as a food market, concentrating on beef, cheese and fresh fish, but since it was redeveloped, its speciality shops, boutiques and restaurants have been an added draw for tourists. Now that it has been restored to its nineteenth-century ambience, the stallholders have given Quincy Market a special festival air with bunting and lights and pavement tables on cobblestones, and guitars strumming late into the night. It is also interesting architecturally. Three 500ft-long buildings, dominated by Faneuil Hall, make up the total market area. One with a gilded pantheon dome became Quincy Market, named after Mayor Josiah Quincy. The others hold the North and South Markets. The market's exotic community atmosphere flourishes despite the fact that its buildings are being increasingly overshadowed by the commercial giants just a block away. An expanse of terraces and concrete, the business and administrative heart of Boston seems almost to be an intrusion on the city's old-world charm.

The city hall at Government Center is Boston's pride. Its severe, unfussy design by a firm of New York architects was picked from 250 entries in a national competition, and has won several architectural awards. Conducted tours can be arranged by telephoning 742 4528.

On the north side of Government Center is the JFK Federal Building, one of several edifices in the Boston area commemorating the assassinated president, and demonstrating the city's respect for its most illustrious contemporary family. In a sense, the Kennedys were Boston's archetypal immigrant family. Patrick Kennedy landed in 1848, and set up as a cooper in Boston. Since the Irish immigrants in the latter half of the nineteenth century had few prospects of employment, and were often discriminated against in society, it was not surprising that JFK's forebears should have stirred political ideas in the family. Patrick's son, John Kennedy's grandfather, was a saloon keeper who died in 1925, by which time his son, Joseph Patrick Kennedy, was well on the way to becoming a millionaire landowner and financier. It was his wealth that helped to make his sons such a vibrant political force in the second half of this century. Joseph Kennedy was born at 151 Meridian Street, Boston, in September 1888, and his famous son John on Beals Street in the suburb of Brookline. The birthplace has been made a national historic site.

Across the Charles River at Harvard is the JFK School of Government, built in the 1970s to teach what is now an important university discipline. The John Fitzgerald Kennedy Library, a few miles drive out of the city at Columbia Point, is the repository of Kennedy memorabilia, and a shrine to the Kennedy years. It holds documents, films, tape recordings and books, and JFK's oval office desk with his famous rocking chair. Visitors to the museum are also treated to a half-hour film on the life and times of John F. Kennedy. It is shown in one of the two theatres in this modernistic, clean, white-faced building, which was funded by a national appeal — one of seven presidential libraries in America, and part of the Government's national archives.

For a bird's-eye view of these and many other landmarks, you need to go to one of the two 'skyscraper' observation decks in Boston — the John Hancock Tower, at St James's Avenue and Trinity Place, or the Prudential Center between Huntington Avenue and Boylston Street. The view from the sixtieth floor of the John Hancock Tower takes in the Brahmin townhouses on Beacon Hill, and reaches as far as New Hampshire, the most mountainous state of New England. It also offers a comprehensive audio and video show, turning the clock back to Boston's early days, with a film of a helicopter flight above the city, and photographic and miniature models of Boston landmarks.

The Prudential Center's skywalk on the fiftieth floor of the fifty-two-storey Prudential Building in the heart of Boston's Back Bay area, provides a forty-three-square-mile panorama of the city, and beyond into the 125 urban communities which are centred on the Boston Peninsula. Together they have a population of nearly 4,000,000. Over 100,000 of these people are students, and this not only because of Harvard. Boston has 74 colleges, several of them part of universities, and some in the heart of the city. Even Harvard's famous Medical School on Shattuck Street is on Boston's side of the water. Among others are Boston University on the Charles River campus, Boston College, the University of Massachusetts' Boston campus at Columbia Point, Suffolk University, Simmons College, North-Eastern University and, in a square bounded by Longwood Avenue, Palace Road, Fenway and Brookline, Emmanuel College, Massachusetts College of Art, and Boston Public Latin School.

Most of these academic riches would probably not have converged on Boston if it had not been for an unknown English immigrant, John Harvard who, in 1637, decided to sail to New England and settle on the other side of the Charles River in Charlestown. He was to die only a year later, at the age of 31, but he left about £1700 — half his estate — and his 400-volume library to a new college that the colonists had founded in 1636. In 1639, the college was named after its benefactor. As the university grew, so did Boston, and as Boston forged ahead so did

Quincy Market, gay with flowers, is part of the Faneuil Hall Marketplace

Harvard. The oldest university in the United States, it has in its 350 years earned a reputation as respected and renowned as any of the great European universities. Harvard now has seventeen departments, nine faculties, ninety-five libraries, seven botanical institutes, two astronomical stations, more than fifty laboratories of science, engineering and medicine, and nine museums devoted to natural history, medicine, art and archeology. Until 1894 it was only accessible to male students. Then Radcliffe College was founded to educate a select few of America's brightest girls. Now part of Harvard, Radcliffe still enrols only 1100 women a year, while the men's colleges can absorb about 15,000 men — more than half of them drawn from outside New England.

The pivot of Harvard is Harvard Square. Around it proud buildings with spires and domes, some dating back to 1720, lend an air of remote maturity to the crowds of laughing and jostling students in the streets. They crowd the shops and restaurants, such as the bar-cum-café rejoicing in the name of the Wursthaus — a German-style beer hall which sells American or German food from a menu peppered with German terminology in an effort, one suspects, to emphasize the food's Teutonic pretensions. Some of the small shops and boutiques cater for the students' more sophisticated tastes. The Harvard Cooperative Society, affectionately known as the 'Coop' —

pronounced to rhyme with 'soup' — despite its mundane beginnings in 1882 as a shelf in a corner fruit store, now houses the largest complete bookstore in the United States with more than 100,000 titles. It also has a massive record library, and with a membership of over 80,000, it is obviously used largely by Bostonians who may never have studied at the university.

Though it has several fine museums and art galleries of its own, Boston would feel impoverished without being able to count among its cultural resources the magnificent range of paintings, sculptures, drawings and prints available at Cambridge. The William Hayes Fogg Art Museum, in Quincy Street, displays oriental and classical works of art and is used as a teaching laboratory for Harvard students, being part of the Fine Arts Faculty. Look out for a collection of English silver, Italian paintings of the late medieval period, French impressionist and post-impressionist works, French Romanesque sculptures and exquisite Chinese bronzes and jades.

The Busch-Reisinger Museum in Kirkland Street concentrates on German art, but there are also Dutch, Austrian, Swiss and Scandinavian canvases. The University Museum in Oxford Street houses several important museums: the Geological and Mineralogical Museum, founded in 1784, which exhibits a large-scale model of a Hawaiian volcano as part of a display of minerals, gem-stones,

meteorites and rocks; the Museum of Comparative Zoology which has the largest turtle shell ever found, the world's oldest reptile egg, a giant sea serpent and the largest collection of ants; the Peabody Museum, which has its main collection in a separate building in Divinity Avenue, but which shows off in its archaeology and ethnology section in the Oxford Street Museum the world's most respected collection of anthropological specimens, including a Neanderthal skull found in Palestine, and central European Iron-Age fossils; and the Botanical Museum, popularly called the Glass Flower Museum, because of its priceless collection of glass flowers and plants. The Blaschka collection dates back to 1877, but Leopold Blaschka and his son, Rudolf, did not complete the collection in their workshop in Dresden, Germany, until 1936. It was commissioned as a memorial to one of Harvard's nineteenth-century luminaries, Dr Charles Elliot Ware. More than 180,000 visitors every year see the exhibits, comprising 784 life-sized models and 3,218 enlarged flowers.

The other towering intellectual centre in Cambridge is the Massachusetts Institute of Technology (MIT) which, since it moved in 1916 to its 125-acre campus extending more than a mile along the banks of the Charles River, has been

The pleasant streets and charming houses of Beacon Hill formed the 'Brahmin' quarter of Boston, where the wealthy families lived

turning out architects, engineers and scientists whose contributions to America's technological achievements are incalculable. Its cultural resources include a library; the Francis Russell Hart Nautical Museum which contains model ships, prints and photographs ranging over 1000 years of boat design; a gallery of contemporary art; the Kresge Auditorium with its unusual three-cornered spherical roof (the auditorium is noted for its superb acoustics); and the cylindrical-shaped chapel with its aluminium belltower. The chapel is surrounded by a moat cleverly designed to reflect light on the inside walls.

Boston's own most treasured art collection — it ranks in importance with the New York Metropolitan Museum of Art, and the Art Institute in Chicago — is the Museum of Fine Arts, in Huntington Avenue. Although it has been in existence since 1870, the museum moved to its present location in 1909, and has recently undergone extensive refurbishing. It shows a wide range of exhibits of Asiatic, classical, Egyptian and near Eastern, American and European decorative and twentieth-century art and sculptures. The

museum also has an impressive collection of nineteenth-century French paintings, and prints dating back to the fifteenth century as well as woven, embroidered, lace and printed fabrics and costumes from all over the world. Attached to the museum is a school, a library, and a research laboratory.

Also in Huntington Avenue is the Symphony Hall, home not only of the world-famous Boston Symphony Orchestra, now over 100 years old, but the equally famous Boston Pops Orchestra.

The rectangular nineteenth-century building is ornate without being fussy, and like many of Boston's imposing buildings, has been liberally decorated with burnished gold inside. The 'pops' season usually lasts from the end of April to June. In July both orchestras present free open-air concerts in the Edward Hatch Memorial Shell on the banks of the Charles River, near the west side of Beacon Hill. Other free concerts are held at the New England Conservatory of Music on Gainsborough Street and Huntington Avenue, and at the Isabella Stewart Gardner Museum at Fenway. This was named after a wealthy eccentric who built up one of the most extensive art collections in America. As a condition of her legacy to the city, she asked in her will for a memorial service to be held in the chapel every year on her birthday.

Boston has more than thirty auditoriums

where theatre and music flourish. The New Metropolitan Center, which opened in Boston's anniversary year, is home to the Boston Ballet as well as providing a welcome addition to the city's cultural facilities. A convenient service operated by a private, non-profit-making organization is Bostix. Its Rotunda ticket booth at Faneuil Hall sells half-price tickets on the day of performance and full-price tickets in advance.

Shopping in Boston is more compact than in many cities of comparable size. Apart from Quincy Market, a prolific shopping area is Washington Street, where there is a large pedestrian shopping mall. Another collection of good shops is further down between Washington and Province Streets and Franklin, Hawley and Temple Streets, where most of Boston's large department stores can be found.

Boston's Back Bay district is bursting with speciality and curio shops. Bounded by Arlington Garden, Boylston Street, Massachusetts Avenue and Charles River, the area was reclaimed from the river in the last century, and amid the nineteenth-century buildings that rose there, the elegant shops, galleries and stores have become a select centre for fashionable and chic merchandise. The Prudential Center is also an Aladdin's cave of prominent stores and shops.

On Charles Street are expensive, attractively stocked antique shops, and here and there, the character of their sales approach is typically British. More even than the shops, the cafés and bars promote the British connection. The 'Pub' proliferates all over Boston. So does the 'Tavern'. Sometimes the 'Publik House' and the 'Saloon Bar' might indulge in more customary American sales techniques, and the message might well read: 'We don't make sandwiches here. We build 'em!'

Boston claims to have very catholic tastes in food — ranging from beans to lobster. Both it provides in profusion. Certainly New England seafood is world-famous. Many restaurants specialize in clam chowder (a fish soup), oysters, and the true Bostonian among fish, scrod, which really is only young and delicious cod. Invariably the seafood is fresh, and served in gargantuan portions. The kind of restaurant is often immaterial for quality or quantity, though prices may vary considerably. Ye Olde Union House in Union Street, the oldest restaurant in Boston — it dates back to 1826 — serves an excellent lobster or oyster meal. But so does the Sheraton Boston Hotel which, with nearly 1400 rooms, is one of the largest hotels in New England.

In central Boston more than fifty hotels between them share accommodation for about 25,000 visitors. The Parker House Hotel, at the corner of School and Tremont Streets, is America's oldest

Boston supports two world-famous orchestras, the Pops and the Symphony

continuously operated hotel. With its burnished gold decor and soft, leather-style armchairs in the lobby, it specializes in what it calls 'classic' luxury. In 1980, conveniently celebrating its 125th anniversary to coincide with the 350 years the city has been in existence, the Parker House was able to look back to 1855 when a successful Boston restaurateur called Harvey Parker acquired the site and decided to open a new kind of hostelry for the fastidious hotel visitor. He ran the place rather like many modern package tour operators handle their business — offering clients an all-inclusive price for accommodation and meals.

Because of its convenient location it soon attracted poets, novelists and philosophers. Its most famous guest was Charles Dickens. On a nine-month speaking tour of America in 1867, Dickens made the Parker House his base, joining what was then known as the Saturday Club, for convivial debate and company. Others who stayed there were Sarah Bernhardt, the famous British actress of the day, and John Wilkes Booth who, eight days after attending a meeting of the club, earned enduring notoriety by assassinating Abraham Lincoln. Charles Dickens

left a manuscript in his own handwriting of four Punch recipes (see highlight). They were in a letter he wrote at the hotel.

About 100 years later, the Parker House was used by John F. Kennedy and his brother Robert to announce their presidential candidacies. And just as Dickens has had a room called after him, so the room the Kennedys used to make the announcement has since been named the Kennedy Room. The Parker House is the nearest major hotel to Logan International Airport, Boston's main airport barely three miles away. It can take as little as fifteen minutes to drive the distance.

Logan Airport is served by more than forty airlines and is the eighth busiest in the country. Taxis are not especially expensive, but you can cut the cost of hiring one to transport you from the airport to the suburbs by using the Share-a-Cab system. Kiosks at several of the airline desks sell half-price tickets for the trip. Alternatively, the Massport Shuttle bus links all the terminals and serves downtown Boston and the outlying areas at six- to twelve-minute intervals. Another shuttle bus service gives tourists the chance to see the historical sights in comfort. A guide does his best to encapsulate Boston's past in a tour lasting an hour or so.

The most widely used of Boston's public transport systems is the Underground. The first subway system to be built in the United States, Boston's is impeccably efficient, frequent, and with its four main lines, serves nearly eighty stations on both sides of the river. Different from the New York subway, where the graffiti are psychedelic, crude and aggressive, Boston's version reflects the softer academic leanings of many of the subway's passengers.

When the students are not crowding into the trains and buses, they can be seen in massive numbers jogging in the parks and on the river banks. The 'emerald necklace' of parks makes Boston a jogger's paradise. And the students' example is

being enthusiastically adopted by worthy Bostonian figures of all sizes, shapes and ages.

Sport is well supported in Boston. Fenway Park, between Lansdowne Street, Van Ness Street and Yawkey Way, can hold more than 30,000 spectators — especially when the local baseball team, the Boston Red Sox, is playing. In the suburbs there is an American football stadium, and at East Boston there is horse-racing on the Suffolk Downs racetrack. If you hire a car — available from airports and all over the city from the major car rental firms — you can easily reach many outdoor leisure centres activities well within a day's drive.

New England's countryside is at its most beautiful in the autumn. The 'fall' colours are so rich in the variations of their rustic shades that to drive along a tree-lined road — and there are few roads in New England which have no trees — provides a feast to the eye. The severity of the winter here takes many visitors by surprise. New England cottages are designed with long overhanging roofs, similar to those in snowy parts of Europe, to keep the snow from doors and windows. In summer, New England's vegetation is greener than in many parts of America, irresistibly reminding the British tourist of the verdant colours of Britain's countryside.

'Where's Boston?' is a question plastered all over the city hoardings. It refers to a permanent showing of an hour-long film describing in photographic montages the variety and scope of Boston's community. It traces the progress the city has made since the 1950s in creating a fresh image to confirm that she has lost the staid attitudes that were once the legacy of her puritanical past. But people are still fond of quoting the words of a cynical Bostonian who once said: 'In New York, they ask you how much you make. In Philadelphia they ask how big your family is. But in Boston all they want to know is what school you went to.'

The Toast is Dickens

Writing to friends in Boston during his stay at the Parker House Hotel in 1867, Charles Dickens enclosed in the letter four of his favourite recipes

for punch. A copy of the note, in his own handwriting, was recently discovered in the hotel archives. This is what he recommended to Mr and Mrs James T. Fields:

Cider Cup: Put into a large jug, 4 or 6 lumps of sugar (according to size) and a thin rind of lemon. Pour in a very little boiling water and thrust a napkin into the top of the jug so as to exclude the air. Leave to stand ten minutes, and then stir well. Add two wine glasses of sherry, and one wine glass of brandy. Stir again. Add one bottle of cider (poured in briskly) and one bottle of soda water. Stir again. Then fill up with ice. If there is any borage* put in a good hand full, as you would put a nosegay into water. Stir up well before serving.

Champagne Cup: Put into a large jug, 4 good lumps of sugar, and the thin rind of a

lemon. Cover up and stir, as above. Add a bottle of champagne, and a good tumbler and a half of sherry. Stir well. Then fill up with ice. Borage as above. Stir up well before serving.

Moselle Cup: 4 good lumps of sugar and the thin rind of a lemon as above. Add a bottle of (still) Moselle, and a tumbler full of sherry. Then, ice as before. A few sprigs of wild thyme or of jasmine, are a better seasoner for this delicate cup than borage. Stir well before serving.

Claret Cup: 4 or 6 lumps as before: give the preference to 6. The thin rind of a lemon as above. Cover up and stir, as above. Add a wine glass of brandy, then a bottle of

claret, then half a bottle of soda water. Then stir well and grate in nutmeg. Then add the ice. If borage be used for this cup, half the cider cup quantity will be found quite sufficient. Stir well before serving.

*The best substitute for borage is a strip or two of the rind of a fresh cucumber. But it must not be left in the cup more than 10 minutes or its flavour will be too strong. It is easily taken out with the spoon as it will probably be on the top of the ice. None of these cups should be made more than a quarter of an hour before serving. Never pour out of the jug, without first stirring.

Boston Directory

The hotels and restaurants listed here are either recommended by the American Automobile Association (AAA) or have been selected because they are of interest to tourists. As a rough guide to cost, they have been classified as either expensive, moderate or reasonable. Hotels all have private bathrooms and colour television.

Hotels

THE COLONNADE: 120 Huntington Ave, tel. 261 2800. 300 rooms. A stylish, modern hotel adjacent to the Prudential Center. 'Intown resort' on the roof with pool, putting green, snack bar and occasional entertainment. Sauna, beauty salon, barber's shop. Pay garage parking. Expensive.

COPLEY PLAZA: 138 St James Ave, tel. 267 5300. 450 rooms. This elegant hotel is sister to New York's famous Plaza. Public rooms are grandly furnished with antiques, and there are mosaic floors, gilded ceilings, wood panelling and original works of art. Pay garage parking available nearby. Two restaurants. Expensive.

COPLEY SQUARE HOTEL: 47 Huntington Ave, tel. 536 9000. 104 rooms. An older hotel near many of Boston's places of interest. Pay garage parking. Coffee shop and famous Hungarian restaurant, the Café Budapest. Reasonable.

57 PARK PLAZA HOTEL — HOWARD JOHNSON'S: 200 Stuart St, tel. 482 1800. 350 rooms. New high-rise hotel near shopping and theatre district. All rooms are well equipped and have balconies. Heated indoor pool, sauna, putting green. Free garage parking. Two restaurants. Moderate.

HARVARD MOTOR HOUSE: 110 Mt Auburn St, tel. 864 5200. 72 rooms. Modern motel one block from Harvard Square. Continental breakfast included in room prices. Free parking. Reasonable.

HOLIDAY INN: 5 Blossom St, tel. 742 7630. 304 rooms. Located near Government Center and many tourist attractions. Outdoor pool.

Lobster Trap Restaurant on top floor, and coffee shop. Free garage parking. Moderate.

HYATT REGENCY CAMBRIDGE: 575 Memorial Dr, tel. 492 1234. 500 rooms. Architecturally one of Boston's showplaces, this striking building on the banks of the Charles River is nicknamed 'The Pyramid on the Charles'. 15 rooms are specially equipped for the handicapped, and one floor is set aside for non-smokers. Attractively furnished rooms, some with balconies. Two restaurants and revolving Spinnaker Lounge on rooftop. Expensive.

LOGAN AIRPORT HILTON: Logan International Airport, East Boston, tel. 569 9300. 559 rooms. The hotel is in the airport compound, but only about 10 minutes' drive from Boston. Modern rooms, inner courtyard with swimming pool. Free transport to air terminals, free parking. Restaurant, coffee shop. Moderate.

MIDTOWN HOTEL: 220 Huntington Ave, tel. 262 1000. 160 rooms. Near Prudential Center, Symphony Hall, business/shopping district and Museum of Fine Arts. Attractive modern rooms. Free garage parking. Heated outdoor pool, sauna, restaurant, coffee shop. Moderate.

SHERATON-BOSTON: Prudential Center, 39 Dalton St, tel. 236 2000. 1318 rooms. Luxury hotel linked by covered passageway to the shops of the Prudential Center. The skyscraper offers panoramic views of Boston from every room; right at the top are the extra-luxurious suites of the Sheraton Towers.

Heated indoor pool, restaurants, cocktail lounges, coffee shop. Pay garage parking. Expensive.

HOTEL SONESTA: 5 Cambridge Pkwy, Cambridge, tel. 491 3600. 200 rooms. In Cambridge but very handy for Boston, and near the Museum of Science and MIT. All rooms have views over the city and the Charles River. Attractive furnishings. Outdoor pool, saunas, restaurant, coffee shop. Free parking. Expensive.

Restaurants

ANTHONY'S PIER 4: 140 Northern Ave, tel. 423 6363. Dramatically set at the end of a pier, with stunning views of the harbour. One of Boston's most popular restaurants, especially noted for its seafood. Moderate.

CAFE BUDAPEST: 90 Exeter St, tel. 734 3388. Hungarian restaurant in the Copley Square Hotel. Attractive old world decor. Cuisine is Continental with strong Hungarian influence. Soups and desserts, all home-made, are particularly excellent. Expensive.

CAFE PLAZA: 138 St James Ave, tel. 267 5300. Deluxe restaurant in the Copley Plaza Hotel. International cuisine in elegant surroundings. Extensive wine list. Specialities include lobster Anita and quenelles of salmon. Closed Sunday. Expensive.

CHARLEY'S EATING AND DRINKING SALOON: 344 Newbury St, tel. 266 3000. Authentic Victorian restaurant-saloon, with waiters dressed to match. Beef and fish dishes very good. Excellent sandwiches are also served. Reasonable.

DURGIN-PARK: 340 N. Market St, tel. 227 2038. A long established, busy, no-nonsense eating place that is a favourite with Bostonians. Good, old fashioned New England food is served in a convivial, if noisy, atmosphere at long tables. Hearty portions of Yankee pot roast, Boston baked beans and baked Indian pudding are specialities. Be prepared to queue, as no reservations are accepted. Reasonable.

FERDINAND'S: 12 Mt Auburn St, Cambridge, tel. 491 4915. Popular French restaurant one block west of Harvard Square. Reasonable.

THE HERMITAGE: 955 Boylston St, tel. 267 3652. Named after Leningrad's magnificent museum, this Russian restaurant is in the Institute of contemporary Art. The menu changes frequently and includes well-known Russian specialities such as borscht, caviar and beef Stroganoff. Closed Sunday evening. Moderate.

JIMMY'S HARBORSIDE RESTAURANT: 242 Northern Ave, tel. 423 1000. Popular waterfront restaurant with a 55-year tradition of excellent seafood — scallops, crab and creamy fish chowder are specialities. Closed Sunday. Moderate.

LEGAL SEA FOODS: Park Square, tel. 426 4444. Over 30 varieties of the freshest imaginable seafood are served at this restaurant, which grew from a small family fish market in Cambridge and is now housed in the Boston Park Plaza Hotel. No reservations, so be prepared to queue. Reasonable.

LOCKE-OBER: 3 Winter Pl, tel. 542 1340. One of Boston's oldest restaurants, established in 1875. Extensive menu of classic dishes; the star is lobster savannah. Surroundings are opulent, with carved panelling, chandeliers and leather chairs. Closed Sunday. Expensive.

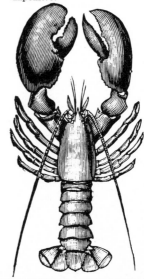

THE MAGIC PAN: 47 Newbury St, tel. 267 9315; Quincy Market, tel. 523 6103. Pancakes rule in these pleasant eating places. Besides 30 varieties of crêpes, the menu also features salads, soups and desserts. Reasonable.

MAISON ROBERT: 45 School St, tel. 227 3370. Said to be one of the finest French restaurants in the USA. There are two dining rooms in the old City Hall: the Bonhomme Richard, where full meals consisting of classic French dishes are served in luxurious surroundings, and Ben's Café (named after Benjamin Franklin), where lighter meals of equally high quality can be eaten at lower cost in a more informal atmosphere. Expensive.

RITZ-CARLTON RESTAURANT: 15 Arlington St, tel. 536 5700. Internationally acclaimed for its superb Continental cuisine, this sophisticated restaurant offers a wide choice of gourmet dishes served in glamorous surroundings. Expensive.

SEVENTH INN: 288 Boylston St, tel. 261 3965. Vegetarian and wholefood restaurant situated near the Public Garden. Fish and organically grown vegetables feature prominently on the menu. Closed Sunday. Reasonable.

TOP OF THE HUB: 800 Boylston St, Prudential Center, tel. 536 1775. The best view in Boston, 52 floors up in the Prudential Building. Entertainment, and dancing. Menu features steaks and local seafood. Moderate.

UNION OYSTER HOUSE: 41 Union St, tel. 227 2750. Boston's oldest restaurant, established in 1826. Traditional New England seafood — clams, oysters, scallops and lobster are very much in evidence. Moderate.

VOYAGEURS: 45½ Mt Auburn St, Cambridge, tel. 354 1718. Striking surroundings range from a room resembling a museum, decorated with jade buddhas and bronze ornaments, to a roof garden with a fountain, goldfish and gardenias. Creative and unusual menu, changed daily, and extensive wine list. Harp or harpsichord music. Open only for dinner. Expensive.

HOBBY-HORSES,
TOPS, SHUTTLECOCKS AND DOLLS,
Dancing Jacks,
DRUMS, TRUMPETS,
Bats and Balls.

Shopping

The most fascinating shopping centres in Boston are undoubtedly the three Faneuil Hall markets, comprising **Quincy Building, North Market** and **South Market**. The halls were originally built in 1826 by Mayor Josiah Quincy and have recently been renovated and restored to their original use. Meat, cheese, seafood, bread and all kinds of grocery stalls and shops are to be found in the Quincy Building; the South Market tends towards jewellery and gifts; the North Market specializes in high fashion. Along North and South Market Streets, open-air cafés lend a touch of European colour to the busy scene. Faneuil Hall itself has a superb Heritage Shop, specializing in early American reproductions — handmade pewter ware, for example.

Two other worthwhile shopping areas are **Downtown Crossing**, a pedestrian precinct near Park Street at the east end of Boston Common, and **Newbury** and **Boylston Streets**, on the west side of the Public Garden. Lovers of antiques can browse along **Charles Street**, which runs between Boston Common and the Public Garden north to Longfellow Bridge. **Harvard Square**, part of the Harvard University complex in Cambridge, across Charles River, is also famous for its antique shops.

Transport

LOGAN INTERNATIONAL AIRPORT: East Boston. Two one-way toll-tunnels, Sumner Tunnel into the city, Callahan Tunnel out of the city, run under the Inner Harbor and link the airport with Boston. An inexpensive limousine service operates to the larger hotels, and for taxis to the outlying suburbs there are

'Share-a-Cab' booths where travellers can arrange to share taxi rides and thus save on the fare.

TAXIS: Taxis are plentiful and relatively inexpensive. The main companies are **Checker**, tel. 536 7000; **Independent Taxi Operators Association**, tel. 426 8700, and **Town Taxi**, tel. 536 5000.

BUSES AND SUBWAY: Buses and the subway (underground) system are run by the Massachusetts Bay Transportation Authority (MBTA). Subway stations are indicated by a circle containing the letter 'T', and each station displays direction and location maps. Bus and subway fares are cheap, but for bus journeys, passengers must have the exact fare. For information, tel. 722 3200.

CAR HIRE: Driving in downtown Boston is not easy, as the combination of a one-way system, old narrow streets, and restricted parking, may easily confuse visitors. For trips out of town, however, a car is always useful. The main agencies are: **Avis**, 60 Park Sq, tel. 267 8500; **Dollar**, 230 Porter St, tel. 569 5300; **Hertz**, Motor Mart Garage, Park Sq, tel. 482 9100, and **National**, Logan International Airport, tel. 567 3261. A complete list of rental agencies will be found in the Yellow Pages of the telephone directory.

TRAINS: Boston has two railway stations: South Station, on Atlantic Avenue at the corner of Sumner Street, is the terminus for trains to and from the south and west; North Station, 120 Causeway Street, near Charles River, handles local trains to and from the north.

CLIMATE: The climate of Boston is not unlike that of Britain — spring and autumn are cool, summer is hot. In winter, however, the temperature is colder than in most parts of Britain and it is wise to be prepared for snow.

Touring Information

AAA: The Massachusetts Division of the AAA has offices at 141 Tremont Street, Boston, tel. 482 8031. There are other branches in Chestnut Hill, tel. 738 6900, and Fairhaven, tel. 997 7811. All are open in office hours, Monday to Friday.

VISITOR INFORMATION: The information centre on the Tremont Street side of Boston Common provides street maps, brochures and information about current events. Throughout the summer it is open daily from 9am to 7pm, and from 9am to 5pm for the rest of the year. The official guide magazine for Boston is called *Panorama*. It is published twice weekly and is usually available at hotels, railway stations and the airport.

SIGHTSEEING: Many bus companies run sightseeing tours around Boston and its surroundings. Gray Line is one well-known company, tel. 426 8800, but a complete list will be found in the Yellow Pages of the telephone directory.
Walking tours are organized from the Boston Common Information Center, tel. 482 2864, starting at 9.30am, Monday to Saturday. See also the box on p.175.
Cruises of Boston Harbor and the Boston Harbor Islands State Park, depart from Rowes Wharf, run by Massachusetts Bay Lines, Inc., tel. 542 8000, and from Long Wharf, run by Bay State Spray Cruises, tel. 723 7800. Cruises along Charles River start from the Museum of Science, tel. 723 2500.

Museums

BOSTON TEA PARTY SHIP AND MUSEUM: Congress St Bridge, Museum Wharf, tel. 338 1773. A full-scale working replica of one of the Boston Tea Party ships can be boarded and is complemented by a museum where the notorious incident is reconstructed in displays and audio-visual presentations.

MUSEUM OF THE AMERICAN CHINA TRADE: 1904 Canton Ave, Milton, tel. 696 1815. All manner of objects brought to America from China by sea captains and merchants are displayed

in a restored mansion. Porcelains, lacquer goods, and oriental silks and embroideries are the main features on display. The museum is closed on Mondays.

CHILDREN'S MUSEUM: Museum Wharf, 300 Congress St, tel. 426 8855. Children and adults can participate in a variety of exhibits here, from filming their own news bulletins to working in a factory, and from climbing down a manhole to dressing up in 'grandmother's attic'. Closed Monday.

MUSEUM OF FINE ARTS: 465 Huntington Ave, tel. 267 9377. One of the world's finest art collections from all ages and cultures, the museum has been established for more than a century. The new west wing houses major special exhibitions. Closed Monday.

HARVARD UNIVERSITY MUSEUM: 24 Oxford St, Cambridge, tel. 495 2248. Archaeology, zoology, botany and geology are the main topics in the four museums that make up this complex. (see also p.188) for this and other museums in Cambridge.

INSTITUTE OF CONTEMPORARY ART: 955 Boylston St, tel. 266 5152. Twentieth-century art of all kinds is on display here, including painting, sculpture, graphic arts, photography and crafts. There is also a varied programme of films, concerts and lectures, with some special attractions for children. Closed Monday.

ISABELLA STEWART GARDNER MUSEUM: 280 The Fenway, tel. 734 1359. The Venetian-style palace of Isabella Gardner, wife of a wealthy Bostonian, is a delightful setting for the many works of art she

collected, including paintings by Titian, Matisse and Whistler. The house has a lovely courtyard filled with glorious flowers. Concerts are held here in summer. The museum is open only in the afternoons. Closed Monday.

MUSEUM OF SCIENCE: Science Park, tel. 723 2500. A 'look-and-touch' museum for all ages. Exhibits range from live animals to computers, from a space module to a life-size model of a Tyrannosaurus Rex. Next door you can learn about astronomy in the Hayden Planetarium.

MUSEUM OF TRANSPORTATION: Museum Wharf, 300 Congress St, tel. 426 7999. An astonishingly varied collection exhibiting every conceivable means of transport: boats, planes, sledges, bicycles, cars and roller skates are just a few of the kinds of exhibit that can be seen here. 'Crossroads' is an activity centre where you can ride in a trolley car, pedal an old-fashioned bike or slide down a fire pole. The history of Boston's transport systems is traced in a major display, 'Boston — A City in Transit'.

USS *CONSTITUTION* MUSEUM: Charlestown Navy Yard, tel. 426 1812. One of America's great fighting ships, launched in 1797, this 44-gun frigate has been restored and is on view to the public. The adjacent museum relates to the history of the ship, which became known as 'Old Ironside' after her involvement with the British in the War of 1812 (see the chapter on Washington D.C.).

'WHERE'S BOSTON?': 60 State St, tel. 661 2425. Quadrophonic sound and several thousand slides are used in this audio-visual portrait of the city. Shows take place daily on the hour.

VENDUE this Day

Places of Interest

BUNKER HILL MONUMENT:
Monument Sq, Charlestown. The Battle of Bunker Hill, one of the significant engagements of the Revolutionary War, took place on 17 June 1775. Although it resulted in a defeat for the American colonists, George Washington subsequently succeeded in driving the British out of Charlestown in 1776. The monument is a 221ft-high granite obelisk, and visitors can climb the 294 steps leading to the top.

BUNKER HILL PAVILION:
55 Constitution Rd, Charlestown, tel. 241 7575. The Battle of Bunker Hill — America's first full-scale battle — is vividly recreated through sights, sounds and other special effects in a specially built theatre, with 14 screens, 22 life-size costumed figures and seven sound channels.

CUSTOMS HOUSE TOWER:
State and India Sts. The observation platform, 500ft high, can be reached by lift, and is a favourite place from which to view the city.

FANEUIL HALL: Faneuil Hall Sq, at Merchants Row. Built in 1742 and given to the city by the merchant Peter Faneuil as a meeting hall, the building came to be known as the 'cradle of liberty' because of the many protest meetings held here before the outbreak of the Revolution. It contains many paintings of famous battles, a library and a military museum.

GIBSON HOUSE MUSEUM:
137 Beacon St. This old brownstone house is furnished in Victorian style, and contains many fascinating curiosities.

GRANARY BURYING GROUND: Tremont and Bromfield Sts. Three of the signatories of the Declaration of Independence are buried here: John Hancock, Samuel Adams and Robert Treat Paine. You can also see the graves of the victims of the Boston Massacre of 1770 — five colonists shot by the British at a meeting which had got out of hand — and that of the wife of Isaac Goose, who was the 'Mother Goose' of the collection of nursery rhymes.

HANCOCK HOUSE: 10 Marshall St, tel. 742 1900. The former home of Ebenezer Hancock, paymaster of the Revolutionary army and brother of John Hancock, is the oldest (1760) brick-built house in Boston. It now houses law offices, but can be visited by appointment.

HARRISON GRAY OTIS HOUSE: 141 Cambridge St. This house, designed by the 18th-century architect Charles Bulfinch, dates from 1796 and contains rooms illustrating the 18th- and 19th-century way of life.

JOHN HANCOCK OBSERVATORY: St James Ave, and Trinity Pl. The view from the 740ft-high observation deck stretches right across Boston, as far as the mountains of New Hampshire.

KING'S CHAPEL: Tremont and School Sts. This was the first Anglican church in New England. Originally founded in 1686, the present church dates from 1754, and has been Unitarian since the late 18th century.

LOUISBURG SQUARE:
Beacon Hill. This lovely old square, with its railed private garden, was and is the centre of wealthy 'old' Boston, where such influential and exclusive families as the Cabots and the Lowells lived. Many of its elegant town houses are still private residences.

NEW ENGLAND AQUARIUM: Central Wharf, Atlantic Ave. The central feature of the aquarium, which houses more than 7000 specimens, is an enormous circular glass tank where sharks and giant turtles can be seen. There is a daily dolphin and sea lion display in a floating amphitheatre.

OLD NORTH CHURCH: 193 Salem St. The oldest (1723) church in Boston, the building is in the style made famous by Sir Christopher Wren. It played a significant part in the American Revolution, for it was from the church steeple that Paul Revere instructed the sexton Robert Newman to signal the approach of the British forces — using one lantern if they were coming by land, two if they were coming by sea.

OLD SOUTH MEETING HOUSE: 310 Washington and Milk Sts. First erected in 1669 the present building dates from 1729. Many historic meetings, particularly those concerned with the Boston Massacre and the Boston Tea Party (see p.173), were held here. The Meeting House contains a fascinating museum of the Revolutionary War.

OLD STATE HOUSE:
Washington and State Sts. Dating from 1713, the Old State House was the official home of Royal Governors of the Colony before the Revolution, and afterwards became the State Capitol. From the balcony the Declaration of Independence was proclaimed in 1776. The interior is a museum of Boston history through the ages. Outside the east front is the site of the Boston Massacre of 1770. Five colonists were killed when British soldiers opened fire on an angry crowd.

PARK ST CHURCH: Park and Tremont Sts. An English architect, Peter Banner, designed this lovely church with its soaring, white steeple, in 1809. William Lloyd Garrison, one of the early American anti-slavery campaigners, delivered his first speech condemning the slave system here.

PAUL REVERE HOUSE:
19-21 North Sq. This is the oldest wooden-frame house in Boston, dating from 1676. Paul Revere, the silversmith who made the famous ride in 1775 to Lexington and Concord to warn his fellow colonists of the approach of the British, bought it in 1770. It has been restored and furnished in period.

PRUDENTIAL CENTER:
Between Huntington Ave and Boylston St. The complex features shops, restaurants, squares and gardens, surrounding the 52-storey Prudential Tower. Skywalk, on the 50th floor, offers superb views over the city.

STATE HOUSE: Beacon and Park Sts. Charles Bulfinch designed this handsome building in 1795 to replace the smaller Old State House. The copper for the gilded dome was purchased from Paul Revere. The Archives Museum in the basement displays many fascinating old documents relating to the early history of the colony.

Parks & Gardens

ARNOLD ARBORETUM:
Arbor Way: tel. 524 1717. One of America's oldest parks, the arboretum was opened in 1872 and is a National Historic Landmark. The 265 acres contain more than 6000 species of labelled ornamental trees, shrubs and vines.

BOSTON COMMON: A historic site and a pleasant place to walk on a sunny day, when the majestic trees provide plenty of cool shade. The Liberty Tree, at the corner of Boylston and Tremont Streets, is a recently planted replacement for the original one, which marked a rallying place for Revolutionary patriots and was cut down by the British in 1775.

BOSTON PUBLIC GARDEN:
Next to Boston Common, this garden is famous for its magnificent displays of flowers. It is at its best in the spring, when thousands of tulips and pansies are in bloom. Trips along the pond can be made in attractive swan boats.

Sport

Fenway Park is the venue for baseball matches and the home team the famous Boston Red Sox. Basketball (Boston Celtics) and hockey (Boston Bruins) take place in **Boston Garden**, and American football can be seen at the **Shaeffer Stadium** in Foxboro.

Horse racing (January to July and September to December) and harness racing (April to October) take place at the **Suffolk Downs Racetrack** in East Boston.

There are several public golf courses and tennis courts, run by the Metropolitan District Commission, tel. 727 5250.

Performing Arts

MUSIC: Boston's big name is the world-famous Boston Symphony Orchestra, whose home is the Symphony Hall, at the corner of Huntington and Massachusetts Aves (tel. 266 1492). The winter season runs from September to April. From early May, the Symphony Hall is devoted to a nine-week season of the Boston Pops Orchestra, where the music ranges from light classical to popular. Later in the summer the 'Pops' are among many musicians who play at the Hatch Shell of the Charles River Esplanade. Free classical concerts are given frequently at the New England Conservatory of Music, 290 Huntington Ave (tel. 262 1120) and at the Berklee College of Music, 1140 Boylston St (tel. 266 1400). The Handel and Haydn Society at 25 Huntington Ave (tel. 266 3605) is America's oldest performing arts organization, approaching its 170th season.

THEATRE: Pre- and post-Broadway productions can often be seen at the Shubert Theater, 265 Tremont St (tel. 426 4520); the Wilbur Theater, 252 Tremont St (tel. 423 4008); and the Colonial Theater, 100 Boylston St (tel. 426 9366). More experimental theatre is sometimes featured at the Charles Playhouse, 74 Warrenton St (tel. 426 6912) and the Boston Repertory Theater, 1 Boylston Place (tel. 423 6580). College productions are often very good, and mostly take place in the winter season.

Tickets for performances and attractions of all kinds can be bought — sometimes at reduced prices — at Bostix, the ticket booth at Faneuil Hall (tel. 723 5181 for recorded information). Closed Mondays.

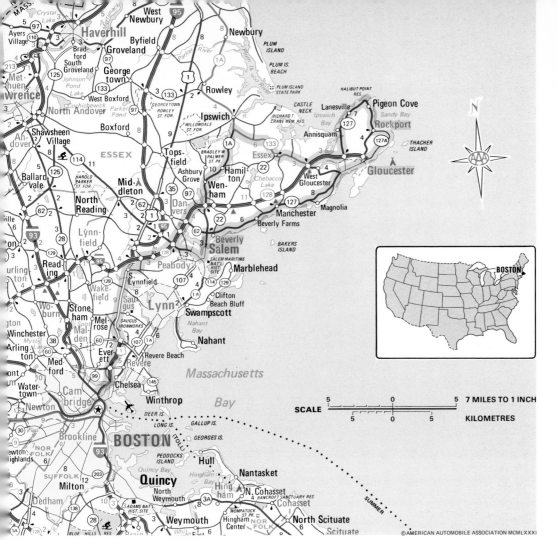

Cape Ann and the North Coast

1 to 2 days — 95 miles

Boston — Saugus — Salem — Beverly — Gloucester — Rockport — Essex — Ipswich — Boston.

Essex County and the rockbound north shore of Boston offer macabre history and beautiful scenery. The rugged coastline from which fearless Yankee fishermen set sail in pursuit of whales, often never to return, boasts surf-pounded beaches, sheltered harbours and picturesque coves. Bursting with historic landmarks, Salem is renowned for the notorious witch-hunts of the late 17th century, which Arthur Miller made the subject of his play *The Crucible,* as well as for its staggeringly successful early Oriental trading, which brought wealth to the town. With such familiar names as Gloucester, Ipswich and Manchester on your route, you are unlikely to forget that this is part of New England. Evidence of the early settlers is scattered throughout the region.

Take the North-east Expressway from downtown Boston and continue north along Interstate 93 for 5 miles, then drive for 10 miles on US 1. At Main Street interchange turn right to Saugus.

Saugus, Massachusetts

This town rose around the success of the Saugus ironworks, established in 1646. The present American iron and steel industry mushroomed from sustained production of cast iron and wrought iron from the works at Saugus. The first dies for coining money and the first fire engine were made here. The Saugus Iron Works National Historic Site, 244 Central Street, is a reconstruction of the earliest industrial site in the States, and includes a blast furnace, a forge and a rolling and slitting mill. In the museum, over five tons of artefacts include a 505lb ironhead used in the original forge. The 17th-century Ironmaster's House has period furnishings. There are working blacksmith demonstrations and guided tours in the summer.

The Scotch-Bordman House (1686) housed Scottish Covenanters brought here from Britain as prisoners to work their sentences at the ironworks. The

The Pirates and Pepper Museum is a reminder of Salem's exotic East India trade. Nearby stands the old Custom House

house retains its original austere appearance.

Continue north for 4 miles on US 1, then turn east on State Route 129 for about 5 miles to State Route 107 and then north to State Route 114 for Salem.

Salem, Massachusetts

Synonymous with witches, Salem was the scene, in 1692, of the notorious witchcraft trials which resulted in the hanging of 19 innocent people. Many women in the town were convinced they were possessed of the devil, and the hysteria spread. Unable to live down its grisly reputation, Salem has capitalized on it and reminders of these and other histories abound in this beautiful seaport, once the sixth most important city of the United States and, until 1630, capital of the Massachusetts Bay Colony. There is so much to see and enjoy here that you need at least a day to do it justice. Salem has a wealth of architectural gems — period houses dating from 1626 to recent times. Washington Square has rose-coloured brick Federal-period mansions built by merchants made wealthy from Oriental trading. Chestnut Street, dating from 1796 is lined with the houses of China Trade Merchants and considered to be one of the most elegant examples of American urban architecture. Residents must sign a legal agreement to follow the colonial theme in their furnishings. Old Salem Market has streets paved in mosaics of stone and brick.

Light-hearted signs showing a witch astride a broomstick are scattered throughout the town to direct morbidly curious tourists to sites involved in the witchcraft trials. The actual Courthouse where the trials occurred is in Washington Square and you may view documents of the witchcraft

trials together with alleged 'tormenting' pins. The Witch House in Essex Street was the home of Judge Jonathan Corwin who in 1692 conducted some of the preliminary witchcraft examinations on the premises.

Near Salem Harbour, at East India Square, 161 Essex Street, is the Peabody Museum. The oldest continuously operating museum in the country, it was founded by sea captains, who displayed treasures from their voyages to the Orient. Young captains held dinner parties in gracious old East India Hall, where the walls are lined with carved wooden figureheads, rare naval paintings and cabinets of early marine implements.

Derby Street houses a number of buildings which comprise the Salem Maritime National Historic Site and which depict the city's successful nautical past. Custom House is the information centre, located on Derby Wharf, which became a centre for shipping after the Revolutionary War and the War of 1812. A museum and slide show in the Custom House outlines the maritime and commercial history of Salem. Next door is Derby House, the first brick house in Salem, built in 1762 for the great Elias Hasket Derby, sea-merchant and one of the first American millionaires (he owned the wharf across the street). There are guided tours around this elegant home.

Adjacent to Derby Wharf is the newly-restored Pickering Wharf. The old waterfront has many gift shops, boutiques, speciality bakeries, ice-cream parlours with outdoor terraces and excellent restaurants. The pier and promenade are softly lit at night, and provide Salem's social centre. Salem Seaport Museum on this wharf has a theatre-in-the-round, multi-media show: *The Voyage of the India Star,* which illustrates Salem's domination of the Sumatra pepper trade in a simulated 1804 voyage to Calcutta and Sumatra by a Salem schooner in search of treasure. The House of Seven Gables, immortalized by Nathaniel Hawthorne in a book of the same name, is a picturesque weatherboarded house just past Derby Wharf at 54 Turner Street. A tour of the house, built by Captain John Turner in 1668, includes six exhibition rooms and a secret staircase. Among several 17th-century houses in the grounds is Hawthorne's birthplace. The Essex Institute, 132-4 Essex Street, includes a museum and six remarkable period houses spanning 300 years, all of which are open to the public. An extraordinary collection of Salem memorabilia, books and manuscripts, furniture and works of art on display, as well as nails from the witch jail

and a section of the tree from which the accused were hanged. It is worth trying to see several of the houses. They range from the simple structure of the 17th-century John Ward House, and the early 18th-century Crowninshield-Bentley House to the elaborate brick façade of the Gardner-Pingree Mansion, a classic example of the work of Samuel McIntire, most celebrated American architect of the early 19th century. Everyday life of each century is reflected in the décor, furnishings, toys and clothes on display.

Also in Essex Street, Ropes Mansion is a gambrel-roofed house filled with fine furniture, Chinese porcelain and relics of the family that occupied the house for about 200 years. A formal city garden displays a wide variety of plants and shrubs.

Off State Route 114, at the end of West Avenue, in Forest River Park, is Pioneer Village, a re-created 1630 settlement. This startlingly vivid reconstruction of early settler days includes wigwams, palisaded log huts, thatched cottages and a blacksmith's forge.

Continue north up Essex Street and drive for 2 miles along Bridge Street, crossing Danvers River and entering Beverly.

Beverly, Massachusetts

One of the most gracious towns in Essex County, this was the affluent home of the distinguished Cabot, Lodge, Lowell and Winthrop families, great industrialists who started the local textile mills. It

was also the birthplace of General Washington's navy.

The Beverly Historical Society occupies the John Cabot Mansion, 117 Cabot Street. Built in 1781, the house contains period furnishings and a research library and museum collections. Other historic houses include the John Balch House of 1636, also in Cabot Street. It is reputed to be one of the oldest frame-built houses in the country.

John Hale House in Hale Street was built in 1694 by the first minister of Beverly, Reverend John Hale, who was instrumental in disentangling the witchcraft fraud.

From Beverly, take State Route 127 and drive 14 miles east to Gloucester.

Gloucester, Massachusetts

A large fishing town and resort, Gloucester has a sheltered harbour, a dramatic rocky coast and excellent beaches. Its association with the sea goes back to the time of the Norsemen who skirted the coast in AD 1001, but more recently the town found fame when Clarence Birdseye invented the fast-freezing process for food here. Rich in sea lore, the grassy Esplanade has a famous bronze statue of a Gloucester fisherman which stares out over the Atlantic in memory of the many men who 'went down to the sea in ships' and lost their lives.

On Roger and Porter Streets, the Gloucester Fishermen's Museum offers visitors the chance to practise crafts. Learn to caulk a boat, shave a mast or handle

The massive granite walls of Hammond Castle, built in 1928, house a superb museum of European antiquities

fishing gear. Films and slides are also shown.

By the water's edge, Beauport, or Eastern Point Boulevard, is a 20-room mansion of various decorative styles designed by American interior designer Henry Sleeper. Inside are numerous American and European antiques collected by Sleeper in his lifetime.

Cape Ann Historical Association

is housed in the Federal-style Captain Elias David House, 27 Pleasant Street, and the museum has exhibits of the town's maritime history and fine seascape paintings by Fitzhugh Lane, as well as china, silver and collections of model schooners.

Overlooking the ocean, the Hammond Museum, 83 Hesperus Avenue, former home of John Hays Hammond Jr, was built from portions of local Rockport granite churches in the style of a medieval castle. It contains extravagant sculptures, paintings and furniture, and a vast organ with 8600 pipes stands in the Great Hall where concerts are given. A courtyard filled with trees and medieval artefacts encloses the towers, battlements and stained glass windows of the castle.

Continue on State Route 127A for 4 miles to Rockport. Turn sharp right about one quarter of a mile short of the town.

Cape Ann and Rockport, Massachusetts

Cape Ann is a picturesque, rocky, atmospheric promontory stretching out into the Atlantic. Here are 25 miles of spectacular coastline with six harbours, 24 coves and more than 20 sandy beaches — a haven for holidaymakers. Nestling in dramatic Sandy Bay is Rockport, a famous old artists' colony, its streets lined with shops and galleries, many housed in one-time fishermen's shacks. The most renowned of these shacks is a faded red building called Motif Number One. Reputed to be the most often painted structure in the USA, the shanty was washed to sea in a winter blizzard of 1978, but has since been reproduced on the basis of scale drawings.

John Heard House, Ipswich, houses a fine collection of furniture

In the centre of town, at 12 Main Street, is the Rockport Art Association, located in an old tavern dating from 1770. Here are held many exhibitions of paintings, graphics and sculpture by over 200 distinguished American artists who are members of the Association. Special events and concerts are also held here.

North of Rockport, at Pigeon Cove, is the intriguing Paper House, a real dwelling, constructed from 1922-42 by the Stenman family entirely of 215 thicknesses of newspapers. The furniture is also made of papers and includes a desk of papers reporting Lindberg's historic flight across the Atlantic in 1927.

South of the town, on State Route 127, is the oldest building in Cape Ann. The James Babson Cooperage Shop of 1658 features tools of the barrel-making trade.

Sewell Scripture House, 40 King Street, contains local historical items, a Marine Room, early American and Victorian rooms, a granite industry exhibit and a library.

Continue north from Rockport on State Route 127 for 7 miles of spectacular coastal driving. Join State Route 128 and travel 3 miles west to the next interchange. Here, turn right on State Route 133 and drive 4 miles to Essex.

Essex, Massachusetts

Situated on the Essex River and home of famed Cape Ann Golf Course, Essex Main Street has a fascinating ship-building museum with a collection which includes shipbuilding tools.

Five-and-a-half miles further west on State Route 133 is the river town of Ipswich.

Ipswich, Massachusetts

This attractive town on Ipswich River has a wealth of beautiful historic homes. Most notable among them is the John Whipple House located at 53 Main Street. Dating from 1638, this house is reputed to be one of the oldest buildings in New England. A fine example of American architecture, the house contains 17th- and 18th-century furnishings and boasts a fine herb garden.

Across the street, the John Heard House, built in 1795, once belonged to a wealthy sea-faring family and contains Chinese ceramics and furniture. One ticket buys admission to both houses.

Close to Ipswich, along Argilla Road, is the Richard T. Crane Jr Memorial Reservation. Wide beaches and marshland make an enjoyable background to swimming, walking and nature studies. There is an interpretive trail which is open all year round. Castle Hill, the former Crane estate, built in the 1920s is now the site of summer concerts and classes in the performing arts. The formal grounds are open to the public and you may picnic at Steep Hill Beach.

The resort town of Crane Beach has a seven mile long sweep of dune-backed sand. Swimming is possible despite the surf as the beach is well-patrolled by lifeguards.

Return from Ipswich on State Route 133 for one mile, then take the right fork on to State Route 1A and drive 8 miles south to Wenham. Continue for 2 miles south of Wenham on State Route 1A, then turn west on State Route 128. After 16 miles, turn left on Interstate 93 and follow it for 10 miles back to Boston.

Rockport's Bearskin Neck area is a maze of old narrow alleys with buildings such as the Lobster Shack and the old pewter shop (detail)

185

Lexington, Concord and Cambridge

1 day — 60 miles

Boston — Medford — Stoneham — Lexington — Concord — Lincoln — South Lincoln — Weston — Waltham — Watertown — Cambridge — Boston.

The first shots of the Revolution resound again on this historic tour through New England. Brave words and deeds of the heroic 'Minutemen' — American patriots who had sworn to be ready to engage battle 'at the minute' — are kept alive by memorabilia at each of the battle sites along the tour. It is fascinating to reconstruct the chain of events that was eventually to lead to the birth of an independent nation. History of a more peaceful nature is offered by the many literary associations of this area, and the tour returns via world-famous Harvard University, across the water from Boston at Cambridge. Distinguished professors such as the poet Henry Wadsworth Longfellow taught here, and his grave, along with those of other eminent Americans, can be seen in Mount Auburn Cemetery.
From Boston take Interstate 93 for a 5-mile journey which leads across the Charles River to Medford (exit 6).

Medford, Massachusetts
Medford is the site of Royall House (1637) which was rebuilt in the 1730s and furnished in the style of that period, with fine

panelling and wood-carving. The house was the headquarters of General Stark and his officers during the siege of Boston. Nearby is a gruesome reminder of bygone days — the original slave quarters. This is the only building of its kind still standing in New England.
From Medford take Interstate 93 for 1½ miles to exit 8 in the Middlesex Fells Reservation. Then take State Route 28 and drive to Stoneham.

Stoneham, Massachusetts
Take the children to the Walter D. Stone Memorial Zoo, where a large variety of birds and mammals can be seen in glass-fronted cages or moated outdoor enclosures. Visitors may bring a packed lunch and picnic on the grass.
Leave Stoneham on State Route 2A, driving through Woburn to Lexington, 6 miles away.

Lexington, Massachusetts
Although it is now practically a suburb of Boston, Lexington retains something of the atmosphere of a small country town. This attractive and historic place is often referred to as 'The

The Mountain Goat enclosures at the Walter D. Stone Memorial Zoo

Birthplace of American Liberty', for in its centre is Lexington Green, the site of the first skirmish of the Revolutionary War, fought on 19 April 1775 between independence-seeking 'Minutemen' and British troops who were on their way to Concord to destroy colonial military supplies that were stored there. This was the occasion of the famous ride by a local silversmith, Paul Revere, who galloped from Boston to Lexington to warn the colonists that the British were coming. Revere warned patriot leaders John Hancock and Samuel Adams, who just had time to escape. About 70 local people, most of them farmers, gathered to fight against the British, but they were outnumbered and were soon defeated and the British moved on to Concord. The line of the Minutemen is marked by an inscribed boulder bearing Captain John Parker's courageous words: 'Stand your ground; don't fire unless fired upon, but if they mean to have a war, let it begin here'. A statue of Parker also stands on the green.
The Hancock-Clark house (1698), where Adams and Hancock were staying when Revere arrived with the news of the British advance, is open to the public and includes period furniture and a museum.
At 1332 Massachusetts Avenue is the Munroe Tavern (1695) which served as the British headquarters and a hospital for those wounded in the battle. It has been restored to its original appearance, as has the Buckman Tavern (1710), which was the rendezvous of the Minutemen.
To complete the picture of the Revolution at Lexington, visit the Old Belfry, off Clark Street. Its

The Minuteman Statue at Lexington commemorates the first engagement (1775) of the American Revolution

© AMERICAN AUTOMOBILE ASSOCIATION MCMLXXXI

bell is a reproduction of the one that sounded the alarm on that historic day in April 1775, summoning the Minutemen to their fate. The old burial ground, beyond the green and to the left of the Unitarian Church, holds the graves of Captain Parker, Governor Eustis and the Reverend John Hancock among others. The oldest gravestone is dated 1690.
Leave Lexington via State Route 2A and travel for 6 miles to Concord.

Concord, Massachusetts
The route continues in the footsteps of Paul Revere and the 700 British troops who followed close on his heels. After their triumph at Lexington, the Redcoats marched to Concord to seize arms which, they believed, were being stockpiled by local farmers. But at Concord they did not have such an easy time.

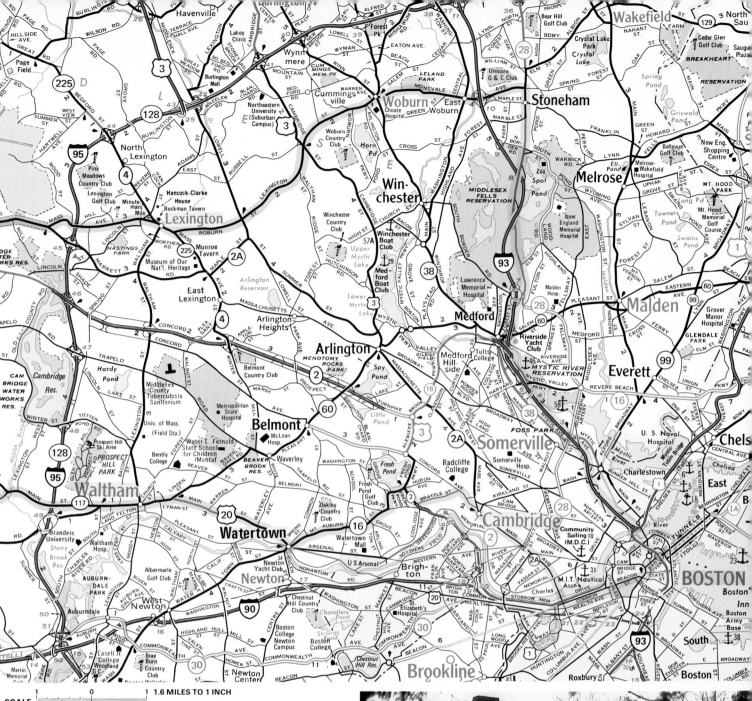

SCALE
1.6 MILES TO 1 INCH
KILOMETRES

Warned by Revere, a force of Concord farmers was waiting for them. Eventually the British were forced to retreat, demoralized and out of ammunition. To the colonists, on the other hand, their victory at the Battle of Concord was a source of tremendous encouragement, spurring them on to full-scale rebellion throughout the country.

The Minutemen National Historical Park encompasses land in Concord as well as Lexington and Lincoln. Details are available from the North Bridge Visitor Centre in Concord. The Battle of Concord, which took place on the old North Bridge over the Concord River, is commemorated by a statue of a Minuteman. It stands to the west of Monument Street.

In contrast to its revolutionary connections, Concord is equally well known for its literary associations. Ralph Waldo Emerson, the essayist and poet, lived here from 1835 until his death in 1882, and his house is open to the public. A stanza of his 'Concord Hymn' is engraved on the statue already mentioned:

By the rude bridge that arched the flood
Their flag to April's breeze unfurled
Here once the embattled farmers stood
And fired the shot heard round the world.

Books, manuscripts, furniture and pictures belonging to the poet Henry Longfellow are displayed in his Cambridge home

Lexington, Concord and Cambridge

A contemporary local author who shared Emerson's passion for self-sufficiency and a return to nature was Henry David Thoreau. His well-known book *Walden* is an account of the two years he spent living alone and quite independently of the outside world at Walden Pond, which lies 1½ miles south of Concord. On the north shore of the 64-acre pond is a sign marking the site where he built his cabin in 1845. The Walden Pond State Reservation now covers about 400 acres, and the pond offers good fishing.

Orchard House, one mile southeast of Concord, was for many years the home of the authoress Louisa May Alcott (1832-88). Her best known book is undoubtedly *Little Women*, published in 1868 and written while she was living here. The story is based on her own memories of a New England childhood. Orchard House is now a museum whose exhibits include a diorama of scenes from the book.

Two houses in Concord have associations with Nathaniel Hawthorne, author of *The Scarlet Letter*. He was born in Salem, but lived here for a time, firstly at the Old Manse, a house in Monument Street built in 1770 by Emerson's grandfather, and later at The Wayside, 1¼ miles east of Concord. Both houses are open to the public.

Sleepy Hollow Cemetery, on Bedford Street, is the burial place of Hawthorne, Emerson, Thoreau and the Alcotts.

Various threads of Concord's history are brought together at the Concord Antiquarian Museum, which contains 15 period rooms furnished with antiques dating from 1685 to 1870, and also a replica of the study where Emerson did much of his writing. A diorama of the Battle of Concord is on display, and other exhibits include Paul Revere's lantern and some of the equipment used by Thoreau at Walden Pond.

The Concord Art Association at 37 Lexington Road hosts exhibitions of contemporary and early American art. The house itself dates from 1720 and has a secret room and a garden with a waterfall. To the north-east of Concord, 253 acres on the banks of the Concord River are devoted to the Great Meadows National Wildlife Refuge.

⎮ Drive out of Concord on the Cambridge Turnpike and join State Route 2. After 2 miles turn off at Bedford Street and drive 1 mile to Lincoln.

Lincoln, Massachusetts
Worth a visit here is the De Cordova Museum, on Sandy Pond Road. A 35-acre park surrounds the castle-like building, which dates from 1880 and is used as a

Concord: the home of Ralph Waldo Emerson, one of America's greatest nineteenth-century poets and thinkers, is a museum of his life and work

centre for the visual and performing arts.

⎮ From Lincoln take unclassified Lincoln Road to South Lincoln, 1 mile away.

South Lincoln, Massachusetts
Drumlin Farm is the home of the Massachusetts Audubon Society, a conservationist group named after the 19th-century naturalist, John James Audubon. It is used as a demonstration farm, with wild and domestic animals and a bird sanctuary, and is open to the public. The Hathaway School of Conservation Education also has its home here.

⎮ From South Lincoln drive for 1 mile on State Route 117 before turning on to Merriam Street. The next stop is Weston, about 2 miles away.

Weston, Massachusetts
This small town is well known to stamp enthusiasts, for it is the home of the Cardinal Spellman Philatelic Museum, situated on the campus of Regis College. The oldest building in Weston is the Josiah Smith Tavern. Dating from 1757, it was a tavern for 90 years, and is now owned by the Society for the Preservation of New England Antiquities.

⎮ Leave Weston on Church Street and join State Route 117. Travel to Waltham.

Waltham, Massachusetts
In 1805 Governor Christopher Gore built a 20-room mansion house here. Built in the Federal style, Gore Place is among America's finest historic houses and is open to the public in summer. Waltham is also the home of the American Jewish Historical Society, where records of Jewish life can be seen.

⎮ From Waltham take US 20 to Watertown, 2½ miles away.

Watertown, Massachusetts
175 North Beacon Street is the home of Perkins School for the Blind. At the central administration building is a library and a museum relating to educating the blind.

⎮ Leave Watertown on State Route 16 then, at Fresh Pond Parkway, change to State Route 2. In ¼ mile, turn on to Brattle Street, then take Concord Avenue which leads straight into Cambridge.

Cambridge, Massachusetts
Across the Charles River from Boston is the historic city of Cambridge.

Most famous of all Cambridge's buildings are those of Harvard University, founded in 1636 and the oldest university in the USA. The nucleus of the university is the original campus, Harvard Yard, where students and visitors mingle. Harvard's buildings could be said to represent the development of American architecture ranging from the red-brick, colonial style façade of Massachusetts Hall (1720), through the 19th-century work of Charles Bulfinch (University Hall)

to the space-age Carpenter Center for the Visual Arts, which was designed by contemporary architect Le Corbusier.

Connected to the university are the Busch-Reisinger Museum, which specializes in Germanic art; the Fogg Art Museum, where ancient, Oriental, Romanesque, Italian and French works of art are on show; Harvard University Library, and the University Museum, where exhibits range from anthropological subjects to geology, botany and zoology. The Ware Collection features exquisite flowers modelled in glass.

Longfellow House, at 105 Brattle Street, is a Georgian-style house where General George Washington had his headquarters in 1775-6, at the beginning of the Revolutionary War. The poet Henry Wadsworth Longfellow later lived here and this was where he wrote *The Village Blacksmith, The Courtship of Miles Standish, Evangeline* and *The Song of Hiawatha*. This was his home from 1837, when he was Professor of Modern Languages at Harvard, until his death in 1882. Some of his books, manuscripts, furniture and pictures are on display.

The huge complex of the Massachusetts Institute of Technology dominates Cambridge. Founded in 1861, the college moved here in 1916 and its campus extends more than a mile along the Charles River Basin. This college has probably supplied the world with more engineers than any other institution of its kind, and the subjects taught also include architecture, humanities and social sciences. Exhibitions of contemporary art take place in the Hayden Gallery, and the campus also features a nautical museum and two pieces of stunning modern architecture by the Finnish architect Eero Saarinen — the Kresge Auditorium and the college chapel.

At Mount Auburn Cemetery visitors can see the graves of several eminent Americans, including Henry Wadsworth Longfellow and his successor as professor at Harvard, James Russell Lowell. Essayist Oliver Wendell Holmes (also a Harvard professor), and Mary Baker Eddy, the founder of the Christian Science movement, are among others buried here.

⎮ Leave Cambridge on State Route 2A, Massachusetts Avenue, and cross the Charles River. Drive along Beacon Street for the return journey to Boston.

John Harvard's statue stands on the campus of the university he helped to found. In the background, the spire of the Memorial Church

Index
of
Place Names

Acknowledgements

The Publishers would like to thank the
following organizations, photographers and
picture libraries for the use of photographs
in this book

Alexandria Tourist Council   Mansell Collection

Barnabys   Mary Evans Picture Library

Biofotos   Metropolitan Dade County

Bruce Coleman Incorporated   Department of Tourism

Bruce Coleman Limited   New England Regional Commission

Camera Press   New York Convention & Visitors Bureau

Colorific!   Paul Miles

Colour Library International   Picturepoint Ltd

Florida Department of Tourism   Richard Surman

Greater Los Angeles Visitor & Convention Bureau   San Francisco Convention & Visitors Bureau

Ian Beames   Spectrum Colour Library

J. Allan Cash Ltd.   United States Travel Service

Joe Coomber   Washington National Gallery of Art

Las Vegas News Bureau   ZEFA